Financial and Accounting Guide

for Nonprofit Organizations

Malvern J. Gross, Jr., C.P.A.
William Warshauer, Jr., C.P.A.

Partners, Price Waterhouse & Co.

Financial and Accounting Guide
for Nonprofit Organizations

REVISED THIRD EDITION

A RONALD PRESS
PUBLICATION

JOHN WILEY & SONS

New York · Chichester
Brisbane · Toronto · Singapore

Library of Congress Cataloging in Publication Data

Gross, Malvern J.
    Financial and accounting guide for nonprofit
organizations.

    "A Ronald Press publication."
    Bibliography: p.
    Includes index.
    1. Corporations, Nonprofit—Accounting.
I. Warshauer, William.   II. Title.
HF5686.N56G76   1983   657'.98   82-21909
ISBN 0-471-87113-3

To the memory of James R. Fako,
our partner and friend

Preface

This book, like its predecessors, has many objectives. Two major objectives are to help the nonprofit organization better communicate its financial activities and financial condition to its members and to the public, and to better manage its financial resources. The book is also intended to aid the governing bodies of such organizations in fully understanding the annual financial reports issued by their organization, thereby assisting them in making more informed judgments. For the treasurer and chief executive of the eleemosynary institution, as well as for the professional accountant, this book provides a wide range of practical and professional guidance.

The Third Edition of this book was significantly expanded to reflect rapidly changing events in nonprofit accounting. The Revised Third Edition is further updated to include recent changes in tax laws and tax forms used by nonprofit organizations. It contains a comprehensive discussion of the AICPA Statement of Position applicable to all nonprofit organizations not covered by one of the earlier-issued AICPA Audit Guides. As chairman of the committee that conceived and drafted this document, one of the authors was privileged to directly participate in this endeavor, which will significantly facilitate establishment of generally accepted accounting principles and reporting practices for the nonprofit sector. The accounting principles and reporting practices presented in the Statement of Position are carefully analyzed and annotated with meaningful interpretive commentary. This discussion will be of particular value to the professional accountant.

The AICPA Statement of Position, in concert with AICPA Audit Guides for colleges and universities, hospitals, and voluntary health and welfare organizations, prescribes accounting principles and reporting practices applicable to virtually every type of nonprofit organization. We take particular satisfaction in the knowledge that the First and Second Editions of this book suggested many of the accounting principles and reporting practices that appear in these AICPA pronouncements on nonprofit accounting.

In the past several years there has been increasing indication that the Financial Accounting Standards Board intends to issue formal accounting standards that will be binding on all nonprofit organizations. The relationship of the AICPA and the FASB and the function of each in the development of accounting principles and reporting practices are carefully examined in the pages that follow.

Throughout the text, based on the extensive experience of the authors with the operations of nonprofit organizations, innovative suggestions are offered. For example, it is recommended that all legally unrestricted funds be reported as a single fund rather than as a series of separate funds, as an aid to the unsophisticated reader or constituent in comprehending the entire financial picture of an organization. A distinction is made between recording unrestricted board-designated endowment funds separately for bookkeeping purposes, and reporting them in a single unrestricted fund in public statements.

The book continues to provide detailed help on tax form preparation, and systematically presents compliance requirements for each state. In addition, it offers several chapters of procedural advice for the smaller organization that includes guidelines for setting up and keeping the books, maintaining proper internal controls, developing and presenting a meaningful budget, and dealing with the mechanics of pooled investments.

Grateful acknowledgment is due to many people for their assistance in the preparation of this Revised Third Edition. While responsibility for the opinions and conclusions expressed are solely the authors', sincere thanks are due for the generous help of their associates, particularly W. W. Britain, C. S. Hartz, R. F. Larkin, B. J. MacCorkindale, D. E. Martin, J. J. McAndrew, J. W. Meyerson, W. E. Offutt, J. F. Rabenhorst and Mrs. R. J. Sylvestre.

MALVERN J. GROSS, JR.
WILLIAM WARSHAUER, JR.

Washington, D.C.
January 1983

Contents

Financial and Accounting Guide

for Nonprofit Organizations

1

Responsibilities of Treasurers and Chief Executive Officers

Nonprofit organizations are among the most influential and powerful institutions in our free society. These organizations range in size from small, local organizations to large national and international ones. Their scope covers almost every activity imaginable—health and welfare, research, education, religion, social organizations, and professional associations. They include foundations, membership societies, churches, hospitals, colleges, and political organizations. It is estimated that there are more than 500,000 nonprofit organizations in the United States and they own property constituting from 10 to 33 per cent of the tax roll in many large cities.

Typically, these organizations are controlled by boards of directors composed of leading citizens who volunteer their time. Where the organization is large enough, or complex enough in operation to require it, the board may delegate limited or broad operating responsibility to a part-time or full-time paid executive, who may be given any one of many alternative titles—executive secretary, administrator, manager, etc. Regardless of size, the board will usually appoint one of its own part-time volunteer members as treasurer; in most cases, the treasurer is second in importance only to the chairperson of the board because the organization's programs revolve around finances. While not always responsible for raising funds, the treasurer is charged with stewardship

3

of these funds and with the responsibility of anticipating problems and difficulties.

The treasurer is usually a businessperson who is extremely active in both professional and community affairs, and so has only a limited amount of time to devote to the organization. Where there is a paid executive, many of the operating duties and responsibilities of the treasurer can be delegated to this executive and, in large organizations, through this executive to a chief accountant or business manager. However, in small organizations there may be no chief executive to delegate to, and in the following pages this will be assumed to be the case, both because small nonprofit organizations predominate, and because it simplifies the presentation. It will further be assumed that the treasurer is not an accountant and doesn't want to become one, but at the same time recognizes the need to understand something about the principles of nonprofit accounting and, more important, financial reporting.

The treasurer has significant responsibilities, including the following:

1. Keeping financial records
2. Preparing accurate and meaningful financial statements
3. Budgeting and anticipating financial problems
4. Safeguarding and managing the organization's financial assets
5. Complying with federal and state reporting requirements

While this list certainly is not all-inclusive, most of the financial problems the treasurer will face are associated with these five major areas.

KEEPING FINANCIAL RECORDS

The treasurer is charged with seeing that the organization's financial records are maintained in an appropriate manner. If the organization is very small, the treasurer will keep the records, probably in a very simple and straightforward manner. If the organization is somewhat larger, a part-time employee—perhaps a secretary—may, among other duties, keep simple records. If the organization is still larger, there may be a full-time bookkeeper, or perhaps even a full-time accounting staff reporting to the chief executive and responsible for keeping the records of the organization. Regardless of size, the ultimate responsibility for seeing that adequate and complete financial records are kept is clearly that of the treasurer. This means that to some extent the treasurer must know what is involved in elementary bookkeeping and accounting, although not at the level of a bookkeeper or a CPA. Bookkeeping and accounting are largely matters of common sense and with the guidance provided in this book there should be no difficulty in understanding basic procedures and requirements.

The important thing to emphasize is that the treasurer is responsible for seeing that reliable records are kept. The detailed procedures to be followed may be delegated to others but it is up to the treasurer to see that the procedures are being followed and that the records are reasonably accurate. This is emphasized because frequently in large organizations the treasurer feels somewhat at a disadvantage being a volunteer with relatively few hours to spend and not an experienced accountant. The bookkeeping staff on the other hand is full-time and presumably competent. There is a natural reluctance for the treasurer to ask questions and to look at the detailed records, to be satisfied that sound bookkeeping procedures are being followed. Yet the responsibility is the treasurer's, and questioning and probing are necessary to ensure that the record-keeping function is being competently performed.

PREPARING ACCURATE AND MEANINGFUL
FINANCIAL STATEMENTS

One of the most important responsibilities of the treasurer is to see that complete and straightforward financial reports are prepared for the board and membership, to tell clearly what has happened during the period. To be meaningful, these statements should have the following characteristics:

1. They should be easily comprehensible so that any person taking the time to study them will understand the financial picture. This characteristic is the one most frequently absent.
2. They should be concise so that the person studying them will not get lost in detail.
3. They should be all-inclusive in scope and should embrace all activities of the organization. If there are two or three funds, the statements should clearly show the relationship between the funds without a lot of confusing detail involving transfers and appropriations.
4. They should have a focal point for comparison so that the person reading them will have some basis for making a judgment. In most instances this will be a comparison with a budget, or figures from the corresponding period of the previous year.
5. They should be prepared on a timely basis. The longer the delay after the end of the period, the longer the period before corrective action can be taken.

These statements must represent straightforward and candid reporting —that is, the statements must show exactly what has happened. This means that income should not be arbitrarily buried in some subsidiary fund or activity in such a way that the reader is not likely to be aware that it has been received. It means that if the organization has a number of "funds," the total income and expenses of all funds should be shown in the financial statements in such a manner that no one has to wonder whether all of the activities for the period are included. In short, the statements have to communicate accurately what has happened. If the statement format is confusing and the reader doesn't understand what it is trying to communicate, then it is not accomplishing its principal objective.

It will be noted that the characteristics listed above would apply equally to the statements of almost any type of organization or business. Unfortunately, financial statements for nonprofit organizations frequently fail to meet these characteristics. There are a number of reasons for this. Probably the most important is that the treasurer is doing the job on a part-time basis and does not have the time to develop a new format or set of statements. It is easier to continue with what has been done in the past. Also there is a marked reluctance on the part of nonaccountants to make changes in statement format because they lack confidence in their abilities to tinker with the "mysteries" of accounting. Furthermore, at just about the time that the treasurer is really becoming conversant with the statements and could start to make meaningful changes, his or her term may expire.

"Grandparent Test"

Since the purpose of any set of financial statements is to communicate to the reader, a good test of whether they accomplish this objective is the "grandparent test." Can these statements be clearly understood by any interested "grandparent" of average intelligence who is willing to take some time to study them? After studying them, will he or she have a good understanding of the overall financial activities for the year? If not, then the statements are not serving their purpose and should be revised and simplified until they do meet this test.

There are illustrations of all types of financial statements throughout this book, as well as suggestions on how to simplify financial statements to make them more readable. If these suggestions are followed, the statements should meet the "grandparent test."

BUDGETING AND ANTICIPATING FINANCIAL PROBLEMS

Another major responsibility of the treasurer is to anticipate the financial problems of the organization so that the board or membership can take steps to solve these problems on a timely basis. A carefully prepared budget is the principal tool that should be used. Budgets can take many different forms, from the very simple to the fairly complex, and all have as their primary objective the avoidance of the "unexpected." Budgets and budgeting techniques are discussed in some detail in Chapter 19.

But there is more to budgeting than merely anticipating the activities of the coming year. Budgeting in a very real sense represents planning ahead for several years in an effort to foresee social and economic trends and their influence on the organization's program. This means that the treasurer must be a forecaster of the future as well as a planner. In many organizations this is done in a very informal, almost intuitive manner. In others, this function is more formalized.

SAFEGUARDING AND MANAGING FINANCIAL ASSETS

Unless the organization is very small there will be a number of assets requiring safeguarding and, again, it is the responsibility of the treasurer to be sure that there are both adequate physical controls and internal controls over these assets.

Physical controls involve making sure that the assets are protected against unauthorized use or theft, and seeing that adequate insurance is provided. Internal controls involve division of duties and record-keeping functions that will ensure control over these assets and adequate reporting of deviations from authorized procedures. Another function of internal control is to provide controls that will help remove undue temptation from the employees of the organization. Chapters 22 and 23 offer guidance on these matters.

Another responsibility of the treasurer is to see that the organization's excess cash is properly invested to insure maximum financial return. One of the accounting techniques often followed by nonprofit organizations is to combine cash from several funds and to make investments on a pooled basis. Chapter 24 discusses the technique of pooling of investments and discusses some of the physical safeguards that should be established.

COMPLYING WITH FEDERAL AND STATE REPORTING REQUIREMENTS

The treasurer and chief executive officer are also charged with complying with the various federal and state reporting requirements. Most tax-exempt organizations, other than churches, are required to file annual information returns with the Internal Revenue Service, and some are even required to pay federal taxes. In addition, certain organizations must register and file information returns with certain of the state governments even though they are not resident in the state. All of these requirements taken together pose a serious problem for a treasurer, who is usually not familiar with either the laws involved or the reporting forms used. Chapters 25, 26, and 27 discuss these requirements in some detail.

SUMMARY

Few positions have more opportunity to influence institutions that affect society than that of the volunteer treasurer of a nonprofit organization. In the past many treasurers have struggled to perform their duties but have become mired in detail or lost in the intricacies of the apparently different accounting and financial principles applicable to nonprofit organizations. One of the principal objectives of this book is to help the treasurer and chief executive officers of such organizations discharge their responsibilities in an effective manner with the least expenditure of time.

PART I

KEY FINANCIAL CONCEPTS

2

Accounting Distinctions Between Nonprofit and Commercial Organizations

Many businesspersons, as well as many accountants, approach nonprofit accounting with a certain amount of trepidation because of a lack of familiarity with such accounting. There is no real reason for this uneasiness because, except for a few troublesome areas, nonprofit accounting follows many of the same principles followed by commercial enterprises. This chapter explores the principal differences and pinpoints the few troublesome areas.

STEWARDSHIP VERSUS PROFITABILITY

One of the principal differences between nonprofit and commercial organizations is that they have different reasons for their existence. In oversimplified terms, it might be said that the ultimate objective of a commercial organization is to realize net profit for its stockholders through the performance of some service wanted by other people, whereas the ultimate objective of a nonprofit organization is to meet some socially desirable need of the community or its members.

So long as the nonprofit organization has sufficient resources to carry out its objectives, there is no real need or justification for "making a profit" or having an excess of income over expense. While a prudent board may want to have a "profit" in order to provide for a rainy day in the future, the principal objective of the board is to fulfill the functions for which the organization was founded. A surplus or profit is only incidental.

Instead of profit, many nonprofit organizations are concerned with the size of their cash balance. They can continue to exist only so long as they have sufficient cash to provide for their program. Thus the financial statements of nonprofit organizations often emphasize the cash position. Commercial organizations are, of course, also very much concerned with cash but if they are profitable they will probably be able to finance their cash needs through loans or from investors. Their principal concern is profitability and this means that commercial accounting emphasizes the matching of revenues and costs.

Nonprofit organizations have a responsibility to account for funds that they have received. This responsibility includes accounting for certain specific funds that have been given for use in a particular project, as well as a general obligation to employ the organization's resources effectively. Emphasis, thus, is placed on accountability and stewardship. To the extent that the organization has received gifts restricted for a specific purpose, it will probably segregate those assets and report separately on their receipt and disposition. This separate reporting of restricted assets is called fund accounting. As a result, the financial statements of nonprofit organizations can often be voluminous and complex because each restricted fund grouping may have its own set of financial statements which summarize all of its activities.

The volume and intricacy of the statements have produced problems in terms of both meaningful disclosure and comparability with the financial statements of commercial enterprises. The financial statements of commercial organizations are easy to understand, relative to those of nonprofit organizations, because there is only a single set of statements, the terminology and format are usually standardized and familiar, and accounting principles are more clearly defined.

PRINCIPAL AREAS OF ACCOUNTING DIFFERENCES

There are five areas where the accounting principles followed by nonprofit organizations often differ from the accounting principles followed by commercial organizations. While the accounting significance of these five areas should not be minimized, it is also important to note that once the significance of each is understood, the reader will have a good understanding of the major accounting principles followed by nonprofit organizations. The principal remaining difficulty will then be designing a set of financial statements which reflect these accounting distinctions and are straightforward and easy to understand. The five areas are as follows.

Cash Versus Accrual Accounting

In commercial organizations the records are almost always recorded on an accrual basis. The accrual basis simply means keeping your records so that in addition to recording transactions resulting from the receipt and disbursement of cash, you also record the amounts you owe others, and others owe you. In nonprofit organizations the cash basis of accounting is frequently used instead. Cash basis accounting means reflecting only transactions where cash has been involved. No attempt is made to record unpaid bills owed by you or amounts due you. Most small nonprofit organizations use the cash basis, although more and more of the medium and larger organizations are now using the accrual basis.

The accrual basis usually gives a more accurate picture of an organization's financial condition than the cash basis. Why, then, is the cash basis frequently used by nonprofit organizations? Principally because it is simpler to keep records on a cash basis than on an accrual basis. Everyone has had experience keeping a checkbook. This is cash basis accounting. A nonaccountant can learn to keep a checkbook but is not likely to comprehend readily how to keep a double-entry set of books on the accrual basis. Furthermore, the cash basis is often used when the nature of the organization's activities is such that there are no material amounts owed to others, or vice versa, and so there is little meaningful difference between the cash and accrual basis.

Sometimes nonprofit organizations follow a modified form of cash basis accounting where certain items are recorded on an accrual basis and certain items on a cash basis. Other organizations keep their records on a cash basis but at the end of the year convert them to the accrual basis by recording obligations and receivables. The important thing is that the records kept are appropriate to the nature of the organization and its needs. Chapter 3 discusses cash and accrual accounting.

Fund Accounting

In commercial enterprises, separate "funds" or fund accounting are not used. Fund accounting is an accounting concept which is not familiar to most businesspersons and can cause real difficulty. In fund accounting, assets are segregated into categories according to the restrictions that donors place on their use. All completely unrestricted assets are in one fund, all endowment funds in another, all building funds in a third, and so forth. Typically in reporting, an organization using fund accounting presents separate financial statements for each "fund." Fund accounting is widely used by nonprofit organizations because it provides stewardship reporting. While this concept of separate funds in itself is not particularly difficult, it does cause problems in presenting financial statements that are straightforward enough to be understood by most readers, i.e., to pass the "grandparent test." Chapter 4 is devoted to a discussion of fund accounting.

Treatment of Fixed Assets

In commercial enterprises, fixed assets are almost always recorded as assets on the balance sheet, and are depreciated over their expected useful lives. In nonprofit accounting, fixed assets may or may not be recorded.

The handling of fixed assets, and depreciation, probably causes more difficulty and confusion than any other type of transaction because everyone seems to have a different idea about how fixed assets should be handled, and there is no single generally accepted principle or practice to follow. Some organizations "write off" or expense the asset when purchased; others record fixed assets purchased at cost and depreciate them over their estimated useful life in the same manner as commercial enterprises. Still others "write off" their fixed asset purchases, and then turn around and capitalize them on the Balance Sheet. Some depreciate; some do not. All of this presents the treasurer with the need for some practical suggestions as to when each approach is appropriate. Fixed asset accounting and depreciation are discussed in Chapters 6 and 7 respectively.

Transfers and Appropriations

In nonprofit organizations transfers are frequently made between "funds." Unless carefully disclosed, such transfers tend to confuse the reader of the financial statements. Some organizations make "appropriations" for specific future projects (i.e., set aside a part of the fund balance for a designated purpose). Often these appropriations are shown, incorrectly, as an expense in arriving at the excess of income over expenses. This also tends to confuse. Transfers and appropriations are not accounting terms used by commercial enterprises. Each is discussed in Chapter 5.

Contributions, Pledges, and Noncash Contributions

In commercial or business enterprises there is no such thing as a "pledge." If the business is legally owed money the amount is recorded as an account receivable. A pledge to a nonprofit organization may or may not be legally enforceable. Some nonprofit organizations record pledges because they know from experience that they will collect them. Others do not because they feel they have no legally enforceable claim. A related problem is where and how to report both restricted and unrestricted contributions in the financial statements. Contributions and pledges are discussed in Chapter 9.

Noncash contributions include donations of securities, equipment, supplies, and services. Commercial enterprises seldom are recipients of such "income." When and at what values it is appropriate to record such noncash contributions is discussed in Chapter 9.

CONCLUSION

The five areas discussed above are the principal differences in accounting found between nonprofit and commercial organizations. While each of these can cause real problems for the casual reader if the statements are not carefully prepared, it is significant to note again that there are only these five areas, and often only one or two will be present in any given organization. It has been noted that part of the reason for these differences stems from the different objectives in nonprofit and commercial organizations. In the one, accountability for program activities and stewardship is the objective. In the other the objective is a proper matching of revenue and costs with the resultant measurement of profitability. The treasurer familiar with commercial financial statements should have no difficulty preparing nonprofit financial statements once the nature of each of these five areas of accounting differences is understood. And if the objectives of financial statements are kept in mind the treasurer should be able to prepare financial statements that meet the "grandparent test" for clarity and effectiveness in communicating with their readers.

3

Cash Versus Accrual Basis Accounting

In the previous chapter it was noted that although more and more of the medium and larger nonprofit organizations are now keeping their records on an accrual basis, most smaller organizations still keep their records on the cash basis of accounting. The purpose of this chapter is to illustrate both bases of accounting, and to discuss the advantages and disadvantages of each.

CASH AND ACCRUAL STATEMENTS ILLUSTRATED

Perhaps the easiest way to fully appreciate the differences is to look at the financial statements of a nonprofit organization prepared on both the cash and accrual basis. The Johanna M. Stanneck Foundation is a "private" foundation with assets of about $200,000. The income from these assets plus any current contributions to the foundation are used for medical scholarships to needy students. Figure 3–1 shows the two basic financial statements that, in one form or another, are used by nearly every profit and nonprofit organization, namely, a Statement of Income and Expenses for a given period, and a Balance Sheet at the end of the period. Figure 3–1 shows these statements on both the cash basis and the accrual basis, side by side for ease of comparison. In actual practice, of course, an organization would report on one or the other basis, and not both bases, as here.

As can be seen most easily from the Balance Sheet, a number of

16

THE JOHANNA M. STANNECK FOUNDATION

STATEMENT OF INCOME, EXPENSES AND SCHOLARSHIP GRANTS*
For the Year Ended December 31, 19X2

	Cash Basis	Accrual Basis
Income:		
Dividends and interest income	$ 8,953	$ 9,650
Gain on sale of investments	12,759	12,759
Contributions	5,500	7,500
Total	27,212	29,909
Administrative expenses:		
Investment advisory service fees	2,000	2,200
Bookkeeping and accounting expenses	2,350	2,500
Federal excise tax	350	394
Other expenses	1,654	2,509
Total ·...........................	6,354	7,603
Income available for scholarships	20,858	22,306
Less: Scholarship grants.................	(17,600)	(21,800)
Excess of income over expenses and		
scholarship grants	$ 3,258	$ 506

*On a cash basis the title should be "Statement of Receipts, Expenditures and Scholarships Paid" to emphasize the "cash" aspect of the statement. There would also have to be a note to the financial statement disclosing the amount of scholarships granted but not paid at the end of the year.

Fig. 3–1. Cash basis and accrual basis statements side by side to highlight the differences in these two bases of accounting.

transactions not involving cash are reflected only on the accrual basis statements. These transactions are:

1. Uncollected dividends and accrued interest income at December 31, 19X2, of $3,550 is recorded as an asset on the Balance Sheet. Since there were also uncollected dividends and accrued interest income at December 31, 19X1, the effect on the accrual basis income as compared to the cash basis income is only the increase (or decrease) in the accrual at the end of the year. In this example, since the cash basis income from this source is shown as $8,953 and the accrual basis as $9,650, the increase during the year must have been the difference, or $697, and the amounts not accrued at December 31, 19X1, must have been $2,853.

2. An uncollected pledge at December 31, 19X2, of $2,000 is recorded as an asset on the Balance Sheet; and because there were no uncollected pledges at the end of the previous year, this whole

THE JOHANNA M. STANNECK FOUNDATION
BALANCE SHEET*
December 31, 19X2

	Cash Basis	Accrual Basis
Assets:		
Cash	$ 13,616	$ 13,616
Marketable securities at cost		
(market value $235,100)	186,519	186,519
Dividends and interest receivable	-	3,550
Pledge receivable	-	2,000
Total assets	$200,135	$205,685
Liabilities:		
Accrued expenses payable	-	$ 1,354
Federal excise tax payable	-	394
Scholarships payable—19X3	-	12,150
Scholarships payable—19X4	-	2,000
Total liabilities	-	15,898
Fund balance.........................	$200,135	189,787
Total liabilities and fund balance	$200,135	$205,685

*On a cash basis the title should be "Statement of Assets and Liabilities Resulting from Cash Transactions."

Fig. 3—1. Continued.

amount shows up as increased income on an accrual basis.

3. Unpaid expenses of $1,354 at the end of the year are recorded as a liability on the accrual basis Balance Sheet, but on the accrual basis expense statements are partially offset by similar items unpaid at the end of the previous year.

4. The federal excise tax not yet paid on 19X2 net investment income is recorded as a liability and as an expense on the accrual basis. The $350 tax shown on the cash basis expenditure statement is the tax actually paid in 19X2 on 19X1 net investment income. (See Chapter 25 for a discussion of taxes as they affect private foundations.)

5. Unpaid scholarships granted during the year are recorded as an obligation. Most of these scholarships will be paid within the following year but one scholarship has been granted that extends into 19X4. As in the case of the other items discussed above, it is necessary to know the amount of this obligation at the prior year end and to take the difference into account in order to relate accrual basis scholarship expenses to cash basis expenditures.

As a result of these noncash transactions, there are significant differences in the amounts between the cash and accrual basis. On the cash basis, expenditures of $17,600 for scholarships are shown, compared to $21,800 on the accrual basis; excess of income of $3,258 compared to $506; and a fund balance of $200,135 compared to $189,787. Which set of figures is more appropriate? In theory, the accrual basis figures are. What then are the advantages of the cash basis, and why should someone use the cash basis?

Advantages of Cash Basis

The principal advantage of cash basis accounting (as previously stated in Chapter 2) is its simplicity, and the ease with which nonaccountants can understand and keep records on this basis. The only time a transaction is recorded under this basis of accounting is when cash has been received or expended. A simple checkbook is often all that is needed to keep the records of the organization. When financial statements are required, the treasurer just summarizes the transactions from the checkbook stubs. This sounds almost too easy, but a checkbook can be an adequate substitute for formal bookkeeping records, provided a complete description is recorded on the checkbook stubs.* The chances are that someone with no bookkeeping training could keep the records of the Johanna M. Stanneck Foundation on a cash basis, using only a checkbook, files of paid bills, files on each scholarship, etc. This would probably not be true with an accrual basis set of books.

Many larger organizations, including many with bookkeeping staffs, also use the cash basis of accounting primarily because of its simpler nature. Often the difference between financial results on a cash and on an accrual basis are not materially different, and the accrual basis provides a degree of sophistication not needed. For example, in the illustration above, what real significance is there between the two sets of figures? Will the users of the financial statements do anything differently if they have accrual basis figures? If not, the extra costs to obtain accrual basis statements have to be considered.

Another reason organizations often keep their records on a cash basis is that they are following the age-old adage of not counting their chickens before they are hatched. They feel uneasy about considering a pledge receivable as income until the cash is in the bank. These organizations frequently pay their bills promptly, and at the end of the period have very little in the way of unpaid obligations. With respect

---

* Chapter 28 discusses cash basis bookkeeping and illustrates how this checkbook approach can be used.

to unrecorded income, they also point out that because they consistently follow this method of accounting from year to year, the net effect on income in any one year is not material. Last year's unrecorded income is collected this year and tends to offset this year's unrecorded income. The advocates of a cash basis say, therefore, that they are being conservative by using this approach.

Advantages of Accrual Basis

With all of these advantages of the cash basis of accounting, what are the advantages of the accrual basis? Very simple—in many instances the cash basis just does not present accurately the financial affairs of the organization. The accrual basis of accounting becomes the more appropriate basis when the organization has substantial unpaid bills or uncollected income at the end of each period and these amounts vary from period to period. If the cash basis were used, the organization would have great difficulty in knowing where it actually stood. These unpaid bills or uncollected income would materially distort the financial statements.

In the illustration above, there probably is not a great deal of difference between the two bases. But assume for the moment that toward the end of 19X2 the foundation had made a grant of $100,000 to a medical school, to be paid in 19X3. Clearly, not recording this large transaction would distort the financial statements.

Nonprofit organizations are becoming more conscious of the need to prepare and use budgets as a control technique.* It is very difficult for an organization to effectively use a budget without being on an accrual basis. A cash basis organization has difficulty because payment may lag for a long time after incurring the obligation. For this reason organizations that must carefully budget their activities will find accrual basis accounting essential.

COMBINATION CASH ACCOUNTING AND ACCRUAL STATEMENTS

One very practical way to avoid the complexities of accrual basis accounting, and still have meaningful financial statements on an annual or semi-annual basis, is to keep the books on a cash basis but make the necessary adjustments on worksheets to record the accruals for statement

* Budgets are discussed in detail in Chapter 19.

purposes. These "adjustments" could be put together on worksheets without the need to formally record the adjustments in the bookkeeping records.*

It is even possible that monthly or quarterly financial statements could be prepared on the cash basis, with the accrual basis adjustments being made only at the end of the year. In this way, it is possible to have the simplicity of cash basis accounting throughout the year, while at the end of the year converting the records through worksheets to accrual basis accounting.

Figure 3–2 gives an example of the type of worksheet that can be used. It shows how the Johnstown Orphanage converted a cash basis statement to an accrual basis statement at the end of the year. Cash basis figures are shown in column 1, adjustments in column 2, and the resulting accrual basis amounts in column 3. The financial statement to the board would show only column 3.

JOHNSTOWN ORPHANAGE
WORKSHEET SHOWING CONVERSION OF CASH TO ACCRUAL BASIS
For the Year Ended December 31, 19X1

	Cash Basis (Col. 1)	Adjustments: Add (Deduct) (Col. 2)	Accrual Basis (Col. 3)
Income:			
Investment income	$225,000	$ 5,000	$230,000
Fees from city	290,000	25,000	315,000
Total	515,000		545,000
Expenses:			
Salaries and wages	430,000	(5,000)	425,000
Food and provisions	50,000	2,000	52,000
Fuel	15,000	1,000	16,000
Maintenance	40,000	1,000	41,000
Children's allowances	10,000	–	10,000
Other	15,000	–	15,000
Total	560,000		559,000
Excess of expenses over income	$ 45,000		$ 14,000

Fig. 3–2.   An example of a worksheet which converts a cash basis statement to an accrual basis statement.

* A simplified accrual bookkeeping system is discussed in Chapter 29 in which the records are kept on a cash basis except at the end of the period when accrual entries are recorded in the books.

Adjustments were made to the cash statement in column 2 as follows:

> *Investment income—*$20,000 of dividends and interest that were received during the current year applicable to last year were deducted. At the same time at the end of the year there were dividends and interest receivable of $25,000 which were added. Therefore, on an accrual basis, a net adjustment of $5,000 was added.
>
> *Fees from the city—*This year the city changed its method of paying fees for children sent to the orphanage by the courts. In prior years the city paid $15 a day for each child assigned at the beginning of the month. This year because of a tight budget the city got behind and now pays in the following month. At the end of the year the city owed $25,000, which was added to income.
>
> *Expenses—*All the unpaid bills at the end of the year were added up and compared to the amount of unpaid bills as of last year (which were subsequently paid in the current year). Here is a summary of these expenses:

	Add unpaid at end of this year	Less paid in current year applicable to last year	Net add (deduct)
Salaries	$15,000	$20,000	$(5,000)
Food	12,000	10,000	2,000
Fuel	3,000	2,000	1,000
Maintenance	5,000	4,000	1,000
Children's allowances	—	—	—
Other	1,000	1,000	—

As can be seen, it is not difficult to adjust a cash basis statement to an accrual basis in a small organization. The bookkeeper just has to go about it in a systematic manner, being very careful not to forget to remove similar items received, or paid, in the current year which are applicable to the prior year.

Actually, in this illustration there is relatively little difference between the cash and accrual basis except for the $25,000 owed by the city due to its change in the timing of payments. Possibly the only adjustment that need be made in this instance is the recording of this $25,000. The problem is that until this worksheet has been prepared there is no way to be sure that the other adjustments aren't material. Accordingly, it is recommended that a worksheet similar to this one always be prepared to insure that all material adjustments are made.

MODIFIED CASH BASIS

Some nonprofit organizations use a "modified cash basis" system of accounting. On this basis of accounting, certain transactions will be recorded on an accrual basis and other transactions on a cash basis. Usually, on a modified cash basis all unpaid bills will be recorded on an accrual basis but uncollected income on a cash basis. However, there are many different variations.

Sometimes only certain types of unpaid bills are recorded. Payroll taxes that have been withheld from employee salaries but which have not yet been paid to the government are a good example of the type of transaction, not involving cash, which might be recorded. Clearly, these taxes are just as much an obligation as the salaries.

On a modified cash basis it is not necessary for the organization to have a complex set of books to record all obligations and receivables. In small and medium-sized nonprofit organizations it is quite sufficient to keep the records on the cash basis and then at the end of the month tally up the unpaid bills and the uncollected receivables and either record these formally in the books through journal entries or record them through a worksheet in the manner described above.*

Under the cash basis, one of the practical ways some smaller organizations use to record all accrued expenses is to hold the disbursement record "open" for the first four or five days of each month. This allows the bookkeeper to pay last month's bills as they arrive about the first of the month and record them in the prior month's records. While the organization actually pays such amounts in the first few days of the new period, it considers the payment as having been made on the last day of the prior period. This means that the organization does not show accounts payable but instead a reduced cash balance. This is frequently a useful practice for reporting internally to the board because it gives reasonable assurance that all expenditures incurred are recorded in the proper period. Of course, in financial statements prepared for external use, such payments subsequent to the end of the period should be shown as accounts payable instead of a decrease in cash.

When Accrual Basis Reporting Should Be Used

There are many advantages of cash basis accounting and reporting, but the accrual basis is ordinarily necessary for fair presentation of the

---

* Chapters 29 and 30 discuss the bookkeeping procedures to formally record accrual basis adjustments in the accounts.

financial statements. Unless the organization does not have any material amounts of unpaid bills or uncollected income at the beginning or end of the period, accrual basis reporting is required to present an accurate picture of the results of operations and of the financial position of the organization.

Accrual basis reporting is also required if an organization is trying to measure the cost of a product or service. It is impossible to know what a particular activity cost during the year if unpaid bills have not been included as an expense in the statement. The same is true where services are provided for a fee but some fees have not been billed and collected during the period. If a board or its membership is trying to draw conclusions from the statements as to the cost or profitability of a particular service, accrual basis statements are essential. The same is true when an organization is on a tight budget and budget comparisons are made with actual income and expenses to see how effectively management has kept to the budget. Without including unpaid bills or uncollected income, such a comparison to budget can be very misleading and useless.*

Generally accepted accounting principles for both commercial and nonprofit organizations include the use of accrual basis accounting. Organizations that have their books audited by certified public accountants, and who wish the CPA to report that the financial statements are prepared in accordance with "generally accepted accounting principles," have to either keep their records on the accrual basis, or make the appropriate adjustments at the end of the year to convert to this basis.†

LEGAL REQUIREMENTS

For some organizations soliciting funds from the public, there are legal requirements with respect to using the accrual basis of accounting. In New York, for example, most nonprofit organizations, other than schools and churches, are required to report to the state on an accrual basis if they have contributions and other revenue of more than $50,000 annually. However, even in New York the requirement is not that the records be kept on an accrual basis, but only that the organization file reports prepared on an accrual basis. This means the organization could still keep cash basis records throughout the year, provided it adjusts them to accrual basis for report purposes. Chapters 25, 26, and 27 dis-

---

* Budgets are discussed in Chapter 19.
† See Chapter 23 for a discussion of "generally accepted accounting principles," independent audits, and auditors' opinions.

cuss the legal reporting requirements for nonprofit organizations. If an organization is required to file reports with one or more state agencies, it should examine the instructions accompanying the report very carefully to see what the reporting requirements are.

CONCLUSION

There are two bases for keeping records—the cash basis and the accrual basis. The vast majority of small nonprofit organizations use the cash basis of accounting, and this is probably an acceptable and appropriate basis. The chief reason for using the cash basis is its simplicity. Clearly, where there are no significant differences between the cash and accrual basis, the cash basis should be used. Where there are material differences, however, the records should either be kept on an accrual basis, or cash basis statements should be modified to reflect the major unrecorded amounts.

4

Fund Accounting

Fund accounting is peculiar to nonprofit organizations.* Most readers of commercial financial statements are not familiar with this type of accounting or its form of reporting. As a consequence, fund accounting more than any other single concept of nonprofit accounting tends to confuse the reader. The purpose of this chapter is to clarify the concept of fund accounting, and discuss its advantages and disadvantages. Chapter 12 discusses the presentation of fund accounting financial statements that will pass the "grandparent test" for clarity.

FUND ACCOUNTING DEFINED

Fund accounting is a system of accounting in which separate records are kept for assets donated to an organization which are restricted by donors or outside parties to certain specified purposes or use. The financial statements usually follow this separate accountability and often separate statements are prepared for each "fund." Assets which carry similar restrictions are usually commingled in a single fund and accounted for together rather than separately.

There is really nothing difficult about fund accounting other than mechanics. It is an accountability or stewardship concept, used principally by nonprofit and governmental organizations that are legally

---

* Readers are cautioned against trying to apply the principles and terminology used in governmental accounting to nonprofit accounting. While both types of accounting follow fund accounting concepts, their application and terminology are different. It is, of course, in large measure because of these differences that this book has been written. Readers interested in governmental accounting will find a number of well-written texts available.

responsible for seeing that certain funds or assets are used only for specified purposes. This need for separate accountability arises whenever a nonprofit organization receives restricted contributions.

For example:

The Johnstown PTA receives a special contribution of $5,000 which the donor specifies is to be used only in connection with an educational program on drug abuse.

The Springtown Methodist Church decides that they need an addition to the Church and a building fund drive is established to raise $100,000. Contributors are told the money will be used only for this building addition.

The Boy Scout Council of Arlington receives a $250,000 gift from a wealthy businessman (an ex-Boy Scout) to be used as an endowment fund.

In each instance, there is a restriction on the contribution and once the organization accepts a restricted gift, it has an obligation to follow the donor's instructions.[*] In fund accounting, restricted contributions are treated as separate "funds," and separate statements are often prepared for each grouping of similar-type funds. In preparing its financial statements, the organization separates the funds which carry restrictions from those that are unrestricted.

Some organizations, as a matter of convenience, establish by board action additional funds in order to segregate certain amounts which the board intends to use for specified purposes in the future. An example of a board-created fund would be an "Unrestricted Investment Fund." The important thing to note about these board-designated funds is that they carry no legal restrictions and represent only an internal designation for the convenience of the organization. By contrast, donor-restricted funds do carry legal restrictions, and the approval of the original donor or the court is usually required to divert these contributions from their original purpose.

CATEGORIES OF FUNDS

An organization that receives many restricted contributions, each having a separate restriction, is faced with the practical problem of

[*] One of the responsibilities of the treasurer is to be sure that controls are established to ensure that restricted funds are expended only for the purpose intended. Usually this control is established through the use of fund accounting. Every new treasurer in an organization should review the disbursement procedures to be sure that restricted funds cannot be inadvertently spent in violation of the restriction.

having to keep track of and report on many separate funds. While it is possible to keep separate records on an almost unlimited number of restricted funds, these separate funds are usually classified by the type of donor restriction. For example, in a college building fund drive, one donor may specify that a gift is to be used for a new chemistry building; another may specify a dormitory. Both represent restricted contributions to a category of fund generally referred to as "Building Funds." For reporting purposes, both gifts would be shown under this broad classification, and detailed records would be kept on both contributions to insure that they are used only for the purposes specified.

In the past an almost infinite variety of names has been given to various categories of funds. However, four categories or groupings of funds are most frequently used by nonprofit organizations for reporting purposes. The description or title indicates the type of general restriction on the funds. The following are the four groupings most commonly encountered.

Current Unrestricted Fund

Several titles are given to the fund that carries out the general activities of the organization. It may be known as the "Unrestricted Fund," "Current Unrestricted Fund," "Operating Fund," "General Fund," "Current Fund," or "Current General Fund." The most common name given is the "Current Unrestricted Fund." This fund contains no restricted assets,* and the board can use the fund as it chooses, to carry out the purposes for which the organization was founded.

All unrestricted contributions, gifts, and income should be recorded in this fund. Except for transactions involving one of the other categories of funds, all transactions of the organization are included in this fund. If the organization never receives restricted gifts or contributions, this fund would show all activity. In that case the organization would not be using fund accounting as it is commonly thought of.

Board-Designated Funds. Board-designated funds are a subcategory of unrestricted funds. They are established when the board acts to transfer or segregate unrestricted funds into a fund that the board intends to use for a specific purpose. In the past it was common to estab-

---

* However, if the amount of donor-restricted funds unspent at the end of the year is relatively small in amount, many organizations will include such amounts in the current unrestricted fund to minimize reader confusion by avoiding the need for a restricted fund. This is not only perfectly acceptable, it is highly desirable. The key requirement is that the Balance Sheet clearly discloses the amount of restricted fund balance remaining at the end of the year.

lish separate board-designated funds which were treated as separate funds, apart from the unrestricted funds. This is still the prevailing practice for colleges and universities. However, the accounting profession recently indicated that for reporting purposes board-designated funds should be included as part of unrestricted funds for most types of nonprofit organizations.*

The reason for this is simply that the artificial separation of certain unrestricted funds confuses the unknowledgeable reader. As discussed elsewhere in this book, one of the most important reporting principles is to keep the reporting and accounting simple enough so that the reader has an opportunity to understand what is happening. The use of a separate board-designated fund will not improve reader comprehension nor does such a fund have any legal significance.

Nevertheless some organizations do establish separate board-designated funds. Although it is usually not a desirable practice, it is acceptable, provided all of these three rules are followed:

1. The board-designated funds must be clearly labeled as "unrestricted" in all statements;
2. In the Statement of Income: †
   a. A columnar reporting approach must be followed ** *and* the board-designated funds must be reported alongside the other unrestricted funds, preferably with the word "unrestricted" appearing across all columns;
   b. A total unrestricted column combining the current unrestricted fund and the board-designated fund(s) must be presented.‡
3. In the Balance Sheet the total of the unrestricted funds must be shown (the Balance Sheet does not have to be in a columnar format; see Figure 13–5, page 197).

An example of an acceptable presentation is shown in Figure 12–1 (page 150).

* See Chapters 13, 15, and 16.

† Throughout this book the authors use the term "Statement of Income" to refer to the statement which shows the revenue, support, contributions and expenses of the organization. Some may object to the use of the word "income" in this title, but the authors' intention is only to simplify the title for the reader's convenience.

** The columnar format approach is discussed in detail in Chapter 12.

‡ There may be circumstances where such totals are not needed. For example, an organization with only two main fund groupings (say an unrestricted fund and a plant fund) plus a board-designated investment fund may find that the use of a separate "total unrestricted" column (i.e., excluding the plant fund) is superfluous. Each organization should evaluate its own financial statements to determine the need for a total unrestricted column in the Statement of Income, but generally such a total column is appropriate.

Current Restricted Fund

Various titles are given to the fund that accounts for monies given to an organization to be spent as part of the normal activities for certain specified purposes. It may be known as "Current Restricted Fund," "Fund for Specified Purposes," "Donor Restricted Fund," or just plain "Restricted Fund." For example, the $5,000 given to the Johnstown PTA for public education on drug abuse would be added to such a fund. Often the funds are relatively small in amount and they are normally used in the year received or in the following year. Generally the aggregate of all these current restricted funds is summarized for financial statement purposes and they are not individually reported in detail.

Most current restricted funds are given for a particular purpose which the organization normally carries out as a part of its activities. At other times the contribution may be for a purpose that is not normally part of the organization's regular activities, or perhaps the money will not be expended for some time. Examples include a contribution to a building fund or to an endowment fund. Contributions restricted for purposes other than current activities are usually reported in another fund category.

The current restricted fund would not include board-designated funds. There is an extended discussion in Chapter 9 on reporting current restricted contributions.

Endowment Fund

This title is given to the fund that contains assets donated to the organization with the stipulation by the donor that only the income earned by these assets can be used. Generally—but not always—the income itself is not restricted and can be used to carry out the organization's principal activities. Occasionally endowment gifts are received which have restrictions on the uses to be made of the income. If term endowment gifts are received, they must be added to the endowment fund for a period of years, after which time the principal can be used as desired by the board. Another possibility is a gift, the income from which is paid to the donor until death; the gift then becomes completely unrestricted.*
Obviously, it is very important to keep track of these restrictions and to properly reflect them in the financial statements.

Some donors, while not formally placing restrictions, may orally ex-

---

* These gifts are usually referred to as "life income" funds or sometimes "annuity" funds. See Chapter 14 (page 205) for a discussion of these funds.

press the "desire" that the gift be put in the endowment fund. However, if the decision is left to the board, such amounts are unrestricted and should be added to the current unrestricted fund. Legally unrestricted gifts should not be added to the endowment fund. All amounts in the endowment fund should bear legal restrictions that the board cannot normally alter.

Fixed Asset Fund

Several titles may be given to the fund in which the cost of fixed assets (land, buildings, furniture and fixtures, equipment, etc.) is recorded. This fund may be referred to as the "Fixed Asset Fund," "Land, Building, and Equipment Fund," or "Plant Fund." Such a fund will usually also include unexpended restricted building fund contributions.*

The principal reason for using this fund is that the board wants to remove these assets from the unrestricted fund. The unrestricted fund will then represent more closely the current activity of the organization, that is, the funds available for current program use. Fixed assets such as buildings are not really available in the sense that they cannot be readily converted to cash and expended. Therefore, many boards believe that fixed assets should be placed in a separate fund.

The use of a separate fixed asset fund is largely a board decision, and there is no reason why a separate fund must be established.† The authors do not recommend the use of a separate fixed asset fund even though this is the predominant practice. A separate fixed asset fund creates considerable confusion for the reader of the statement, without offering any real advantage. Fixed assets are a necessary part of the resources that are available to the board for carrying out the purposes for which the organization was formed; creating a separate fixed asset fund implies that fixed assets are not available to the board for day-to-day operations.

Segregating fixed assets into a separate fund also causes considerable bookkeeping and reporting problems, with the increased likelihood that the reader will not understand the statements. This is particularly

* The AICPA Statement of Position applicable to certain nonprofit organizations provides that unexpended building fund gifts be reflected in a "deferred income" account until such time as the restriction is met through the acquisition of the building or asset. See Chapter 16 (page 260) for a discussion of this approach.

† The AICPA Hospital Audit Guide provides that fixed assets should be reported in the "unrestricted" fund and not as a separate fund. The AICPA Audit Guides for Colleges and Universities and Voluntary Health and Welfare Organizations both illustrate the use of a separate fixed asset fund. The 1978 AICPA Statement of Position indicates either approach is acceptable.

true if the organization records depreciation on its fixed assets in the current unrestricted fund. As is explained in more detail in Chapter 7, charging depreciation in the current unrestricted fund and then transferring this depreciation to the fixed asset fund is very confusing. Few readers will understand this transfer.

Concern has been expressed about including the fixed asset fund in the unrestricted fund, because part or even all of the fixed assets may have been purchased with gifts restricted for the purchase of fixed assets. Can such fixed assets be included in the unrestricted fund? Where fixed assets have been purchased with restricted funds, prevailing opinion asserts that once the acquisition has been made the restriction has effectively been met and is therefore removed. If the asset is sold at a subsequent date and there is a legal question whether the proceeds are restricted or unrestricted, the proceeds may be classified as restricted at that time.

If a fixed asset fund is combined as part of the unrestricted fund, unspent restricted building fund contributions would normally be included as part of the "Current Restricted Fund." Also, where the fixed asset fund is combined with the current unrestricted fund, the title of the fund is usually changed to the "Unrestricted Fund."

There is an extended discussion of accounting for fixed assets in Chapter 6.

Other Fund Groupings

In addition to the above funds, other specialized fund groupings may be encountered. For example, colleges and universities often have "Loan or Scholarship" funds and "Retirement of Indebtedness" funds. Usually the title is descriptive of the nature of these resources.

Need To Limit Number of Funds

Occasionally a donor will give such a large sum of money, often for endowment purposes, that the board will want to create a separate fund bearing the name of the donor, rather than including this separate fund in the financial statements with all other similar funds. Examples would be the "George Beauchamp Scholarship Fund" or the "Josie Henderson Memorial Fund." The principal reason for this separate reporting is to give the donor public recognition for a substantial gift.

The objective is fine, but it does create presentation problems since an organization could find itself with a substantial number of funds in the financial statements. When this happens, there is a risk that the reader will become confused. Unless there are only one or two "name" funds, they should all be summarized and included under one of the major categories of funds discussed above. At the same time public recognition can be given by preparing a supporting schedule showing the details of each "name" fund. If this schedule is skillfully prepared it will not detract significantly from the clarity of the main statement. An example of such reporting is shown in Figure 12–8 (page 160).

OTHER CLASSIFICATIONS OF FUNDS

In recent years a number of accountants have urged a different type of classification for purposes of reporting. Instead of reporting a classification based on the uses which will be made of the funds, it is suggested that the funds be classified more broadly by the degree of availability for current usage. Some have proposed using the classification "unrestricted" and "restricted" while others propose the classification "expendable" and "nonexpendable." Both have merit.

Unrestricted and Restricted

Under this approach the organization continues to keep its records on a fund accounting classification basis as described above, but at the time of preparing financial statements the funds are combined for reporting purposes into only two classifications: "unrestricted" and "restricted." These classifications would include:

Unrestricted
  Current unrestricted fund
  Fixed asset fund, except for unexpended gifts for fixed assets *

Restricted
  Current restricted fund
  Unexpended gifts for fixed assets
  Endowment fund

The theory behind this approach is that the board has basically only two kinds of funds—those over which it has complete control and those over which it has only partial control. This approach is designed to

---

* Some will argue that fixed assets should be classified as restricted in this type of classification approach. There are valid arguments on both sides but the authors recommend they be treated as unrestricted.

clearly show this distinction. An example of financial statements prepared on this basis is shown in Figure 14–4 (page 226).

Expendable and Nonexpendable

The other classification approach summarizes the funds based on their availability for current expenditure to further the organization's objectives:

Expendable
  Current unrestricted funds
  Current restricted funds

Nonexpendable
  Fixed asset funds *
  Endowment funds

The theory behind this approach is that the board has basically only two kinds of funds—those which are currently expendable for the organization's program, and those which are not. The nonexpendable are more in the nature of "capital-type" funds.

A TYPICAL SET OF "FUND" FINANCIAL STATEMENTS

Figure 4–1 shows the simplified statements of a nonprofit organization having four separate funds—a current unrestricted fund, a current restricted fund, a fixed asset fund, and an endowment fund. This presentation is typical of a small organization using fund accounting. The format makes separate accountability of each fund quite evident. It also shows the main problem associated with fund accounting—the difficulty in getting an overall picture of the organization's affairs without a careful review of all the statements.

The principal advantage of fund accounting is that the activities of each fund are reported separately. There is no question of accountability since the reader can see exactly what has taken place. This is the stewardship aspect.

* The reader may wonder why fixed assets are treated as nonexpendable here whereas the authors treated them as unrestricted earlier. The logic of this approach deals more with whether they can be expended—i.e., directly spent—than with the question of restriction. As previously discussed, fixed assets are used in the current activities of the organization and in this sense are "spent." Yet on balance the authors feel that with the expendable/nonexpendable classifications, fixed assets should be treated as nonexpendable.

McLEAN COMMUNITY SERVICE CENTER

CURRENT UNRESTRICTED FUND
STATEMENT OF INCOME, EXPENSES, AND CHANGES IN FUND BALANCES
For the Year Ended August 31, 19X1

Income:

Contributions and gifts	$ 85,000	
Service fees	110,000	
Investment income from Endowment Fund .	20,000	
Other income	13,000	
Total income		$228,000

Expenses:

Salaries	130,000	
Rent	43,000	
Utilities	12,000	
Other.	10,000	
Total expenses		195,000
Excess of income over expenses		33,000
Fund balance, beginning of year		7,000
Less—Transfer to Fixed Asset Fund		(25,000)
Fund balance, end of year		$ 15,000

Fig. 4–1. A typical set of income statements where each fund is reported in a separate statement.

The principal disadvantage of fund accounting is that it is difficult to comprehend the total activities of the organization without a careful review of all the statements and perhaps a little bit of pencil pushing. For example, what was the total excess of income over expenses for all funds? To answer this question it is necessary to add three figures and to be careful to pick out the right figures ($33,000 + $1,000 + $71,000 = $105,000).

The statement presentation in Figure 4–1 is a quite simple form. Some organizations incorrectly record unrestricted investment income in the endowment fund and then transfer this income to the current unrestricted fund below the caption "excess of income over expenses." In this illustration, $20,000 would have been shown in the endowment fund and would then have been shown in the current unrestricted fund as a transfer. This would have been incorrect. Unrestricted endowment income is by definition unrestricted and all such income should be reported in the current unrestricted fund. If this income had been

McLEAN COMMUNITY SERVICE CENTER

CURRENT RESTRICTED FUND
STATEMENT OF CONTRIBUTIONS, EXPENSES, AND
CHANGES IN FUND BALANCES*
For the Year Ended August 31, 19X1

Contributions		$ 24,000
Expenses:		
Athletic awards	$15,000	
Citizenship program	5,000	
Other.	3,000	
Total expenses		23,000
Excess of contributions over expenses		1,000
Fund balance, beginning of year		10,000
Fund balance, end of year		$ 11,000

McLEAN COMMUNITY SERVICE CENTER

FIXED ASSET FUND
STATEMENT OF CHANGES IN FUND BALANCES
For the Year Ended August 31, 19X1

Fund balance, beginning of year	$ 50,000
Add—Transfer from General Fund	25,000
Fund balance, end of year	$ 75,000

McLEAN COMMUNITY SERVICE CENTER

ENDOWMENT FUND
STATEMENT OF INCOME AND CHANGES IN FUND BALANCES*
For the Year Ended August 31, 19X1

Income:	
Contributions and gifts	$ 25,000
Gain on sale of investments	46,000
Total	71,000
Fund balance, beginning of year	250,000
Fund balance, end of year	$321,000

*The title used in actual practice would probably be "Statement of Changes in Fund Balances." See Chapter 12 for a discussion of this type of statement.

Fig. 4—1.   Continued.

handled incorrectly as a transfer, the excess of income in the current unrestricted fund would appear to have been an excess of $13,000, because the transfer-in of the $20,000 would have appeared after the excess-of-income caption. Few readers would realize from this incorrect presentation that the current unrestricted fund actually had an excess of income of $33,000.

The way to simplify fund accounting statements is to show all funds on a single statement in columnar format. In this format each fund is shown in a separate column side by side. These statements have been recast in this columnar format and are shown in Figure 12–1 (p. 150).

Interfund Borrowing

As was previously noted, one of the problems with having a number of separate "funds" is that there is sometimes difficulty in keeping all the transactions completely separate. For example, in the McLean Community Service Center illustration, the current unrestricted fund often runs out of cash over the summer months and the board authorizes a cash loan from the other funds. In theory there is no difficulty in keeping track of these borrowings, but it does create one more area where the reader who is not careful or knowledgeable can become confused. Figure 4–2 shows the Balance Sheet for the four funds used by the McLean Community Service Center. Notice the number of interfund transactions.

Note that the current unrestricted fund has borrowed $31,000—that is, $3,000 from the current restricted fund, $5,000 from the fixed asset fund, and $23,000 from the endowment fund. While this is perfectly clear to the person knowledgeable about fund accounting, or to the careful reader, some readers are neither knowledgeable nor careful.

One word of caution with respect to interfund borrowings. A fund should not borrow from another fund unless it is clear that the borrowing fund will have the financial resources to repay. It is not appropriate to finance a deficit operation through interfund borrowing.

It should also be observed that before funds are borrowed from legally restricted funds, advice should be sought from legal counsel as to whether such borrowings are permissible. It would appear entirely inappropriate for an organization to raise funds for a building addition and then "lend" such amounts to help finance general operations of the organization.

The statements presented above were fairly simple statements. There were only four funds, and the restricted funds were carefully combined to eliminate unnecessary detail. Some organizations, however, attempt

McLEAN COMMUNITY SERVICE CENTER

BALANCE SHEET
August 31, 19X1

Assets		Liabilities and Fund Balance	
CURRENT UNRESTRICTED FUND			
Cash	$ 50,000	Accounts payable	$ 17,000
Pledges receivable	13,000	Due to other funds	31,000
			48,000
		Fund balance	15,000
	$ 63,000		$ 63,000
CURRENT RESTRICTED FUND			
Cash	$ 11,000	Accounts payable	$ 3,000
Due from Current Unrestricted Fund	3,000	Fund balance	11,000
	$ 14,000		$ 14,000
FIXED ASSET FUND			
Due from Current Unrestricted Fund	$ 5,000	Fund balance	$ 75,000
Equipment	70,000		
	$ 75,000		$ 75,000
ENDOWMENT FUND			
Cash	$ 3,000	Fund balance	$321,000
Due from Current Unrestricted Fund	23,000		
Investments	295,000		
	$321,000		$321,000

Fig. 4-2. A typical Balance Sheet where each fund is reported separately.

to break out the restricted funds into a number of separate funds—one for each major donor. As the number of funds increases, there will be more transfers between funds and the complexity will increase. Fund accounting and reporting can become very difficult, not so much because the concepts are difficult but because of the confusion to the reader created by so many funds. It is not enough merely to report the activities of the organization; it is equally important that the statements be effective in communicating what has actually happened. If this is not accomplished, the statements have not served their purpose and the treasurer has failed in a most important responsibility. Chapter 12 discusses alternative presentations to help simplify the financial statements.

ELIMINATION OF FUNDS FOR REPORTING PURPOSES

More and more nonprofit organizations are re-evaluating the need to report their financial affairs on a "fund accounting" basis. Instead they are presenting a consolidated Statement of Income showing all activity for the year, and a consolidated Balance Sheet carefully disclosing in line captions or in footnotes all pertinent information on the restricted funds. This approach gives appropriate recognition that a nonprofit organization is a single entity and not a series of separate entities called "funds."

This does not mean the organization will not keep detailed records on a fund accounting basis. It certainly will have to do so or it will lose track of donor-imposed restrictions. Rather, it means that for reporting purposes the organization will carefully combine all the activity for the year in a meaningful manner. This is not easy to do but, if carefully done, adds greatly to the reader's understanding of the organization's overall financial picture.

CONCLUSION

Fund accounting is simply a common-sense answer to the problem of recording and reporting funds given to an organization for a restricted purpose. There is nothing particularly difficult about the concepts involved, but as the number of funds increases there is considerable risk that the reader of the financial statements will not fully understand the relationship among the funds and therefore will lose sight of the overall financial affairs of the organization. For this reason great care must be taken in preparing the financial statements where fund accounting is involved.

5

Interfund Transfers and Appropriations

As pointed out in the previous chapter, the use of fund accounting, while often necessary, creates a certain amount of confusion and adds to the problem of meeting the "grandparent test." In this chapter two other problem areas will be explored. One relates to the use of "transfers" to allocate assets between funds, and the other relates to the use of appropriations to authorize future expenditure of funds for specific purposes. Both add to the complexity of financial statements. Transfers between funds are frequently unavoidable; appropriations, on the other hand, serve very little purpose and should be avoided.

TRANSFERS BETWEEN FUNDS

Nonprofit organizations following fund accounting procedures utilize a number of different funds, some restricted, such as funds for specific purposes, and some unrestricted, such as board-designated funds. The board has the right to transfer assets between unrestricted funds and in certain circumstances between restricted and unrestricted funds. For example, if the board has established a board-designated investment fund, it may from time to time transfer funds from a current unrestricted fund to this fund. Or, alternatively, it may find at some time that it needs some of the funds previously transferred and will, in turn, transfer some of these funds back to the current unrestricted fund. Another example would be the transfer of unrestricted assets to the fixed asset fund (where a separate fixed asset fund is maintained) to pay for fixed assets purchased in whole or part with unrestricted funds.

Transfers can very easily confuse the readers of financial statements if they are not properly shown. Special care must be taken in preparing the statements to insure that "transfers" will be understood.

Presentation of Transfers

Several principles should be followed in the presentation of "transfers" in the financial statements. The first and most important is that a transfer should not be shown in a manner that suggests the transfer is an expense to the transferring fund or income to the receiving fund. The easiest way to avoid this is to show the transfer in a separate Statement of Changes in Fund Balances or, if that separate statement is not used, in the Statement of Income, Expenses, and Changes in Fund Balances after the caption "Fund balances, beginning of year."

Transfers should not be shown as an expense or as income because only transactions which result in expense or income to the organization as a whole are shown in the expense or income sections of a financial statement. A transfer is purely an internal action involving neither. For this reason great care must be taken to avoid a presentation that suggests the transfer is either an income or an expense item.

Transfers in a Combined Statement of Income, Expenses, and Changes in Fund Balances. The most effective manner in which to present a transfer between funds with a minimal risk of misunderstanding is in a columnar statement, with the activity of each fund shown in a separate column, side by side.* This is a desirable format because the reader can easily see both sides of the transfer: the funds going out of one fund and the funds going into the other fund.

Figure 5–1 shows this columnar presentation for a Statement of Income, Expenses, and Changes in Fund Balances. The Board of the Corvallis YMCA decided to transfer $40,000 from its current unrestricted fund to an unrestricted investment fund. Notice how this is handled in a columnar format. The transfer is shown after the caption "Fund balance, beginning of year." In this way there is no inference that the transfer had anything to do with either income or expenses of the current unrestricted fund for the year. Rather, it is inferred that a portion of the fund balance accumulated over many years was transferred to another board-controlled fund.

---

* Chapter 12 discusses the use of columnar format statements and their advantages and disadvantages. The reader may want to refer to this discussion since no attempt will be made to discuss this format in this chapter although it will be used throughout.

CORVALLIS YMCA

STATEMENT OF INCOME, EXPENSES, AND CHANGES IN FUND BALANCES
For the Year Ending December 31, 19X1

| | Unrestricted | | Funds for | |
	Current Fund	Investment Fund	Specified Purposes	Combined All Funds
		(in thousands)		
Income:				
Membership	$255			$255
Community fund	50			50
Program activities	372			372
Contributions and other income	45		$17	62
Investment income	13			13
Gain on sale of investments . .	15			15
Total income	750		17	767
Expenses:				
Program	326			326
General administration	265			265
Property repairs and maintenance	50			50
Depreciation	35			35
Other	14		7	21
Total expenses	690		7	697
Excess of income over expenses	60		10	70
Fund balance, beginning of year	415	$200	10	625
Transfer between funds	(40)	40		
Fund balance, end of year	$435	$240	$20	$695

Fig. 5–1.　Reporting a transfer in a columnar format Statement of Income, Expenses, and Changes in Fund Balances.

Transfers in Statement of Changes in Fund Balances.　Some organizations do not present a combined Statement of Income, Expenses, and Changes in Fund Balances. They have either two separate statements —a Statement of Income and Expenses and a Statement of Changes in Fund Balances—or only a Statement of Income and Expenses. If two separate statements are presented, the transfer should be shown in the Statement of Changes in Fund Balances. It should not be shown in the Statement of Income and Expenses since a transfer represents an adjustment of the fund balance rather than an item of income or expense.

CORVALLIS YMCA
STATEMENT OF INCOME AND EXPENSES
For the Year Ending December 31, 19X1

| | Unrestricted | | Funds for | |
	Current Fund	Investment Fund	Specified Purposes	Combined All Funds
		(in thousands)		
Income:				
Membership	$255			$255
Community fund	50			50
Program activities	372			372
Contributions and other income	45		$17	62
Investment income	13			13
Gain on sale of investments	15		—	15
Total income	750		17	767
Expenses:				
Program	326			326
General administration	265			265
Property repairs and maintenance	50			50
Depreciation	35			35
Other	14		7	21
Total expenses	690		7	697
Excess of income over expenses	$ 60		$10	$ 70

STATEMENT OF CHANGES IN FUND BALANCES
For the Year Ending December 31, 19X1

| | Unrestricted | | Funds for | |
	Current Fund	Investment Fund	Specified Purposes	Combined All Funds
		(in thousands)		
Fund balance, beginning of the year	$415	$200	$10	$625
Excess of income over expenses	60		10	70
Transfer between funds	(40)	40	—	—
Fund balance, end of the year	$435	$240	$20	$695

Fig. 5–2. Reporting a transfer when a separate Statement of Changes in Fund Balances is presented.

Figure 5–2 shows the Corvallis YMCA transfer of funds using both statements.

Transfers in Statement of Income and Expenses. A third possibility is that the organization will not show the changes in fund balance either in the income statement or as a separate statement. This might occur where the only change between the beginning and ending fund balance is the excess of income for the year. In that instance it is necessary to report the transfer in the Statement of Income and Expenses. Figure 5–3 shows the transfer after the caption "Excess of income over expenses."

CORVALLIS YMCA

STATEMENT OF INCOME, EXPENSES, AND TRANSFERS
For the Year Ending December 31, 19X1

	Unrestricted		Funds for Specified Purposes	Combined All Funds
	Current Fund	Investment Fund		
			(in thousands)	
Income:				
Membership	$255			$255
Community fund	50			50
Program activities	372			372
Contributions and other income	45		$17	62
Investment income	13			13
Gain on sale of investments . .	15			15
Total income	750		17	767
Expenses:				
Program	326			326
General administration	265			265
Property repairs and maintenance	50			50
Depreciation	35			35
Other	14		7	21
Total expenses	690		7	697
Excess of income over expenses	60		10	70
Transfer between funds	(40)	$40	—	—
Excess of income after transfer	$ 20	$40	$10	$ 70

Fig. 5–3. A transfer reported in a Statement of Income and Expenses. This presentation would not be acceptable if a separate Statement of Changes in Fund Balances is also presented.

This approach is acceptable only if a Statement of Changes in Fund Balances is not presented either separately or as part of the income statement. In practice, this approach is seldom encountered since most organizations will include a "change in fund balance section" at the bottom of the income statement as shown in Figure 5–1.

Transfer of Income or Deficit

The boards of some organizations create a separate board-designated investment fund and then use "transfers" as a device to reduce or increase the current unrestricted fund balance to a predetermined level. The casual reader is likely to be misled where this transfer is reported directly on the Statement of Income and Expenses (rather than on a Statement of Changes in Fund Balances). This is often what the board has in mind.

Figures 5–4 and 5–5 show two examples of this type of transfer, and at the same time provide perfect illustrations of why fund accounting is so hard for most readers to understand when separate statements are presented for each fund. In each of the examples the casual reader is likely to look at only the last figure in the statement: the $500 excess of income over expenses and transfers. These are the wrong figures to focus on. What should be observed is a $15,000 excess of income in Figure 5–4 and an $8,000 deficit in Figure 5–5.

Transfers are made at the "discretion" of the board, and if this type of transfer is made the board can "window dress" the statements to suit

---

THE JOHNSTOWN MUSEUM
STATEMENT OF CURRENT UNRESTRICTED FUND INCOME, EXPENSES AND TRANSFERS
For the Year Ending December 31, 19X1

Income		$157,000
Less—Expenses.....................................		(142,000)
Excess of income over expenses......................		15,000
Less—Transfers to:		
Building fund	$ 4,500	
Board-designated investment fund	10,000	14,500
Excess of income over expenses and transfers		$ 500

Fig. 5–4.   An example of a transfer which reduces the current unrestricted fund income. The casual reader is likely to confuse this transfer with an expense, and may wrongly conclude the excess of income is $500.

THE SMITHVILLE MUSEUM

STATEMENT OF CURRENT UNRESTRICTED FUND INCOME,
EXPENSES AND TRANSFERS
For the Year Ending December 31, 19X1

Income	$102,000
Less—Expenses	(110,000)
Excess of expenses over income	(8,000)
Add—Transfer from board-designated investment fund	8,500
Excess of income and transfers over expenses	$ 500

Fig. 5–5. A transfer which covers a current unrestricted fund deficit for the year. The casual reader is likely to confuse this transfer with income, and may wrongly conclude the excess of income is $500.

its objectives. In Figure 5–4 it appears that the board may be somewhat embarrassed by the surplus and has disposed of it by transferring it to other funds. Perhaps the motivation is fund raising. Many believe that it is hard to convince contributors that money is needed if the fund shows a big surplus. While the careful reader will recognize the surplus, the casual reader, or the reader who does not understand that transfers are made at the discretion of the board, may think the net income for the year was only $500. In Figure 5–5 it could appear that the board allowed expenses to get out of hand and has tried to cover up the deficit. Again, only the careful reader will understand that the transfer is merely a bookkeeping device.

The real problem with these two transfers is not that they were made, but that they were reported in a manner that suggests the transfers were items of income or expenses. This confusion would not exist if the transfer had been made in a separate Statement of Changes in Fund Balances, or in a separate "changes in fund balance section" of the income statement.

At the same time, where separate board-designated funds are used, transfers should not be made to keep the current unrestricted fund balance at "zero" or at some artificially low amount. Transfers to board-designated funds should be made only when it is obvious that there are surplus funds in the current unrestricted fund that are not likely to be needed in the foreseeable future. Likewise, transfers should not be made to the general fund from board-designated funds just to cover a particular year's deficit as long as there is a surplus remaining from prior years. Transfers should be made to the current unrestricted fund only when the balance in that fund has become so small that cash is needed from other funds for operations.

Other Transfers

Occasionally there are other transfers between funds. In some instances expenditures for "current" activities are made from the current unrestricted fund but are later paid for by a current restricted fund. This is often handled as a transfer. However, it would be more straightforward to include the expense directly in the current restricted fund, rather than including it in the unrestricted fund and then showing it as a transfer. The fact that the bookkeeping took place in one fund does not mean the organization cannot report the expense directly in the fund that ultimately paid for it.

Another type of transfer involves depreciation expense which is shown in the unrestricted fund but is then transferred to the plant fund. Chapter 7 shows several illustrations of this type of transfer.

APPROPRIATIONS

An "appropriation" is an authorization to expend funds in the future for a specific purpose. An appropriation is not an expenditure nor does it represent an obligation that has already been incurred. It is only an internal authorization indicating how the board intends to spend part of the fund balance. Once funds have been "appropriated," they are usually set up in a separate account, but as part of the fund balance or net worth of the organization. They are not shown as a liability. All that happens when the board makes an appropriation is that part of the fund balance is set aside for a particular purpose. Since appropriations are made by the board, it can subsequently reverse its action and restore these funds to the general use of the organization.

In many ways an appropriation is very similar to a "transfer between funds" and often the two terms are used interchangeably. If monies are . going from one fund to another fund, a "transfer" is involved. Occasionally the treasurer will use the word "appropriation" instead of the word "transfer." This may confuse the readers, who usually don't understand what an appropriation is. If a transfer is being made between funds, the word "transfer" is correct and should be used.

If amounts are being set aside within a single fund, an appropriation or "designation" of the fund balance is involved. In this circumstance it is better to use the word "designated" since it is more descriptive of what the board has done.

Reporting Treatment

Figure 5–6 shows a simplified presentation of an appropriation where a separate Statement of Changes in Fund Balances is *not* used. Figure 5–7 shows a two-year presentation where a separate Statement of Changes in Fund Balances is used; the presentation is prepared in the second year, when the actual expenditure is made.

Appropriation accounting is both confusing and subject to abuse. It is confusing because very few readers understand exactly what an appropriation is. Most readers do not realize that an appropriation is not an expenditure but only a nonbinding, internal "authorization" for a future expenditure. Appropriation accounting is also confusing because the presentation in the financial statements is often not made in a straight-

---

THE BETHLEHEM SERVICES ORGANIZATION

STATEMENT OF INCOME, EXPENSES, AND UNAPPROPRIATED FUND BALANCE
Year Ending December 31, 19X1

(in thousands)

Income, ...	$100
Less—Expenses	80
Excess of income over expenses	20
Unappropriated fund balance, beginning of year	80
Less—Appropriated for Project A	(15)
Unappropriated fund balance, end of year	$ 85

BALANCE SHEET
December 31, 19X1

Cash		$100
Other assets		100
Total assets		$200
Accounts payable.		$100
Fund balance		
Appropriated—Project A	$15	
Unappropriated.	85	100
		$200

Fig. 5–6. Handling an appropriation in the financial statements, when a separate Statement of Changes in Fund Balances is not used. The authors discourage the use of the term "appropriation."

THE BETHLEHEM SERVICES ORGANIZATION

STATEMENT OF INCOME AND EXPENSES

(in thousands)

	Year Ending December 31, 19X1	Year Ending December 31, 19X2
Income	$100	$100
Expenses:		
Other than Project A	80	80
Project A	–	13
Total expenses	80	93
Excess of income over expenses.....................	$ 20	$ 7

STATEMENT OF CHANGES IN FUND BALANCES

	Year Ending December 31, 19X1	Year Ending December 31, 19X2
Appropriated:		
Balance, beginning of year	–	$ 15
Add—Appropriation for Project A	$ 15	–
Less--Appropriation no longer needed	–	(15)
Balance, end of year	15	–
Unappropriated:		
Balance, beginning of year	80	85
Excess of income over expenses for the year..........	20	7
Less—Appropriated for Project A	(15)	–
Add—Appropriation no longer needed	–	15
Balance, end of year	85	107
Fund balance	$100	$107

BALANCE SHEET

	December 31, 19X1	December 31, 19X2
Assets	$200	$207
Liabilities.......................................	$100	$100
Fund balance:		
Appropriated*: for Project A	15	
Unappropriated	85	107
Total liabilities and fund balance	$200	$207

*Sometimes the word "allocated" or the word "designated" will be used instead of "appropriated."

Fig. 5–7. An example of the recommended manner in which to report an appropriation, and the subsequent year's reversal when the actual expenditure is made.

THE BETHLEHEM SERVICES ORGANIZATION
STATEMENT OF INCOME AND EXPENSES
Year Ending December 31, 19X1

(in thousands)

Income		$100
Expenses:		
Total expenses	$80	
Appropriation for Project A	15	
Total expenses		95
Excess of income over expenses and appropriation		$ 5

Fig. 5–8. An example of an improper presentation of an appropriation. Even though the appropriation is clearly disclosed, most readers will assume the excess income for the year is $5,000.

forward manner. When the term "appropriation" appears on a financial statement the casual reader is probably uncertain of its meaning.

Appropriation accounting is subject to abuse because it is frequently used to give the appearance of an expenditure of funds out of the income for the year. This can occur when, incorrectly, the appropriation is treated as though it were an expenditure, as shown in Figure 5–8. This treatment presents a net income figure which appears lower than it actually is, and while it is understandable that a board interested in raising funds finds it difficult to go "hat-in-hand" if the income statement shows a large excess of income for the preceding year, the presentation is not permitted by current accounting pronouncements.

This is not to suggest that the board may not have a specific and very real project in mind when it makes an appropriation. Many organizations have sizable projects that only take place every few years. Often the board wants to provide for the funds over a period of time. The key point is that financial statements should represent transactions that have taken place in the past and not transactions that may take place in the future.

Appropriation Accounting Is Not Recommended

Appropriation accounting creates more confusion than clarification. It fails the "grandparent test." When an organization wants to set aside funds to provide for some future need, no bookkeeping entry is required. The board should perhaps put the desired amount in a savings account or earmark part of the investment securities. Neither action would result in a bookkeeping entry or a presentation problem.

Essential Rules Where "Appropriation" Accounting Is Used

Notwithstanding the reservations about the use of the term "appropriations," some organizations will continue to use this term. For these relatively few organizations, the following rules must be followed to provide a straightforward and meaningful presentation of what transpires and to conform to "generally accepted accounting principles": °

1. Appropriations should be made only for specific projects or undertakings. There should be no appropriations for general, undetermined contingencies or for any indefinite future losses. The unexpended balance of a department's budget should not be carried over to future period(s) in the guise of an appropriation.
2. All new appropriations and all remaining appropriations from prior years should be specifically authorized by the board each year. This function should not be delegated. All prior-year appropriations should be carefully reviewed to be certain they are still necessary. If all or part of a prior-year appropriation is no longer applicable, it should be reversed.
3. The appropriation must not be included as part of expenses. An example of an improper presentation is shown in Figure 5–8.
4. The appropriation should preferably be reported in a separate Statement of Changes in Fund Balances, as illustrated in Figure 5–7. If a separate Statement of Changes in Fund Balances is not used, the appropriation should be reported in the separate "change in fund balance section" of the income statement. Under no circumstances should the appropriation be reported before the caption "Excess of income over expenses."
5. When the expense is incurred in a subsequent period out of the funds previously appropriated, such expense must be included in the Statement of Income and Expenses for that year, as illustrated in Figure 5–7. It is not appropriate to charge such expense directly against the "appropriation" since to do so has the effect of concealing the expense. The reader has a right to know what has been incurred.
6. When an expenditure has been made, and charged to expense as provided in rule 5 above, the appropriation must be reversed in the same manner as it was set up. Figure 5–7 shows this reversal.

° All three AICPA Audit Guides and the Statement of Position addressed to the FASB indicate that appropriations may not be charged to expense, and are only a form of segregation of fund balance. See Chapters 13 through 16. The rules listed here comply with the requirements of these pronouncements.

7. The appropriation on the Balance Sheet must appear in the net worth or fund balance section, not in the liability section (see Figure 5–7).

Footnote Disclosure.   There is one final alternative for the organization wanting to use the term "appropriation" but not wanting to confuse the reader. That is to make no reference to appropriations on any of the statements and handle the disclosure only in footnotes. If this approach is followed, the footnotes to the Balance Sheet would disclose the amount appropriated. For example such a footnote might read:

Of the total fund balance of $100, $15 has been appropriated by the board for future use in Project A.

Even clearer wording would result if the word "designated" was substituted for the word "appropriated." This fully discloses the appropriation but eliminates all of the confusion on the statements. This approach is easiest to understand and therefore is recommended.

CONCLUSION

Confusing and complicated? Absolutely, and this is one of the major reasons why appropriation accounting or the use of the term "appropriation" should be avoided. Appropriation accounting serves little legitimate purpose and usually confuses the readers, including the board members themselves. If a board is truly concerned about setting aside a "reserve" or appropriation for some future year, it need only decide that it will not spend that amount. Furthermore, there is no reason why the monies represented by the appropriation can't be invested or put in a separate savings account. This is not to minimize the practical problem of actually setting this money aside and not spending it. This is always difficult. But appropriation accounting is not the answer.

6

Fixed Assets—Some Accounting Problems

Fixed assets and their depreciation present difficult accounting and reporting problems for nonprofit organizations. Some organizations record and report fixed assets, some do not. Some record and report depreciation, some do not. Until recently there was no area of nonprofit accounting in which opinion was so divided. This chapter summarizes current accounting thinking, presents alternatives for recording fixed assets, and offers several recommendations as to when each is appropriate. The next chapter discusses the related problem of depreciation.

NATURE OF THE PROBLEM

Fixed assets present a problem because many nonprofit organizations handle their affairs on a cash basis. When these organizations need to purchase a new building or equipment they turn to their membership to raise cash for these purchases in a building or equipment fund drive. Having raised the money and purchased the building, they feel there is relatively little significance in having the fixed asset on the organization's Balance Sheet except as a historical record of what it cost.

This is in contrast to a commercial enterprise which is dependent upon recovering the cost of the fixed asset through the sale of goods or services to outsiders. In a commercial business it is entirely appropriate to record the asset on the Balance Sheet and to depreciate (i.e., to systematically allocate) the cost of the asset over its estimated useful life. Depreciation is an expense which is charged against income for the period. If income from the sale of goods or services is not large enough to recover all the expenses including depreciation charges, the commercial enterprise is considered to have suffered a loss. If such losses occur over an extended period of time the enterprise will, of course, go bankrupt.

One of the principal reasons why recording fixed assets is so controversial is that the nature of nonprofit organizations is such that there usually is no compelling need to record the asset and then to depreciate it over a period of time. The element of matching income and costs has historically been of little interest to nonprofit organizations. This is changing.

Another factor is that nonprofit organizations frequently have as their principal asset buildings acquired many years ago. Because of inflation and growth in real estate values, these buildings and land are frequently worth several times their cost. To many it seems incongruous to depreciate a building on the basis of original cost when the building is known to be presently worth more than this amount.

Further, if fixed assets were originally purchased out of a special building or equipment fund drive, it is difficult to justify recording them on the books and then depreciating them since this depreciation represents a charge against current income. Effectively it appears that the cost of the building has been reported (and incurred) twice, once when the funds were originally raised and once when the assets are written off through the depreciation charge. Some believe it is unethical to raise funds for fixed assets in a building fund drive and subsequently to seek to recover the costs of such assets from the users of the facility or from future donors. Of course, the building or asset can be recorded and not depreciated but this goes against the grain of accounting for fixed assets as used by commercial enterprises. The result of all this is that many approaches are followed and there is much confusion.

ALTERNATIVES FOR HANDLING FIXED ASSETS

There are two basic alternative approaches for recording fixed assets, and a third, not recommended, hybrid approach.* These are:

* Part III of this book discusses the various published Audit Guides for nonprofit organizations as well as the AICPA Statement of Position. These documents prescribe the fixed asset and depreciation procedures that are acceptable for certain categories of organizations. Readers should refer to this discussion if the financial statements prepared by their organizations are to be described as being prepared in accordance with "generally accepted accounting principles." See Chapter 23 for a discussion of the significance of generally accepted accounting principles.

1. Immediate write-off approach, where assets are written off as purchased, in the Statement of Income and Expenses.
2. Capitalization approach, where the full cost of the asset is capitalized and recorded on the Balance Sheet. This is now the "generally accepted" accounting principle.
3. Write-off, then capitalize approach, where the asset is written off in the Statement of Income and Expenses but then capitalized on the Balance Sheet. This hybrid approach is not recommended.

Each of these three approaches is discussed in detail in the following sections. Each can be used for both accrual basis and cash basis organizations.

Immediate Write-Off Method

The "immediate write-off" approach is the simplest and the most frequently used. The organization treats all fixed asset purchases as any other category of expense, and does not capitalize the purchases as assets. The purchase is included as another expense in the Statement of Income and Expenses.

A good example would be the Rathskeller Youth Center,° which raised $25,000 for building alterations in 19X1. In 19X2, the Center purchased furniture and fixtures for $5,000. In this illustration the Center is on an accrual basis of accounting, but the principles would be the same if it were on a cash basis.

The Rathskeller Youth Center's Statement of Income and Expenses and Balance Sheet for these two years are shown in Figure 6–1.

Advantages.   The principal advantage is simplicity. In the first year, a building fund drive was conducted to raise income for the building alterations, and this statement shows clearly the income and expenditures for this purpose. The amount shown as excess of income over expenses represents the actual amount which remained after all bills were paid and pledges collected. While this is not the cash balance of the Center, it has much the same significance. With this presentation there is no confusion as to the amount available for the board to spend.

This approach recognizes that while the Center has a building which is essential to its continued operation, the building has no value in terms of meeting the day-to-day cash requirements.

° The Rathskeller Youth Center is located in a small town and provides a place where teenagers can congregate. The center occupies a small building that a wealthy businessman donated for this purpose. Operating expenses are covered principally from donations from the general public, although each teenager pays a small membership fee to belong.

RATHSKELLER YOUTH CENTER
STATEMENT OF INCOME AND EXPENSES

	Year Ending December 31,	
	19X1	19X2
Income:		
Membership fees	$ 4,000	$ 5,000
Contributions:		
General	37,900	39,600
Building Fund	25,000	–
Total income	66,900	44,600
Expenses:		
Salaries	11,000	10,000
Building maintenance	5,000	5,200
Coffee and food	12,800	12,600
Music and entertainment	2,000	2,400
Other	8,000	5,900
Building alterations	25,000	–
Furniture and equipment	–	5,000
Total expenses	63,800	41,100
Excess of income over expenses	$ 3,100	$ 3,500

BALANCE SHEET

	December 31,	
	19X1	19X2
Assets:		
Cash	$ 2,000	$ 4,000
Pledges receivable	6,500	6,700
Total assets	$ 8,500	$10,700
Liabilities:		
Accrued salaries	$ 3,000	$ 2,000
Accounts payable	400	100
Total liabilities	3,400	2,100
Fund balance:		
Beginning of year	2,000	5,100
Excess of income over expenses	3,100	3,500
End of year	5,100	8,600
Total liabilities and fund balance	$ 8,500	$10,700

Fig. 6–1. An example of the statements of an organization that follows the immediate write-off method of handling fixed assets.

Disadvantages.   The principal disadvantage is that the historical cost of the Center's building is not reflected on the Balance Sheet and therefore the fund balance does not truly represent the "net worth" of the organization. In addition, the Balance Sheet does not account for the asset by reflecting its existence and the organization seems much smaller in size than it actually is. Most members take pride in seeing fixed assets reflected in the financial statements. The absence of a building in the statements can be upsetting to many people, particularly those who have made large contributions toward its construction.

Another disadvantage, although not applicable in this case, is that by writing off the asset all at one time, no allocation of cost is made against future years' revenue-producing projects. This is discussed in Chapter 7. A related problem is that by writing off fixed assets as purchased, there can be considerable fluctuation in such expenditures between years. In this instance, observe that the furniture and equipment purchases of $5,000 in 19X2 were not matched by similar purchases in 19X1.

A further disadvantage is that this method is not "generally accepted" and an organization could not describe its financial statements as being prepared in accordance with generally accepted accounting principles. A CPA would therefore be required to qualify the opinion on these statements and to indicate that the statements were not prepared in accordance with generally accepted accounting principles. See Chapter 23 for a discussion of the significance of qualified opinions.

Capitalization Method

The second approach is for the organization to capitalize all of its fixed asset purchases. However, even when fixed assets are capitalized, it still is appropriate to write off small equipment purchases to avoid the paperwork of keeping track of them. Many organizations "expense" amounts under $100; others have higher limits of $500 or $1,000 depending on their size.

Figure 6–2 shows the Statement of Income and Expenses and Balance Sheet under this capitalization approach. Organizations that want an unqualified opinion from their CPA will have to follow this method. Under this capitalization approach, depreciation could be taken, or, alternatively, the fixed assets could be written down from time to time as their value decreases. This subject is covered in Chapter 7.

Advantages.   The principal advantage is that the fixed assets purchased are reflected on the Balance Sheet. This makes it possible for the reader to see the amount of assets for which the board is re-

RATHSKELLER YOUTH CENTER

STATEMENT OF INCOME AND EXPENSES

	Year Ending December 31,	
	19X1	19X2
Income:		
Membership fees	$ 4,000	$ 5,000
Contributions:		
General	37,900	39,600
Building Fund	25,000	–
Total income	66,900	44,600
Expenses:		
Salaries	11,000	10,000
Building maintenance	5,000	5,200
Coffee and food	12,800	12,600
Music and entertainment	2,000	2,400
Other	8,000	5,900
Total expenses	38,800	36,100
Excess of income over expenses....................	$28,100	$ 8,500

BALANCE SHEET

	December 31,	
	19X1	19X2
Assets:		
Cash	$ 2,000	$ 4,000
Pledges receivable	6,500	6,700
Land and original building	90,000	90,000
Building alterations............................	25,000	25,000
Furniture and equipment	20,000	25,000
Total assets	$143,500	$150,700
Liabilities:		
Accrued salaries	$ 3,000	$ 2,000
Accounts payable	400	100
Total liabilities.............................	3,400	2,100
Fund balance:		
Beginning of year	112,000	140,100
Excess of income over expenses	28,100	8,500
End of year.................................	140,100	148,600
Total liabilities and fund balance	$143,500	$150,700

Fig. 6–2. An example of the statements of an organization that follows the capitalization method of handling fixed assets.

sponsible. In this instance it will be noted that prior to 19X1 the Center had acquired land and building of $90,000 and furniture and fixtures of $20,000. The fund balance reflects the cost of these significant assets.

A major advantage is that by reflecting fixed assets on the Balance Sheet, the organization can then follow depreciation accounting techniques. As discussed in the next chapter, this results in a more accurate reflection of the cost of services rendered.

Many businesspersons feel more comfortable when financial transactions are recorded on this capitalization method since commercial businesses also capitalize (and depreciate) their fixed assets.

Disadvantages.   Readers may find this income statement more difficult to understand. The biggest risk is that they will confuse the large excess of income over expenses with the amount of "cash" available to the board·for use. The readers may be left with the impression that in 19X1 the Center has excess income of $28,100, and therefore does not need any contributions. This is a risk.

Another related concern is that the reader will look at the fund balance on the Balance Sheet and will likewise confuse the $140,100 fund balance as an amount that is available for current spending.

Write-Off, Then Capitalize Method

An organization can combine these two approaches and write off purchases of fixed assets on its Statement of Income and Expenses and then turn around and capitalize or record the assets on its Balance Sheet. It is a hybrid approach and is not recommended because of its complexity.*

The theory is that a nonprofit organization should charge off all purchases as incurred but still show the asset on the Balance Sheet. This allows the organization to show the expenditure for the fixed assets, which reduces the amount of the excess of income over expenses. One of the disadvantages of the capitalization method discussed above is thus eliminated. In this case, the building alterations have been paid

---

* This method of handling fixed assets was originally recommended in the 1964 edition of *Standards of Accounting and Financial Reporting for Voluntary Health and Welfare Organizations* (see Chapter 13) and was widely followed between then and 1974. However, with the issuance of the 1974 AICPA Audit Guide which states that such organizations are required to capitalize fixed assets and follow depreciation accounting, this method can no longer be considered generally accepted. The 1974 revised edition of *Standards of Accounting and Financial Reporting for Voluntary Health and Welfare Organizations* deleted all reference to the "write-off, then capitalize" method. It will probably be several years before this approach completely disappears, and for this reason a discussion of it is included in this chapter.

for from contributions which are reflected in the Statement of Income
and Expenses and the organization does not look to recover the building
cost through charges to income over a period of years through depreciation.

The second part of this approach is to "reinstate" or add back these
written-off assets on the Balance Sheet. This adding back can be seen
in the fund balance section of Figure 6–3, where $25,000 is added to
the fund balance in 19X1 to reinstate the assets written off on the
Statement of Income and Expenses. In this way the Balance Sheet
reflects the cost of the assets and more fairly shows the net worth of
the organization. From time to time these assets are removed from the
Balance Sheet as the assets decline in value by directly reducing the
carrying value on the Balance Sheet.*

Obviously the most confusing part of this approach is the adding back
or capitalizing of the fixed assets in the fund balance section of the Balance
Sheet.

Advantages.   Most of the advantages of both the immediate write-off
and the capitalization methods are present in this hybrid approach. The
reader sees the expenditure for the fixed assets in the Statement of
Income and Expenses, and the excess of income over expenses has been
reduced by this purchase, offset by any contributions that may have
been received for such asset purchases in the current year. Accordingly,
the reader is not misled into thinking there is a large excess of income
which can be expended. At the same time, by capitalizing the asset in
the Balance Sheet the accountability for the asset is not lost.

Disadvantages.   The capitalizing of the asset directly in the fund
balance is very confusing, and there is a high degree of risk that the
reader won't understand it. It appears to mix apples and oranges in
that it is saying purchases of fixed assets should be handled on more
or less a cash basis in the Statement of Income and Expenses but on an
accrual basis in the Balance Sheet. This is inconsistent and seems
illogical.

Another related disadvantage is that under this method there is no
way to provide depreciation charges in the Statement of Income and
Expenses since the asset has already been written off. As more fully
discussed in the next chapter, it is frequently appropriate to provide
depreciation charges in order to try to match income and costs. While
this may or may not be appropriate in the case of the Rathskeller Youth
Center, it will be for many other types of nonprofit organizations. Accordingly, this method should not be used by organizations where deprecia-

---

* This direct write-down is illustrated on page 74.

RATHSKELLER YOUTH CENTER

STATEMENT OF INCOME AND EXPENSES

	Year Ending December 31,	
	19X1	19X2
Income:		
Membership fees	$ 4,000	$ 5,000
Contributions:		
General	37,900	39,600
Building Fund	25,000	–
Total income	66,900	44,600
Expenses:		
Salaries	11,000	10,000
Building maintenance	5,000	5,200
Coffee and food	12,800	12,600
Music and entertainment	2,000	2,400
Other	8,000	5,900
Building alterations	25,000	–
Furniture and equipment	–	5,000
Total expenses	63,800	41,100
Excess of income over expenses	$ 3,100	$ 3,500

BALANCE SHEET

	December 31,	
	19X1	19X2
Assets:		
Cash	$ 2,000	$ 4,000
Pledges receivable	6,500	6,700
Land and building	90,000	90,000
Building alterations	25,000	25,000
Furniture and equipment	20,000	25,000
Total assets	$143,500	$150,700
Liabilities:		
Accrued salaries	$ 3,000	$ 2,000
Accounts payable	400	100
Total liabilities	3,400	2,100
Fund balance:		
Beginning of year	112,000	140,100
Excess of income over expenses	3,100	3,500
Building and equipment capitalized	25,000	5,000
End of year	140,100	148,600
Total liabilities and fund balance	$143,500	$150,700

Fig. 6–3. An example of the statements of an organization that follows the write-off, then capitalize, method of handling fixed assets.

tion is appropriate. Another related disadvantage is that if asset purchases fluctuate from year to year, they can have a significant effect on the excess of income over expenses. This would not be so if the assets were capitalized and depreciated. Only the depreciation charge would then appear in the Statement of Income and Expenses.

Finally, it should again be noted that this method does not follow generally accepted accounting principles and organizations following this approach will find that their CPAs will be required to qualify their opinion.

SEPARATE BUILDING FUND

No distinction has been made in the illustrations in this chapter between restricted and unrestricted contributions for the building fund. These contributions have been treated as though they were unrestricted, for ease in illustrating the various ways in which fixed assets can be handled. If, however, these contributions were "restricted," they would normally be reported in a separate restricted fund, or in a building or fixed asset fund as discussed in Chapter 4.

Immediate Write-Off

If a separate building or fixed asset fund were used, the principles outlined in this chapter would still apply. In the immediate write-off approach, restricted building fund contributions would be added to a separate building fund when received. As expenditures were made, they would be shown as expenses of that fund. The amount remaining in the fund at any time would be the unexpended restricted gifts. Since under this approach assets are not capitalized, the Balance Sheet would normally only have cash and a fund balance in the building fund. Effectively, the building fund would follow the procedures discussed in Chapter 4 for current restricted funds (see Figure 4-1).

In some instances, the organization might purchase fixed assets out of unrestricted funds, as is the case with the $5,000 of furniture and equipment purchased in 19X2. Since unrestricted funds are involved, the $5,000 would be shown as an expense of the unrestricted fund.

Capitalization

If the capitalization approach were followed, the fixed assets on the Balance Sheet would be reflected in a separate fixed asset fund in a manner similar to that shown in Figure 6-4.

RATHSKELLER YOUTH CENTER

STATEMENT OF INCOME AND EXPENSES
For the Years Ending December 31, 19X1 and 19X2

	December 31, 19X1		December 31, 19X2	
	Current Unrestricted	Fixed Assets	Current Unrestricted	Fixed Assets
Income:				
Membership fees	$ 4,000		$ 5,000	
Contributions	37,900	$25,000	39,600	
Total income	41,900	25,000	44,600	
Expenses:				
Salaries . . . . ., ...	11,000		10,000	
Building maintenance	5,000		5,200	
Coffee and food	12,800		12,600	
Music and entertainment . .	2,000		2,400	
Other	8,000		5,900	
Total expenses	38,800		36,100	
Excess of income over				
expenses	$ 3,100	$25,000	$ 8,500	

BALANCE SHEET

	December 31, 19X1		December 31, 19X2	
	Current Unrestricted	Fixed Assets	Current Unrestricted	Fixed Assets
Assets:				
Cash	$ 2,000		$ 4,000	
Pledges receivable	6,500		6,700	
Land and original building .		$ 90,000		$ 90,000
Building alterations		25,000		25,000
Furniture and equipment .		20,000		25,000
Total assets.	$ 8,500	$135,000	$10,700	$140,000
Liabilities:				
Accrued salaries	$ 3,000		$ 2,000	
Accounts payable	400		100	
Total liabilities	3,400		2,100	
Fund balance:				
Beginning of year	2,000	$110,000	5,100	$135,000
Excess of income over				
expenses	3,100	25,000	8,500	
Interfund transfer	—	—	(5,000)	5,000
End of year	5,100	135,000	8,600	140,000
Total liabilities and fund				
balance	$ 8,500	$135,000	$10,700	$140,000

Fig. 6—4. An example of statements of an organization that records contributions and fixed assets in a separate Fixed Asset Fund.

Observe in this approach that restricted contributions are reflected directly in the fixed asset fund at the time they are received. Observe also that the fixed assets purchased by these restricted funds are reflected directly in this fund.

But reflecting fixed assets in a separate fund creates a problem. What should be done with fixed assets purchased with unrestricted funds, in this case the $5,000 of furniture and equipment in 19X2? Should the fixed assets be left in the current unrestricted fund (since they were purchased with unrestricted funds) or transferred into the fixed asset fund? The answer is to transfer the assets to the fixed asset fund since it makes no sense to have fixed assets spread among several funds. This transfer is shown in the fund balance section of the Balance Sheet.

This results in a fixed asset fund which contains a combination of restricted and unrestricted amounts—unexpended restricted contributions, and fixed assets purchased using both restricted and unrestricted contributions. While this makes it more difficult to characterize the fund as either restricted or unrestricted, the presentation is less confusing. However, observe that the fixed asset fund should not contain any unexpended unrestricted funds. The transfer from the current unrestricted fund should take place only at the time fixed assets are purchased with unrestricted funds.

The authors do not recommend the use of a separate fixed asset fund, for the reasons discussed in Chapter 4, but prefer that fixed assets be included in the unrestricted fund. If the organization follows this recommendation, it will still record restricted contributions in a separate restricted building fund. However, at the time fixed assets are purchased from these restricted funds, a transfer would be made from the restricted building fund to the unrestricted fund for the cost of the assets purchased. This transfer would also be reported in the manner shown in Figure 6–4 but the transfer would be in the opposite direction. The column headings would then change to "unrestricted fund" and "building fund."

Write-Off, Then Capitalize

If the hybrid write-off, then capitalize approach to handling fixed assets were followed, a combination of the above procedures would also apply. Restricted contributions received would be reported in a separate fixed asset fund, and the disbursement for the assets would be reported as an expense. The Balance Sheet would then show—in a separate fixed asset fund—the capitalization of the assets as illustrated in Figure 6–3.

Assets purchased with unrestricted funds would be transferred to the fixed asset fund as shown on Figure 6–4.

CONCLUSION AND RECOMMENDATIONS

As discussed in the first chapter, the most important principle to be considered in keeping records and preparing financial statements is that they be successful in communicating to their readers what has happened during the year. If the statements are too complicated, they fail in this respect and their usefulness is limited. The organization should adopt methods of accounting and reporting appropriate to its activities and to the users of its statements.

The first approach, i.e., immediate write-off, would appear appropriate for small or possibly medium-sized organizations with relatively unsophisticated readers or for organizations on the cash basis. This is particularly so if the primary concern is raising enough cash each year to cover expenses, whether the organization is on the cash or accrual basis. The bookkeeping complexities of the capitalization method just do not seem warranted, particularly because the financial statements prepared on an accrual basis often leave the reader with the wrong impression of the results of operations.

On the other hand, if the organization is larger, or is already on the accrual basis, the second approach, i.e., capitalization, is probably appropriate. If the organization merely writes off, or expenses, all fixed assets as purchased, the reader could lose track of what assets the organization has and part of the stewardship potentially is lost. Also, a larger organization is less likely to keep its fixed assets for an indefinite period of time. It is more likely to outgrow its building, sell it, and buy a new one. It may also have other types of fixed assets which will be replaced from time to time, such as office equipment and vehicles.

Organizations should capitalize their assets if they have a reason to match revenues and costs or if they want to determine cost of services being rendered. A direct write-off approach distorts the result of operations for these organizations. Instead, assets should be capitalized and the costs recovered through depreciation charges. The capitalization method is the only one that can be considered as a "generally accepted accounting principle" and for this reason is the method which must be followed by organizations wanting an unqualified opinion from their CPAs.

The third approach, i.e., write-off, then capitalize, is not recommended. This approach appears to depart too much from generally accepted accounting principles. Very few readers will understand it and most will usually become confused. Furthermore, this method effectively precludes an organization from depreciating its assets through its income statement, which means that organizations that must show total costs of a service cannot use this method.

Finally, where an organization follows the recommended capitalization approach, the authors do not recommend carrying the fixed assets in a separate fixed asset fund. As more fully discussed in Chapter 4, carrying fixed assets in a separate fund causes confusion for most readers, particularly where depreciation accounting techniques are followed.

7

Fixed Assets—Depreciation

Depreciation, a problem related to fixed assets, can be difficult for nonprofit organizations to handle. If the organization follows the immediate write-off method of handling fixed assets, there are no assets on the Balance Sheet to depreciate. But many organizations do record fixed assets and are faced with the very basic question of whether to depreciate these assets. This has been a controversial question until recently; depreciation accounting is now becoming more generally accepted.

ARGUMENTS AGAINST TAKING DEPRECIATION

A number of reasons are advanced for not taking depreciation. Probably the most relevant is that depreciation is a concept associated with commercial enterprises, which determine profit through the matching of income and cost. Nonprofit organizations are usually not concerned with determining profit nor with a direct matching of income and cost. For them, depreciation serves little purpose.

Another reason often suggested is that nonprofit organizations frequently raise the funds they need for major fixed asset additions through special fund drives. When it comes time for the replacement of these assets, additional funds will be raised through similar drives. Therefore, there is no need to recover the costs of assets from income in the form of a depreciation charge.

Another consideration advanced is that, with inflation, the market value of fixed assets often increases as fast or faster than the decline in asset value associated with deterioration through passage of time. Depreciation is often thought of, incorrectly,* as a method of trying to measure loss in value. Many ask why depreciate an asset that is worth twice what it cost 25 years ago?

Another practical argument is that depreciation is difficult to show in the financial statements, particularly when fund accounting is followed. If depreciation serves no real purpose, why confuse the reader with book-keeping entries that don't involve cash?

WHY DEPRECIATION SHOULD BE RECORDED

Depreciation accounting is now required for most nonprofit organizations that want to describe their financial statements as being in accordance with "generally accepted accounting principles." But aside from these requirements, the authors believe that depreciation accounting is applicable to most nonprofit organizations for a number of reasons.

Most nonprofit organizations provide services that are measured in terms of costs. Depreciation is a cost. By not including this cost the reader is misled into thinking the actual costs were less than they really were. The board of an organization is charged with the responsibility of efficiently using all of the resources available to it to carry out the program of the organization. By excluding a significant amount from the costs of the program, the board gives the reader the impression that the program has been carried out more efficiently than is actually the case.

Most nonprofit organizations, even those that raise funds for major fixed asset additions through special fund-raising drives, must replace certain assets out of the recurring income of the organization. If no depreciation is taken and these assets are written off as purchased, two things happen. First, the organization deludes itself into thinking its income is sufficient to cover its costs whereas, in reality, it is not. Second, the excess of income over expenses of the organization will fluctuate widely from year to year relative to the timing of asset replacement and the replacement cost of the asset.

This will precipitate disproportionately high expenses in some years, which will depress the excess of income over expenses; in other years,

* Depreciation is defined by the Committee on Terminology of the American Institute of Certified Public Accountants as follows: "Depreciation accounting is a system of accounting which aims to distribute the cost or other basic value of tangible capital assets, less salvage (if any), over the estimated useful life of the unit (which may be a group of assets) in a systematic and rational manner. It is a process of allocation, not of valuation. Depreciation for the year is the portion of the total charge under such a system that is allocated to the year. Although the allocation may properly take into account occurrences during the year, it is not intended to be a measurement of the effect of all such occurrences." Copyright © 1961 by the American Institute of Certified Public Accountants, Inc.

the amount written off will be unrealistically low, inflating net income, and will not reflect the true cost to the organization of providing programs or services.

Some nonprofit organizations sell products or provide to outsiders services which are also available from commercial enterprises. Depreciation is especially appropriate for those assets involved with this revenue-producing function. Once the organization engages in the sale of goods or services, it has an interest in matching income and costs in a manner similar to commercial enterprises. If no depreciation is taken, there is an appearance of profit which may not be appropriate.

A nonprofit organization that sells products or services to government agencies, Blue Cross, or other organizations where a "reimbursement" formula is involved or potentially involved, should charge depreciation. The reasons for taking depreciation are much the same as those noted in the preceding paragraph. If no depreciation is taken on the books it is always difficult to justify using a depreciation factor in a rate-making or reimbursement situation. On the other hand, if depreciation has consistently been recorded on the books over a period of time, it will be difficult for the governmental or other agency to argue against using a depreciation factor in setting the rate or reimbursement base.

Although an organization does not now sell a service to a governmental agency, perhaps it will in the future. It is conspicuous to start taking depreciation only when a product or service is first charged to an agency. Many organizations have found, much to their surprise, that at some point they have undertaken a project involving government reimbursement. A good example is a professional engineering society that undertakes to do research under a government grant on a cost-reimbursement basis.

Furthermore, nonprofit organizations are subject to federal income taxes on "unrelated business income." Depreciation is a cost that should be recorded to reduce the profits subject to tax. Depreciation should be charged even if there is no profit because there may be profits in the future. It is always difficult to change accounting principles at a later date and start taking depreciation if the activity starts becoming profitable. Chapter 25 discusses the problems of unrelated business income.

As can be seen, depreciation is appropriate for most organizations that follow the practice of recording fixed assets on their Balance Sheet.* Since depreciation is a concept that is used by commercial organizations, it should cause relatively little confusion in financial statements.

---

* Depreciation is not applicable, however, to those organizations following the hybrid write-off, then capitalize method discussed in Chapter 6 because the asset has already been written off at the time it was purchased.

PRESENTATION IN THE FINANCIAL STATEMENTS

The presentation of depreciation in the financial statements is straightforward and similar to that used by commercial enterprises. Figure 7–1 shows depreciation in the financial statements of the Corvallis YMCA.°

CORVALLIS YMCA

STATEMENT OF INCOME AND EXPENSES
(Condensed)

	Year Ending December 31,	
	19X1	19X2
Income (in total)	$721,000	$767,000
Expenses:		
Other than depreciation	676,000	662,000
Depreciation	33,000	35,000
Total expenses	709,000	697,000
Excess of income over expenses	$ 12,000	$ 70,000

BALANCE SHEET
(Condensed)

	December 31,	
	19X1	19X2
Current assets (in total)	$ 68,000	$ 78,000
Investments in marketable securities at cost (market		
value $135,000 in 19X1 and $183,000 in 19X2)	132,000	176,000
Fixed assets:		
Land	50,000	50,000
Building	450,000	450,000
Equipment	120,000	130,000
Total	620,000	630,000
Less—Accumulated depreciation	(106,000)	(141,000)
Net fixed assets	514,000	489,000
Total assets.	$714,000	$743,000
Liabilities (in total)	$ 89,000	$ 48,000
Fund balance (in total).	625,000	695,000
	$714,000	$743,000

Fig. 7–1. An example of the financial statements of an organization that records depreciation.

° The Corvallis YMCA financial statements were presented in greater detail on page 42.

The Corvallis YMCA has both its own building and substantial amounts of equipment. While it receives some support from the public, most of its income is received from program fees. Accordingly the organization follows the practice of capitalizing all fixed assets and depreciating them. The building is depreciated over a fifty-year life, and all equipment over a five-year life. Depreciation has been included in the Statement of Income and Expenses, calculated as follows:

	19X1	19X2
Building (50 years):		
Cost: $450,000 (2%/year)	$ 9,000	$ 9,000
Equipment (5 years):		
Cost: $120,000 (20%/year)	24,000	
Cost: $130,000 (20%/year)		26,000
Total	$33,000	$35,000

The captions and presentation are familiar and should cause no problem in a single-fund organization. Considerable difficulty arises, however, if the organization has a separate plant fund and wishes to provide the depreciation charge in the current unrestricted fund. The problem is a mechanical one of transferring the accumulated depreciation created by the depreciation charge from the current unrestricted fund to the plant fund, since the accumulated depreciation should be in the plant fund where the assets are recorded.

Here is an example of how this transfer can be made where there are separate plant funds:

MORRISTOWN HISTORICAL SOCIETY
STATEMENT OF INCOME, EXPENSES, AND TRANSFERS

	Current Unrestricted Fund	Plant Fund	Total All Funds
Income................	$100,000	$ 8,000	$108,000
Expenses:			
Other than depreciation	(90,000)		(90,000)
Depreciation............	(5,000)		(5,000)
Excess of income over expenses .	5,000	8,000	13,000
Fund balance, beginning of year .	50,000	100,000	150,000
Transfer of depreciation to plant fund	5,000	(5,000)	—
Fund balance, end of year	$ 60,000	$103,000	$163,000

Things would be simpler if the depreciation charge were included directly in the plant fund and not shown as a transfer. The principal reason why this is usually not done is that the organization wants to show depreciation in the current unrestricted fund to match income and costs. Here is how the statement would look if the depreciation were included directly in the plant fund:

MORRISTOWN HISTORICAL SOCIETY
STATEMENT OF INCOME AND EXPENSES

	Current Unrestricted Fund	Plant Fund	Total All Funds
Income.	$100,000	$ 8,000	$108,000
Expenses:			
Other than depreciation	(90,000)		(90,000)
Depreciation.		(5,000)	(5,000)
Excess of income over expenses .	10,000	3,000	13,000
Fund balance, beginning of year .	50,000	100,000	150,000
Fund balance, end of year	$ 60,000	$103,000	$163,000

This simplifies the presentation. Furthermore, in a columnar approach the reader's attention is probably going to focus primarily on the "total all funds" column, and the figures are exactly the same for both presentations in this column.

The real confusion occurs when, instead of preparing the statements in a columnar approach, the organization prepares separate statements for each of the funds, as was illustrated on pages 35 and 36. It is difficult for the readers of the statements to fully understand transfers between funds. This is particularly true with depreciation because the concept of transferring depreciation back and forth is a difficult one to comprehend.

Because of these problems of presentation, it is recommended that whenever depreciation expense is shown in the current unrestricted fund, all fixed assets should be included in this same fund. There would be no separate plant fund and thus there would be no need to transfer depreciation between funds. The financial statement presentation becomes greatly simplified. This approach is recommended by the Hospital Audit Guide and is illustrated in Figures 15–1 and 15–2.

DIRECT WRITE-DOWN OF FIXED ASSETS CAPITALIZED

Some organizations capitalize fixed asset purchases but do not write off such assets through regular depreciation charges in the Statement of Income and Expenses. Instead they continue to carry these assets in the Balance Sheet at their original cost. Where this approach is followed, it may still be necessary to periodically write down the carrying value of these assets so that the Balance Sheet is not overstated.

There are two approaches for handling this write-down in value. The first is to directly reduce both the asset carrying value and the fund balance by the amount of the write-down. Under this approach the write-down does not appear at all in the Statement of Income and Expenses. The write-down would appear in a Statement of Changes in Fund Balances.° This is the approach followed in the 1973 AICPA Audit Guide for Colleges and Universities discussed in Chapter 14.

The other approach is to show the write-down in the Statement of Income and Expenses, appropriately labeled. Here is how this latter approach would appear:

MORRISTOWN HISTORICAL SOCIETY
STATEMENT OF INCOME AND EXPENSES

Income.		$108,000
Expenses:		
Operating expenses.	$90,000	
Write-down of worn-out office equipment and automobile	3,500	93,500
Excess of income over expenses.		$ 14,500

This second approach is the one preferred by the authors because the reader is clearly shown all expenses in one statement. If the write-down were made directly to the fund balance, the reader is not as likely to know the total expenses of the organization. At the same time, if this second approach is followed, the organization should rethink its policy of not providing depreciation. The advantage of regular depreciation charges is that they are regular, and no one year is charged with a disproportionately high amount of expense.

° If a Statement of Changes in Fund Balances is not used, the write-down could appear directly on the Balance Sheet, in the fund balance section (see Figure 7–2).

If the organization follows the write-off, then capitalize method, discussed and not recommended in Chapter 6, fixed assets are written off in the Statement of Income and Expenses when purchased and then capitalized on the Balance Sheet. In this case it is not appropriate to make a charge for depreciation on the income statement since the asset was completely written off when purchased. But the Balance Sheet amount should be reduced from time to time to reflect any decrease in value of the fixed assets. The reduction of the fixed asset amount must be recorded directly on the Balance Sheet. Figure 7–2 shows the Balance Sheet of the Rathskeller Youth Center where a direct reduction in asset values is made. The figures are the same as in Figure 6–3. Since the Statement of Income and Expenses is not affected by this direct write-down, the statement shown in Figure 6–3 is still applicable.

RATHSKELLER YOUTH CENTER
BALANCE SHEET

	December 31, 19X1	December 31, 19X2
Assets:		
Cash	$ 2,000	$ 4,000
Pledges receivable	6,500	6,700
Land and building	90,000	90,000
Building alterations	25,000	25,000
Furniture and equipment	10,000	13,000
Total assets	$133,500	$138,700
Liabilities:		
Accrued salaries	$ 3,000	$ 2,000
Accounts payable	400	100
Total liabilities	3,400	2,100
Fund balance:		
Beginning of year	112,000	130,100
Excess of income over expenses	3,100	3,500
Building and equipment capitalized	25,000	5,000
Write-off of worn-out equipment	(10,000)	(2,000)
End of year	130,100	136,600
Total liabilities and fund balance	$133,500	$138,700

Fig. 7–2. An example of a Balance Sheet for an organization that periodically writes off fixed assets in the Balance Sheet as a direct reduction of the fund balance.

FUNDING DEPRECIATION

Some organizations in addition to depreciating their fixed assets also set aside cash to be used for subsequent replacement of their fixed assets. This is referred to as "funding" the depreciation, and it involves simply the physical segregation of cash, often in a separate savings account. The only bookkeeping entry would be to record the movement of cash from one bank account to the other. The Balance Sheet would probably show this segregation, as follows:

BALANCE SHEET
(In Part)

Assets:

Cash	$15,000
Savings account (for replacement of equipment).	10,000
Receivables.............................	10,000
Equipment (net of accumulated depreciation of $10,000)	40,000
Total assets	$75,000

At the time the equipment is replaced, the amount of cash in the savings account reserved for this equipment would be used toward the cost of its replacement.* The cash has been segregated as a matter of convenience. The only advantage of this "funding" is that cash has been physically set aside, and will be less likely to be used on other things. This technique is primarily a form of discipline.

Separate Plant Fund

Sometimes depreciation will be charged in the plant fund and a transfer of cash made from the current unrestricted fund to the plant fund to fund the depreciation. When this is done, the effect is to transfer part of the net worth of the current unrestricted fund to the plant fund. This can be very confusing, particularly if separate statements are presented for the current unrestricted fund and the plant fund. If, on the other hand, the statements are shown in columnar form, the reader can clearly see what has happened. The following condensed income

---

* It should be noted that because of inflation or technological advances the setting aside of funds equal to depreciation on an historical cost basis will probably not cover the cost of replacement.

statement shows depreciation in the plant fund and the transfer of an equal amount of the fund balance (in the form of cash) from the current unrestricted fund to the plant fund:

MORRISTOWN HISTORICAL SOCIETY
STATEMENT OF INCOME, EXPENSES, AND CHANGES IN FUND BALANCES

	Current Unrestricted Fund	Plant Fund	Total All Funds
Income	$100,000	$ 8,000	$108,000
Expenses:			
Other than depreciation	(90,000)		(90,000)
Depreciation		(5,000)	(5,000)
Excess of income over expenses	10,000	3,000	13,000
Fund balance, beginning of year	50,000	100,000	150,000
Transfer to plant fund	(5,000)	5,000	—
Fund balance, end of year	$ 55,000	$108,000	$163,000

Another possibility is that the organization will record depreciation in the current unrestricted fund and then transfer this depreciation to the plant fund in the manner illustrated on page 71, and also "fund" the depreciation in the manner illustrated above. If this were done, the combination would look like this:

MORRISTOWN HISTORICAL SOCIETY
STATEMENT OF INCOME, EXPENSES, AND CHANGES IN FUND BALANCES

	Current Unrestricted Fund	Plant Fund	Total All Funds
Income	$100,000	$ 8,000	$108,000
Expenses:			
Other than depreciation	(90,000)		(90,000)
Depreciation	(5,000)		(5,000)
Excess of income over expenses	5,000	8,000	13,000
Fund balance, beginning of year	50,000	100,000	150,000
Transfer of depreciation expense to plant fund	5,000	(5,000)	—
Transfer of assets to plant fund	(5,000)	5,000	—
Fund balance, end of year	$ 55,000	$108,000	$163,000

The effect of these transfers is a wash as far as their effect on the fund balance of each of these two funds. However, often the board will not transfer an amount exactly equal to the depreciation. There is no reason why both transfers can't be netted for statement presentation. If, as in this instance, they net out to zero, no transfer need be shown at all. The entries would still be made on the books but to show both transfers in the statement would be confusing to most readers.

The use of "funding" techniques for depreciation is acceptable under present usage but the authors feel the complexities, particularly when a separate plant fund is involved, outweigh the advantages. Therefore this approach is not recommended.

TRANSFERS OF REPLACEMENT FUNDS TO THE PLANT FUND

Some organizations do not provide depreciation at all in the income statement. Instead, they transfer an amount (usually cash) from the current unrestricted fund to the plant fund as a "replacement fund" to build up cash for future acquisitions. As in the preceding example, this transfer is not an expense but represents a transfer of part of the fund balance of the current unrestricted fund to the separate plant fund. Here is an example:

MORRISTOWN HISTORICAL SOCIETY

STATEMENT OF INCOME, EXPENSES, AND CHANGES IN FUND BALANCES

	Current Unrestricted Fund	Plant Fund	Total All Funds
Income	$100,000	$ 8,000	$108,000
Less expenses (excludes depreciation)	(90,000)		(90,000)
Excess of income over expenses	10,000	8,000	18,000
Fund balance, beginning of year	50,000	100,000	150,000
Transfer to plant fund replacement fund	(5,000)	5,000	–
Fund balance, end of year	$ 55,000	$113,000	$168,000

The amount transferred to the plant fund builds up over the years and represents a fund from which future purchases or replacement of present buildings and equipment can be made. The amount of this transfer can vary from year to year. The board will often establish a policy to transfer amounts exactly equal to a charge for depreciation although no depreciation has been charged against income. The effect on the fund balance of the current unrestricted fund in such circumstances is exactly the same as though depreciation had been taken. The difference is that the reported excess of income over expenses excludes depreciation.

The use of a replacement fund is not recommended. If the board deems it prudent to set aside funds for future replacement, this suggests it should be depreciating its assets. While replacement cost may be greater than the original cost being depreciated, depreciation should still be taken and charged against income each year. To the extent that the board wants to set aside additional funds it may do so, but such amounts should not be confused with depreciation.

Further, by making a transfer of unrestricted funds to the plant fund, the board has mixed restricted and unrestricted funds. This violates the principles in several of the Audit Guides and the Statement of Position discussed in Part III. If the board wants to use a "replacement fund" concept, it should do so as part of the unrestricted fund (i.e., a segregation of part of the unrestricted fund balance).

CONCLUSION

Once the question of capitalizing or writing off fixed assets when purchased has been resolved, the question of whether to depreciate the assets recorded on the Balance Sheet is also largely resolved. If the asset has been written off, no depreciation is appropriate. If fixed assets have been recorded and the organization wants to follow "generally accepted accounting principles," depreciation accounting is required for most nonprofit organizations. Even where depreciation accounting is not mandatory, it is clearly applicable where an organization is trying to measure the cost of services rendered or where the organization must look to replacing its assets periodically from current income.

8

Investment Income,
Gains and Losses, and
Endowment Funds

In the past ten to fifteen years increasing attention has been given to investments and the rate of return on endowment funds, particularly in view of inflation and rising costs. Traditionally, organizations with endowments tended to invest largely in fixed-income bonds or preferred stocks. When common stocks were acquired only the bluest of blue chips were considered.

Beginning in the late 1960s, more and more nonprofit organizations reduced their dependence on fixed-income issues (e.g., bonds) and began investing sizable portions of their portfolios in common stock. Common stock possessed higher risk than bonds but was purchased because of its potential for future growth. Although this primarily resulted in substantially less current income from interest and dividends, these organizations felt it would be more than offset over a period of years by capital gains resulting from both inflation and real growth.* This is often referred to as the "total return" approach to investing. However, this new emphasis created accounting and reporting problems. The purpose of this chapter is to discuss the accounting principles that are generally followed by nonprofit organizations in recording their investments in

---

* The stock market performance of the 1970's has disillusioned many organizations that eagerly adopted this approach when it first received wide publicity. Many of its ardent supporters have gone back to the more traditional emphasis on fixed-income securities and blue chip common stocks.

endowment and other restricted and unrestricted funds. The accounting implications of the emphasis on total investment return are also reviewed.

ACCOUNTING PRINCIPLES

In discussing the accounting principles followed for investment income, it is important to distinguish between the two types of income which arise from investments. The first is interest and dividends, which are usually referred to as investment income. The second is the capital gain (or loss) arising at the time investments are sold. Traditionally, gains or losses have not been thought of as "income" but rather as part of principal. In the discussion that follows the accounting principles applicable to each of these two types of income will be discussed.

Investment Income on Unrestricted Funds

All dividends and interest income on unrestricted funds, including board-designated funds, should be recorded in a current unrestricted fund Statement of Income and Expenses or in a combined Statement of Income, Expenses, and Changes in Fund Balances. It is not appropriate to record such income directly in a separate Statement of Changes in Fund Balances; such income must be shown in a Statement of Income and Expenses so the reader will be fully aware of its receipt.

Unrestricted Investment Income on Endowment Funds

Unrestricted investment income on endowment funds should also be reported directly in the current unrestricted fund, in the same manner as other unrestricted investment income. It is not appropriate to first report such unrestricted investment income in the endowment fund and then to transfer it to the current unrestricted fund. The reason for this is that only donor-restricted income is reported in the endowment fund. If the terms of the donor's endowment gift are that the income is automatically unrestricted income, then this income is never restricted and should not be reported in the endowment fund. This presentation applies even where a columnar statement presentation is used in which all funds are shown side by side.

Some argue that with a columnar statement format it is acceptable to report the income first in the endowment fund column and then to transfer it to the current unrestricted fund, perhaps showing the transfer in the income section rather than below the caption "Excess of income over expenses." Their argument is that in this way it is easier for the reader to see the total endowment income in relation to the size of the endowment fund, and thus to form a judgment on management's investment skill. While this argument has merit, the chance of the reader's being confused when a transfer is shown is too great to justify such a presentation. The amount of investment income arising from endowment funds can still be shown as a separate line item in the income statement, to distinguish it from other sources of unrestricted investment income. (See Figure 4–1.)

Restricted Investment Income

The use of income from certain endowment funds, and usually from all other restricted funds, may be restricted for a specified purpose. This income should be reported directly in the appropriate restricted fund. For example, the donor may have specified that the investment income from an endowment fund gift is to be used for a specific project. In this situation the investment income arising from this gift should be reported directly in the fund for specified purposes and not reported first in the endowment fund and then transferred.

Some donors will specify that the investment income is to be added to the endowment principal for a period of years, after which time the income, and perhaps the accumulated income and principal, will become unrestricted. In this situation the investment income would, of course, be reported in the endowment fund.

Gains or Losses on Unresricted Funds

Gains or losses on board-designated investment funds are not restricted except as the board might designate. For this reason gains or losses on such unrestricted funds should always be recorded directly in the current unrestricted fund. Except for the college Audit Guide, all of the current AICPA pronouncements concur with this treatment.

There is a difference in practice as to where unrestricted gains should be shown on the statement. Some organizations take the position—with which the authors concur—that there is little real difference among dividends, interest, and capital gains. All represent income to the organization, and traditionally are more or less interchangeable; that is, if high-grade blue chips are held, capital gains will be minimal, but if more speculative low-dividend-paying stocks are held there is the promise of higher gains. When this approach is taken, unrestricted capital gains are usually reported in the same section of the financial statements as dividends and interest income. The other approach is to separate capital gains from dividends and interest income by showing the capital gains in a separate section of the financial statements, but above the "Excess of income over expenses" caption. Either is acceptable.

Gains or Losses on Endowment Funds

Traditionally, gains or losses on endowment investments have not been considered income but adjustments of the principal of the fund. Thus, gains or losses on an endowment fund are usually added back to the principal of that fund and all of the restrictions associated with the principal are considered applicable to these gains. Presumably the theory for this treatment is that, with inflation, capital gains largely reflect a price-level adjustment of the original principal.* In addition many lawyers have felt that, historically, this treatment was required by law.

As a result, capital gains or losses on endowment funds are usually not reported as unrestricted gains or losses in the current unrestricted fund. Instead they are usually reported in the endowment fund, either in a Statement of Income and Expenses, or in a separate Statement of Changes in Fund Balances. The authors' preference is to reflect such gains in a combined Statement of Income, Expenses, and Changes in Fund Balances, with the gains shown as part of income in either the endowment fund or the current unrestricted fund, according to the legal facts as to the nature of such gains or losses.† An example of this type of presentation is shown in Figure 12–1. An alternative approach is shown in Figure 16–2 in which such gains are reported as "nonexpendable additions." This latter approach is the one recommended by the AICPA Statement of Position.

It is argued by many that capital gains are not income and therefore must be shown in the changes in fund balance section of the statements. This approach, while acceptable under present guidelines for certain types of organizations, is not recommended. In many ways gains on investments are income in the same sense that interest and dividends are income, except where by law or donor restriction they are required to be added to principal. As such the reader has a right to know the

---

* It should be noted that in the case of bonds and other fixed-income securities inflation is usually ignored. If inflation were considered, a portion of the fixed income would have to be retained as an addition to principal if the original purchasing value of the principal were to be maintained. This approach, while logical, is not followed, and would not be considered an acceptable approach at this time.

† The answer to whether such gains are in fact legally restricted must be addressed by legal counsel to each organization. The laws vary from state to state.

amount of such gains. When gains are included directly in the changes in fund balance section of the statement, the effect is often to bury them. The reader has a right to know the total excess of income over expenses, including such gains. There should be no need to look at two or more statements, or, where only a Statement of Changes in Fund Balances is used, to have to interpret how various items cause the fund balance to change.

Some organizations do not keep track of the gains or losses by individual "name" funds within the endowment fund, but place all such gains (or losses) in a separate fund within the endowment fund with the title "Gains or Losses on Investments." This fund is accumulated over a period of years in the endowment fund and is effectively kept in perpetuity. While this may be an easy mechanical approach at the time the gains or losses arise, the authors believe it more appropriate to distribute such gains and losses to each name fund on an equitable basis at the time they occur. It is virtually impossible to judiciously allocate such amounts at a future date.

As is discussed later in this chapter, there is now some question whether gains on endowment funds are legally restricted. As is noted, a number of states now permit nonprofit organizations to include realized and in some instances unrealized gains as part of income from restricted funds. The authors believe that where it is determined that gains are legally unrestricted, all such gains should be reported in the same manner as gains arising from investments of unrestricted funds.*

Unrealized Gains and Losses

So far our discussion on gains or losses has been focused on realized gains or losses. Gains and losses are realized in an accounting sense only when the investments involved have actually been sold. What about unrealized gains and losses—increases or decreases in market value of investments currently held over their original cost?

Prior to 1973, investments could only be carried at cost. Under this method gains are not recognized until such time as the investment is sold and the gain "realized." In 1973/4 two Audit Guides † were issued which indicated these organizations could carry their investments either at cost or at market. In 1978 the AICPA Statement of Position addressed

---

* However, readers should note that in certain situations a contrary treatment is required for organizations covered by one of the Audit Guides or the Statement of Position.

† Voluntary Health and Welfare Organizations, and Colleges and Universities. (See Chapters 13 and 14.)

to the FASB held that nonprofit organizations not covered by an Audit Guide could carry both their marketable and other types of investments at either the lower of cost or market (or amortized cost for certain marketable debt securities) or market. Prior to 1978 hospitals had to carry investments at cost. Subsequent to this date, they can carry equity investments at market only if market value is lower than aggregate cost; otherwise they are still required to carry investments at cost. (See page 246.) When investments are carried at market, gains (and losses) are recognized on a continuing basis.

Investments Carried at Cost. Where an organization carries its investments at cost and not at market, gains can be recorded only when they are realized. The theory behind this is that until such time as an investment is actually sold there can be no assurance that the market value of the investment won't decline to or even below the original cost. Therefore no gain is recorded until such time as the investment is sold and the gain is realized by conversion to cash.*

On the other hand, if the market value of an investment is less than cost, consideration must be given to writing down the carrying value to the market value. Needless to say, there is a great deal of reluctance to write down investments as market prices decline below cost.†

The question is frequently asked whether marketable securities must be written down if it is believed that the decline is merely "temporary." This is difficult to answer. Certainly, market values fluctuate both up and down. It is not the intent of this principle to require a write-down every time market values go below the cost of an investment. The general principle is that if an investment's carrying value is permanently "impaired" either a provision for loss should be set up or the investment written down.

To answer the question of what constitutes "permanent" impairment, it is necessary to look at the nature of the individual securities. If they are being held temporarily or if, based on past buying and selling experience, the probability is that many of the individual stocks or bonds will be sold within the next year or two, then a provision for decline in market value should be set up. On the other hand, this is optional

---

* There is an exception to this general rule. Where an organization "sells" securities between the organization's own funds, i.e., between, say, an unrestricted board-designated investment fund and an endowment fund, the transfer is treated as though it were a sale with a third party, and the gain or loss recognized. The rationale is that otherwise the transaction would not be equitable to the funds involved.

† The Statement of Position discussed in Chapter 16 requires a write-down of marketable securities from cost to market where the aggregate market value of marketable securities by fund group is less than cost. See page 264 for a discussion of the treatment of the write-down.

if the decline in value appears truly temporary or if the investments are bonds which, based on past experience, can reasonably be expected to be held until maturity. For example, in the case of stocks, if the loss is caused by a general downward movement in the stock market, as distinct from a downward movement in the price of the particular stock held, there may be little reason to write down the security. A key factor is whether it can be reasonably expected that the organization will sustain a loss.*

Where it appears necessary to write down part of the carrying value of the investments, the provision for decline should appear in the Statement of Income, Expenses, and Changes in Fund Balances in the same place in the statement as realized gains or losses are presented (see below). Perhaps a caption should be used such as "Provision for decline in market value of investments." The provision set up in this manner should be disclosed in the Balance Sheet and netted against the carrying value of the investments.

In subsequent periods actual losses when realized would be charged to this provision. When it is apparent that the remaining portion of the provision is no longer required, it should be reversed in exactly the same manner as set up, i.e., in the Statement of Income, Expenses, and Changes in Fund Balances, with a caption such as "Add—Reserve for decline in market value no longer needed."

One final observation. There is a tendency to resist setting up a provision when market prices go down since this publicly acknowledges a loss. This is particularly so when one believes the decline is temporary. The alternative is to bury one's head in the sand and pretend there is no loss. This disguises the market value of securities held and may precipitate an even more unfortunate result—inaction with respect to investment decisions. If a loss has already been recognized there will be no reason not to sell a security at the appropriate time.

Presentation of Gains or Losses in the Financial Statements

The presentation of gains or losses in the Statement of Income, Expenses, and Changes in Fund Balances can vary depending on whether such gains or losses are considered unrestricted or restricted, and whether

---

* The Financial Accounting Standards Board (FASB) in its Statement of Financial Accounting Standards No. 12, *Accounting for Certain Marketable Securities*, requires most organizations to carry marketable equity securities at the lower of aggregate cost or market. However, paragraph five specifically states that Statement No. 12 does *not* apply to nonprofit organizations. It is possible that the FASB may at some point remove this exemption, in which case this requirement would apply.

the organization makes a distinction between capital-type transactions and other types of transactions.

Unrestricted Realized Gains or Losses. Unrestricted realized gains or losses can be shown in the income section of the statement, or toward the bottom of the statement to separate investment income, including gains, from operating income, as shown below:

STATEMENT OF INCOME, EXPENSES, AND CHANGES IN FUND BALANCES

Operating income (in total)	$125,000	
Expenses (in total)	(150,000)	
Excess of expenses over operating income		$(25,000)
Add—Nonoperating income:		
Contributions	20,000	
Interest and dividends	10,000	
Capital gains.	25,000	
Total nonoperating income		55,000
Excess of income over expenses.		$30,000

Sometimes investment income, excluding gains or losses, is shown in the operating income section, with gains or losses shown in the non-operating income section. This splitting of investment income and gains is acceptable but not recommended by the authors. As is discussed in the next section, organizations are increasingly concerned with the total return on invested funds, which includes gains.

Restricted Realized Gains or Losses. Restricted realized gains or losses can be presented in the financial statements in the same manner as unrestricted realized gains, discussed above, except, of course, in the appropriate restricted fund column.

Alternatively, some organizations are treating restricted gains and losses separately as "capital additions" or "nonexpendable income," and reporting such amounts as shown at the top of the next page.

Note that in this approach the nonexpendable additions represent only amounts which cannot be spent for current activities—in this case the endowment gift and the gain. However, the current unrestricted fund gain of $10,000 is expendable and therefore is reflected outside of the nonexpendable additions section. This approach was introduced by the 1978 AICPA Statement of Position and is discussed more fully in Chapter 16.

	Current Unrestricted	Endowment
Income:		
Unrestricted gains	$ 10,000	
Dividends and interest	5,000	
Other.	95,000	
Total	110,000	
Expenses (in total)	(105,000)	
Excess of income over expenses before capital additions.	5,000	
Nonexpendable additions:		
Endowment gift	–	$10,000
Gains on investments	–	25,000
Excess of income and capital additions over expenses	$ 5,000	$35,000

Presentation Where Investments Are Carried at Market. Where investments are carried at market, the increase or decrease in market value would be recorded as illustrated below:

STATEMENT OF INCOME, EXPENSES, AND CHANGES IN FUND BALANCES

Income:		
Contributions	$ 55,000	
Program activities	115,000	
Interest and dividends	50,000	
Net increase (decrease) in carrying value of investments	(20,000)	
Total income		$200,000
Expenses (in total)		(165,000)
Excess of income over expenses		35,000
Fund balance, beginning of year		100,000
Fund balance, end of year		$135,000

BALANCE SHEET
(In Part)

Cash		$ 60,000
Investments at market (cost $275,000)		350,000
Other assets		60,000
Total assets		$470,000

In presenting unrealized gains or losses in the Statement of Income, Expenses, and Changes in Fund Balances, there appears little purpose in reporting realized gains or losses separately from unrealized gains or losses. In fact, to report the two separately can result in an awkward presentation.

For example, assume an organization sells for $130 an investment that was purchased in a prior year at a cost of $100, but which had a market value at the beginning of the year of $150. From an economic standpoint, the organization had a loss during the year of $20 (carrying value of $150 vs. sales price of $130). Yet, from the standpoint of reporting realized gains, there is a gain of $30 (cost of $100 vs. sales price of $130). If the realized gain were separately reported, the presentation would be:

Realized gain	$ 30
Less gain previously recognized	(50)
Net loss	$ (20)

This presentation is likely to confuse most readers. Since there appears to be no real significance to reporting these two portions separately, the following presentation would appear more appropriate:

Net increase (decrease) in carrying value of investments . . .	$ (20)

FIXED RATE OF RETURN CONCEPT

As was noted above, one of the traditional principles followed by non-profit organizations having endowment funds is that realized gains are added to the principal of the endowment fund, and are not recognized as "income." Only dividends and interest are considered income. This creates a dilemma. If an organization's $1 million endowment fund is invested in 5 per cent bonds, income would be $50,000 a year. If, instead, it were invested in common stocks, that pay 2 per cent in dividends but can be expected to double in value every ten years, annual income would be $20,000. Obviously if the doubling assumption is correct, over the ten-year period the organization will realize far more from the common stocks than from the bonds:

	Common Stocks		Bonds
Interest/dividends over 10 years	$ 200,000		$500,000
Increase in value over 10 years	1,000,000		—
	$1,200,000	or	$500,000
Average per year	$ 120,000		$ 50,000

Under traditional accounting practices if the organization wants maximum current income, the "bonds" in this illustration are the correct choice of investment. But from an economic standpoint, it is the wrong choice. Should the accounting treatment influence an economic or investment decision?

Interfund Transfer of Realized Gains

A number of large institutions have adopted an accounting approach to this problem which involves a transfer to the unrestricted fund of a portion of the previously realized and unrealized gains from the endowment and board-designated investment fund. The amount thus transferred is then used for current operations. Typically the board determines the amount of the transfer by first deciding what rate of return it could achieve if it emphasized interest and dividends rather than capital growth. This rate of return is often selected as the "spending rate." This "spending rate" is then compared to the actual dividends and interest income. The deficiency is the amount transferred.

For example, using the illustration above, if the board felt confident that over a period of time its common stock investments would realize a 5 per cent return after considering inflation, the amount of dividends plus "transfer" should equal 5 per cent of the $1 million, or $50,000. Figure 8–1 shows how this transfer would be presented in both the unrestricted fund and the endowment fund.

Transfer Must Not Be Reported in the Income Section. Note that in Figure 8–1 the transfer from the endowment fund is presented in the changes in fund balance section, below the caption "Excess of income over expenses." Some organizations have—incorrectly—presented the transfer in the income section. This incorrect presentation is shown in Figure 8–2; it is not acceptable under generally accepted accounting principles.*

---

* See Chapters 18 and 23 for a discussion of generally accepted accounting principles.

	Unrestricted Fund	Endowment Fund
Income:		
Program income	$100,000	
Dividend income	20,000	
Realized gains.		$ 50,000
Total income.	120,000	50,000
Expenses.	(140,000)	
Excess (deficit) of income over expenses	(20,000)	50,000
Fund balance, beginning of year	50,000	1,000,000
Transfer of a portion of realized gains		
from endowment fund.	30,000	(30,000)
Fund balance, end of year	$ 60,000	$1,020,000

Fig. 8–1.   An example of how the transfer from the endowment fund to the unrestricted fund should be presented under the total return approach.

	Unrestricted Fund	Endowment Fund
Income:		
Program income	$100,000	
Dividend income	20,000	
Realized gains.		$ 50,000
Transfer of portion of realized gains		
from endowment fund.	30,000	(30,000)
Total income.	150,000	20,000
Expenses.	(140,000)	
Excess of income over expenses	10,000	20,000
Fund balance, beginning of year	50,000	1,000,000
Fund balance, end of year	$ 60,000	$1,020,000

Fig. 8–2.   An example of an unacceptable presentation in which the transfer from the endowment fund is reported in the income section of the unrestricted fund.

Many readers have difficulty understanding why accountants will not permit this transfer to be shown as income since the amount transferred will be used for current purposes just as though it were dividends and interest. What troubles many accountants is that inclusion of the transfer in the income section (Figure 8–2) allows the board to arbitrarily determine what its excess of income over expenses will be. If the board were to consistently transfer all of the legally available realized gains rather than only an arbitrarily determined portion, most accountants would not be troubled by reflecting such amounts as income. It is when the board decides to transfer only a portion that it appears to the accountant that the potential for income manipulation exists. This is not to suggest that the method the board uses in determining its "spending rate" is not rational, but it is still arbitrary. For this reason, when the board decides to transfer such gains, the presentation of this transfer should be shown outside of the income section in the fund balance section, as shown in Figure 8–1.

It should be emphasized, however, that accountants are not trying to tell the board how to handle its investments or how much of the organization's resources should be utilized for current operations. This is outside the accountant's purview or interest. However, it is within the accountant's sphere to indicate how the board's action—in this case the transfer of funds—should be presented in the financial statements so as not to mislead the reader. Looking at Figure 8–1 no one can misinterpret the results of the year's activities in the current unrestricted fund—a deficit of $20,000. However, it would be an unusual reader who would not conclude from Figure 8–2 that the current unrestricted fund had an excess of $10,000.

Fixed Return from an Independent Investment Fund

Because of the popularity of the total return approach, several independent investment funds have been established which provide the nonprofit organization with a flat "spending rate" amount each year. These are set up in much the same way as mutual funds. Probably the best known of these independent investment funds is The Common Fund in which a number of colleges have invested. If the institution elects, The Common Fund will return annually 5 per cent of the market value of the institution's share of the Fund rather than actual dividends, interest, and realized gains.

Accounting for Fixed Annual Payment.   The accounting for this 5 per cent return must be handled in exactly the same manner as it would be if the organization were making its own investments in its own separate endowment fund. It is not acceptable to record the full 5 per cent payment as dividend income. Therefore it is necessary for the organization to know the amount of its share of the actual dividends and realized gains of the outside investment fund. Its share of the actual dividends is recorded as unrestricted fund income and its share of the actual total realized gains is recorded as gains in the endowment fund, without regard to the 5 per cent cash payment received from the investment fund. The carrying value of the organization's share of this investment fund is thus increased or decreased to the investment fund's cost basis just as though there were no separate investment fund.

The excess of the 5 per cent cash payment over the dividends and interest earned represents a return of a portion of the organization's investment in this outside fund. If the organization wishes to utilize this excess for general purposes, it should account for this excess as a transfer from the endowment fund to the unrestricted fund, as in Figure 8–1. In short, the accounting for the dividends and interest and realized gains is completely independent of the 5 per cent cash payment. It is dependent on the underlying actual results of the investment fund.

Here is an example. Assume that the organization described above makes a $1 million cash investment in an outside investment fund, which constitutes 10 percent of the total independent investment fund's assets. Here is the activity for the first year:

	Outside Investment Fund	Our Organization's Share (10%)
Balance beginning	$10,000,000	$1,000,000
Dividend income	200,000	20,000
Realized gains	500,000	50,000
Less 5% payments	(500,000)	(50,000)
Balance ending	$10,200,000	$1,020,000
Unrealized appreciation	$ 500,000	$ 50,000

The appropriate reporting for our organization, assuming it carries its investments at cost, would be the same as contained in Figure 8–1.

Accounting Where Investments Are Carried at Market. If the organization followed the practice of recording its investments at market, then $50,000 would be recorded in the endowment fund as realized gains. The $30,000 transfer would again be handled as in Figure 8–1.

Inflation Index To Protect Principal

It should be noted that the discussion so far has not touched on the budgeting considerations that an organization's board may consider in establishing the amounts to be transferred from the endowment fund to the unrestricted fund. The most common approach is the "spending rate" approach described above, in which the board decides on the amount to be spent in total and then, after deducting actual dividends and interest, transfers the balance. It is referred to as the spending rate because often it is arrived at, in part at least, by determining what income could be achieved if emphasis were placed on current income rather than on growth.

Inflation Protection Approach. The authors believe this spending rate approach is backward. The more appropriate approach is for the board to first establish the rate at which the endowment fund must be increased to protect it from inflation. Transfers to the unrestricted fund should then be made only to the extent that gains exceed the amount which has to be added to principal to protect it from inflation.

There is a significant difference between the spending rate approach and this inflation protection approach. The spending rate approach may or may not protect the principal against inflation, depending on the assumptions used in arriving at the spending rate. Yet the first concern of the board should be to protect the principal against inflation. Only if there are gains in excess of this requirement should transfers be made to the unrestricted fund.

Figure 8–3 shows how an inflation index could be used to determine the amount to be transferred. Assuming inflation of 5 per cent a year,° again our original principal of $1 million, 2 per cent dividends, and realized gains of $50,000, $40,000, and $120,000 in each of three years, the amount which would be transferred in each of three years would be calculated as shown in Figure 8–3.

In this illustration a constant inflation rate of 5 per cent has been

	19X1	19X2	19X3
Principal at beginning of year, adjusted for inflation	$1,000,000	$1,050,000	$1,102,500
Add inflation factor of, say, 5%.	50,000	52,500	55,125
Principal end of year as adjusted for inflation	$1,050,000	$1,102,500	$1,157,625
Dividends	$ 20,000	$ 20,000	$ 20,000
Realized gains	50,000	40,000	120,000
Total	70,000	60,000	140,000
Less amount retained as an adjustment for inflation	(50,000)	(52,500)	(55,125)
Balance, for current operations	$ 20,000	$ 7,500	$ 84,875

Fig. 8–3. An example showing how the amount of the transfer would be calculated under the total return approach using an inflation protection approach.

° Perhaps wishful thinking on the authors' part.

assumed. In actual practice, the rate would vary and the board would, of course, peg its rate to the appropriate government index.

The advantage of this approach is that all income—dividends and gains—is transferred except that portion which must be retained as an inflation adjustment to protect the value of the endowment fund. This means that the full impact of the board's investment decisions will be felt, whether conservative or speculative.

Income does fluctuate because of the magnitude and timing of realized capital gains. Notice that in Figure 8–3 only $7,500 of income is available in 19X2. Possibly one refinement is to provide that the amount of the transfer should be averaged over a three-year period. This would have the effect of dampening large changes due to the timing of the realized gains.

Market Value Approach.   An increasing number of nonprofit organizations carry their endowment fund investments at market value, and the inflation index approach outlined above can be followed by these organizations. Carrying investments at market, of course, eliminates the fluctuation due to the timing of realized gains. At the same time, it should be noted that a general stock market decline at the end of any one year could also result in a loss rather than income. Again, a three-year moving average might become appropriate.

For those nonprofit organizations that carry their investments at cost, the board could still adopt the market value approach solely for the purpose of determining the amount of realized gains to be transferred. Figure 8–4 shows how this would be handled.

	19X1	19X2	19X3
Dividends	$ 20,000	$ 20,000	$ 20,000
Realized gains	50,000	40,000	120,000
Unrealized gains—			
increase (decrease)	50,000	80,000	(20,000)
Total	120,000	140,000	120,000
Less amount retained as an adjustment for inflation (see Figure 8-3)	(50,000)	(52,500)	(55,125)
Balance, for current operations	$ 70,000	$ 87,500	$ 64,875

Fig. 8–4. An example showing how the amount of the transfer would be calculated using an inflation protection approach and recognizing unrealized gains in the calculation.

Presentation in the Financial Statement. Under present accounting rules, the board can follow either of the approaches discussed above for determining the amount of realized gains or losses to transfer, but the transfer must not be reported as income. This means that the amounts reported as income in the unrestricted fund calculated as shown in Figure 8–3 or 8–4 would be the amounts of actual dividends and the balance would have to be reported as a transfer. In some years it is possible that such dividends would exceed the amount available. When this happens a transfer must be made back to the endowment fund. Figure 8–5 shows this presentation for the organization which calculates the amount of the transfer on the basis of realized gains only (as calculated in Figure 8–3).*

	Unrestricted Fund		
	19X1	19X2	19X3
Income:			
Program income	$ 100,000	$ 100,000	$ 100,000
Dividend income	20,000	20,000	20,000
Total	120,000	120,000	120,000
Expenses.	(140,000)	(140,000)	(140,000)
Excess of expenses over income	(20,000)	(20,000)	(20,000)
Transfer of portion of realized gains from endowment funds			64,875
Transfer of portion of unrestricted fund to endowment fund to protect principal from inflation.		(12,500)	
Excess (deficit) of income and transfer over expenses	$ (20,000)	$ (32,500)	$ 44,875

Fig. 8–5. An illustration showing the presentation in the unrestricted fund of transfers which have been calculated using an inflation protection approach.

May Realized Gains Be Legally Transferred?

Implicit in the above discussion is the assumption that at least part of the realized gains on funds donated to an organization for endowment

---

* Some organizations might object to transferring some of their dividend income to the endowment fund. One modification might be to not make such transfers back to the endowment fund but instead to reduce future years' transfers to the unrestricted fund by the amount of such deficiencies. If this modification were followed, the 19X3 transfer in Figure 8–4 would be $52,375 ($64,875 less $12,500).

purposes can, in fact, be transferred to the unrestricted fund of the organization. Is this a valid assumption?

Changing Attitude on Income Transfer.   Over the years there has been a tendency to assume that the law requires endowment funds and the realized gains on the sales of endowment fund investments to be inseparable and sacrosanct. There now appears to be some authoritative support for the view that the realized gains on endowment funds may also be transferred to the unrestricted fund. In 1969, in a widely publicized report to the Ford Foundation entitled "The Law and the Lore of Endowment Funds," W. L. Cary and C. B. Bright concluded:

If the managers of endowment funds wish to seek long-term appreciation in their investments, the need of their institutions for current yield should not dissuade them. We find no authoritative support in the law for the widely held view that the realized gains of endowment funds can never be spent. Prudence would call for the retention of sufficient gains to maintain purchasing power in the face of inflation and to guard against potential losses, but subject to the standards which prudence dictates, the expenditure of gains should lie within the discretion of the institution's directors.

Latitude Under State Law.   Subsequent to Cary and Bright's report, a number of states have adopted legislation which specifically permits most nonprofit organizations to include capital gains in usable income to the extent the board deems "prudent." In fact, the model uniform law provides that not only realized gains may be considered usable income but also unrealized gains.

Endowment Fund Distinction for Colleges and Universities.   There is another important factor to consider. Many colleges and universities * combine two types of endowment funds—board-designated investment funds and true donor-restricted endowments—into a single fund for investment purposes. There is a great deal of difference between the two. In the first the restriction is internally and voluntarily created whereas in the other the restriction is donor-fixed and legally sanctioned.

There would appear to be no question that the board may transfer to the unrestricted fund not only the realized gains but also the principal of board-designated investments. After all, the board's designation was voluntary and it could therefore reverse its designation and transfer such funds to the unrestricted fund. Board-designated investment funds usually constitute a substantial portion of the endowment funds of most large educational institutions.

---

* Most other types of nonprofit organizations are prohibited from combining board-designated investments and endowment funds for reporting purposes.

9

Contributions, Pledges, and Noncash Contributions

So far we have not discussed the problems of recording and reporting the principal resource most nonprofit organizations depend upon—contributions. At first it might appear that this is a fairly straightforward subject that would not involve significant difficulty. In fact, the opposite is true. An organization can receive contributions with a wide range of restrictions attached. Not only must these contributions be recorded in the right fund and reported in such a way that the reader is fully aware of their receipt and restrictions, but there is considerable controversy surrounding the timing of the recording of such gifts as income.

Some contributions are made in the form of pledges which will be paid off over a period of time; accounting questions often arise as to whether such pledges should be recorded and if so, when they should be recognized as income. Also, an organization can receive a variety of noncash contributions ranging from marketable securities, buildings, and equipment to contributed services. All of these present accounting and reporting problems for the organization.

TYPES OF SUPPORT

A nonprofit organization can receive several types of support. Each of the following types will be discussed in a separate section of this chapter:

1. Unrestricted contributions

2. Current restricted contributions
3. Grants for specific projects
4. Noncurrent restricted contributions
5. Bequests
6. Contributed services
7. Other noncash contributions
8. Pledges

UNRESTRICTED CONTRIBUTIONS

It was noted in Chapter 4 that all unrestricted contributions should be reported in the current unrestricted fund. This principle is fairly well accepted and followed by most nonprofit organizations. What is not uniformly followed is the method of reporting such unrestricted contributions. Some organizations have followed the practice of adding unrestricted contributions directly to the fund balance either in a separate Statement of Changes in Fund Balances or in the fund balance section where a combined Statement of Income, Expenses, and Changes in Fund Balances is used. Others report some or all of their contributions directly in an unrestricted investment fund, and worse still, some report unrestricted contributions directly in the endowment fund as though such amounts were restricted. The result of all these practices is to make it difficult for the readers of the financial statements to recognize the amount and nature of contributions received. Often this is done in an attempt to convince the readers that the organization badly needs contributions.

All unrestricted contributions should be reported in a Statement of Income and Expenses, or if a combined Statement of Income, Expenses, and Changes in Fund Balances is used, such unrestricted contributions should be shown before arriving at the "Excess of income over expenses" caption. It is not acceptable to report unrestricted contributions in a separate Statement of Changes in Fund Balances or to report such gifts directly in an endowment fund.

Presentation in the Income Statement

The presentation of unrestricted contributions within the Statement of Income and Expenses can be handled in one of several ways. For smaller organizations and for organizations where fees for services rendered are not a significant factor, contributions are usually reported in the top section of the statement along with all other sources of income, as follows:

Income:

Contributions	$50,000
Other income	10,000
Total	60,000
Expenses (in total)	(55,000)
Excess of income over expenses	$ 5,000

For other organizations it is more appropriate to separate contributions from service fee income in order to arrive at an excess or deficit before contributions are added. The following is a simplified example of this type of presentation:

Service fees	$150,000
Less expenses	(175,000)
Excess of expenses over service fees before contributions	(25,000)
Contributions	40,000
Excess of income over expenses	$ 15,000

Note that in both examples contributions are shown above the excess of income over expenses for the period so the reader can see the net results of all unrestricted activities.

Multicolumn Presentation

Some organizations prefer to present unrestricted investment funds separately in a columnar presentation. This is done to emphasize that fund assets are considered by the directors to be unavailable for operating expenses. An example of this type of presentation would be:

	Unrestricted		
	Operating	Investment	Total
Support and revenue:			
Other unrestricted income	$200,000		$200,000
Bequests	125,000		125,000
Total	325,000		325,000
Expenses (in total)	(195,000)		(195,000)
Excess of support and revenue over expenses .	$130,000		$130,000
Transfer bequests to investment fund	(125,000)	$125,000	
Fund balance:			
Beginning of year	60,000	300,000	360,000
End of year	$ 65,000	$425,000	$490,000

Several points should be noted. First, observe that all three columns are clearly labeled "unrestricted" so the reader will not mistake the investment column for a restricted endowment fund. Second, note that a "total" column is included. The purpose, of course, is to clearly show the reader the total of all unrestricted funds available to the organization. Third, note that all unrestricted income is reported in the unrestricted operating fund column. This is because, prior to a board decision to designate amounts for other purposes, all unrestricted income is legally available for operations. The board designation of bequests to be held for investment is reflected as an interfund transfer to the unrestricted investment fund.

CURRENT RESTRICTED CONTRIBUTIONS

Current restricted contributions are contributions that can be used to meet the current expenses of the organization, although restricted to use for some specific purpose. Current restricted contributions cause reporting problems, in part because the accounting profession has not yet resolved the appropriate reporting treatment for these types of gifts.

The principal unresolved accounting problem relates to the question of what constitutes "income" or "support" to the organization. Simply worded, is a gift which can only be used for a specific project "income" to the organization at the time it is received, or does this restricted gift represent an amount which should be looked on as being held in a form of escrow until it is expended for the restricted purpose If it is looked on as something other than income, what is it—deferred income, or part of a restricted fund balance?

Obviously if a current restricted gift is considered income or support · in the period received—whether expended or not—the accounting is fairly straightforward. But if the other view is taken, the accounting can become quite complex.

Inherent in the discussion of this issue is the question of whether a nonprofit organization is a single entity, or a series of separate entities called "funds." If the latter view is taken, the organization's primary reporting focus is on the individual funds and more particularly on the unrestricted fund, with the restricted fund reporting being more to show stewardship of these unexpended resources.

Perhaps an example will best illustrate the problem. The Johnstown Eye Foundation received a contribution of $50,000 to be used for salary costs of the staff of a mobile eye clinic which visits elementary schools to test children's vision in the greater Johnstown area. In the first year only $40,000 of the $50,000 was expended for this purpose. In addition to the mobile clinic contribution, the Johnstown Eye Foundation had other unrestricted contributions and income of $320,000 and expenses of $315,000. The reporting problem relates to how and where to report the $50,000 contribution and the $40,000 of expenses. There are three alternative approaches:

1. Report the current restricted gift of $50,000 as income in total in the year received, and then reflect the unexpended balance of $10,000 in a current restricted fund balance at the end of the year (Figure 9–1).
2. Report the current restricted gift of $50,000 initially as a direct addition to the current restricted fund balance and then recognize as income the $40,000 actually expended during the period (Figure 9–2).
3. Report the current restricted gift of $50,000 initially as a deferred contribution in the Balance Sheet, and then recognize as income the $40,000 actually expended during the period (Figure 9–4).

Each of these approaches is discussed below.

Report as Income in Full in the Year Received

The first approach is to report a current restricted gift as income or support in full in the year received, either in a separate current restricted fund or as part of a "current" fund.* In this approach gifts are recognized as income as received and expenditures are recognized as incurred. The unexpended income is reflected as part of the fund balance. Figure 9–1 shows the Statement of Income, Expenses, and Changes in Fund Balances and the Balance Sheet for the Johnstown Eye Foundation, following this approach.

The reader can clearly see from this presentation that the Johnstown Eye Foundation received gifts of $50,000 and expended $40,000 and that the organization had unspent current restricted gifts of $25,000 from previous years.

The implication of this presentation is that the $50,000 is income at

---

* The use of a separate current restricted fund is illustrated in Figure 9–1. However, many organizations choose not to use a separate current restricted fund, but instead have a single current or general fund. This is perfectly acceptable provided appropriate disclosures are made of unexpended balances and, where material, the sources of such contributions.

THE JOHNSTOWN EYE FOUNDATION

STATEMENT OF INCOME, EXPENSES, AND CHANGES IN FUND BALANCES
For the Year Ended June 30, 19X1

	Unrestricted	Current Restricted	Total
Income:			
Restricted contributions		$ 50,000	$ 50,000
Other income	$320,000		320,000
Less—Expenses	(315,000)	(40,000)	(355,000)
Excess of income over expenses .	5,000	10,000	15,000
Fund balance, beginning of year .	100,000	25,000	125,000
Fund balance, end of year	$105,000	$ 35,000	$140,000

BALANCE SHEET
June 30, 19X1

	Unrestricted	Current Restricted	Total
Cash	$ 40,000	$ 38,000	$ 78,000
Other assets	85,000	–	85,000
Total	$125,000	$ 38,000	$163,000
Accounts payable	$ 20,000	$ 3,000	$ 23,000
Fund balance	105,000	35,000	140,000
Total	$125,000	$ 38,000	$163,000

Fig. 9–1. **An example of a set of financial statements in which current restricted income is reported as income in total in the year received, in a separate
current restricted fund.**

the time received, and that while there may be restrictions on the use
of the funds, the board truly considers the $50,000 as funds of the Johns-
town Eye Foundation, reportable as such.

Observe, however, that in this approach a current restricted gift received on the last day of the reporting period will also be reflected as
income, and this would increase the excess of support over expenses
reported for the entire period. Many boards are reluctant to report such
an excess in the belief this may discourage contributions or suggest that
the board has not used all of its available resources. Those who are

concerned about reporting an excess of income over expenses are there-fore particularly concerned with the implications of this approach: a large unexpected current restricted gift may be received at the last min-ute, resulting in a large excess of income over expenses.

Others, in rejecting this argument, point out that the organization is merely reporting what has happened and to report the gift otherwise is to hide its receipt. They point out that in reality all gifts, whether re-stricted or unrestricted, are restricted and only the degree of restriction varies; unrestricted gifts must be spent realizing the goals of the organi-zation, and therefore such gifts are restricted to this purpose even though a particular use has not been specified by the contributor.

There are valid arguments on both sides. The approach shown in Figure 9–1 is the one recommended in the AICPA Audit Guide for Voluntary Health and Welfare Organizations and therefore is very widely followed.

Report as Income When Expended

The second approach is to report the current restricted gift initially as a direct addition to the fund balance of the current restricted fund, and then to recognize the gift as "income" at the time it is actually expended. The theory is that the gift is "earned" only when the organization com-plies with the restriction imposed by the donor, which occurs when the gift is spent for the restricted purpose.

In this type of approach a separate Statement of Changes in Fund Balances is often used. This avoids some of the confusion that results from adding the gift directly to the fund balance. If a combined State-ment of Income, Expenses, and Changes in Fund Balances is utilized the reader is usually confused by seeing the gift apparently reported twice in the income statement; first the entire gift is reported as an addition to the fund balance, and then the same gift is reported as income when it is actually spent. Figure 9–2 shows an example of the use of two statements.

Observe that the amount of current restricted contributions reported as such ($40,000) exactly offsets the amount of expenses. This is char-acteristic of this approach. Essentially a current unrestricted gift is not considered "income" until the restriction attached to the gift is met, which usually occurs when the gift is spent.

In this presentation the exact offsetting of current restricted income and expenses is obvious and confusing. Few nonaccountant readers un-derstand why the two should be equal. Further, observe that the dual

THE JOHNSTOWN EYE FOUNDATION

STATEMENT OF INCOME AND EXPENSES
For the Year Ended June 30, 19X1

	Current Unrestricted	Current Restricted	Total
Income:			
Contributions		$40,000	$ 40,000
Other	$320,000		320,000
Total	320,000	40,000	360,000
Expenses (in total)	(315,000)	(40,000)	(355,000)
Excess of income over expenses .	$ 5,000	—	$ 5,000

STATEMENT OF CHANGES IN FUND BALANCES
For the Year Ended June 30, 19X1

	Current Unrestricted	Current Restricted	Total
Fund balance, beginning of year .	$100,000	$25,000	$125,000
Add—Excess of income over expenses	5,000	—	5,000
Gifts received		50,000	50,000
Gifts utilized		(40,000)	(40,000)
Fund balance, end of year	$105,000	$35,000	$140,000

Fig. 9–2. An example of reporting a current restricted gift initially as a direct addition to the current restricted fund balance, and then recognizing the gift as "income" when expended.

column approach in Figure 9–2 effectively forces the preparation of a separate Statement of Changes in Fund Balances for both the unrestricted and current restricted fund.

This approach has been traditionally followed by nonprofit organizations, and it is recommended in the AICPA Audit Guides for Hospitals, and for Colleges and Universities.

In a variation of this second approach, presented in Figure 9–3, the current restricted contribution which was spent is reported in the current *un*restricted fund. The point here is that once the gift restriction has been met, it is no longer restricted and thus is recognizable as unrestricted income under this accounting approach.

THE JOHNSTOWN EYE FOUNDATION

STATEMENT OF CURRENT UNRESTRICTED FUND INCOME,
EXPENSES, AND CHANGES IN FUND BALANCES
For the Year Ended June 30, 19X1

Income:	
Restricted contribution utilized.	$ 40,000
Other income	320,000
Total.	360,000
Expenses (in total)	(355,000)
Excess of income over expenses.	5,000
Fund balance, beginning of year	100,000
Fund balance, end of year	$105,000

CURRENT RESTRICTED FUND
STATEMENT OF CHANGES IN FUND BALANCES
For the Year Ended June 30, 19X1

Fund balance, beginning of year	$ 25,000
Add—Gifts received.	50,000
Less—Gifts utilized	(40,000)
Fund balance, end of year	$ 35,000

Fig. 9–3. An alternate example of reporting a current restricted gift as income at the time expended. In this approach a separate Statement of Changes in Fund Balances is usually used for the current restricted fund.

Report as Deferred Contribution Until Expended

A third approach is beginning to find favor among accountants: all current restricted gifts are added to a deferred account until the restrictions have been met. This deferred account is reflected on the Balance Sheet outside of the fund balance section, as a type of liability. This approach is shown in Figure 9–4.

In this approach there is no current restricted fund as such. Essentially unexpended restricted gifts are looked on as liabilities until the restrictions lapse and the gifts are reported as income. Note that the $35,000 in "Deferred restricted income" shown in Figure 9–4 represents $10,000 of the recent $50,000 contribution which is yet to be expended, plus $25,000 in unspent current restricted gifts from previous years.

THE JOHNSTOWN EYE FOUNDATION

BALANCE SHEET
June 30, 19X1

Assets (in total)	$163,000
Liabilities	23,000
Deferred restricted income	35,000
Fund balance	105,000
	$163,000

STATEMENT OF INCOME, EXPENSES, AND CHANGES IN FUND BALANCES
For the Year Ended June 30, 19X1

Income:	
Restricted contributions utilized	$ 40,000
Other income	320,000
Total	360,000
Expenses (in total)	(355,000)
Excess of income over expenses	5,000
Fund balance, beginning of year	100,000
Fund balance, end of year	$105,000

Fig. 9–4. An example of a set of financial statements in which a current restricted gift is treated as deferred income at the time received and then recognized as income as expended.

Many, of course, object to this because they believe a current restricted gift should be reflected in the fund balance since such amounts are rarely returned to the donor. They also observe that it is very difficult for the reader to see the total activity of the organization because some gifts are being added directly to the deferred account. Those who favor this approach argue that it is less confusing than the preceding approach (adding directly to the current restricted fund balance) and does not result in the sharp fluctuations in income of the first approach (reporting current restricted gifts as income in full in the year received).

This approach is the one recommended in the AICPA Statement of Position for organizations not covered by one of the AICPA Audit Guides.* However, in the Statement of Position the point is strongly made

---

* See Chapter 16.

that the recognition of the gift as income occurs when and as the restrictions lapse, either through spending of the specific monies involved, or through spending of other, unrestricted monies which also meet the requirements of the restriction. Thus, in the Statement of Position, income recognition is triggered not by the spending of the gift, but rather by the event that lifts the restriction.

GRANTS FOR SPECIFIC PROJECTS

Many organizations receive grants from third parties to accomplish specific projects or activities. These grants differ from current restricted gifts principally in the degree of accountability the recipient organization has in reporting back to the granting organization on the use of such monies. In some instances the organization receives a grant to conduct a specific research project, the results of which are turned over to the grantor. The arrangement is similar to a private contractor's performance on a commercial for-profit basis. In other instances the organization receives a grant for a specific project and must specifically account for the expenditure of the grant in detail. In both instances the grantor is explicit in indicating how the grant is to be used and requires a complete accounting including a return of unexpended funds.

The line between current restricted gifts and grants for specific projects can get fuzzy. Most donors of current restricted gifts are explicit as to how their gifts are to be used, and often the organization will initiate a report back to the donors on the use of their gifts. However, current restricted gifts usually do not have the degree of specificity that is attached to grants for specific projects and they usually are smaller in amount.

In almost every instance where the grantor is a government agency the term "grant" will be used rather than "gift." A quid-pro-quo can be said to exist; that is, the grantor expects to receive a specific product or the accomplishment of a specific service in exchange for a specific grant, and can demand an accounting of how the funds were used.

Accounting for Grants

Grants should be accounted for on an "as-earned" basis. This means that amounts given to the organization in advance of their expenditure should be treated as deferred grant income until such time as expenditures are made which can be charged against the grant. At that time grant income should be recognized to the extent earned. Where expenditures have been made but the grantor has not yet made payment, a receivable should be set up to reflect the grantor's obligation.

Some organizations record the entire amount of the grant as a receivable at the time awarded, offset by deferred grant income on the liability side of the Balance Sheet. This is particularly appropriate where the payment schedule by the grantor will not coincide with the schedule of work performed by the organization. Thus, collection of the grant award is separated from recognition of the grant as revenue. This is an acceptable approach although some discretion needs to be exercised for grants that extend into future periods. If the grantor can subsequently modify or cancel the grant unilaterally, the grant should probably not be recorded as a receivable until it is earned.

Figure 9–5 shows an example of a Balance Sheet in which there is both a grant receivable and deferred grant income. The receivable could result either from the recording of a grant award for work not yet accomplished (in which case the offset would be deferred grant income) or from work performed under a grant agreement that has not yet been collected.

This accounting is very similar to the "deferred" approach for handling current restricted funds, discussed above. Where the organization follows this approach for handling current restricted funds, the importance of distinguishing between a current restricted gift and a grant disappears since the accounting is the same.

THE D.E. MARTIN RESEARCH CENTER

BALANCE SHEET
September 30, 19X1

Cash	$ 30,000
Grant receivable.	50,000
Other assets	30,000
Total assets	$110,000
Accounts payable	$ 5,000
Deferred grant income	20,000
Fund balance	85,000
Total liabilities and fund balance	$110,000

Fig. 9–5. An example of a Balance Sheet which has both a receivable from a grantor and deferred grant income.

NONCURRENT RESTRICTED CONTRIBUTIONS

Noncurrent restricted contributions are given for a specific purpose other than to meet the current expenses of the organization. The two most common examples of noncurrent contributions would be gifts for endowment and gifts for building or plant expansion. Such gifts are distinctive in that they will not be used in the current operations of the organization to pay for services that the organization regularly carries out. The restrictions on the use of these gifts are always designated by the donor, not by the board. Board-designated gifts are unrestricted gifts.

These noncurrent restricted gifts are sometimes referred to as "non-expendable" or "capital" gifts because they are akin to the capital of a profit-oriented entity. While building fund gifts will be "expended" for building, the resulting asset is not expended as such, except over time through depreciation. Both types of gifts have the effect of increasing the "fund balance" or "capital" of the organization.

Accounting Treatment for Endowment Fund Gifts

Endowment fund contributions should be reported directly in the endowment fund. If a Statement of Income and Expenses is presented which includes an endowment fund, obviously the gift should be reported in that statement. Alternatively, if a Statement of Changes in Fund Balances is the only statement presented for the endowment fund, the gift would obviously be shown in that statement and should be clearly labeled as such.

There are several approaches and variations for reporting endowment gifts in a Statement of Income and Expenses. Usually a multicolumn presentation is followed to separate operating income from endowment fund gifts, as shown here:

	Unrestricted	Endowment	Total
Support and Revenue:			
Contributions	$125,000	$50,000	$175,000
Other	200,000	—	200,000
Total	325,000	50,000	375,000
Less—Expenses (in total)	(310,000)	—	(310,000)
Excess of support and revenue over expenses	$ 15,000	$50,000	$ 65,000

Another approach which has received considerable attention as a result of the AICPA Statement of Position is the use of a "nonexpendable additions" section in the statement. In this approach such gifts are reflected in a section titled "Nonexpendable additions" or "Capital additions." This section immediately follows the caption "Excess of income over expenses before nonexpendable additions." (See Figure 16–2 and the related discussion.)

Accounting Treatment for Plant Fund Gifts

Plant fund contributions can be accounted for in one of two ways. Most organizations account for such gifts in the same manner as for endowment fund gifts; that is, they recognize the gift at the time received. However, some organizations that follow the deferred income approach in recognizing current restricted funds (discussed earlier in the chapter) take the position that plant fund gifts should also be treated as deferred gifts until such time as the gift is used for asset purchases. When the asset is purchased, the gift is recognized as income.

While there is logic to this deferred approach if the organization is following the deferred approach for current restricted funds, the authors prefer the more conventional approach of recognizing the receipt of the gift at the time received. A plant fund gift is not being used for current purposes, and the argument that a large gift will distort the excess of operating income over expenses therefore does not apply. Further, the return of unspent plant fund gifts is almost unheard of, which is not entirely true with current restricted gifts.°

BEQUESTS

Often an organization is informed that it is a beneficiary under a decedent's will long before the estate is probated and distribution made. When should such a bequest be recorded—at the time the organization first learns of the bequest or at the time of receipt?

Recording as an Asset

A bequest should be recorded as an asset at the time the organization can first be certain it will be a beneficiary and the amount of the bequest is known. Thus, if an organization is informed that it will receive a bequest of a specific amount, say $10,000, it should record this $10,000 as an asset.

° However, readers should note that the AICPA Statement of Position requires plant fund gifts to be deferred until expended for plant.

If instead the organization is informed that it will receive 10 per cent of the estate, the total of which is not known, nothing would be recorded although footnote disclosure would be necessary. Still a third possibility exists if the organization is told that while the final amount of the 10 per cent bequest is not known, it will be at least some stated amount. In that instance the minimum amount would be recorded with footnote disclosure of the contingent interest.

Observe that a bequest should not be recorded until the legal process is far enough along for the organization to be certain it will be a beneficiary. If challenges to the will are likely it would be more prudent to leave the bequest out of the financial statements until the uncertainty is resolved.

Recording as Income

So far we have discussed the recording of the bequest as an asset. The related question is: When should the bequest be recognized as income?

If the bequest is unrestricted, or is restricted for endowment, it should be recorded as income in the unrestricted fund or the endowment fund at the time the bequest is recorded as an asset. However, if the bequest is restricted for a current purpose or for plant additions it should be treated in the same manner as any other current restricted or plant fund gift. For example, if current restricted funds are handled using the deferred income approach discussed earlier, then the bequest should also be handled in this manner.

CONTRIBUTED SERVICES

Many organizations depend almost entirely on volunteers to carry out their program functions. The question frequently asked is: Should such organizations place a value on these contributed services and record them as "contributions" in their financial statements?

The answer is "yes" under certain limited circumstances. These limited circumstances exist only when *all* of the following conditions are satisfied:

1. The services must be an essential part of the organization's activities which if not handled by volunteers would in fact be handled by paid staff;
2. There must be reasonably good control over the employment of such services;
3. There must be an objective basis on which to value these services;

4. The services being provided must benefit persons outside of the organization;

5. The amounts involved must be such that their omission would materially distort the organization's financial statements.

Services as an Essential Part of an Organization's Program

Probably the most important requirement is that the services being performed are an essential part of the organization's program. The key test is whether the organization would hire someone to perform these services if volunteers were not available. This also suggests that the organization would have the financial ability to hire staff if volunteers were not available.

This is a difficult criterion to meet. Many organizations have volunteers involved in peripheral areas which, while important to the organization, are not of such significance that paid staff would be hired in the absence of volunteers. But this is the acid test: If the volunteers suddenly quit, would the organization have the financial capacity and inclination to hire replacements?

Control Over Employment

When a person volunteers services to an organization, there usually is no agreement to do everything the organization wants at the time the organization wants it done. The volunteer reserves the right, as it were, to pick and choose. If ordered to do an unpleasant task, the volunteeer has the option of balking and saying "no" far more readily than a paid employee. Volunteers may tend to socialize more while "on the job." All of this is recognized by nonprofit organizations and is taken into account in planning jobs to be done with volunteer help. As a result, most nonprofit organizations do not have the same degree of control over their volunteers as over their paid employees.

One of the controls that must be exercised is some form of time record. It does not need to be elaborate but should contain a day-by-day record of the number of hours worked. Many organizations use a simple daily sign-up sheet on which volunteers indicate the number of hours they have worked. At the end of each reporting period these sheets can be tallied to determine the total hours worked.

Basis on Which To Value Services

It is usually not difficult to determine a reasonable value for volunteer services where the volunteers are performing clerical services. As indicated above, by definition the services to be recorded are only those for which the organization would in fact hire paid staff if volunteers were not available. This suggests that the organization should be able to establish a reasonable estimate of what costs would be involved if employees had to be hired.

In establishing such rates it is not necessary to establish individual rates for each volunteer. Instead, the volunteers can be grouped into three or four general categories and a rate established for each category.

Some organizations are successful in getting local businesses to donate one of their executives on a full- or part-time basis for an extended period of time. In many instances the amount paid by the local business to the loaned executive is far greater than the organization would have to pay for hired staff performing the same function. The rate to be used in establishing a value should be the lower rate. This also helps to get around the awkwardness of trying to discern actual compensation.

Services Benefit Those Outside the Organization

This criterion was proposed for the first time in the 1978 AICPA Statement of Position, discussed in Chapter 16. It is designed to eliminate those situations where the services being rendered by the volunteers benefit only the organization or, in the case of a membership organization, its members. For example, the services of volunteers of trade associations or religious organizations would not be recorded where the activities are primarily for the benefit of the members or the organization.

This is not to suggest that such volunteer time is not important but rather recognizes that there is less reason to record such amounts for these organizations since the public is not directly involved.

Materiality in Amount

If the above criteria are met, an organization should still not record a value unless the services are material in amount. It is expensive to keep. the records necessary to meet the reporting requirements and unless the resulting amounts are significant it is wasteful for the organization to record them.

Accounting Treatment

The dollar value assigned to contributed services should be reflected as income in the section of the financial statements where other unrestricted contributions are shown. In most instances it is appropriate to disclose the amount of such services as a separate line.

On the expense side, the value of contributed services should be allocated to program and supporting service categories based on the nature of the work performed. The amounts allocated to each category are not normally disclosed separately. If volunteers were used for constructing fixed assets, the amounts would be capitalized rather than being charged to an expense category. Figure 9–6 shows a simplified example of reporting for contributed services.

The footnotes to the financial statements will normally disclose the nature of contributed services and the valuation techniques followed.

OTHER NONCASH CONTRIBUTIONS

Frequently an organization will receive contributions which are not in the form of cash. Typical examples are stocks and bonds, supplies, equipment, a building, etc. These contributions should be recorded if they are significant in amount *and* if there is a reasonable basis for valuation.

The value recorded should be the fair market value at the date received. Marketable stocks and bonds present no serious valuation problem. They should be recorded at their market value on the date of receipt or, if sold shortly thereafter, at the amount of proceeds actually received. However, the "shortly thereafter" refers to a sale within a few days or perhaps a week after receipt. Where the organization deliberately holds the securities for a period of time before sale, the securities should be recorded at their fair market value on the date of receipt. This will result in a gain or loss being recorded when the securities are subsequently sold (unless the market price remains unchanged).

Supplies and equipment should be recorded at the amount which the organization would normally pay for similar items. If an organization normally gets a special discount on supplies and equipment because of its nonprofit status, this lower price should be used. The valuation of a donated building or nonmarketable securities is more difficult and it is usually necessary to get an outside appraisal to determine the value.

Occasionally a nonprofit organization will be given use of a building or other facilities either at no cost or at a substantially reduced cost. A value should be reflected for such a facility in the financial statements, both as income and as expense. The value to be used should be the fair market value of facilities which the organization would otherwise rent if the contributed facilities were not available. This means that if very expensive

THE KANAB COMMUNITY SERVICE ORGANIZATION

STATEMENT OF INCOME, EXPENSES, AND CHANGES IN FUND BALANCES
For the Year Ended June 30, 19X1

Income:		
Service fees	$200,000	
Contributions	50,000	
Value of contributed services	75,000	
Total income		$325,000
Expenses:		
Program services:		
Assistance to the elderly	100,000	
Assistance to the poor	100,000	
Assistance to youth	50,000	
Total program		250,000
Supporting services:		
Administration	40,000	
Fund raising	10,000	
Total supporting		50,000
Total expenses		300,000
Excess of income over expenses		25,000
Fund balance, beginning of year		100,000
Fund balance, end of year		$125,000

Fig. 9–6. An example of a Statement of Income, Expenses, and Changes in Fund Balances in which a value is reported for contributed services of volunteers.

facilities are donated the valuation to be used should be the lower value of the facilities which the organization would otherwise have rented.

Where a donor indicates that the organization can use such rent-free facilities for more than a one-year period, the organization should reflect as income only the current period's value for such facilities. The value of future periods' facilities should be recorded in each future year. Normally no amount would be reflected in any of the financial statements for such future values although footnote disclosure would be appropriate.

PLEDGES

A pledge is a promise to contribute a specified amount to an organization. Typically, fund-raising organizations solicit pledges because a donor either does not want to or is not able to make a contribution in cash in the amount desired by the organization at the time solicited. As with consumer purchases, the "installment plan" is a way of life. Organizations find donors are more generous when the payments being contributed are small and spread out over a period of time.

A pledge may or may not be legally enforceable. The point is moot because few organizations would think of trying to legally enforce a pledge. The unfavorable publicity that would result would only hurt future fund raising. The fact that the pledge is not legally enforceable is, therefore, not germane. The only relevant criteria are will the pledge be collected and is the pledge material in size.

If these criteria are satisfied, then the accounting question is: Should a pledge be recorded as an asset at the time the pledge is received? If the answer is "yes," the next question is: When should the pledge be recognized as income? Thus, there are two questions—the recognition of the pledge as an asset, and the recognition of the pledge as income. The timing may be entirely different.

Recording as an Asset

For many organizations pledges are a significant portion of their income. The timing of the collection of pledges is only partially under the control of the organization. Yet over the years most organizations find they can predict with reasonable accuracy the collectible portion of pledges, even when a sizable percentage will not be collected. Accordingly, the authors recommend that pledges be recorded as assets and an allowance established for the portion that is estimated to be uncollectible.

There is considerable difference of opinion on this subject, and the AICPA Audit Guides and the Statement of Position take different positions. Here is a summary of the various positions:

Audit Guide for Hospitals: "All pledges . . . should be accounted for in the financial statements."

Audit Guide for Colleges and Universities: "Pledges . . . should be disclosed in the notes unless they are reported in the financial statements."

Audit Guide for Voluntary Health and Welfare Organizations: ". . . pledges shall be recorded [in the financial statements] when obtained."

Statement of Position for Certain Nonprofit Organizations: "Pledges an organization can legally enforce should be recorded . . . ."

As can be seen, three of the four documents agree with the authors' recommendation that pledges be recorded, but there is some difference between the documents as to which pledges should be recorded.

Since the Statement of Position affects so many types of organizations, it is likely that its approach will become very widespread. It provides that the organization should only record pledges which could be legally enforced.° While there is logic to this type of criterion, it seems much more pertinent to deal with the fundamental question of whether, in fact, the pledges will be collected. If the answer is "yes," it would appear appropriate to record the pledge, with, of course, an appropriate allowance for the estimated uncollectible portion.

The authors have difficulty with the position taken in the College Guide. It would appear that the authors of this Guide could not decide which position was appropriate—that is, recording pledges, or only disclosing their existence in the footnotes. Perhaps as the FASB † gets into the nonprofit area the inconsistencies among the various Guides will be narrowed or eliminated.

Pledges for Extended Periods.   The authors would offer one limitation to their recommendation that pledges be recorded as assets. Occasionally donors will indicate that because they believe an organization is doing such important work they will make an open-ended pledge of support for an extended period of time. For example, if a donor promises to pay $500 a year for fifty years, would it be appropriate to record as an asset and deferred pledge income the full fifty-years' pledge? No; obviously this would distort the financial statements. Most organizations follow the practice of not recording pledges for future years' support beyond a fairly short period—say two or at the most three years. They feel that long-term pledges are harder to collect and the delinquency factor is much greater. These arguments have validity, and organizations should consider very carefully before recording pledges for support in future periods beyond the following one or two years.

Recognition as Income

The second, related question is: When should a pledge be recognized as income? Consider for example the situation where an organization receives a pledge of $1,500 to be paid $500 this year, $500 next year, and $500 the following year. Should the $1,500 be recorded as income at the time the pledge is received, or should only the amount that will be received in the current year ($500) be recorded? The answer depends on the donor's intention.

Donors' Silence on Intentions.   If donors are silent about their intentions, the authors believe the presumption should be that they intend their

° See page 260.
† See Chapter 18.

pledge to be used in the year they have indicated they will make payment. In the interim, the pledge would be recorded as an asset (i.e., as a pledge receivable), but would also be reflected as "deferred" income in the Balance Sheet. In our example, the donor has agreed to give $500 a year for three years and since no contrary intention has been indicated, the presumption is that the future payments were intended to be used in the two future years; $500 should be recorded in the current year as income and $1,000 as deferred pledge income. At the end of the initial year the Balance Sheet would appear as follows:

BALANCE SHEET

Assets:		
Cash	$1,100	
Pledges.	1,000	
Total assets		$2,100
Liabilities:		
Accounts payable	$ 200	
Deferred pledge income.	1,000	
Total	1,200	
Fund balance	900	
Total liabilities and fund balance		$2,100

As can be seen, $1,000 has been deferred. Each year $500 would be transferred from deferred income and recorded as current income.

Even here there is a difference of opinion in the authoritative literature. While the Statement of Position concurs with the authors' recommendations, the Audit Guides for Voluntary Health and Welfare Organizations and for Hospitals take a different position. They say that if donors are silent as to their intentions, the pledges should be recognized as income currently, and not be deferred. This overlooks the reality that organizations normally cannot spend money before they get it and it is hard to see how the donors could have expected the organization to do so. From this the authors draw the conclusion that donors do not intend an organization to spend their gifts until the periods in which they have indicated they will pay off their pledges.

Donors' Specification of Intentions. The other possibility is that the donors are very specific as to when they intend their gifts to be used. Often they will want to support a current year's project, but for financial or tax reasons do not want to make payment until the following year.

Again the principle is to recognize the gifts on the basis of the donors' intentions. In our previous example, if it were the donor's intention to have the full $1,500 recorded as income in the current year, this intent should be followed and the entire $1,500 should be recorded as a current year's contribution.

Even here, if a very large and unusual pledge received for a current year's project is to be paid off over a long period of time (say, three to five years), the organization should consider carefully the advisability of recording this pledge in the current year. In that circumstance the potential risk of not collecting this large amount has to be carefully considered. If this amount were not collected the current year's statements could be seriously misleading.

Building Fund Pledges.   If a pledge of $1,500 is made toward a building or capital fund, the full $1,500 is normally recorded as income of the building fund at the time the pledge is received. The reason for this different treatment is that a building fund is not usually associated with a specific year's activities as such. Also, organizations will often borrow to cover construction costs with the pledges as part of the basis for assuming that the loan can be paid off when due.

The Statement of Position for Certain Nonprofit Organizations takes the position that organizations should record unexpended plant fund contributions as deferred income until expended for fixed assets. This would also be followed with respect to building fund pledges. (See Chapter 16.)

Allowance for Uncollectible Pledges

A key question is how large the allowance for uncollectible pledges should be. Most organizations have past experience to help answer this question. If over the years, 10 per cent of pledges are not collected, then unless the economic climate changes, 10 per cent is probably the right figure to use. Care must be taken, however, because while an organization's past experience may have been good, times do change—as many organizations have discovered to their sorrow.

Another factor to consider is the purpose for which the pledge will be used. Some people will hesitate to default on a pledge for a worthwhile current year's project but may be less conscientious about a pledge for a building fund or a long-term project.

Another point to keep in mind in setting up an allowance is that a pledgor who defaults on an installment once is likely to do so again. If the default brings no notice from the organization the pledgor assumes the contribution is not really needed, and it will be easier to skip the next

payment. So once a donor becomes delinquent on even a single installment, a 100 per cent allowance for the total pledge, not just for the delinquent portion, should be considered. In addition, the organization should
review the amount of allowance needed for other nondelinquent pledges;
once there are signs of any delinquency the overall collection assumptions
may be in doubt. If so, the organization should be conservative and set up
additional allowances.

PART II

FINANCIAL STATEMENT PRESENTATION

10

Cash Basis Financial
Statements

Most small and some medium-sized nonprofit organizations keep their records on a cash basis of accounting.* As was discussed in some detail in Chapter 3, for many organizations the cash basis is the best one. Probably the most important reason for this is the simplicity of record keeping. Another reason is that cash basis financial statements are the easiest type of statements to prepare and understand since the accounting principles are so straightforward.

SIMPLE CASH BASIS STATEMENT

Figure 10–1 shows the financial statement of a typical small church that keeps its records on the cash basis. It also follows the principle of writing off all fixed assets as purchased so there are no fixed assets to be reflected in a Balance Sheet.

Characteristics

This statement shows not only cash receipts and disbursements but also the cash balance of the church. Since there are no receivables or payables in cash basis accounting, the only asset reflected is cash. This

---

* Note, however, that "generally accepted accounting principles" require accrual basis statements. Organizations that want an opinion from their CPA which states that their financial statements are prepared in accordance with "generally accepted accounting principles" must prepare their statements on an accrual basis.

ALL SAINTS CHURCH

STATEMENT OF CASH RECEIPTS, DISBURSEMENTS,
AND CASH BALANCE
For the 12 Months Ending December 31, 19X2

	Actual	Budget
Receipts:		
Plate collections	$ 4,851	$ 5,000
Envelopes and pledges.	30,516	32,200
Special gifts.	5,038	4,000
Nursery school fees.	5,800	6,000
Total	46,205	47,200
Disbursements:		
Clergy	14,325	15,000
Music	8,610	8,400
Education	6,850	7,000
Church office	5,890	6,200
Building maintenance	4,205	4,300
Missions	2,000	2,000
Other	3,318	1,600
Total	45,198	44,500
Excess of cash receipts over disbursements	1,007	$ 2,700
Cash balance, January 1, 19X2	4,300	
Cash balance, December 31, 19X2	$ 5,307	

Fig. 10–1. An example of a simple cash basis statement that combines both the activity for the year and the ending cash balance.

being so, this presentation shows the readers everything they would want to know about the cash transactions for the twelve months.

The words "receipts" and "disbursements" have been used, rather than the words "income" and "expenses." Traditionally "receipts" and "disbursements" are used in cash basis statements since both words signify an event that has taken place (i.e., cash has been received or disbursed). The words "income" and "expense" usually refer to accrual basis statements. Also, note that the words "net income" have not been used since they usually refer to profit-oriented (i.e., business) entities.

Budget Comparison

One of the first principles to be remembered in preparing financial statements—whether cash basis or accrual basis—is that the reader should be given a point of reference to help in judging the results. This can be a comparison with last year's statement or it can be a comparison with the budget for the current year. The important thing is that the reader's attention is directed to deviations from either past experience or anticipated results. In Figure 10–1 a comparison with the budget gives the reader a point of reference. A careful examination will show where receipts and disbursements have deviated from what was expected. In this illustration, the reader will note that "envelopes" and "plate collections" have not met expectations. Most expenditures (except "other" disbursements) have been close to the budget.

SIMPLE STATEMENT WITH LAST YEAR'S FIGURES AND BUDGET

While the statement in Figure 10–1 has a comparison with the budget, some organizations also add last year's figures. An even more elaborate statement would contain a column showing the amount of deviation of actual receipts and disbursements from the budget. Figure 10–2 shows the same statement but with these additional columns to help the reader quickly pinpoint problem areas.

Quickly look down the column labeled "Actual better (worse) than budget." See how rapidly the three significant items that have deviated from the budget can be spotted. This is the advantage of the deviation column.

Comparison with Last Year's Actual Figures

The 19X1 comparison column gives additional information to help the reader interpret the current year's statement. For example, note that in 19X2 every category of receipts is up from 19X1, as is every category of disbursements. The thoughtful reader has to ask whether the board wasn't overly optimistic in budgeting receipts of almost $7,000 more than the prior year. Perhaps on that basis the less-than-budget envelope and pledge receipts for 19X2 do not look as bad. At the same time, the reader will observe that the board went ahead and spent more than was budgeted. This comparison with both last year's actual and this year's budget helps the reader to obtain insight into the financial statement.

At the same time, including last year's actual figures may be more distracting than helpful for some readers. In preparing financial statements, careful consideration must be given to the needs and limitations of the reader. Careful thought must be given to the degree of sophistication which is appropriate. Accordingly, statements for the board might contain this full four-column presentation while the statements for the

ALL SAINTS CHURCH

STATEMENT OF CASH RECEIPTS, DISBURSEMENTS,
AND CASH BALANCE
(SHOWING A COMPARISON WITH LAST YEAR AND BUDGET)
For the 12 Months Ending December 31, 19X2

	Actual 19X1	Actual 19X2	19X2 Budget	Actual Better (Worse) Than Budget
Receipts:				
Plate collections	$ 4,631	$ 4,851	$ 5,000	($ 149)
Envelopes and pledges	28,722	30,516	32,200	(1,684)
Special gifts.............	1,650	5,038	4,000	1,038
Nursery school fees.......	5,650	5,800	6,000	(200)
Total	40,653	46,205	47,200	(995)
Disbursements:				
Clergy	13,400	14,325	15,000	675
Music	7,900	8,610	8,400	(210)
Education	5,651	6,850	7,000	150
Church office	4,317	5,890	6,200	310
Building maintenance	3,105	4,205	4,300	95
Missions	1,500	2,000	2,000	–
Other.................	3,168	3,318	1,600	(1,718)
Total	39,041	45,198	44,500	(698)
Excess of cash receipts over disbursements	1,612	1,007	$ 2,700	($1,693)
Cash balance, January 1	2,688	4,300		
Cash balance, December 31 ..	$ 4,300	$ 5,307		

Fig. 10–2. An example of a simple cash basis statement that shows last year's actual figures and this year's budget to give the reader a basis for drawing a conclusion.

church membership could contain only the two-column presentation in Figure 10–1. Or, perhaps the appropriate information for the membership may be the two "actual" columns.

COMBINED CASH BASIS INCOME STATEMENT AND BALANCE SHEET

In Chapter 2 it was noted that cash basis accounting reflects only transactions involving cash. This means that a cash basis Balance Sheet does not show accounts receivable or accounts payable since no cash has been involved. However, there are assets and liabilities that do result from cash transactions and these assets and liabilities should be reflected on the Balance Sheet. Three types of transactions are frequently reflected in a cash basis Balance Sheet: those involving securities or investments, fixed assets, and loans payable.

Securities or investments can arise either from an outright purchase for cash, or as a result of a donation. If they result from a donation, they should be treated as "cash" income and be recorded as an asset. Fair market value at the date of receipt should be used for valuation purposes.

The purchase of fixed assets for cash may or may not be reflected on the Balance Sheet depending on the principles being followed for fixed asset accounting. Chapter 6 discussed the problems of accounting for fixed assets.

Occasionally a cash basis organization will borrow money from a bank or from an individual. A good example is a church that has a drop in contributions over the summer months and needs a short-term loan to tide it over until fall pledge collections pick up. These loans are "cash" transactions and should be reflected on the Balance Sheet.

Figure 10–3 shows an example of a statement showing assets resulting from cash transactions. The Friends of Evelyn College is a small nonprofit organization whose function is to raise funds among alumnae for the ultimate benefit of their alma mater.

Characteristics

Note the second line of the title—"Net assets resulting from cash transactions." Another title sometimes used is "Fund balance resulting from cash transactions." Normally the use of the words "balance sheet" is avoided since these words imply the accrual basis.

This format provides a description of the assets held at the end of year right on the Statement of Income Collected and Expenses Disbursed. This makes it possible for the reader to obtain a total picture of the organization by looking at only one statement. This simplicity is a real advantage.

This organization has used the words "income collected" and "expenses disbursed" whereas in Figures 10–1 and 10–2 the words "receipts" and "disbursements" were used. It was previously noted that the words "income" and "expense" generally refer to accrual basis accounting and should be avoided in cash basis statements. Here, however, the use of the words "collected" and "disbursed" clearly indicate that cash transactions are involved and therefore there is no reason not to use these titles.

THE FRIENDS OF EVELYN COLLEGE, INC.

STATEMENT OF INCOME COLLECTED, EXPENSES DISBURSED,
AND NET ASSETS RESULTING FROM CASH TRANSACTIONS
For the Year Ended December 31, 19X2

Income collected:

Contributions received	$146,797	
Interest income	2,150	
Total		$148,947

Expenses disbursed:

Grants to Evelyn College	125,000	
Audit fee	573	
Other expenses	832	
Total		126,405
Excess of income collected over expenses disbursed		22,542
Net assets, January 1, 19X2		20,604
Net assets, December 31, 19X2		$ 43,146

Net assets comprised:

Cash	$ 943	
U.S. treasury bills, at cost which approximates market	47,211	
Marketable securities at contributed value (market value $6,958)	4,992	
		$ 53,146
Less: Loan payable to bank		(10,000)
		$ 43,146

Fig. 10–3. An example of a simple cash basis financial statement which combines in a single statement both income and expenses for the year and the assets and liabilities at the end of the year.

The term "net income" is more familiar to most than the phrase used in this illustration, "Excess of income collected over expenses disbursed" or the phrase used in Figures 10–1 and 10–2, "Excess of cash receipts over disbursements." As was previously noted, the words "income" and "expense" usually refer to accrual basis transactions. Still, many like to use the words "net income" in cash basis statements because they feel the reader understands this term better than one of the other expressions. If the organization wants to use the words "net income," it should then add the words "on a cash basis" so there can be no confusion.

Note that the market value is shown parenthetically on both the U.S. treasury bills and the marketable securities. As is discussed in Chapter 8, marketable securities are often carried at cost. However, it is important to show the market value on the statements so that the reader can see how much unrealized appreciation (or depreciation) there is.

SEPARATE STATEMENT OF RECEIPTS AND DISBURSEMENTS
AND STATEMENT OF NET ASSETS

It is not always possible to combine a Statement of Assets with the Statement of Receipts and Disbursements. This is particularly true where the Statement of Receipts and Disbursements is long and complicated or where the assets and liabilities are voluminous. Figure 10–4 shows the first two years' operation of a private swim club that purchased land and built- a pool, borrowing part of the monies needed. Two statements are used although the cash balance is also shown on the Statement of Cash Receipts and Disbursements.

Cash Basis Emphasized

All cash transactions have been included in this Statement of Cash Receipts, Disbursements, and Cash Balance, but all transactions not involving income or expenses as such have been segregated to aid the reader. If these transactions had not been segregated it would have been more difficult for the reader to see what the on-going pattern of income and expenses would be.

Notice that in this presentation the statement comes down to the cash balance at the end of the year. The purpose of this is to accent the most important asset. The statement could have stopped at the "Excess of cash receipts over disbursements" caption, but by showing the cash balance the importance of cash is emphasized. This is important for organizations with constant cash problems.

Mortgage Repayments

The mortgage principal repayment is shown as an "other cash" transaction. This allows the reader to see the cash position at the end of the year. On an accrual basis neither the loan proceeds nor the mortgage principal repayment would be shown.

Certain Assets Not Capitalized

Notice that the lawn furniture has not been considered a fixed asset. This is because lawn furniture will be replaced every year or two and therefore there is little point in setting it up as a fixed asset. Cash basis organizations normally do not depreciate assets, and if these assets were recorded they probably would have to be depreciated since they have such a short life.

CROMWELL HILLS SWIM CLUB

STATEMENT OF CASH RECEIPTS, DISBURSEMENTS, AND CASH BALANCE
RESULTING FROM CASH TRANSACTIONS
For the Years Ended December 31, 19X1 and 19X2

	19X1	19X2
Income collected:		
Membership dues	$25,000	$25,000
Interest income	125	300
Total	25,125	25,300
Expenses disbursed:		
Salaries of manager	2,000	2,200
Salaries of life guards	12,000	13,000
Payroll taxes	820	730
Pool supplies	2,000	2,200
Mortgage interest	1,200	2,300
Lawn furniture	800	—
Other miscellaneous	1,380	670
Total	20,200	21,100
Excess of income collected over expenses disbursed	4,925	4,200
Other cash transactions-receipts (disbursements):		
Mortgage principal repayments	(3,800)	(5,700)
Members' capital contributions	50,000	—
Bank loan received	40,000	—
Land acquisition	(25,000)	—
Pool construction cost	(62,500)	—
Net other cash transactions	(1,300)	(5,700)
Excess of cash receipts over (under) disbursements for the year	3,625	(1,500)
Cash balance, beginning of the year		3,625
Cash balance end of the year	$ 3,625	$ 2,125

Fig. 10—4. Cash basis statements where cash balance is shown in the Statement of Cash Receipts and Disbursements, and a separate Statement of Net
Assets is also presented.

STATEMENT OF INCOME
WITH CERTAIN CASH TRANSACTIONS OMITTED

There is still another way to show the Cromwell Hills Swim Club
statements. In this presentation certain cash transactions which affect
the Balance Sheet are not shown in the Statement of Income. In 19X1

CROMWELL HILLS SWIM CLUB

STATEMENT OF NET ASSETS RESULTING FROM CASH TRANSACTIONS
December 31, 19X1 and 19X2

	19X1	19X2
Net Assets		
Cash	$ 3,625	$ 2,125
Fixed assets, at cost:		
Land	25,000	25,000
Pool	62,500	62,500
Total assets	91,125	89,625
Less—Bank Loan	(36,200)	(30,500)
Net assets	$54,925	$59,125
Represented by		
Capital contributions..........................	$50,000	$50,000
Excess of income collected over expenses disbursed:		
Beginning of the year	—	4,925
For the year	4,925	4,200
End of the year..............................	4,925	9,125
	$54,925	$59,125

Fig. 10–4.   Continued.

these are the loan of $40,000, repayment of $3,800, and the purchases of land and pool of $87,500. Figure 10–5 shows how statements presented on this basis would look.

Characteristics

As noted above, the Statement of Income Collected, Expenses Disbursed, and Capital Contributed does not contain all cash transactions. Those transactions affecting only the Statement of Assets are not reflected. As a result the last line on the Statement of Income is no longer the cash balance, but "Excess of income collected and capital contributed over expenses disbursed." This means that the emphasis on the cash balance is gone, and this creates a risk that the reader may misinterpret the meaning of this "excess" line. Most will readily recognize that the $54,925 in 19X1 is not the cash balance at the end of the year, but some may think the club had a "cash" surplus in 19X2 of $4,200. Many will fail to realize that there was a mortgage principal repayment of $5,700 and that the actual cash balance decreased $1,500 during the year.

CROMWELL HILLS SWIM CLUB

STATEMENT OF INCOME COLLECTED, EXPENSES DISBURSED, AND CAPITAL CONTRIBUTED
For the Years Ended December 31, 19X1 and 19X2

	19X1	19X2
Income collected:		
Membership dues	$25,000	$25,000
Interest income	125	300
Total	25,125	25,300
Expenses disbursed:		
Salaries of manager	2,000	2,200
Salaries of life guards	12,000	13,000
Payroll taxes	820	730
Pool supplies	2,000	2,200
Mortgage interest	1,200	2,300
Lawn furniture	800	—
Other miscellaneous	1,380	670
Total	20,200	21,100
Excess of income collected over expenses disbursed	4,925	4,200
Capital contributed	50,000	—
Excess of income collected and capital contributed over		
expenses disbursed	$54,925	$ 4,200

STATEMENT OF NET ASSETS RESULTING FROM CASH TRANSACTIONS
December 31, 19X1 and 19X2

	19X1	19X2
Cash	$ 3,625	$ 2,125
Fixed assets, at cost:		
Land	25,000	25,000
Pool	62,500	62,500
Total assets	91,125	89,625
Less—Bank loan	(36,200)	(30,500)
Net assets	$54,925	$59,125

Fig. 10–5. An example of cash basis statements where certain cash transactions are not reflected in the Statement of Income Collected, Expenses Disbursed, and Capital Contributed.

In this presentation, the Statement of Assets could have been added at the bottom of the Statement of Income in a manner similar to that of Figure 10–3. Figure 10–6 shows how this would look in condensed form. This is a better approach because the reader does not have to make the transition from one statement to another, or to understand the title at the top of the second statement.

MODIFIED CASH BASIS STATEMENTS

In Chapter 2 it was noted that cash basis organizations often reflect certain noncash transactions in their financial statements. This may be a large receivable from a brokerage house for securities that have been sold at the end of the year, or it may be a large bill owed to someone which would materially distort the statements if omitted. In each case these transactions are reflected in the statements to avoid material distortions.

There is absolutely nothing wrong with an organization's including such noncash transactions in the statements. The important thing is that the statements be meaningful. Care should be taken, however, to label noncash transactions in the statement so the reader knows they have been included.

CROMWELL HILLS SWIM CLUB
CONDENSED STATEMENT OF INCOME COLLECTED, EXPENSES
DISBURSED, CAPITAL CONTRIBUTED, AND NET ASSETS
For the Years Ended December 31, 19X1 and 19X2

	19X1	19X2
Income collected	$25,125	$25,300
Expenses disbursed	(20,200)	(21,100)
Excess of income collected over expenses disbursed	4,925	4,200
Capital contributed	50,000	—
Excess of income collected and capital contributed over		
expenses disbursed	54,925	4,200
Net assets, beginning of the year	—	54,925
Net assets, end of the year	$54,925	$59,125
Net assets comprised:		
Cash	$ 3,625	$ 2,125
Land (at cost)	25,000	25,000
Pool (at cost)	62,500	62,500
Total assets	91,125	89,625
Less—Bank loan	(36,200)	(30,500)
Net assets	$54,925	$59,125

Fig. 10–6. **An example of a cash basis statement in which the Statement of Income is combined with a Statement of Net Assets.**

CONCLUSION

More nonprofit organizations use cash basis than accrual basis accounting. Except where fixed assets and loans are involved, cash basis statements are very simple to prepare and understand. And even with the complication of fixed assets and loans, it is possible to present meaningful statements that most readers will understand. In developing the appropriate financial statement presentation the treasurer should consider carefully what emphasis is desired. If the cash position of the organization is the crucial item, then the statement should come down to the cash balance at the end of the period. If cash is not a problem, the last line should be either the caption "Excess of income over expenses on the cash basis" or "Net assets at the end of the year." This is largely a matter of judgment and of knowing the readers of the statements and their level of sophistication.

11

Accrual Basis Financial
Statements

In the previous chapter several cash basis statements were illustrated. One of the reasons cash basis accounting is followed is the simplicity of record keeping. Unfortunately for many organizations cash basis accounting is just not appropriate. They have too many unpaid bills at the end of the year or too much uncollected revenue. The only meaningful basis of accounting for these organizations is the accrual basis.[*]

Accrual basis accounting is more complicated, but this does not mean that the financial statements prepared on an accrual basis need be complicated or hard to understand. The key, however, is careful planning. This is the laying out of the financial-statement format so that the statements tell the organization's story as simply and effectively as possible. Easy-to-understand financial statements do not just happen; they must be carefully prepared with the reader in mind.

In this chapter three sets of accrual basis financial statements are discussed. Each has been prepared with the reader in mind. Many of the accounting principles discussed in previous chapters are also illustrated in these statements.

SIMPLE ACCRUAL BASIS STATEMENTS

Camp Squa Pan is a typical medium-sized boys' camp sponsored by a local YMCA but operated as a separate entity. It was started in

[*] "Generally accepted accounting principles" require accrual basis statements. Organizations that want an opinion which states that their financial statements are prepared in accordance with generally accepted accounting principles from their CPA must prepare their statements on an accrual basis.

CAMP ŚQUA PAN, INC.

STATEMENT OF INCOME, EXPENSES, AND CHANGES IN FUND BALANCES
For the Years Ended December 31, 19X1 and 19X2

	19X1	19X2
Income:		
Campers' fees	$203,760	$214,400
Interest	212	412
Total income	203,972	214,812
Expenses:		
Salaries	89,606	93,401
Food...	36,978	40,615
Repair and maintenance	25,741	29,415
Horse care and feed	3,983	4,010
Insurance	6,656	6,656
Advertising and promotion	2,563	2,201
Depreciation	12,570	13,601
Other miscellaneous	21,141	26,415
Total expenses	199,238	216,314
Excess of income over (under) expenses	4,734	(1,502)
Fund balance, beginning of the year	55,516	60,250
Fund balance, end of the year	$ 60,250	$ 58,748

Fig. 11–1. An example of a simple accrual basis Statement of Income, Expenses, and Changes in Fund Balances.

the late 1940's with a contribution of $50,000 from the local YMCA, and over the years has broken even financially. Figures 11–1 and 11–2 show the financial statements on an accrual basis.

Income

The principal transaction reflected in these statements, which would have been handled differently on a cash basis, is the receipt in the current year of camp deposits for the following year. In 19X1 the camp notices were sent out in October and many deposits had been received by December 31. In 19X2, however, the notices didn't get out until almost Christmas and very few deposits had been received. If Camp Squa Pan had been on a cash basis, the income for 19X2 would have been substantially less, since the $18,275 of deposits received in 19X1 for 19X2 camp fees would have been 19X1 income. Offsetting this would have been the $1,610 of deposits received in 19X2 for 19X3

CAMP SQUA PAN, INC.

BALANCE SHEET
December 31, 19X1 and 19X2

ASSETS

	19X1	19X2
Current assets:		
Cash	$ 13,107	$ 9,997
U.S. treasury bills at cost which approximates		
market	10,812	–
Accounts receivable.	1,632	853
Prepaid insurance	2,702	1,804
Total current assets	28,253	12,654
Fixed assets, at cost:		
Land	13,161	13,161
Buildings	76,773	76,773
Furniture and fixtures.	22,198	23,615
Automobiles	13,456	14,175
Canoes and other equipment	12,025	12,675
	137,613	140,399
Less: Accumulated depreciation.	(71,242)	(76,629)
Net fixed assets	66,371	63,770
Total assets . . . .·.	$ 94,624	$ 76,424

LIABILITIES AND FUND BALANCE

	19X1	19X2
Current liabilities:		
Accounts payable and accrued expenses	$ 4,279	$ 3,416
Camp deposits	18,275	1,610
Total current liabilities	22,554	5,026
Deferred compensation payable	11,820	12,650
Fund balance:		
Original YMCA contribution	50,000	50,000
Accumulated excess of income over expenses	10,250	8,748
Total fund balance	60,250	58,748
Total liabilities and fund balance	$ 94,624	$ 76,424

Fig. 11–2.   An example of a simple accrual basis Balance Sheet.

camp fees. Here is what 19X2 income would have looked like on a cash basis:

19X2 accrual basis income	$214,400
Less 19X2 deposits received in 19X1	(18,275)
Plus 19X3 deposits received in 19X2	1,610
19X2 cash basis income	$197,735

As can be seen, there is a $16,665 difference between the cash and accrual bases. This difference is material when measured against the excess of expenses over income in 19X2 of $1,502. On a cash basis this excess would have been $18,167 and the cash basis statements would have been misleading.

Depreciation

Depreciation is recorded by Camp Squa Pan. As is more fully discussed in Chapter 7, nonprofit organizations that capitalize their fixed assets should also depreciate them. In this case the camp director felt the building and equipment would deteriorate with time and he knew there was little likelihood that the YMCA would make another major contribution for new buildings or equipment. Accordingly, he concluded that it was appropriate to depreciate the fixed assets and to include depreciation as an expense so that he would be forced to set camp fees high enough to recover these depreciation costs.*

Fund Balance

The camp uses the term "fund balance" on its Balance Sheet. This term is similar in meaning to "stockholders' equity," "net worth," "capital," or "net assets." Since nonprofit organizations do not normally have stockholders as such, the term "stockholders' equity" is not appropriate. However, the terms "net worth," "net assets," or even "capital" are all terms that are used to represent the aggregate net value of the organization. In this case, Camp Squa Pan has kept the composition of the fund balance segregated on the Balance Sheet between the original YMCA contribution and the accumulated excess of income over expenses of the camp. Many organizations keep amounts separated in this way on their financial statements, although this is a matter of preference more than anything else. From a practical standpoint, the historical source of the funds is of little significance for a nonprofit organization except where there are restrictions which relate to these balances. In the example here, there is no reason why a single line could not have been shown with the title "fund balance" and the amount $58,748.

---

* There are a number of accounting policies which each organization must determine. The handling of fixed assets and depreciation is a good example. Since there are a number of acceptable alternatives, each organization should disclose the accounting policies it has adopted in its notes to the financial statements so that all readers will be fully aware of them.

A minor point to note is that the camp has set up a deferred compensation liability for its caretaker who lives at the camp year round. This will be paid to him sometime in the future, probably when he retires. The point to note is that if the organization has a commitment for this type of expense, it should be recorded currently on an accrual basis.

ACCRUAL BASIS STATEMENTS—
FUND-RAISING ORGANIZATION

The United Fund Drive of Richmond Hill is a typical community fund-raising organization. It solicits contributions on behalf of about twenty agencies serving the Richmond Hill area. Its annual drive takes place in late September. A substantial portion of the contributions is raised through pledges to be paid from payroll deductions over the period October through May. After the annual drive is completed and the board knows how much has been received or pledged, it makes allocations to the various agencies that will receive funds. As the cash is received it is turned over to these agencies. The records are kept on an accrual basis and pledges are recorded. The fiscal year ends on July 31. Figures 11–3 and 11–4 show the comparative financial statements for the six-month periods ending January 31, 19X1 and 19X2.

Pledges

The Statement of Income, Allocations, and Fund Balance clearly shows both the total pledges and the amount that is estimated to be uncollectible. Many organizations are reluctant to record pledges until received. Yet experience shows that a fairly consistent pattern of collection will usually exist for most organizations. There is no reason why pledges, less the anticipated uncollectible portion, should not be recorded. In this case, if pledges were not recorded, the financial statements would have little meaning.

Fiscal Period

Obviously the organization's fiscal year-end should not fall in the middle of the period when both collections and payment of the allocations are in process. This is what would happen if December 31 were the year-end. In this case the year-end is July 31 since all pledges are

UNITED FUND DRIVE OF RICHMOND HILL, INC.
STATEMENT OF INCOME, ALLOCATIONS AND FUND BALANCE

	6 Months Ending January 31,	
	19X1	19X2
Income available for allocation:		
Pledges	$597,342	$726,661
Interest income...............................	90	765
Less—Provision for uncollectible pledges	(31,161)	(39,192)
	566,271	688,234
Less—Administrative expenses	(25,344)	(27,612)
Income available for allocation	540,927	660,622
Allocations to agencies:		
American Red Cross	42,759	50,000
Richmond Hill Area Urban League	17,640	28,025
Big Brothers	—	13,971
Boy Scouts of America	70,220	72,385
Camp Fire Girls	40,531	40,905
Black Affairs Council	13,816	15,000
Child Guidance Clinic	6,010	—
Day Care Center	—	15,000
Family and Children's Service	107,026	116,760
Girl Scouts	40,422	56,000
Goodwill Industries............................	30,650	32,700
Legal Aid Society	11,719	10,700
Salvation Army	36,757	40,967
Summer Youth Program	—	10,000
Visiting Nurse Association	4,010	6,689
Hebrew Community Center	25,783	28,038
Y.M. and Y.W.C.A.............................	42,392	43,075
Richmond Hill Hospital.........................	68,127	65,069
	557,862	645,284
Excess of income over (under) allocations	(16,935)	15,338
Fund balance, August 1	24,237	9,502
Fund balance, January 31	$ 7,302	$ 24,840

Fig. 11—3. An example of an accrual basis Statement of Income and Allocations for a typical united fund drive.

normally paid by May 31. At July 31 the organization will have collected and paid to agencies all of the previous year's fund drive pledges. For newly formed organizations the year-end date must be elected on a timely basis for federal tax reporting purposes. Page 419 discusses this requirement.

UNITED FUND DRIVE OF RICHMOND HILL, INC.

BALANCE SHEET

	January 31, 19X1	January 31, 19X2
ASSETS		
Cash	$ 38,727	$ 59,805
Pledges receivable, less allowance for uncollectible pledges of $31,161 in 19X1 and $39,192 in 19X2	168,516	229,517
Total assets.	$207,243	$289,322
LIABILITIES AND FUND BALANCE		
Allocated to agencies	$557,862	$645,284
Less: Payments to date	(361,536)	(389,517)
Net unpaid	196,326	255,767
Payroll taxes and accounts payable	3,615	8,715
Total liabilities	199,941	264,482
Fund balance	7,302	24,840
Total liabilities and fund balance	$207,243	$289,322

Fig. 11–4.   An example of an accrual basis Balance Sheet for a typical united fund drive.

Income Statement Format

There is considerable detail on the Statement of Income, Allocations, and Fund Balance, but it all concerns the principal function of the drive, allocations to agencies. While there are some administrative expenses, no details have been shown because to do so would distract from the main purpose of the statement. Presumably the board would receive a supporting schedule accounting for these expenses.

Notice the caption "Income available for allocation." It is important in statements of fund-raising organizations that the amount which is actually available for the purposes for which the organization exists be clearly shown. An alternative presentation would be: *

* The Second Edition of *Standards of Accounting. and Financial Reporting for Voluntary Health and Welfare Organizations* illustrates a presentation similar to this one, although following the terminology of the AICPA Audit Guide for Voluntary Health and Welfare Organizations (i.e., Revenue, Support, Program Services, Supporting Services). See Chapter 13 and pages 196–200.

	19X2
Income	$688,234
Expenses:	
Allocations to agencies (in detail)	645,284
Administrative expenses (in detail)	27,612
Total	672,896
Excess of income over expenses	$ 15,338

There is certainly nothing wrong with this format except that it is too easy to get lost in the details of the administrative expenses and miss the central point, that $645,284 was distributed to agencies out of an available amount of $660,622 ($688,234 less $27,612). The administrative expenses are a real cost of raising the income and should be shown as a deduction from the gross income raised.

Functional Reporting

The Voluntary Health and Welfare Organization Audit Guide discussed in Chapter 13 provides for reporting of expenses on a functional basis, with a distinction between program and supporting functions and a further division of the supporting function into administrative and fund raising. Figure 11–3 does not specifically use the words "program" and "supporting"; however, since the program function of a community fund-raising drive is to collect and allocate funds, its entire fund-raising effort is in reality the program. The only fund-raising costs which would be "supporting" would be efforts made to raise funds for the organization itself, as, for example, a building fund drive.

Balance Sheet Format

Notice that, to make it easier for the reader, on the Balance Sheet the gross amount allocated to agencies has been shown and then payments-to-date have been deducted to arrive at the net amount still payable. It would certainly be correct to show only one figure, the remaining $255,767, but then it would be more difficult for readers to understand exactly what that figure represented. They might mistakenly conclude this was the total amount allocated.

Notice that the estimated uncollectible amount of pledges is shown on the Balance Sheet. This gives the readers some idea as to the percentage that is expected to be collected.

ACCRUAL BASIS STATEMENTS—
INTERNATIONAL ORGANIZATION

There are many large nonprofit organizations, some of which have international operations. This does not mean, however, that the financial statements are necessarily complex or involved. The financial statements of Children Overseas Inc. are a good example. Children Overseas Inc. is a large organization serving poor and destitute children in eleven countries. Its funds are raised principally by encouraging contributions toward the support of particular children. Figures 11-5, 11-6, 11-7 show the financial statements of this large international organization.

One of the first things that may strike the reader is that the figures are shown only in thousands of dollars. There is no point in carrying figures out to the last dollar. Round off to the significant figure. The extra digits only make the reader work harder and incorrectly suggest that there is significance in the detail. Where there is concern that the absence of the extra digits reduces the impact of the numbers, another alternative is to use zeros to replace amounts rounded (i.e., $8,206 becomes $8,206,000). In this way readability is retained along with the usual impact of the amounts.

Income Statement Format

The Consolidated Statement of Income, Expenses, and Changes in Fund Balances (Figure 11-5) shows some detailed sources of income, but only total expenses. A separate supporting statement (Figure 11-6) shows the details of the expenses by country, for the interested reader. It would have been possible to include much of this "by country" detail on the Statement of Income, but this could very well have confused the reader by having too much detail. The supporting schedule has been carefully prepared to help the reader see how it ties into the income statement ($8,206; $2,353; $583 and $11,142). This makes it easy for the reader to become quickly oriented when looking at this supporting schedule. If the organization had wanted to give even more detail in this supporting schedule, it could have used a wide sheet of paper and listed the details by type of expenses down the side and by country

CHILDREN OVERSEAS INC.

CONSOLIDATED STATEMENT OF INCOME, EXPENSES, AND CHANGES IN FUND BALANCES

(in thousands)

	For the Year Ended June 30	
	19X1	19X2
Income:		
Pledges for children	$ 9,210	$ 9,073
Gifts for special purposes	1,372	1,514
Contributions, endowment gifts, and		
bequests.	450	661
Government refunds	155	82
Investment and miscellaneous income	44	74
Provision for unrealized loss on		
investments	(44)	—
Reduction in provision for unrealized		
loss on investments no longer needed	—	92
Total income	11,187	11,496
Expenses (Figure 11-6):		
Aid and services to children	8,649	8,206
Supporting operations	2,081	2,353
Promotion and advertising.	454	583
Total expenses	11,184	11,142
Excess of income over expenses	3	354
Fund balance (deficit), beginning of year	(514)	(511)
Fund balance (deficit), end of year.	$ (511)	$ (157)

Fig. 11–5. An example of a comparative Statement of Income, Expenses, and Changes in Fund Balances for a large international nonprofit organization.

CHILDREN OVERSEAS INC.

ANALYSIS OF EXPENSES BY COUNTRY

(in thousands)

Country	Year Ended June 30, 19X2				19X1 Total
	Aid and Services to Children	Supporting Operations	Promotion and Advertising	Total	
United States	—	$1,287	$425	$ 1,712	$ 1,767
Canada	—	192	70	262	122
Australia	—	74	88	162	7
Bolivia	$ 165	59	—	224	107
Brazil	419	59	—	478	392
Colombia	1,116	85	—	1,201	1,223
Ecuador	841	65	—	906	907
Greece	957	100	—	1,057	1,214
Hong Kong	851	80	—	931	1,226
Indonesia	67	38	—	105	43
Korea	1,308	98	—	1,406	1,438
Peru	588	85	—	673	592
Philippines	1,165	61	—	1,226	1,257
Vietnam	729	70	—	799	889
19X2 Total · · · · · · · ·	$8,206	$2,353	$583	$11,142	
19X1 Total	$8,649	$2,081	$454		$11,184

Fig. 11–6.   An example of a supplementary statement showing details of expenses. This statement would provide details not shown on the Statement of Income and Expenses.

across the page. It would have taken a wide sheet, but here (in part) is the way it would have looked:

	Total	Bolivia	Brazil	Colombia
		(in thousands)		
Aid and services to children:				
Monthly cash grants	$4,317	$ 68	$200	$ 542
Purchased goods	636	8	49	107
Gifts for special purposes	1,461	15	40	143
Health services	650	29	38	158
Special services and projects	305	17	25	50
Social workers	472	14	37	65
Shipping and warehousing . .	145	6	6	18
Translation costs	220	8	24	33
Total	$8,206	$165	$419	$1,116

CHILDREN OVERSEAS INC.

CONSOLIDATED BALANCE SHEET
(in thousands)

	June 30 19X1	June 30 19X2
ASSETS		
Cash	$ 563	$ 704
Investments, at cost less provision for unrealized loss of $137,000 in 19X1 and $45,000 in 19X2 which approximates market	1,066	1,331
Accounts receivable:		
Estimated unpaid pledges and gifts due from foster parents.	155	135
Foreign government refunds	24	18
U.S. government refunds	3	3
Other receivables	—	22
Prepaid expenses	73	35
Land, building, and equipment, net of allowance for depreciation of $85 in 19X1 and $105 in 19X2	60	65
Total assets.	$ 1,944	$ 2,313
LIABILITIES AND FUND BALANCE		
Liabilities:		
Advance payments for children.	$ 1,963	$ 1,992
Accounts payable and accrued payroll taxes	84	48
Estimated statutory severance pay liability	92	101
Unremitted gifts for special purposes	316	329
Total liabilities	2,455	2,470
Fund balance (deficit)	(511)	(157)
Total liabilities and fund balance	$ 1,944	$ 2,313

Fig. 11–7. An example of a Balance Sheet for a large international nonprofit organization.

The key thing to remember is that if details are going to be given they should have totals that tie in to the main schedule so the reader knows exactly what the details represent. For example, in this partial schedule, the $8,206 ties in to the Statement of Income.

Provision for Unrealized Losses

In Chapter 8 it was noted that nonprofit organizations should consider setting up a provision for a decline in value in investments where the market is less than cost. These statements present an example of how to set up such a provision and how to reverse it when it is no longer needed. In 19X2 the market value went back up and part of the reserve was no longer needed. Note that it has been reversed in exactly the same manner as it was set up.[*]

As was discussed in Chapter 8, many consider investment income and gains on investments to be similar in nature and both reportable in the same section of the statement. In Figure 11–5, investment income and the provision for unrealized loss are reported in the same section.

CONCLUSION

The illustrations in this chapter show many of the features of accrual basis financial statements for nonprofit organizations. There are many possible format variations, but readability is the key consideration that must be considered when preparing financial statements. What does the organization want to tell its reader? Once it is determined what information to include, it should be possible to design a statement format that will communicate this information to both sophisticated and unsophisticated readers.

---

[*] Of course, in this example it could be argued that the provision should not have been set up since part of it was not ultimately needed. However, in this instance because of a fund deficit the board felt it prudent to provide a provision since there appeared to be a possibility that part of the investments would have to be sold.

12

Fund Accounting Financial Statements

One of the characteristics of nonprofit organizations is that they have a stewardship responsibility to their members and to the public for the funds they receive. This stewardship frequently results in a type of accounting referred to as "fund accounting." The principles of fund accounting were discussed in Chapter 4.

Fund accounting offers many advantages if the financial statements are carefully prepared. It can provide a form of presentation that clearly shows the reader what financial activity has taken place within each of the individual funds. Unfortunately, all too often instead of clarifying the financial situation, fund accounting confuses the reader because the statements are not put together with the reader in mind. They may be technically accurate statements but they fail in their principal objective, communication.

On pages 35 and 36 the fund accounting statements of McLean Community Service Center were presented. Refer back to these statements, and observe that there are four separate income statements, one for each fund. Note there is a transfer between funds and that to determine the overall excess of income of the Center the reader really has to have a pencil to add up several numbers. Observe also that there may be some hesitation in knowing which numbers to add together.

This presentation is typical of fund accounting and no technical fault can be found with these statements. However, the reader may have some difficulty in ascertaining the overall financial picture of the Center. The important question is, therefore, not whether the statements are technically accurate, but whether the reader will understand them. If the reader gives up after only a quick review then the statements have failed to accomplish their objective. This is the problem of fund accounting statements—they can be so complex that the reader gets lost or doesn't understand the terminology of the statements. The objective of this chapter is to show how to present fund accounting statements that will have the maximum chance of being understood by the average reader.

COLUMNAR FORMAT PRESENTATION

One of the things that can be done to simplify fund accounting is to present the activities of all funds in a single statement in columnar format. In this type of presentation the activity of each fund is shown in a separate column, side by side. In this manner it is possible to see all the funds at one time. Figures 12–1 and 12–2 show the McLean Community Service Center's statements recast in this columnar format.

Characteristics and Advantages

Once the reader has become oriented to this format, it is possible to see at a glance the total activity of the Center.

It is significant that the Center received net income of $105,000 for the year, and not $33,000, which is the first impression that the reader gets when looking at only the separate current unrestricted fund statement in Chapter 4. In this presentation the total income of the other funds can also be seen, and by being given a total the reader doesn't have to work to get the overall results of operations. While the $71,000 of endowment fund income may not be available for general purposes, it represents a real asset that will generate unrestricted income in the future. The reader should be fully aware of this amount.

Some accountants will argue against showing a "total all funds" column. They point out that this implies that all of the funds can be used for any purpose, whereas in reality there are restrictions. In this example, two thirds of the excess of income of $105,000 is endowment fund gifts and gains which cannot be used currently.* They feel that to add the two together is mixing apples and oranges. This is true to a point, but as long as the column headings across the page are reasonably descriptive as to the type of restrictions involved, no one can be seriously misled by this

---

* With respect to the $46,000 of gains on endowment fund investments, there now appears to be some question whether such amounts are legally restricted. See pages 95–96.

THE McLEAN COMMUNITY SERVICE CENTER

STATEMENT OF INCOME, EXPENSES, AND CHANGES IN FUND BALANCES
For the Year Ending August 31, 19X1

	Current		Fixed Asset Fund	Endowment Fund	Total All Funds
	Unrestricted Fund	Restricted Fund			
Income:					
Contributions and gifts	$ 85,000	$24,000		$ 25,000	$134,000
Service fees	110,000				110,000
Investment income from endowment	20,000				20,000
Gains on sale of investments				46,000	46,000
Other	13,000				13,000
Total income	228,000	24,000		71,000	323,000
Expenses:					
Program	107,000	23,000			130,000
Management and General	76,000				76,000
Fund raising	12,000				12,000
Total expenses	195,000	23,000			218,000
Excess of income over expenses	33,000	1,000	$50,000	71,000	105,000
Fund balance, beginning of year	7,000	10,000	25,000	250,000	317,000
Interfund transfers	(25,000)				—
Fund balance, end of the year	$ 15,000	$11,000	$75,000	$321,000	$422,000

Fig. 12–1. An example of a columnar Statement of Income, Expenses, and Changes in Fund Balances.

THE McLEAN COMMUNITY SERVICE CENTER

BALANCE SHEET
August 31, 19X1

	Current		Fixed Asset Fund	Endowment Fund	Total All Funds
	Unrestricted Fund	Restricted Fund			
Cash	$50,000	$11,000		$ 3,000	$ 64,000
Pledges receivable	13,000				13,000
Investments				295,000	295,000
Equipment.			$70,000		70,000
Interfund receivable (payable).	(31,000)	3,000	5,000	23,000	—
Total assets	32,000	14,000	75,000	321,000	442,000
Less—Accounts payable . . .	(17,000)	(3,000)			(20,000)
Fund balance	$15,000	$11,000	$75,000	$321,000	$422,000

Fig. 12–2.   An example of a columnar Balance Sheet.

columnar approach.* Furthermore, the reader who doesn't understand the significance of the separate statement presentation is more likely to be misled and may come away thinking the excess of income was only $33,000.

Transfer and Fund Balance Section

Notice the ease in handling the transfer from the current unrestricted fund to the fixed asset fund. While any transfer can cause confusion, the confusion is minimized when both sides of the transaction are shown in a single statement as they have been here. Notice that the transfer has been shown in the fund balance section. As is discussed in Chapter 5, this helps to remove any suggestion that the transfer is an expense or income.

When several funds are shown in a columnar format, often one or more of the funds will have very little activity and a number of the captions will not be applicable. This is particularly so in this instance with the fixed asset fund. Yet the blank spaces should not detract from the statement, and the very absence of figures in this column is informative because it tells the reader that, in fact, there has been no activity.

Expenses are grouped according to functional category. In this instance all of the expenditures in the current restricted fund are shown as program expenses, and no detail is given. This may not be satisfactory, in which case a supporting schedule could be prepared showing the details of the $23,000. But even if a supporting schedule is prepared the figures should still be shown "in total" in the columnar statement. Otherwise the reader will not be able to see the total picture. There is a risk of confusion in having the same figures in two statements but this can be minimized by putting a caption on the separate supporting statement along the lines "Included in total on Statement of Income, Expenses, and Changes in Fund Balances." See Figure 12–8.

Statement Omitting Changes in Fund Balances

It will be noted that in Figure 12–1 the statement is labeled Statement of Income, Expenses, and Changes in Fund Balances. Many organizations prefer to omit reference to "changes in fund balance" and present only a Statement of Income and Expenses, and a Balance Sheet. When this is done, the change in fund balance for the year is shown in the fund balance section of the Balance Sheet. Figure 12–3 shows in condensed

* If there is any question about the reader's understanding the restrictions, a detailed description should be included in the notes to the financial statements, appropriately cross-referenced to the column heading.

THE McLEAN COMMUNITY SERVICE CENTER

STATEMENT OF INCOME AND EXPENSES
For the Year Ending August 31, 19X1
(condensed)

| | Current | | Fixed Asset Fund | Endowment Fund | Total All Funds |
	Unrestricted Fund	Restricted Fund			
Income (in total)	$228,000	$24,000		$71,000	$323,000
Expenses (in total)	(195,000)	(23,000)			(218,000)
Excess of income over expenses	$ 33,000	$ 1,000		$71,000	$105,000

BALANCE SHEET
August 31, 19X1
(condensed)

| | Current | | Fixed Asset Fund | Endowment Fund | Total All Funds |
	Unrestricted Fund	Restricted Fund			
Total assets	$ 32,000	$14,000	$75,000	$321,000	$442,000
Accounts payable	$ 17,000	$ 3,000			$ 20,000
Fund balance, beginning of the year	7,000	10,000	$ 50,000	$ 250,000	317,000
Excess of income over expense	33,000	1,000		71,000	105,000
Interfund transfer	(25,000)		25,000		—
Fund balance, end of the year	15,000	11,000	75,000	321,000	422,000
Total liabilities and fund balance	$ 32,000	$14,000	$75,000	$321,000	$442,000

Fig. 12–3. An example of a columnar Statement of Income and Expenses and a Balance Sheet in which the changes in fund balances are shown in the Balance Sheet.

form the McLean Community Service Center's statements with only a Statement of Income and Expenses and a Balance Sheet that shows the change in fund balance directly in the fund balance section.

This presentation has the advantage of emphasizing the excess of income over expenses. The unsophisticated reader is more likely to remember the last figure in a set of statements than one in the middle, no matter how well labeled. In Figure 12–1 the excess of income over expenses of $105,000 for all funds is clearly shown, but several lines from the bottom of the page. In Figure 12–3 the $105,000 is shown twice, including the last line. If an organization wants to emphasize this excess line, then this presentation has some advantage.

One of the major disadvantages of this presentation is that the transfer between funds has been shown in the Balance Sheet. As discussed in Chapter 5, transfers should be reported apart from the Statement of Income and Expenses to avoid any inference that the transfer is an expense or an income item, but this presentation is somewhat awkward. This can be overcome by using a separate Statement of Changes in Fund Balances. Figure 12–4 shows a Statement of Changes in Fund Balances in which the only changes are the excess of income over expenses and the transfer between funds.

McLEAN COMMUNITY SERVICE CENTER
STATEMENT OF CHANGES IN FUND BALANCES
For the Year Ending August 31, 19X1

| | Current | | Fixed | | |
	Unrestricted Fund	Restricted Fund	Asset Fund	Endowment Fund	Total All Funds
Fund balance, beginning of the year..........	$ 7,000	$10,000	$50,000	$250,000	$317,000
Excess of income over expenses	33,000	1,000		71,000	105,000
Transfers between funds.............	(25,000)		25,000		.—
Fund balance, end of the year	$15,000	$11,000	$75,000	$321,000	$422,000

Fig. 12–4. An example of a separate Statement of Changes in Fund Balances in columnar format.

STATEMENT OF CHANGES IN FUND BALANCES

Many organizations show all activity for the year for each fund other than the current unrestricted fund in a Statement of Changes in Fund Balances. Where this is done, the only Statement of Income and Expenses is for the current unrestricted fund. Figure 12–5 shows an example of this approach.

The difficulty with this separate Statement of Changes in Fund Balances is that the reader may not know how to interpret it. For example, the current unrestricted fund is included in this statement even though there is a separate Statement of Current Unrestricted Fund Income and Expenses. Many readers will not comprehend the relationship of this column with the Statement of Income and Expenses and they may be confused. Also, while all of the changes in the other funds have been carefully labeled as to what each item represents, nowhere is the reader told what the relationship of the activity in this statement is to the activity in the Statement of Current Unrestricted Fund Income and Expenses. Few will recognize that the fund balance of all funds has increased $105,000 during the year.

Those who favor this separate Statement of Changes in Fund Balances argue that one of the major advantages of this form of statement is that the reader is not likely to confuse current unrestricted fund income with restricted fund income. They feel that in a statement labeled Statement of Income, Expenses, and Changes in Fund Balances (Figure 12–1) the reader may conclude that $105,000 is available for any purpose, which is certainly not correct. The format in Figure 12–5 is somewhat neutral in terms of identifying certain of the additions to the funds as "income." Many believe that this is desirable and that, for example, gains on sale of investments in the endowment fund are not income and should not be shown as income.* They feel the same way about restricted contributions. The organization does not have an unrestricted right to these funds and, in theory, would have to return them if they were not spent for the purposes designated. Accordingly, they say, these funds are held in trust until expended, and should not be shown in a manner that suggests they are income as such.

Recommendation

There is some merit to all of these arguments. The authors, however, do not recommend the use of this separate Statement of Changes in

* Gains on investments are discussed in Chapter 8.

McLEAN COMMUNITY SERVICE CENTER

STATEMENT OF CURRENT UNRESTRICTED FUND INCOME AND EXPENSES
For the Year Ending August 31, 19X1
(condensed)

Income (in total)	$228,000
Expenses (in total)...............................	(195,000)
Excess of income over expenses....................	$ 33,000

STATEMENT OF CHANGES IN FUND BALANCES
For the Year Ending August 31, 19X1

| | Current | | Fixed | | |
	Unrestricted Fund	Restricted Fund	Asset Fund	Endowment Fund	Total All Funds
Fund balance, beginning of the year	$ 7,000	$10,000	$50,000	$250,000	$317,000
Excess of income over expenses	33,000				33,000
Restricted contributions		24,000		25,000	49,000
Gain on sale of investments........				46,000	46,000
Expended for restricted purpose...........		(23,000)			(23,000)
Interfund transfers.....	(25,000)		25,000		—
Fund balance, end of ... the year...........	$15,000	$11,000	$75,000	$321,000	$422,000

Fig. 12–5. An example of columnar statements illustrating the use of a separate Statement of Changes in Fund Balances. In this approach, a Statement of Income and Expenses is presented only for the current unrestricted fund.

Fund Balances. Instead, the combined Statement of Income, Expenses, and Changes in Fund Balances illustrated in Figure 12–1 is recommended. The major reason for this recommendation is that most readers will not fully understand the significance of the separate statement presentation and will not comprehend the overall financial picture of the organization. It is certainly accurate to say that restricted funds are not available for general purposes but the board would not have accepted such funds if it did not believe that they would contribute to the objectives of the organization. Accordingly, it is important that the reader see all of the activities, and not just those that result from unrestricted income and expense. The board can guard against misinterpretation by carefully labeling each column heading and, if appropriate, describing the restrictions in footnotes.

If an organization insists on using a separate Statement of Changes in Fund Balances, it is recommended that all funds be shown in a columnar format as in Figure 12–5. Otherwise the reader is even less likely to see the overall financial activity for the year.

A COMPLICATED SET OF FUND FINANCIAL STATEMENTS

The McLean Community Service Center statements are relatively straightforward and not particularly complicated. In many organizations, this simplicity does not exist. The thing that most frequently complicates the statements is showing a number of "name" funds. These are frequently endowment funds, but may also include funds for specified purposes and possibly unrestricted investment funds. One characteristic of "name" funds is that the donor's name is associated with the fund. As was discussed in Chapter 4, the use of "name" funds, if carried to an extreme, can cause confusion because it adds detail. The real risk is that the reader will not see the forest for the trees.

There are two principal financial statements that most readers want to see. Most important is a Statement of Income and Expenses and, of lesser importance, the Balance Sheet. If all transactions have been skillfully summarized on these two statements, it is then possible to provide a third schedule that shows the appropriate detail of the information on the two primary statements. The key to successful presentation in this third schedule is showing totals that tie back into the Statement of Income and Expenses.

The J. W. M. Diabetes Research Institute financial statements are a good example of how substantial detail can be provided on "name" funds without detracting from the reader's overall understanding of the results of operations. While these statements relate to a medical service and research institute, the form would essentially be the same for almost any type of organization. Figures 12–6, 12–7, and 12–8 show these statements.

Overall Impression of Complexity

The reader's first impression of these statements may be that they "look" complicated and will be hard to understand. This is particularly so with respect to Figure 12–8 which shows changes in the individual "name" funds. Before studying this statement, however, take a few minutes to study the first two statements (Figures 12–6 and 12–7) to get an

J. W. M. DIABETES RESEARCH INSTITUTE

STATEMENT OF INCOME, EXPENSES, AND
CHANGES IN FUND BALANCES
For the Year Ending June 30, 19X2

| | Unrestricted | | Funds for | | Total |
	General Fund	Investment Fund	Specified Purposes	Endowment Funds	All Funds
Income:					
Grants and contracts	$424,701				$ 424,701
Contributions and legacies	341,216		$ 27,515	$ 122,504	491,235
Investment income ...	92,793		16,556	1,640	110,989
Gain on sales of investments	33,660		33,486	229,334	296,480
Total	892,370		77,557	353,478	1,323,405
Expenses:					
Client services	461,313		21,500		482,813
Research	242,988		32,856		275,844
Administration	112,044				112,044
Total	816,345		54,356		870,701
Excess of income over expenses for the year .	76,025		23,201	353,478	452,704
Fund balance, beginning of the year	845,200	$258,925	257,594	1,888,247	3,249,966
Interfund transfers	(35,000)	42,119		(7,119)	—
Fund balance, end of the year	$886,225	$301,044	$280,795	$2,234,606	$3,702,670

Fig. 12–6. An example of a columnar Statement of Income, Expenses, and Changes in Fund Balances in which activity for all funds is reported.

overall impression of what has happened during the year. Look first at the "total all funds" column on the Statement of Income and Expenses and the description of the items of income and expense. The reader should focus on the total picture before looking at some of the detail by individual funds. The same thing should be done with the Balance Sheet. Look first at the total, and only then at the detail by funds.

The statement of activity by individual "name" funds is more difficult. The stewardship concept has been introduced in considerable detail on this statement. Apart from the many individual "name" funds, this statement also shows these funds segregated by the type of restriction associated with each fund. Some funds contain restrictions only with respect to the original principal; others restrict both the income and the prin-

J. W. M. DIABETES RESEARCH INSTITUTE
BALANCE SHEET
June 30, 19X2

| | Unrestricted | | Funds for | | |
	General Fund	Investment Fund	Specified Purposes	Endowment Funds	Total All Funds
ASSETS					
Current assets:					
Cash	$ 174,860	$ 2,315	$ 20,515	$ 15,615	$ 213,305
Marketable securities, at cost (market value $3,250,000) ..		256,610	255,310	2,231,080	2,743,000
Contract receivables ..	7,500				7,500
Other receivables	2,345				2,345
Inventories of books and supplies	14,200				14,200
Total current assets	198,905	258,925	275,825	2,246,695	2,980,350
Fixed assets at cost:					
Land	100,000				100,000
Buildings...........	1,749,250				1,749,250
Vehicles	25,500				25,500
Total	1,874,750				1,874,750
Less: Accumulated Depreciation	(1,056,200)				(1,056,200)
Net fixed assets	818,550				818,550
Total assets	$1,017,455	$258,925	$275,825	$2,246,695	$3,798,900
LIABILITIES AND NET WORTH					
Accounts payable	$ 47,845				$ 47,845
Withholding taxes	6,300				6,300
Grants paid in advance ..	42,085				42,085
Interfund payable (receivable)	35,000	$ (42,119)	$ (4,970)	$ 12,089	—
Total liabilities	131,230	(42,119)	(4,970)	12,089	96,230
Fund balances	886,225	301,044	280,795	2,234,606	3,702,670
Total liabilities and fund balances	$1,017,455	$258,925	$275,825	$2,246,695	$3,798,900

Fig. 12–7.   An example of a columnar Balance Sheet.

J. W. M. DIABETES RESEARCH

STATEMENT OF CHANGES IN INDIVIDUAL UNRESTRICTED INVESTMENT FUND,

For the Year Ending

(All income and expenses have been shown in total on the Statement of Income,

		Investment Income		Capital Gains (Losses)	
	Contributions and Legacies	Reported Directly in General Fund	Other	Reported Directly in General Fund	Left in Fund
* Unrestricted Investment Fund:					
Elmer C. Bratt Fund		$11,651		$33,660	
*Funds for specified purposes:					
Charity Fund	$ 3,000		$ 6,683		$ 19,307
Library Fund	18,615		603		1,756
Staff pensions	4,150		3,742		10,811
Malmar Repair Fund	700		5,078		312
100th Anniversary Fund	1,050		450		1,300
Total funds for specified purposes	$ 27,515		$16,556		$ 33,486
Endowment funds:					
Principal and income restricted:					
The Malmar Fund					($ 3,015)
Clyde Henderson Fund			$ 1,150		8,165
Evelyn I. Marnoch Fund			490		(2,156)
			1,640		2,994
*Principal only restricted:					
The Roy B. Cowin Memorial Fund.		$73,859			213,369
The Lillian V. Fromhagen Fund		2,392			6,911
Donna Comstock Fund	$ 16,153	1,670			3,661
Josephine Zagajewski Fund	100,000	2,250			
The Peter Baker Fund	6,351	688			1,580
	122,504	80,859			225,521
* Restrictions lapsed in 19X1:					
The Alfred P. Koch Fund		283			819
Total endowment funds	$122,504	$81,142	$ 1,640		$229,334

*Funds have been "pooled" for investment purposes. See Chapter 24 for a discussion of pooled investments.

Fig. 12—8. An example of a supplementary statement illustrating fairly complex fund

cipal. While this statement is complicated, there is a great deal of information on the statement that the reader should be able to understand if some time is taken to study it. On the other hand if the reader isn't interested in this detail, the overall Statement of Income and Expenses still clearly summarizes all income and expenses. This is a key point—everything is summarized in total, and readers are required to look at detail only to the extent they wish to do so.

One final observation about the overall impression these statements make. If these same statements had been presented in a separate statement format, including separate statements for each "name" fund, the resulting set of statements would most certainly have discouraged and

INSTITUTE

FUNDS* FOR SPECIFIED PURPOSES, AND ENDOWMENT FUNDS
June 30, 19X2
Expenses and Changes in Fund Balances)

Disbursed for Specified Purpose	Other Interfund Transfers Add (Deduct)	Net Change in Fund	Fund Balance Beginning of Year	Fund Balance End of Year
	$42,119	$ 42,119	$ 258,925	$ 301,044
($ 9,200)		$ 19,790	$ 148,516	$ 168,306
(18,156)		2,818	13,511	16,329
(21,500)		(2,797)	83,167	80,370
(5,500)		590	2,400	2,990
		2,800	10,000	12,800
($54,356)		$ 23,201	$ 257,594	$ 280,795
		($ 3,015)	$ 110,700	$ 107,685
		9,315	25,601	34,916
		(1,666)	10,871	9,205
		4,634	147,172	151,806
		213,369	1,641,300	1,854,669
		6,911	53,165	60,076
		19,814	28,160	47,974
		100,000		100,000
		7,931	12,150	20,081
		348,025	1,734,775	2,082,800
	($ 7,119)	(6,300)	6,300	—
	($ 7,119)	$346,359	$1,888,247	$2,234,606

how changes in individual name funds can be presented for a accounting structure.

probably confused all but a few readers. There would be just too much detail; few readers would be able to get any meaningful understanding of the overall financial picture of this organization. So while the supplementary summary on individual "name" funds may seem complex, the alternative would be far less comprehensible.

Statement of Income, Expenses and Changes in Fund Balances

On the Statement of Income, Expenses, and Changes in Fund Balances the number of columns has been limited to the four fund groupings that have distinctive significance. While there are varying degrees of restrictions associated with the endowment funds, no attempt is made to indicate these on the face of the statement because this represents a detail that can best be left to a supporting statement. It is important that the reader not get lost in detail on the summary statement.

Transfers. There are two transfers between funds in this statement. The first is a transfer from the endowment fund of a term endowment on which the restrictions have lapsed. This transfer of $7,119 * went directly to the unrestricted general fund since this amount became unrestricted. The second transfer is a transfer from the unrestricted general fund to the unrestricted investment fund, in the amount of $42,119. In the unrestricted general fund column, only the net amount of $35,000 is shown.

It should be noted that there are no contributions or gains shown directly in the unrestricted investment fund. All unrestricted contributions or gains are shown in the unrestricted general fund. The board can then transfer any portion of such income to the unrestricted investment fund but it should not show such income directly in that fund. Unrestricted income must be reported initially in the unrestricted general fund.

Unrestricted Investment Income. It will be noted that unrestricted investment income of $92,793 ($81,142 from endowment funds and $11,651 from unrestricted investment funds) has been shown directly in the unrestricted general fund. It would not have been appropriate for the board to have left this amount in the endowment and unrestricted investment funds since this income contains no restrictions as to its use. To assist the reader in seeing how much income each separate fund earned, this unrestricted income is also shown in the Statement of Changes in Individual Funds in the column "Reported directly in general fund." Inclusion of this column in the statement is optional.

Gains and Losses. Endowment fund gains aggregating $229,334 have

---

* This $7,119 was a term endowment, the restrictions on which lapsed in 19X1. Since the restrictions had lapsed, this fund became an unrestricted fund and the principal and accumulated gains were transferred to the unrestricted general fund. Some argue that the $7,119 of lapsed term endowment should be shown as unrestricted general fund income rather than as a transfer. Their argument is that this amount is now available for unrestricted purposes and thus is unrestricted income. Usually, such persons also take exception to the use of an "income" statement in connection with the endowment fund preferring instead a Statement of Changes in Fund Balances. Thus they argue that the original receipt of the term endowment has not been previously reflected in income. However, if statements are being presented in a columnar format, as here, the receipt of the original term endowment was included as part of income for the endowment fund, and thus part of total all funds income. Accordingly, it would be wrong to again include the same item in income, albeit, unrestricted general fund income.

been shown in the endowment fund column. While there is some legal question whether endowment fund gains are restricted and must be added to endowment principal,* it is generally accepted that they are. On the other hand, unrestricted investment fund gains should be reported in the unrestricted general fund. These gains, as with investment income, represent unrestricted income and should be reported as such. There is no reason why the board can't transfer all or part of these gains back to the unrestricted investment fund, but this should be handled as a transfer.†

Comparison with Last Year's Figures.   An additional column may be added to either the Balance Sheet or the Statement of Income and Expenses to show last year's actual figures so the reader has a point of reference. This comparison is usually to the total all funds column, although sometimes a comparison is made only to the unrestricted general fund. If the comparison column is to the total all funds column, then this additional column should be next to the current year's total column to make it easier for the reader. If the comparison is only to the unrestricted general fund it should be set up as shown below.

Instead of a comparison to last year's figures, the comparison could have been to this year's budget.

| | Unrestricted | | | Funds | | |
| | General Fund | | Invest- | for | Endow- | |
	Last Year	This Year	ment Fund	Specified Purposes	ment Funds	Total All Funds
Income:						
Tuition and fees	$689,188	$724,701				$ 724,701
Contributions	23,444	41,216		$27,515	$ 22,504	91,235
Legacies					100,000	100,000
Investment income	83,598	92,793		16,556	1,640	110,989
Gain on sale of investment	11,345	33,660		33,486	229,334	296,480
Total ..	$807,575	$892,370		$77,557	$353,478	$1,323,405

* See page 95.
† Where a columnar format statement is used, as here, it is permissible to report unrestricted investment fund gains or losses and investment income directly in the unrestricted investment fund column.

Balance Sheet

Fixed assets have not been set up as a separate fund. Instead, they have been included as a part of the unrestricted general fund. This greatly simplifies the problem of depreciation since depreciation can then be handled in exactly the same manner as it would be handled by a commercial enterprise. The presentation problems in handling depreciation if a separate plant fund is used are discussed more fully in Chapter 7.

One of the principal reasons why many prefer to see fixed assets in a separate fund is that the unrestricted general fund balance then represents the current assets of the organization. In our illustration the fund balance of $886,225 is mostly represented by fixed assets. If the plant fund assets had been shown separately, the unrestricted general fund balance would have been only $67,675. But this lower figure has limited significance because there are other unrestricted current assets that are available for general purposes if the board chooses to use them. These other unrestricted current assets are, of course, the $301,044 of unrestricted investment funds. Many, including the authors, recommend that *all* unrestricted funds, including both fixed assets and unrestricted investment funds, be combined into the unrestricted general fund. In this instance, the fund balance would then be $1,187,269.

One effective way of showing this "unrestricted" total while still keeping the present format is to split the fund balance figures on the balance sheet into two amounts, restricted and unrestricted. Here is how this would look:

| | Unrestricted | | Funds for | | |
	General Fund	Investment Fund	Specified Purposes	Endowment Funds	Total All Funds
Fund balances:					
Restricted ..			$280,795	$2,234,606	$2,515,401
Unrestricted	$886,225	$301,044			1,187,269
	$886,225	$301,044	$280,795	$2,234,606	$3,702,670

Some will argue that the fixed asset amounts should not be included in the "unrestricted" figure since the organization could not exist without its buildings. This may be so, but there is no reason why the institute has to use its present buildings. They could be sold and new ones built on less expensive land or in a better location. These are all decisions that the board is free to make and, being free to make them, the assets are unrestricted.

Balance Sheet Format.   In the McLean Community Service Center statements the Balance Sheet (Figure 12-2) was set up to show total assets less liabilities equaling the fund balance:

Total assets	$442,000
Less—Liabilities	(20,000)
Fund balance	$422,000

In the J. W. M. Diabetes Research Institute statements (Figure 12-7) the more conventional Balance Sheet approach was followed showing total assets equaling the sum of the liabilities and fund balance:

Total assets	$3,798,900
Liabilities	$ 96,230
Fund balance	3,702,670
Total liabilities and fund balance	$3,798,900

Either approach is acceptable. The first is more appropriate for organizations with relatively few categories of liabilities, and therefore for smaller organizations.

Statement of Changes in Individual Funds

Notice the line at the top of Figure 12-8: "All income and expenses have been shown in total on the Statement of Income, Expenses, and Changes in Fund Balances." This or a similar statement helps readers to recognize that they don't have to add the income and expenses shown on this statement to the amounts shown on the Statement of Income, Expenses, and Changes in Fund Balances (Figure 12-6) in order to get total income and expenses. While technically there is no requirement that this type of caption be shown, it helps in understanding the nature of this statement. Most of the totals shown on this statement can be tied in directly to the Statement of Income, Expenses, and Changes in Fund Balances.

Restricted Income From Endowments.   Income on endowment funds that are restricted to a specified purpose should be reported directly in that fund. Normally the endowment fund would not directly disburse restricted income except to another fund. Note that in the Malmar endowment fund no investment income has been shown. Actually $4,970 of income was received but it was reported directly in the fund for

J. W. M. DIABETES RESEARCH INSTITUTE

ANALYSIS OF EXPENSES AND COMPARISON WITH BUDGET AND LAST YEAR'S ACTUAL

For the Year Ending June 30, 19X2

	Actual Last Year	Budget This Year	Actual This Year	Client Services	Research	Administration
Salaries and payroll taxes	$581,615	$615,000	$618,686	$425,851	$133,588	$ 59,247
Retirement benefits	23,151	33,000	33,833	21,463	8,720	3,650
Major medical	3,656	4,500	4,578	3,155	1,013	410
Clinic supplies	34,616	42,000	41,374	29,488	11,886	
Office supplies	3,518	6,900	8,356		5,500	2,856
Laboratory supplies	47,717	40,000	33,596		33,596	
Insurance	5,751	6,000	5,951			5,951
Telephone	3,748	5,000	6,116		3,800	2,316
Depreciation	39,516	43,000	43,525	2,856	30,309	10,360
Contracted repairs and maintenance	14,819	9,600	15,054			15,054
Utilities and fuel	19,151	20,000	19,268		11,316	7,952
Other	36,118	35,000	40,364		36,116	4,248
Total	$807,376	$860,000	$870,701	$482,813	$275,844	$112,044
Budget		$860,000		$480,000	$280,000	$100,000
Actual last year	$807,376			$451,254	$251,348	$104,774

Fig. 12–9. An example of an analysis of expenses by both function and types of expense, along with a comparison to both budget and last year's actual.

specified purposes in a separate fund maintained for this income (Malmar Repair Fund). This $4,970 plus $108 of income earned on this restricted fund balance is the $5,078 reported as investment income.

There are two other endowment funds with restrictions on the income. In both instances the income has been left in the endowment fund. Presumably the donor specified that the income was to be accumulated for a period of time before it could be spent. There is no disclosure of the terms of the fund on the statement, but if they were significant a footnote could be added to tell the reader. However, unless the terms of the restriction are significant, footnote details should be avoided.

There is no reason why unrestricted investment funds couldn't also have "names" associated with them. Here all of the unrestricted investment funds are shown as the Elmer C. Bratt Fund. The board could also have had several other "name" funds, all part of the total unrestricted investment fund.

While it is not obvious from this statement, most of the investments are "pooled" together and individual funds have a percentage or share interest in the total investment portfolio. Since all of the individual funds are "pooled" together, each gets its proportionate share of income and gains or losses on the sale of investments. Chapter 24 discusses the mechanics of "pooling" investments.

Other Supporting Statements

There are other statements that could be included with the three statements we have just discussed. For example, many readers might want to see a great deal more of the details of the expense categories than are shown in total on the Statement of Income and Expenses, and perhaps also a comparison with the budget or last year's actual figures. Figure 12–9 shows an example of this type of supporting schedule. Again, as with all supporting or supplementary statements, the format must be so designed that the reader clearly sees how the figures tie into the main statement.

The reader interested in detail gets a great deal of information from looking at this type of analysis. There is a comparison both with budget for the year and with last year's actual expenses, by type of expense and function. It must be remembered that the more detail provided, the greater the risk that the reader will get lost in the detail. Financial statements are not necessarily improved by providing details or additional supporting schedules. In fact, often they detract from the overall effectiveness.

SUMMARY OR CONDENSED STATEMENTS

Frequently for fund-raising purposes or for the general information of the membership, the board will want to distribute summary or condensed financial statements. Often the board will prefer not to show a large excess of income since this might discourage fund raising. In the case of the J. W. M. Diabetes Research Institute, the board might want to show only the unrestricted general fund activities, which as will be recalled, had an excess of income of $76,025. Yet actually the institute had a total "all funds" excess of $452,704.

The board may prefer issuing statements for only the unrestricted general fund. This is not recommended. At some point the credibility of the board and its statements may come into question if some of the readers feel information is being withheld.

There are two acceptable approaches open to the board. The first would be to present a condensed statement showing income and expenses for all funds but clearly indicating the amount of the excess of income that was donor-restricted. Figure 12–10 shows this presentation.

J. W. M. DIABETES RESEARCH INSTITUTE

CONDENSED SUMMARY OF INCOME AND EXPENSES
For the Year Ending June 30, 19X2
(in thousands)

Income:		
Grants and contracts...................	$425	
Contributions and legacies...............	491	
Investment income	111	
Gain on sale of investments	296	
Total income		$1,323
Expenses:		
Client services	483	
Research	275	
Administration....................	112	
Total expenses..................		870
Excess of income over expenses		$ 453
Excess restricted by donor	377	
Unrestricted	76	
Total		$ 453

Fig. 12–10. An example of a condensed Summary of Income and Expenses for all funds, suitable for inclusion in an annual report or fund-raising literature.

J. W. M. DIABETES RESEARCH INSTITUTE

SUMMARY OF UNRESTRICTED INCOME AND EXPENSES
(Note)
For the Year Ending June 30, 19X2
(in thousands)

Income:

Grants and contracts.................	$425	
Contributions and legacies	341	
Investment income	93	
Gain on sale of investments	33	
Total income		$892
Expenses:		
Client services......................	461	
Research..........................	243	
Administration	112	
Total expenses.....................		816
Excess of unrestricted income over		
expenses..........................		$ 76

Note: In addition to the above unrestricted income and expenses, the institute received restricted contributions and legacies of $150,000, of which $122,000 was added to the endowment fund and $28,000 to the funds for specified purposes. In addition, the institute realized gains on sales of investments of $263,000 and received investment income of $18,000. Of these amounts, $231,000 was added to the endowment fund and $50,000 to the funds for restricted purposes. The institute also expended an aggregate of $54,000 from funds for specified purposes.

Fig. 12–11. An example of a condensed Statement of Unrestricted Income and Expenses which provides footnote disclosure of the amount of restricted income and expenditures.

The second approach is to present a statement showing the income and expenses of all funds over which the board has control (i.e., the unrestricted general fund and the unrestricted investment funds), and then showing in a footnote the activity in the other funds. Figure 12–11 shows this second presentation.

A reader who wishes to can convert this second condensed statement into an all-inclusive statement. The important thing is that the board cannot be accused of hiding the large gains in the endowment fund from the reader. This is particularly important since legal questions are now starting to be raised about the availability of capital gains for general purposes.

It would be entirely inappropriate, however, to eliminate the unrestricted investment fund activities from the condensed statement of unrestricted income. Unrestricted investment funds have all of the characteristics of unrestricted general funds since the board can act at any time to convert unrestricted investment funds back into unrestricted general funds. These funds must be considered part of general unrestricted funds any time when condensed financial statements are presented.

CONCLUSION

This chapter has presented a number of illustrations to help the reader more readily understand the complexities of presenting fund accounting financial statements. The use of the columnar approach has been discussed because it offers many advantages over presenting separate statements for each fund, the approach followed by many organizations. It has been indicated that it is extremely important that these statements be all-inclusive so that the reader can get a broad overall picture of the activities of the organization before getting down into the detail. Several illustrations were given showing how typical detail can be presented with a minimum risk of confusing the reader. Finally, condensed or summary financial statements were discussed and the importance of disclosing all income, either in the body of the statement or in footnotes was emphasized. Failure to do so creates a credibility gap which can only hurt the organization.

PART III

ACCOUNTING AND REPORTING GUIDELINES

13

Voluntary Health and Welfare Organizations

In 1974 the American Institute of Certified Public Accountants issued a revised * "Audit Guide" prepared by its Committee on Voluntary Health and Welfare Organizations. This Audit Guide was prepared to assist the independent auditor in examinations of voluntary health and welfare organizations. Included in this revised Audit Guide is a discussion of accounting and reporting principles which should be followed by this type of organization. This chapter summarizes the accounting and reporting principles discussed in this Guide.

Neither the Accounting Principles Board nor its predecessor, the Accounting Procedures Committee of the American Institute of Certified Public Accountants, issued any pronouncement on what may be considered "generally accepted" accounting principles for nonprofit organizations. To date, the successor to· the Accounting Principles Board, the Financial Accounting Standards Board, likewise has not issued any pronouncements.†

Applicable to Many Categories of Organizations

"Voluntary health and welfare organizations" are those nonprofit organizations which "derive their revenue primarily from voluntary contributions from the general public to be used for general or specific pur-

---

* The original Audit Guide was issued in 1967.

† Chapter 18 discusses in more detail the formal rule-making procedures of the accounting profession, and in particular the relationship of the FASB and the AICPA.

poses connected with health, welfare, or community services." * Note that there are two separate parts to this definition: first, the organization must derive its revenue from voluntary contributions from the general public, and second, the organization must be involved with health, welfare, or community services.

Many organizations fit the second part of this definition, but receive a substantial portion of their revenues from sources other than public contributions. For example, an opera company would not be a voluntary health and welfare organization because its primary source of income is box office receipts, although it exists for the common good. A YMCA would be excluded because normally it receives most of its revenues from program fees.

In the pages that follow, the reader will observe that most of the principles followed are similar to those used by other categories of nonprofit organizations, and most were discussed in the first part of this book, which dealt with accounting principles. The reader should refer to this earlier discussion for any detail of how the principles outlined are actually applied. The purpose of this and the succeeding chapters is merely to outline the practices and principles discussed in specific Audit Guides.

FUND ACCOUNTING

Classification of Funds

The Guide † lists the funds commonly used, and the types of transactions normally associated with each fund. The fund groupings listed by the Guide and the type of transactions recorded in each are discussed below.

Current Unrestricted Fund. This fund "accounts for all resources over which the governing Board has discretionary control to use in carrying on the operations of the organization . . . except for unrestricted amounts invested in land, buildings and equipment that may be accounted for in a separate fund." ** These are all of the completely unrestricted assets of the organization, including board-designated endowment funds or other resources allocated by the board for some specific purpose.

---

* Page v, *Audits of Voluntary Health and Welfare Organizations.* Copyright ©
1974 by the American Institute of Certified Public Accountants, Inc.
  † Hereafter in this chapter the word "Guide" refers to *Audits of Voluntary Health and Welfare Organizations, ibid.*
    ** Page 2, *ibid.*

Prior to the issuance of this Guide many voluntary health and welfare organizations set up separate board-designated funds which were reported on separately from the other unrestricted activities of the organization. This Guide specifically provides that all such unrestricted income, expenses, assets, and liabilities must be reported in a single fund so that the reader can quickly see the total amount the board has at its disposal. This a major and significant change. It means that for these organizations board-designated funds must be included in the current unrestricted fund for financial statement purposes. The prior practice followed by many organizations of "designating" certain gifts as endowments (and then reporting these gifts directly in the endowment fund) is no longer permissible.

This does not prevent the board from "designating" certain portions of the "current unrestricted fund" *balance* for specific purposes, but such designations must be reported only in the fund balance section of the Balance Sheet. See the discussion below on "Appropriations."

Current Restricted Fund.   These are the amounts which have been given to the organization for a specific "operating" or "current" purpose. Excluded from this classification would be amounts given for endowment purposes or for building funds. Typically these current restricted gifts are for purposes which the organization normally carries on, as distinct from some purpose not directly related to the organization's objectives.

Current restricted funds would, of course, include only amounts given to the organization by outside persons. They would not include amounts which the board had "designated" for some future purposes.

Land, Building, and Equipment Fund.   This is used to record the organization's net investment in its fixed assets. Also included in this fund are donor-restricted contributions which have been given for the purpose of purchasing fixed assets.

While the Guide provides for this separate land, building, and equipment fund, it does not prohibit the organization from combining this fund (excluding unexpended donor-restricted building fund gifts) with the current unrestricted fund. Many organizations in the past have preferred to use a separate fixed asset fund, principally so that the current unrestricted fund would exclude long-term assets such as fixed assets or other funds. This meant that the current unrestricted fund was then a form of "current working capital" fund. Under this new Guide, however, the use of separate board-designated endowment or other funds is no longer permitted. As a result many organizations have concluded that there is no practical reason for segregating fixed assets in a separate fund and have combined their fixed asset fund and their current un-restricted fund. When this is done the title of the current unrestricted fund would become "unrestricted fund."

The major reason why this Guide still permits the use of a separate fixed asset fund is principally historical usage. That is, most nonprofit organizations have traditionally carried their fixed assets in a separate fund and the authors of the Guide concluded that the continued use of this separate fund would not distort the financial picture, provided the plant fund is reported with all other funds in a single columnar-format statement. (See Figure 13–1, page 186.) The authors would have pre-ferred, however, that the plant fund were combined with the current unrestricted fund in the same manner as recommended in the earlier issued Audit Guide for hospitals, discussed in Chapter 15 (see Figure 15–1, page 236).

Endowment Fund. This fund is to be used for all assets donated to the organization with the stipulation by the donor that only the income earned can be used. Generally the income itself is not restricted and can be used to carry out the organization's principal activities, although occasionally gifts are received which have restrictions on the uses to be made of the income. It is also possible to receive gifts that are restricted for a period of years, after which time the principal can be used as desired by the board. Another possibility is an endowment gift under which the income earned on the principal of the gift is paid to the donor during his or her life but becomes completely unrestricted at his or her death.

It is important to note that this endowment fund is to be used only for gifts that have been restricted by the donor. Occasionally a donor, while not formally placing restrictions on a gift, will orally express the "desire" that the gift be put in the endowment fund. However, if the decision is left to the board, such amounts are unrestricted, and should be added to the current unrestricted fund. Legally unrestricted gifts cannot be added to the endowment fund. All amounts in the endowment fund must bear legal restrictions that the board cannot normally alter.

Custodian Fund. These are funds "established to account for assets received by an organization to be held or disbursed only on instructions of the person or organization from whom they were received." * Since these funds are not normally the property of the organization they are not reflected in the Statement of Support, Revenues and Expenses, and Changes in Fund Balances.

* Page 3, *ibid.*

ACCOUNTING PRINCIPLES

Summarized in the following paragraphs are the accounting principles (or practices) that are prescribed by the Audit Guide for voluntary health and welfare organizations.

Accrual Basis

The Guide concludes that the accrual basis of accounting is normally necessary for financial statements prepared in accordance with generally accepted accounting principles. While cash basis statements are not prohibited, the auditor cannot issue an opinion on cash basis financial statements which states that the statements are prepared in accordance with generally accepted accounting principles unless these financial statements do not differ materially from the statements prepared on the accrual basis. The same caution is made with respect to modified accrual basis statements.*

Unrestricted Gifts

All unrestricted gifts and donations are recorded as revenue or "support" of the current unrestricted fund. As noted above, in the past some organizations have internally restricted certain donations but such self-imposed restrictions in no way change the characteristics of the gift and such gifts must be reported in the current unrestricted fund.

Restricted Gifts

Normally there would be only three types of restricted gifts: gifts for a "current" purpose (reported in the current restricted fund); gifts for building fund purposes (reported in the land, building, and equipment fund); and gifts for endowment (reported in the endowment fund).

Current Restricted Gifts.   The Guide states that all current restricted gifts and other income should be reported in the year in which received (or pledged). Traditionally such income has been recorded only to the extent actually expended, on the theory that it is not income until expended for the restricted purpose.

Now, under the new rules, if a donor makes a contribution for a

---

* Modified accrual basis statements (also called modified cash basis statements) are discussed in Chapter 3.

current restricted purpose of $50,000 but the organization expends only $40,000 during the current year, the full $50,000 would still be reported as income. This is contrary to the practice provided in the Audit Guides for colleges and hospitals and in the AICPA Statement of Position for certain nonprofit organizations.* See pages 100–107 for a comprehensive discussion of the various alternatives for reporting current restricted income.

Building Fund Gifts.   These gifts would be reported in the fixed asset fund. As was noted above, however, the Guide does not prohibit combining the fixed asset fund and the current unrestricted fund. If this combining is done, restricted building fund gifts would then be reported in the current restricted fund.†

Endowment Fund Gifts.   As noted above, these gifts would be reported in a separate endowment fund, and only legally restricted gifts would be reported here.

Timing of Reporting of Gifts

Current unrestricted and restricted gifts are reported as income in full in the year for which the gift *is intended*. If the donor is silent as to intent, the presumption is that the gift is intended for the year in which made. Where it is appropriate to defer recording the gift as income to a future period (because of a donor timing restriction) the gift would be reported in the Balance Sheet as a "deferred credit." (See Figure 13–3, on page 194.)

In many instances, of course, there will be some question as to the donor's intent. For example, if a calendar-year organization normally solicits contributions in the late fall of the year with the clear understanding in its solicitation literature that the amounts raised will be used for the organization's upcoming year beginning January 1, it is reasonable to presume that contributions raised are intended for the future year and those received before December 31 should not be reported as income. On the other hand, if a large unsolicited gift is unexpectedly received toward the end of the year (say, on December 15), the entire amount of this gift should be recorded as income in the current year. The fact that the contribution is an extraordinarily large one and that it occurs toward the end of the year does not justify deferring its recognition as income. There must be clear evidence that the donor

* See Chapters 14, 15, and 16.

† If a significant amount of restricted building fund gifts were received, the title of the fund would probably have to be changed, or possibly two separate funds used (i.e., current restricted fund and restricted building fund gifts).

intended the gift for a future period in order to justify excluding it from income in the year in which it is received (or pledged).

Bequests. A special problem occurs with respect to bequests. Often the organization will be notified that it is a beneficiary under a will but a significant period of time will elapse before the organization receives the cash. The exact amount of the bequest may not be known until shortly before it is received.

The question frequently asked is when to record a bequest as income. The general answer is to record a bequest at the time the organization is first reasonably certain of the amount it will receive. If the organization is informed that it will receive a fixed dollar amount, the gift should be recorded at the time it is so informed, recognizing the gift as income of the appropriate fund. If the organization is informed that it will receive a percentage of an estate and that its share will definitely exceed a certain amount, then this "certain" amount would be recorded with an adjustment when the final distribution is made. On the other hand, if the organization is told only that it is a beneficiary and that there will be a sizable payment, the amount of which cannot be estimated, no amount should be recorded although footnote disclosure should be made.

Pledges

Pledges represent assets and should be recorded as assets. The same is true with allocations from "United Fund" campaigns that have been made but not received in cash at the end of the period. Appropriate provision for uncollectible pledges should be established based on prior experience.

Investment Income

All unrestricted investment income (dividends and interest) must be reported directly in the current unrestricted fund in the revenues section. Endowment income which has been restricted to a specified purpose would be reported directly in the current restricted fund. Investment income from current restricted fund investments or plant fund investments is normally considered "restricted" and would be reported in the fund generating the income.

Gains or Losses on Investments

Gains or losses (and appreciation or depreciation where investments are carried at market; see below) on *unrestricted* investment funds would be reported in the current unrestricted fund, in the revenue section. Gains or losses (and appreciation or depreciation) on endowment funds are usually considered to be restricted and would be reported directly in the endowment fund. Likewise, gains or losses on current restricted fund investments and plant fund investments would normally be reported in the respective fund.

As can be seen in Figure 13–1 (page 186), gains or losses on investments are reported in the "revenues" section of the Statement of Support, Revenues and Expenses, and Changes in Fund Balances. Prior to the issuance of the Guide, gains or losses on endowment funds were typically added directly to the fund balance of that fund and not reported as income (i.e., revenue).

Where an organization carries its investments at market, the unrealized appreciation or depreciation would also be reported in the "revenues" section of this statement. It would not be appropriate, for example, to report a realized gain in the "revenues" section and then the unrealized appreciation (representing the increase in market value during the year) at the bottom of the statement after the caption "Excess of revenues over expenses." When an organization decides to carry investments at market, its appreciation (or depreciation) is "revenue" and is reported in the same manner as realized gains or losses.

Total Return Concept

Where the board wishes to transfer some of the realized or unrealized gains on endowment fund investments to the current unrestricted fund (and assuming it has the legal right to do so), the transfer must be shown below the caption "Excess of revenues over expenses." It is not permissible to treat this transfer as income in the revenues section. This can be seen in Figure 13–1 where a transfer of $50,000 from the endowment fund has been reported. For a more complete discussion of accounting under the total return investment concept, see pages 88 to 95.

Carrying Value of Investments

The Guide provides that an organization can carry its investments either at market or at cost. Previously, marketable securities could be carried only at cost or, in the case of donated securities, at the fair market value at the date of receipt. This is an important change which many organizations will want to consider carefully.

Carried at Cost. If an organization carries its investments at cost, market value should be disclosed in the financial statements. If the market value of the portfolio as a whole is less than cost and such decline is of a permanent nature, it may be necessary to write down the portfolio or to provide a provision for loss. This same approach can be taken with respect to an individual investment where there is a permanent impairment. But note that this is necessary only where the decline is of a "permanent" nature; short-term fluctuations normally do not require a write down or establishment of a provision for loss.

Carried at Market.   If the organization carries its investments at market, it must do so for all of its investments. It may not pick and choose which investments to carry at market.° Unrealized appreciation or depreciation would be reported in the same manner as gains or losses on investments are reported. See the discussion on gains and losses above.

Fixed Asset Accounting

Prior to the issuance of the Guide, the practices followed by voluntary health and welfare organizations in handling fixed assets included every conceivable combination of methods. The Guide, however, has changed this with dramatic suddenness.† It provides that an organization must capitalize its fixed assets *and* must follow depreciation accounting procedures. This means that this category of organization will be following fixed asset accounting practices similar to those followed by business entities.

Reason for Depreciation.   In discussing the question of depreciation accounting, the Guide states:

The relative effort being expended by one organization compared with other organizations and the allocation of such efforts to the various programs of the organization are indicated in part by cost determinations. Whenever it is relevant to measure and report the cost of rendering current services, depreciation of assets used in providing such services is relevant as an element of such measurement and reporting process. Although depreciation can be distinguished from most other elements of cost in that it requires no current equivalent cash outlay, it is not optional or discretionary. Assets used in providing services are both valuable and exhaustible. Accordingly, there is a cost expiration associated with the use of depreciable assets, whether they are owned or rented, whether acquired by gift or by purchase, and whether they are used by a profit-seeking or by a not-for-profit organization.

Where depreciation is omitted, the cost of performing the organization's ser-

---

° This is a different position from that taken in the Statement of Position for nonprofit organizations not covered by the three Audit Guides. See page 267.

† See Chapters 6 and 7 for a comprehensive discussion of fixed assets and depreciation accounting.

vices is understated. Depreciation expense, therefore, should be recognized as a cost of rendering current services and should be included as an element of expense in the Statement of Support, Revenue, and Expenses of the fund in which the assets are recorded and in the Statement of Functional Expenditures.°

There are, of course, many strong arguments for not recognizing depreciation and these are discussed at some length in Chapter 7. However, for this category of organization these arguments are fairly moot because the Guide requires that depreciation accounting be followed. If depreciation accounting is not followed, the CPA will be required to qualify the opinion.

Retroactive Recording.   Of course, this does not mean that every $10 purchase must be capitalized and depreciated. The cut-off point is left to the organization to determine and many may conclude that this cut-off should be fairly high to minimize record keeping. While obviously each organization will have to make its cut-off decision based on its size and extent of fixed asset activity, the authors would think most organizations would establish a cut-off between $100 and $250.

The Guide also recognized that there would be some initial implementation problems when the Guide became effective in 1974. It provided that the organization should reconstruct the amount of fixed assets and accumulated depreciation as though the organization had followed this accounting principle all along.

The Guide also provided that if an organization was unable to reconstruct its cost basis for its fixed assets (or the fair market value at the date of receipt in the case of donated fixed assets), it could use a "cost" appraisal. A cost appraisal differs from a current value appraisal in that the appraiser attempts to determine what the asset would have cost at the time it was originally purchased, and not at today's prices.

Fixed Assets Where Title May Revert to Grantors.   Some organizations purchase or receive fixed assets under research or similar grants in which, at the completion of the grant period, title to these fixed assets reverts to the grantor.

Should these assets be recorded and depreciated? Typically the grant period closely approximates the useful life of these assets and the grantor in fact seldom asks for their return. The right to reclaim these assets usually is in the grant award mainly to protect the grantor in the event the grant is prematurely terminated. Under these circumstances, a fixed asset, whether purchased or donated, should be recorded as an asset and depreciated as with any other asset. If the aggregate amount

° Page 12 of the Guide.

of these assets which might have to be returned were material, disclosure of the relevant facts would, of course, be appropriate.

Donated Services

Donated services are not normally recorded except where their omission would make the financial statements misleading. If this would be the case, donated services would still only be recorded when:

1. There is "a clearly measurable basis for the amount."
2. The "organization exercises control over the employment and duties" of the person donating the services.
3. "The services performed are a normal part of the agency's program. . . ." *

Certain categories of services would not normally be recorded; these include supplementary efforts of volunteers which are in the nature of services to beneficiaries of the organization, volunteers assisting in fund-raising drives, and professional personnel assisting in research and training activities without pay.

But where all of the requirements listed above are met, and where the amounts are material, there is no option. Donated services must be recorded or the CPA will be required to qualify the opinion.

Donated Materials

Donated materials are normally recorded as a contribution at their fair market value, appropriately disclosed. The principal exception would be where the amounts are not significant or where there is no readily measurable basis for valuing such materials. In addition, donated materials that merely pass through the hands of the organization to a beneficiary are normally not recorded since the organization is merely acting as an agent for the donor.

Donated Securities

Donated securities are treated in the same way as donated cash; that is, if the donated securities are to be used for a donor-specified purpose or endowment then the gift would be recorded directly in the appropriate fund at the fair market value at the date of receipt. If the gift is not restricted by the donor, of course, the gift would be recorded

* Page 21 of the Guide.

directly in the current unrestricted fund in the same manner as any other cash gift.

Donated Equipment and Fixed Assets

Donated fixed assets would be recorded at their fair market value as revenue of the fixed asset fund, provided a separate fixed asset fund were used. If, on the other hand, the donated asset will be sold shortly after receipt and the cash received therefrom will be unrestricted, these fixed asset gifts would be recorded in the current unrestricted fund at the time of initial receipt.

Appropriations

The board is permitted to "appropriate" or designate a portion of the unrestricted fund balance for some special and specific purpose. This appropriation or designation, however, would be reported only in the fund balance section of the Balance Sheet. The appropriation or designation may *not* be shown as a deduction on the Statement of Support, Revenues and Expenses, and Changes in Fund Balances.

Accordingly, it is not appropriate for an organization to charge expenditures directly against "appropriated" balances. The expenditure must be included in the Statement of Support, Revenues and Expenses, and Changes in Fund Balances. All an appropriation does is to allow the board to designate *in the fund balance section* of the Balance Sheet how it intends to spend the unrestricted fund balance in the future.

For example, the unrestricted current fund balance of the National Association of Environmentalists of $135,516 (Figure 13–3) could be split into several amounts, representing the board's present intention of how it plans to use this amount. Perhaps $50,000 of it is intended for Project Seaweed, and the balance is available for undesignated purposes. The fund balance section of the Balance Sheet would appear:

```
Fund balance:
  Designated by the board for
    Project Seaweed  . . . . . . . . .    $ 50,000
  Undesignated, available for
    current purposes  . . . . . . . . .     85,516
                                         $135,516
```

As monies are expended for Project Seaweed in subsequent periods, they would be recorded as an expense in the Statement of Support, Revenues and Expenses, and Changes in Fund Balances. At the same time the amount of the fund balance designated by the board for Project Seaweed would be reduced and the amount "undesignated" would be increased by the same amount. See pages 47–52 for a comprehensive discussion of appropriation accounting techniques.

FINANCIAL STATEMENTS

The Guide provides for three principal financial statements:

1. Statement of Support, Revenues and Expenses, and Changes in Fund Balances (Figure 13–1, page 186)
2. Statement of Functional Expenses (Figure 13–2, page 192)
3. Balance Sheet (Figure 13–3, page 194)

The statements presented in the Guide are for illustrative purposes only and the Guide points out that variations from the ones presented may be appropriate. However, as noted below, expenses must be reported on a functional basis and supporting services such as management and general, and fund raising must be separately disclosed. Further, the Guide indicates that the major categories of expenses going into each of the functional classifications must also be disclosed, either in a formal Statement of Functional Expenses (Figure 13–2) or in notes to the financial statements.

Statement of Support, Revenues and Expenses, and Changes in Fund Balances

Figure 13–1 shows a Statement of Support, Revenues and Expenses, and Changes in Fund Balances for the National Association of Environmentalists. This is the format shown in the Guide with some modifications (discussed below).

Functional Classification of Expenses.   Traditionally, nonprofit organizations have reported in terms of amounts spent for salaries, rent, supplies, etc. (i.e., a natural expense classification). This Guide takes a major step forward when it states that the organization exists to perform services and programs and therefore should be reporting principally in terms of its individual program activities or functions. Figure 13–1 shows the expenses of the National Association of Environmentalists reported on a functional basis. This type of presentation requires management to tell the reader how much of its funds were expended for

NATIONAL ASSOCIATION OF ENVIRONMENTALISTS

STATEMENT OF SUPPORT, REVENUES AND EXPENSES, AND CHANGES IN FUND BALANCES
For the Year Ended December 31, 19X2

	Current Funds		Fixed Asset Fund	Endowment Fund	Total All Funds
	Unrestricted	Restricted			
Support:					
Contributions and gifts	$213,000		$10,000		$223,000
Bequests	60,000			$ 21,500	81,500
Total support	273,000		10,000	21,500	304,500
Revenues:					
Membership dues	20,550				20,550
Research projects	89,500	$38,400			127,900
Advertising income	33,500				33,500
Subscriptions to nonmembers.	18,901				18,901
Dividends and interest income	14,607				14,607
Appreciation of investments				33,025	33,025
Total revenues	177,058	38,400		33,025	248,483
Total support and revenues.	450,058	38,400	10,000	54,525	552,983
Expenses:					
Program services:					
"National Environment" magazine.	108,240		2,260		110,500
Clean-up month campaign.	124,308		2,309		126,617
Lake Erie project	83,285	26,164	5,616		115,065
Total program services	315,833	26,164	10,185		352,182
Supporting services:					
Management and general	30,355		3,161		33,516
Fund raising	5,719		250		5,969
Total supporting services	36,074		3,411		39,485
Total expenses	351,907	26,164	13,596		391,667
Excess (deficit) of revenues over expenses	98,151	12,236	(3,596)	54,525	161,316
Other changes in fund balance:					
Equipment acquisitions from unrestricted funds	(30,000)		30,000		-
Transfer of endowment fund gains	50,000			(50,000)	-
Fund balance, beginning of year	17,365	5,915	67,266	230,010	320,556
Fund balance, end of year	$135,516	$18,151	$93,670	$234,535	$481,872

Fig. 13–1. Income statement in the columnar format recommended in the AICPA Audit Guide for Voluntary Health and Welfare Organizations.

each program category and the amounts spent on supporting services, including fund raising.

Further, the Guide states that this functional reporting is not optional. The Statement of Support, Revenues and Expenses, and Changes in Fund Balances must be prepared on this functional or program basis or the CPA will be required to qualify the opinion, stating that the statements were not prepared in accordance with generally accepted accounting principles.

Many organizations will have to develop reasonably sophisticated procedures to be able to allocate expenses between various categories. An excellent reference source is the revised edition (1974) of *Standards of Accounting and Financial Reporting for Voluntary Health and Welfare Organizations*, discussed on pages 196–200. Also, United Way of America has published a comprehensive book to guide "human service organizations" in identifying their program classifications. This book is referred to as *UWASIS—United Way of America Services Identification System.*

Fund-Raising Expenses Disclosed.   The Statement of Support, Revenues and Expenses, and Changes in Fund Balances must also clearly disclose the amount of supporting services. These are broken down between fund raising and other management and general expenses. This distinction between supporting and program services is required, as is the separate reporting of fund raising. Absence of either the functional reporting approach or information on fund raising would result in a qualified opinion by a CPA.

When fund raising is combined with program functions such as the joint mailing of fund-raising and educational materials, the total cost should be allocated between the program function and fund-raising expense on the basis of the use made of the material.

Columnar Presentation.   The statement presentation is in a columnar format and, as can be observed in Figure 13–1, includes *all* four funds on one statement. This represents a significant departure from the statement format recommended in the Audit Guide for hospitals (discussed in Chapter 15), and from past practice. This format, however, is very similar to the format recommended in earlier chapters of this book.

It should be noted that this statement provides a complete picture of all activity of this organization for the year—not just the activity of a single fund. Further, by including a "total all funds" column on the statement, the reader is quickly able to see the total activity and does not have to add together several funds to get the total picture. This represents a major advance in nonprofit accounting.

The illustrated financial statements in the Guide show figures in the "total all funds" column for both the revenues and expenses categories. The illustrated statements do not, however, show figures in this total column for the caption "Excess of revenues over expenses" or for the captions that follow (i.e., other changes, fund balance beginning of year, fund balance end of year). The reason these totals were omitted is that the authors of the Guide were troubled by adding unrestricted and restricted revenues and expenses together to get a total. This is a continuation of the historic reluctance many accountants have shown in adding together what they feel are apples and oranges.

At the same time, the Guide's authors felt that they had to show total expenses for all funds because depreciation was being reported in a separate column, and, as noted above, depreciation is an expense which has to be reported as part of the functional expenses for the period. Only by showing a total of the expenses of the several columns would the reader see the total expense picture. Thus, somewhat reluctantly, the authors included a "total all funds" column for the expenses (and revenues). They chose not to include a total column for the "excess of revenues" and the "fund balances" captions because of their concern that the reader might misinterpret these amounts.

It seems somewhat inconsistent that while the Guide shows revenues and expenses in total, it does not show the net of these two amounts or the fund balances at the beginning and end of the year. However, nothing in the Guide indicates a prohibition from showing total-all-funds amounts for these other captions, as has been done in Figure 13–1. Further, in the years since the issuance of the Guide in 1973, most organizations have elected to show total figures for all captions.

Unrestricted Activity in Single Column.   One of the most significant features of this presentation is that all legally unrestricted revenues and expenses are reported in the single column, "current unrestricted" fund. The use of a single column in which all unrestricted activity is reported greatly simplifies the presentation and makes it more likely that "grandparent" will be able to comprehend the total picture of the organization. Further, a number of interfund transfers are eliminated because under the earlier Audit Guide separate board-designated funds were permitted whereas here the organization is *required* to combine all unrestricted activity in this single column.

Many organizations, of course, will want to continue to keep board-designated accounts within their bookkeeping system. This is fine. But, for reporting on the activity for the year, all unrestricted funds must be combined and reported as indicated in this illustration.

While not recommended, there would appear to be no prohibition to an organization's including additional columns to the *left* of this total "unrestricted" column to show the various unrestricted board-designated categories of funds which make up the total unrestricted fund column. However, where an organization does so it must clearly indicate that the total current unrestricted fund column represents the total unrestricted activity for the year and that the detailed columns to the left are only the arbitrarily subdivided amounts making up this total. Probably an organization is better advised to show such detail in a separate supplementary schedule, if at all.

Where an organization chooses to show its unrestricted fund broken into two columns, and has only one fund with restricted resources, it may be acceptable to eliminate the total unrestricted column in the interest of simplicity. An example of the column headings might be:

Unrestricted		Current	Total
General Fund	Investment Fund	Restricted Fund	All Funds

The key to whether this would be acceptable is the extent of activity in the various columns. For example, if the current restricted fund in the above illustration were relatively minor in amount, then the "total all funds" column would largely reflect the total unrestricted fund (i.e., the general fund and the investment fund). This is a judgmental question.

Current Restricted Column.   The "restricted" column represents those amounts which have been given to the organization for a specified purpose other than for endowment or fixed asset additions. It should be observed that the amounts reported as revenues in this fund represent the total amount the organization received during the year, and not the amount of such funds that was actually expended. As noted earlier in this chapter, gifts or grants which have time restrictions placed on them by the donor and could not be expended during the current period would not be reported as revenues but would be shown as deferred income on the Balance Sheet.

Use of Separate Fixed Asset Fund.   The Guide provides for the use of a separate plant fund, although, as noted earlier, it does not require its use. The organization could combine the fixed asset fund with the current unrestricted fund and report such activity as part of that fund. This, of course, has certain advantages since it would reduce the number of columns and would eliminate the need for certain interfund transfers.

One of the reasons why this separate plant fund was presented is that the industry committee * objected strongly to the fixed asset capitalization and depreciation accounting requirements. One argument expressed against depreciation was a concern that certain organizations had to budget their income and expenses exclusive of depreciation. For this reason the industry committee was reluctant to follow depreciation

---

* Joint Liaison Committee of the National Health Council, the National Assembly for Social Policy and Development, Inc., and the United Way of America.

accounting practices, but agreed to do so provided the depreciation provision was reported directly in a separate fixed asset fund column, and not in the unrestricted fund column. Thus in Figure 13–1 the depreciation for this organization is reflected entirely in the plant fund column.

Another argument many make against combining the plant fund with the unrestricted fund is that fixed assets are often purchased with donor-restricted gifts. There is a legal question of whether the original restrictions remain with the fixed assets once purchased. In the event of sale many believe the cash proceeds would remain restricted, and for this reason feel it inappropriate to combine the two funds.

Appreciation of Investments.   This organization has elected to carry its investments at market. Obviously this means that the organization must reflect appreciation (or depreciation) on its Statement of Support, Revenues and Expenses, and Changes in Fund Balances. In this instance the net appreciation of investments was $33,025. Assuming there were no sales or purchases of investments during the year, this amount would have been determined by comparing the market value of the investments at the end of the year with the market value at the beginning of the year. Normally, however, there will be some realized gain or loss during the year. While there is no technical objection to reporting the realized gain or loss separately from the unrealized appreciation (or depreciation), there seems little significance to this distinction. See page 88 for a discussion of the reasons why.

Activity of Restricted Funds Reported as Revenues and Expenses.   It is significant to note that the Guide has reported changes in the three restricted funds (current restricted fund, endowment fund, and fixed asset fund) in an income statement format and has reported the excess of revenues over expenses of these restricted funds. In the past many have argued that such restricted fund activity should not be reported in an income statement format but rather as "changes" in fund balance without any indication of the net change for the year. (See Figure 12–5 and the accompanying discussion in Chapter 12.)

This change is significant because it now permits the reader to see the total activity of the organization—both restricted and unrestricted. Thus the Guide appears to be saying that we have a single entity on which we are reporting as distinct from several subentities for which there is no total. In this example, the total excess of revenues over expenses was $161,316, whereas the activity of the unrestricted funds resulted in an excess of only $98,151. Certainly the reader has a right to know of these other amounts in a manner which will permit seeing a total picture.

Other Changes in Fund Balance. This section represents interfund transfers. Since all unrestricted funds are reported as a single fund there are very few such transfers. In this illustration $30,000 of equipment was purchased from current unrestricted funds. Since all fixed assets are reported in the fixed asset fund, this $30,000 has to be transferred from the current unrestricted fund to the fixed asset fund.

The second transfer shown in Figure 13–1 is a transfer of endowment fund gains from the endowment fund to the current unrestricted fund. This transfer was made under a "total return" approach.*

Statement of Functional Expenses

Figure 13–2 is a statement which analyzes functional or program expenses and shows the natural expense categories which go into each functional category. It is primarily an analysis to give the reader insight as to the major types of expenses involved.

Obviously in order to arrive at the functional expense totals shown in the Statement of Support, Revenues and Expenses, and Changes in Fund Balances an analysis must be prepared which shows all of the expenses going into each program category.

The Statement of Functional Expenses merely summarizes this detail for the reader. In many instances the allocation of salaries between functional or program categories should be based on time reports and similar analyses. In other instances the allocation will be made on the basis of floor space. Obviously each organization will have to develop time and expense accumulation procedures that will provide the necessary basis for allocation.

The Guide would seem to give some leeway to an organization whose principal expenses are salaries and only one or two other major expenses. Under those circumstances it might be possible to present this information in notes to the financial statements rather than in a separate statement.

Depreciation. In the illustrative financial statements in the Guide, depreciation expense is shown as the very last item on the statement and all other expenses are subtotaled before depreciation is added. This presentation was illustrated in the Guide because of the concern of many nonprofit organizations in showing depreciation as an expense. By subtotaling all expenses before adding depreciation, the Guide emphasizes the somewhat different nature of depreciation expense. The authors disagree and for this reason have included depreciation among

---

* See pages 89–91 for a comprehensive discussion of transfers under the total return concept of endowment fund investments.

NATIONAL ASSOCIATION OF ENVIRONMENTALISTS
STATEMENT OF FUNCTIONAL EXPENSES
For the Year Ended December 31, 19X2

	Total All Expenses	Program Services				Supporting Services		
		"National Environment" Magazine	Clean-up Month Campaign	Lake Erie Project	Total Program	Management and General	Fund Raising	Total Supporting
Salaries	$170,773	$24,000	$68,140	$60,633	$152,773	$15,000	$3,000	$18,000
Payroll taxes and employee benefits	22,199	3,120	8,857	7,882	19,859	1,950	390	2,340
Total compensation	192,972	27,120	76,997	68,515	172,632	16,950	3,390	20,340
Printing	84,071	63,191	18,954	515	82,660	1,161	250	1,411
Mailing, postage, and shipping	14,225	10,754	1,188	817	12,759	411	1,055	1,466
Rent	19,000	3,000	6,800	5,600	15,400	3,000	600	3,600
Telephone	5,615	895	400	1,953	3,248	2,151	216	2,367
Outside art	14,865	3,165	11,700	–	14,865	–	–	–
Local travel	1,741	–	165	915	1,080	661	–	661
Conferences and conventions	6,328	–	1,895	2,618	4,513	1,815	–	1,815
Depreciation	13,596	2,260	2,309	5,616	10,185	3,161	250	3,411
Legal and audit	2,000	–	–	–	–	2,000	–	2,000
Supplies	31,227	–	1,831	28,516	30,347	761	119	880
Miscellaneous	6,027	115	4,378	–	4,493	1,445	89	1,534
Total	$391,667	$110,500	$126,617	$115,065	$352,182	$33,516	$5,969	$39,485

Fig. 13–2. An analysis of the various program expenses showing the natural expense categories making up each of the functional or program categories.

the other expense categories in Figure 13–2. Either presentation is acceptable.

Balance Sheet

Figure 13–3 shows a Balance Sheet for the National Association of Environmentalists. The statement illustrated in the Audit Guide presents the more conventional Balance Sheet format in which each fund is reported as a separate sub-Balance Sheet. Figure 4–2 on page 38 is an example of such a Balance Sheet. Figure 13–3 has been presented in a columnar format because the authors feel this presentation is more meaningful to most readers. The Guide does not prohibit a columnar presentation but indicates that care must be taken to ensure that the restricted nature of certain of the funds is clearly shown.

Comparison Column.   In Figure 13–3 we have shown the totals for the previous year to provide a comparison for the reader. Obviously in a columnar presentation it is practical to show this comparison with the previous year for only the "total all funds" column, although it is possible also to show a comparison for a second column, as is illustrated on page 163. *

Designation of Unrestricted Fund Balance.   While it is a little more awkward to show when the Balance Sheet is presented in a columnar fashion as in Figure 13–3, it is still possible to disclose the composition of the unrestricted fund balance of $135,516. This is shown earlier in this chapter, on page 184.

Investments Carried at Market.   As previously noted, the National Association of Environmentalists carries its investments at market rather than at cost. The Guide indicates that where this is done the statement should disclose the unrealized appreciation (or depreciation). This particular organization has disclosed this information in footnotes to the financial statements rather than on the face of the statement itself.

RECOMMENDED SIMPLIFIED PRESENTATION

While the Audit Guide for voluntary health and welfare organizations significantly strengthens both the accounting and reporting principles for this category of organizations, there are several further steps

* Many accountants object to including this total comparison column, saying that sufficient information on the nature of the restricted portions is not reported. There is some validity to this argument but the authors feel this total column is preferable to no comparison.

NATIONAL ASSOCIATION OF ENVIRONMENTALISTS

BALANCE SHEET

December 31, 19X2 and 19X1

| | December 31, 19X2 | | | | | December 31, 19X1 |
| | Current Funds | | | | | Total |
	Unrestricted	Restricted	Endowment Funds	Fixed Asset Funds	Total All Funds	All Funds
ASSETS						
Current assets:						
Cash	$ 52,877	$22,666	$ 8,416	$ 2,150	$ 86,109	$ 11,013
Savings accounts	50,000				50,000	918
Accounts receivable	3,117				3,117	269,289
Investments, at market	76,195		226,119		302,314	769
Pledges receivable	4,509	1,000			5,509	281,989
Total current assets	186,698	23,666	234,535	2,150	447,049	
Fixed assets, at cost				111,135	111,135	72,518
Less: Accumulated depreciation				(19,615)	(19,615)	(6,019)
Net fixed assets				91,520	91,520	66,499
Total assets	$186,698	$23,666	$234,535	$ 93,670	$538,569	$348,488
LIABILITIES AND FUND BALANCES						
Current liabilities:						
Accounts payable	$ 48,666	$ 1,015			$ 49,681	$ 25,599
Deferred income	2,516	4,500			7,016	2,333
Total current liabilities	51,182	5,515			56,697	27,932
Fund balance	135,516	18,151	$234,535	$ 93,670	481,872	320,556
Total liabilities and fund balances	$186,698	$23,666	$234,535	$ 93,670	$538,569	$348,488

Fig. 13–3. A Balance Sheet prepared in columnar format.

that the Guide might have taken which would have aided readers' comprehension of these statements. Most of the improvements the authors recommend involve elimination of detailed reporting on a fund-by-fund basis.

Figures 13–4 and 13–5 show such a simplified Statement of Income, Expenses, and Changes in Fund Balances, and the Balance Sheet for the National Association of Environmentalists. The principal change has been to eliminate the reporting on each fund, and to report only on the entity as a whole.* This does not mean that it is not important to inform the reader of the amount of restricted resources which have been received and are unspent at the end of the year. Obviously this is important and can be determined by comparing the beginning and ending restricted fund balances in the Balance Sheet. What is not of particular importance, however, is the detail of all of the transactions that took place during the year or even of the composition of the restricted assets at the end of the year. Rather, the interested reader should be primarily concerned with the amount of restricted funds remaining at the end of the year. This is clearly shown in the detail presented in the fund balance section of the Balance Sheet (Figure 13–5).

CONCLUDING COMMENTS ON THE GUIDE

The AICPA Audit Guide for voluntary health and welfare organizations is a significant step forward in reporting for a major category of nonprofit organizations. Its relatively direct approach will add greatly to the ability of the nonaccountant to understand financial statements.

The requirement of reporting expenses on a functional or program basis should have a major impact on these organizations because functional reporting will emphasize the purpose of the organization's existence. In reporting on this basis the reader will be given a basis for judging how effectively the organization's resources have been used.

The Guide has also eliminated much of the confusion caused by fund accounting in the past by reporting restricted and unrestricted funds in a single statement. Thus the Guide seems to confirm what most nonaccountants have always known (but which accountants tend to forget): each organization is a single entity, not a collection of separate entities.

* There have been a number of other changes, including a change in some of the captions (principally the substitution of the word "income" for the words "support and revenues"). Note also that because we have presented all funds together there is no need to show interfund transfers.

NATIONAL ASSOCIATION OF ENVIRONMENTALISTS

STATEMENT OF INCOME, EXPENSES, AND CHANGES IN FUND BALANCES

Year Ended December 31, 19X2

Income:

Contributions and gifts	$223,000	
Bequests	81,500	
Membership dues	20,550	
Research projects	127,900	
Advertising income	33,500	
Subscriptions to nonmembers	18,901	
Dividends and interest income	14,607	
Appreciation of investments	33,025	
Total income		$552,983

Expenses:

Program services:

"National Environment" magazine	110,500	
Clean-up month campaign	126,617	
Lake Erie project	115,065	
Total program services		352,182

Supporting services:

Management and general	33,516	
Fund raising	5,969	
Total supporting services		39,485
Total expenses		391,667

Excess of income over expenses		161,316
Fund balance, beginning of year		320,556
Fund balance, end of year		$481,872

Fig. 13–4.   A simplified Statement of Income and Expenses in which no distinction is made between restricted and unrestricted funds.

THE EVOLUTION OF STANDARDS

In 1964, two national organizations in their respective fields of health and social welfare, the National Health Council and the National Assembly for Social Policy and Development, published a book for use

NATIONAL ASSOCIATION OF ENVIRONMENTALISTS
BALANCE SHEET

	December 31	
	19X2	19X1
ASSETS		
Current assets:		
Cash	$ 86,109	$ 11,013
Savings accounts	50,000	
Investments, at market.	302,314	269,289
Accounts receivable	3,117	918
Pledges receivable.	5,509	769
Total current assets	447,049	281,989
Fixed assets, at cost	111,135	72,518
Less: Accumulated depreciation	(19,615)	(6,019)
Net fixed assets	91,520	66,499
Total assets	$538,569	$348,488

LIABILITIES AND FUND BALANCES

Current liabilities:		
Accounts payable.	$ 49,681	$ 25,599
Deferred income	7,016	2,333
Total current liabilities	56,697	27,932
Fund balance:		
Restricted by donors for:		
Endowment.	234,535	230,010
Fixed asset purchases	2,150	1,617
Current purposes.	18,151	5,915
Total restricted	254,836	237,542
Unrestricted:		
Invested in fixed assets	91,520	66,499
Designated for Project Seaweed	50,000	
Undesignated, available for current use	85,516	16,515
Total unrestricted.	227,036	83,014
Total fund balance	481,872	320,556
Total liabilities and fund balance	$538,569	$348,488

Fig. 13–5.   A simplified Balance Sheet in which restricted funds are disclosed only in the fund balance section.

by affiliated organizations to assist them in establishing uniform standards of accounting and reporting. This book, *Standards of Accounting
and Financial Reporting for Voluntary Health and Welfare Organizations,* was one of the first major attempts to analyze the needs of the
readers of financial statements of voluntary health and welfare organizations and to prescribe standards of both accounting and reporting for
member organizations. It was written because prior thereto contributors
could not compare the financial statements of member organizations
since each organization followed accounting principles it felt appropriate and each had a different concept of what the reader of financial
statements should be told. The standards of accounting and reporting
prescribed in this book provided a framework which, when followed,
made it possible for readers to make meaningful comparisons of the
financial statements of several organizations.

While the standards prescribed were initially seen as being applicable
only to the member organizations of these two national organizations,*
this book's influence was felt by all voluntary health and welfare organizations, in part because until recently there was no other definitive
source of accounting principles, or reporting standards, to which they
could refer.

A number of the accounting principles recommended in this 1964
book were controversial and were not uniformly accepted by accountants
or by nonprofit organizations.† Nevertheless the book provided a set
of "standards" which had great impact on nonprofit accounting, particularly for voluntary health and welfare organizations. In large part
because of this influence and because many accountants found some
of the principles recommended by Standards ** difficult to accept, it

---

* There are many well-known organizations associated with the National Health
Council or the National Assembly for Social Policy and Development. These include,
among others, the American Cancer Society, Boy Scouts of America, National Jewish
Welfare Board, YMCA, the American Red Cross, and The Salvation Army.

† The two major areas with which many CPAs had difficulty were the handling
of fixed assets and the form of recommended financial statements. Standards recommended that all fixed assets be written off as purchased but then later capitalized and
reported in the Balance Sheet. This is the "write-off, then capitalize" method discussed on page 59. It is contrary to the way commercial organizations handle fixed
assets and many could not accept such a contrary treatment. Further, to many this
method was just too complicated to be understood.

The form of financial statement recommended, the Summary of Financial Activities,
was a unique form of financial statement in which all income and expenditures of the
organization were reported, regardless of source or restriction. While this concept was
excellent, the format of the statement was just too complicated and hard to understand
and few readers—including CPAs—really comprehended the information it contained.

** To the end of this chapter references to "Standards" refers to *Standards of Accounting and Financial Reporting for Voluntary Health and Welfare Organizations,*
published in 1964. "Revised Standards" refers to the 1974 edition.

became necessary for the authors of Standards and the accounting profession to reach agreement on appropriate principles for such organizations. Accordingly two committees were formed: a Committee of CPAs under the AICPA and a separate Industry Committee formed by the authors of Standards and referred to as the Joint Liaison Committee.[*] These Committees worked together over a several-year period to reconcile the differences between Standards and practices which CPAs felt represented "generally accepted accounting principles." At the conclusion of this period, the AICPA published in 1974 its Audit Guide, discussed earlier in this chapter. While the Joint Liaison Committee was not enthusiastic about all of the principles contained in the Audit Guide, they were able to endorse it and to urge their members and affiliated organizations to adhere to its principles.

Accordingly, in 1974 the second edition of *Standards of Accounting and Financial Reporting for Voluntary Health and Welfare Organizations* was published.[†] It was revised to conform with the AICPA Audit Guide and there are no significant differences in accounting and reporting principles between the two publications.

INFLUENCE OF STANDARDS ON THE AUDIT GUIDE

Without question, Standards had a significant impact on the accounting and reporting principles prescribed in the AICPA Audit Guide. Perhaps the most important impact was from Standards' insistence that an organization must present on a single financial statement all of its activities for the year, both unrestricted and restricted. Without the influence of Standards and the efforts of the Joint Liaison Committee, the Audit Guide would have followed pretty much the format recommended in the Hospital Audit Guide. As discussed in Chapter 15, the Audit Guide for hospitals recommends reporting all unrestricted funds

---

[*] This Committee consisted of representatives of the original two national organizations sponsoring Standards, and representatives of the United Way of America.

[†] United Way of America joined the National Health Council and the National Assembly for Social Policy and Development, Inc. in the sponsorship of the second edition. In 1974, United Way of America was in the process of completing a major book, *Accounting and Financial Reporting—A Guide for United Ways and Not-For-Profit Human Service Organizations.* The accounting principles and reporting formats recommended in this book are consistent with those in both the Audit Guide and Revised Standards. In addition, it offers considerable advice, including a comprehensive chart of accounts, forms, and documentation specifically addressed to this category of nonprofit organizations. It can be obtained from United Way of America, Alexandria, VA 22314.

together in one statement but reporting restricted funds in separate statements. This makes it difficult for the reader to see the total picture.

A Useful Reference

This book provides considerable assistance to the reader and offers much more detailed instruction than does the Audit Guide. The Audit Guide is intended to be only an outline of principles for the CPA's guidance. Revised Standards is intended to be a manual for the accountant within an organization applying these principles. It is an important reference book for the organization following the principles outlined in the AICPA Audit Guide.*

* It can be obtained from the National Health Council, New York, NY 10019.

14

Colleges and Universities

Among the most influential types of nonprofit institutions are colleges and universities. The extent of their influence is suggested by the fact that there are more than eight million students currently attending institutions of higher learning. There are approximately 3,000 colleges and universities and they must depend in large part on support from gifts and contributions from alumni and the general public. These institutions have the same need to report on their activities and to effectively communicate their financial needs as do other nonprofit organizations. The problems of reporting are complicated for these institutions by their historical reliance on fund accounting techniques. The purpose of this chapter is first to outline and discuss the accounting principles which are generally accepted for colleges and universities, and then to offer suggestions on how to simplify the financial statements to help the reader more easily understand them.

AUTHORITATIVE PRONOUNCEMENTS

The American Council on Education published in 1953 *College and University Business Administration*, of which a substantial portion deals with the principles of accounting and reporting. Republished in 1968,* this book was until 1973 generally accepted as the most authoritative source of accounting and reporting principles applicable to colleges and universities. Because of its wide use, it became generally known by the

* *College and University Business Administration*, Revised Edition, American Council on Education, Washington, DC, 1968.

acronym "CUBA." This acronym will be used throughout this chapter and refers to the 1968 edition.

AICPA Audit Guide

In 1973 * the Committee on College and University Accounting and Auditing of the American Institute of Certified Public Accountants issued an Audit Guide for use by CPAs in their examination of the financial statements of these institutions. As with the other industry guides † it contains not only guidance to the CPA on auditing procedures, but also a comprehensive discussion of accounting and reporting principles for such institutions. Accordingly, the Audit Guide has now become the authoritative source for principles of accounting and reporting for colleges and universities.** Throughout this chapter the principles outlined herein will be as discussed in this Audit Guide except where the authors indicate their preference for alternative treatment.

To a large extent this Audit Guide has codified principles of accounting and reporting discussed in CUBA. In fact, a number of representatives of the National Association of College and University Business Officers (NACUBO) worked with the AICPA Committee throughout the development of this Audit Guide so that the Guide represents a joint effort of both the accounting profession and college and university business officers.

NACUBO "Administrative Service"

The 1968 edition of CUBA has now been superseded by a looseleaf administrative service titled "College and University Business Administration—Administrative Service," published by NACUBO. The Audit Guide for colleges and universities has been incorporated as a part of this Service. Changes in terminology of the captions of the financial statements, interpretations of the Audit Guide, and other changes as occur from time to time are reflected on a current basis in this Service.

---

* In 1974 the Guide was effectively modified through the issuance of a Statement of Position which modified somewhat the description and classification of revenues, expenditures, and transfers of current funds. See page 305 for a discussion of the purpose and function of a Statement of Position.

† See Chapter 13 for a discussion of the Audit Guide for voluntary health and welfare organizations and Chapter 15 for the Audit Guide for hospitals.

** See page 304 for a discussion of the significance of Audit Guides and their relationship to generally accepted accounting principles.

FUND ACCOUNTING

Fund accounting is followed by colleges and universities in a classical manner and no other type of institution is as wedded to fund accounting. This results from a historical reliance on outside gifts, many of which involved restrictions, and thus the need to keep track of these restricted resources. Also, because of a continuing reliance on outside financial help, these institutions often felt it prudent to set aside funds from current unrestricted gifts to function as endowment funds and thus to provide future endowment income. All of this encouraged the use of fund accounting and resulted in problems of communicating with nonaccountant readers of financial statements.

Classification of Funds

Generally the number of major fund groupings is limited to five: *

1. Current funds
   a. Unrestricted
   b. Restricted
2. Loan funds
3. Endowment and similar funds
4. Annuity and life income funds
5. Plant funds
   a. Unexpended
   b. Renewal and replacement
   c. Retirement of indebtedness
   d. Investment in plant

Within these major groupings there are often several subgroupings. Figure 14–1 (pages 208–209) shows the format of the Statement of Changes in Fund Balances for Mary and Isla College and the subgrouping of both current and plant funds can be seen.

Current Funds.   These are the funds that are available for the general operations of the institution. Usually a distinction is made between those current funds that are unrestricted and those that are restricted by an

---

* There is a sixth fund group—agency funds. These are funds that are in the custody of the institution but do not belong to it. An example would be funds belonging to student organizations on deposit with the institution. Agency funds are not discussed or illustrated in this chapter because they are not funds of the institution. Reference should be made to the Audit Guide and to the Administrative Service by interested readers.

outside party for a current purpose. Generally each type of activity for the year is presented in a separate column, with the columns side by side in the financial statements.

The balance in the current *restricted* fund represents the unexpended balance of amounts which have been received for a specific current purpose and, in theory, these amounts would have to be returned if the institution were not to use the funds for the restricted purpose.

The balance in the current *unrestricted* fund represents only that amount which the board has chosen to leave in this fund. As is discussed below, the board can transfer into and out of the current unrestricted fund and there is little significance to the balance in this fund at any given time. Unfortunately, few nonaccountant readers understand this and many mistakenly assume that a low current unrestricted fund balance is an indication the organization is in poor financial condition, which may or may not be the case. This can be seen in Figure 14–3 (page 216), in which the net increase of $160,000 suggests that Mary and Isla College is in dire financial straits. Notice, however, immediately above this net increase that the board has chosen to transfer $600,000 from this fund to other funds.

Loan Funds. These are funds which are available for granting loans to students and, to a lesser extent, to faculty. These funds are not available for other uses. The principal of restricted gifts where only the income can be used for loans should be shown as part of the endowment fund, and income as earned and available for loans should be transferred to the loan fund.

Endowment Funds. This fund grouping includes three types of funds classified as endowment and similar funds:

1. Endowment funds, where the donor has stipulated that the principal is to be kept intact in perpetuity and only the income therefrom can be expended either for general purposes or for a restricted purpose.
2. Term endowments, where the donor has provided that upon the passage of time or the happening of a specific event the endowment principal can then be utilized either for a specific purpose or for the general operation of the institution. Term endowments are usually not reported separately in the principal financial statements except where they are sizable.
3. Quasi-endowment, where the board, as distinct from the donor, has set aside unrestricted current funds to be used as endowment. Quasi-endowment funds are also known as "Board-Designated Endowment," or "Funds Functioning as Endowment." The amount of quasi-

endowment funds should be clearly shown in the financial statements or notes thereto.

Annuity or Life Income Funds. These are amounts where only the principal, and not the income to be earned thereon, has been given to the institution. The income is usually reserved by the donor for a specified period of time and the institution agrees to pay either a specified sum or the actual income earned to the donor for this period. The principal of these gifts represents an asset owned by the institution but until the income or annuity restrictions lapse, clearly these amounts do not represent funds which have the same value as unrestricted funds. For this reason these amounts should not be combined with endowments or other funds for reporting purposes.

Plant Funds. Plant funds consist of four subgroupings:

1. Unexpended funds. These funds are amounts which are to be used for plant additions or modernization. Such funds will also include cash and other investments which have been transferred to this fund for plant purposes.
2. Funds for renewal or replacement. These funds represent amounts transferred from current funds for renewal or replacement of existing plant. Such amounts represent a form of funding in lieu of depreciation. In reporting, often these funds are combined with unexpended funds.
3. Funds for retirement of indebtedness. These are the amounts set aside by the board for debt service (interest and principal) often under a mandatory contractual arrangement with the lender. These funds can also include amounts set aside by the board at its discretion.
4. Investment in plant. This represents the cost of plant including land and equipment. Actual cost, or market value at date of gifts is used.

All plant or fixed assets are reported in the plant fund. The current funds show plant activities to the extent that funds for additions, renewal or replacement, and retirement of indebtedness are transferred from the current fund to the plant fund. Also, the current fund will show plant activities to the extent that equipment purchases charged directly through current fund expenditures will subsequently be recorded in the plant fund as additions to the net investment in plant.

While the Guide illustrates the use of all four subgroupings, some institutions combine several or all of these for reporting purposes, showing the balances of each subgrouping only in the Balance Sheet.

THE THREE PRINCIPAL FINANCIAL STATEMENTS

Three principal financial statements are used by colleges and universities, as follows:

1. Statement of Changes in Fund Balances (Figure 14–1, pages 208–209).
2. Balance Sheet (Figure 14–2, pages 214–215).
3. Statement of Current Funds Revenues, Expenditures, and Other Changes (Figure 14–3, page 216).

There are frequently other supporting statements which provide detail that should tie in with these three principal statements. While the supporting statements provide information which the board or other specific users of the statements may want, it is important not to confuse the general reader of the financial statements by providing more detail than is appropriate. The discussion in this chapter will be confined to the three principal statements listed above. A reader interested in further information should refer to the Administrative Service.

It is important to recognize the premise from which the Guide has prescribed accounting and reporting principles. The Guide states:

Service, rather than profits, is the objective of an educational institution; thus, the primary obligation of accounting and reporting is one of accounting for resources received and used rather than for determination of net income.°

Thus it is essential to recognize that the Guide does not attempt to prescribe accounting and reporting principles that would assist the reader in, understanding whether the institution had an excess of revenues over expenditures for the period. This is not the purpose. Its purpose is only of "accounting for resources received and used."

The key, then, to understanding college financial statements is to recognize what type of transaction is included in each of these three statements, and to understand the principles of fund accounting. The following paragraphs describe the type of transactions in each of these principal statements. A description of some of the accounting and reporting principles appears in a later section of this chapter.

Statement of Changes in Fund Balances

The most important of the three financial statements is the Statement of Changes in Fund Balances. This statement summarizes all of the activity

° Page 5 of the Guide.

of the institution for the entire period. Figure 14–1 shows the Statement of Changes in Fund Balances for Mary and Isla College.

Notice that this format essentially follows an income statement format (i.e., revenues less expenditures equals net change for the year). This is a significant change from the format of the Statement of Changes in Fund Balances previously recommended by CUBA. That form of statement was the more typical Statement of Changes in Fund Balances in which the first line was the balance at the beginning of the year, then the additions were shown, then the deductions, and finally, the fund balance at the end of the year. An example of this superseded format can be seen in Figure 12–5 on page 156.

The significance of the new format is that it presents a reasonably concise summary of the net change in the institution for the entire year. While most business officers (and many accountants) flinch at the comparison, this "net change" has much the same significance as "excess of revenues over expenditures," particularly when all funds are viewed together.

Total All Funds. The illustrative financial statements in the Audit Guide do *not* show a "total all funds" column, as is illustrated in Figure 14–1, and the Guide discourages such a total column. The Guide indicates, however, that the use of a total column is permitted provided care is taken to ensure that the restricted nature of certain of the funds is clearly shown. As has been repeatedly noted, the authors recommend the use of a total column and accordingly have included one in this and subsequent illustrations.°

Revenues and Other Additions. The reader should note that while this statement is in an income statement format, the captions are not pure. Observe that the caption is "Revenues and other additions." The "other additions" are a number of items which do not constitute revenue in a traditional accounting sense, but which are normally added to the fund balance of a particular fund. In this illustration the "other additions" are the $1,000,000 expended for plant facilities, and the $170,000 for retirement of indebtedness.† As is illustrated in Figure 14–4, the authors recommend eliminating such "nonrevenue" additions from this financial

---

° Those readers not familiar with the arguments for and against the inclusion of such a "total all funds" column will find a discussion on pages 149–152.

† Many would also argue that the gifts, bequests, capital gains, and other "revenue" in the funds other than the current unrestricted fund are also "other additions." They feel that these amounts are not revenue and are only additions to the fund balance which should not be looked upon as revenue. The authors disagree and feel that such amounts do represent revenue. Note that the same basic format is used in the Audit Guide for voluntary health and welfare organizations (see Figure 13–1) and the authors of that Guide consider the "revenue" caption appropriate.

MARY AND

STATEMENT OF CHANGES

For the Year

	Current Funds		Loan
	Unrestricted	Restricted	Funds
Revenues and other additions:			
Unrestricted current fund revenues	$3,385,000		
Gifts and bequests—restricted		$400,000	$10,000
Grants and contracts—restricted		200,000	
Investment income—restricted		10,000	
Realized gains on investments.			
Interest on loans receivable			5,000
Expended for plant facilities			
Retirement of indebtedness			
Total.	3,385,000	610,000	15,000
Expenditures and other deductions:			
Educational and general expenditures	2,300,000	550,000	
Auxiliary enterprises expenditures	95,000		
Refunded to grantors		10,000	
Expended for plant facilities			
Retirement of indebtedness			
Interest on indebtedness.			
Disposal of plant facilities			
Loans written off.			3,000
Total	2,395,000	560,000	3,000
Net increase/(decrease) before transfers.	990,000	50,000	12,000
Transfers among funds—additions/			
(deductions):			
Mandatory:			
Principal and interest	(220,000)		
Renewals and replacements	(50,000)		
Unrestricted gifts allocated	(600,000)		
Portion of unrestricted quasi-endowment			
funds investment gains appropriated	40,000		
Total	(830,000)		
Net increase/(decrease) for the year	160,000	50,000	12,000
Fund balance, beginning of year	650,000	85,000	84,000
Fund balance, end of year	$ 810,000	$135,000	$96,000

Fig. 14–1.   An example of a Statement of Changes in Fund Balances in

ISLA COLLEGE

IN FUND BALANCES

Ended June 30, 19X1

| Endowment and Similar Funds | Plant Funds | | | | Total All Funds |
	Unexpended	Renewal and Replacement	Retirement of Indebtedness	Investment in Plant	
					$ 3,385,000
$ 160,000	$ 65,000				635,000
					200,000
5,000	20,000	$ 10,000			45,000
150,000					150,000
					5,000
				$ 1,000,000	1,000,000
				170,000	170,000
315,000	85,000	10,000		1,170,000	5,590,000
					2,850,000
					95,000
					10,000
	900,000	100,000			1,000,000
			$170,000		170,000
			50,000		50,000
				85,000	85,000
					3,000
	900,000	100,000	220,000	85,000	4,263,000
315,000	(815,000)	(90,000)	(220,000)	1,085,000	1,327,000
			220,000		
		50,000			
550,000	50,000				
(40,000)					
510,000	50,000	50,000	220,000		
825,000	(765,000)	(40,000)		1,085,000	1,327,000
4,210,000	1,200,000	150,000	100,000	21,615,000	28,094,000
$5,035,000	$ 435,000	$110,000	$100,000	$22,700,000	$29,421,000

the basic format recommended by the AICPA Audit Guide (see page 206).

statement in order to provide a pure revenue and expenditure classification.

In this presentation certain information is presented in summary form. For example, the $3,385,000 shown as unrestricted current funds includes a number of categories of income, including all unrestricted gifts, and investment income. The detail of this $3,385,000 is shown in the Statement of Current Funds Revenues, Expenditures, and Other Changes (Figure 14–3). For this reason this second statement (or one containing similar information) is necessary in order for the reader to see some detail of the sources of income of the institution.

The *restricted* gifts and bequests reported in the current restricted fund represent the total amount which has been received during the year, and not the amount actually expended. It will be observed that in the Statement of Current Funds Revenues, Expenditures, and Other Changes (Figure 14–3) the amount reported as current restricted revenues is the exact amount actually expended. This inconsistency in presentation causes considerable reader confusion. For a more complete discussion of the principles followed in reporting current restricted funds the reader should refer to pages 100–107.

Expenditures and Other Deductions. As with the "Revenues and other additions" caption, there are also a number of nonexpense categories included in this caption. In part that is why the word "expenditure" is used instead of the word "expense." "Expenditure" implies disbursement whereas "expense" implies accrual basis "cost." The principal nonexpense categories are the $1,000,000 expended for plant facilities and $170,000 of retirement of indebtedness. It may be noted that both of these items are also shown in the "Revenue and other additions" section of this statement, but in different fund columns. If these were eliminated in both sections, the amounts shown as revenues and expenditures would represent fairly pure amounts.

As in the revenue section there is no detail shown for the $2,300,000 of educational and general expenditures. Again, this is because these amounts are reported in more detail in the Statement of Current Funds Revenues, Expenditures, and Other Changes (Figure 14–3).

Net Increase (Decrease) Before Transfers. This caption is *not* included in the illustrated Statement of Changes in Fund Balances in the Audit Guide, perhaps in part because the authors of the Guide were reluctant to imply that these amounts represented anything similar to "excess of revenues over expenditures," which certainly they are not. Yet it does seem useful for the reader to know what the results of each fund's activity were before the transfers are made between funds. For example, observe that the net increase in the current unrestricted fund before transfers was $990,000. Without this subtotal most readers would probably focus on the $160,000 net increase after transfers.

Those who argue against this subtotal point out that some of the transfers are required under mandatory debt arrangements and have many of the characteristics of an expenditure. They feel that the reader focusing on the $990,000 is likely to be misled into thinking that this is truly the amount available for expenditure by the board.

The Guide does not prohibit such a subtotal and in fact several members of the Audit Guide Committee felt that the Guide's illustrated statements should include this subtotal. The authors believe this caption is useful and would encourage all colleges and universities to include it.

Transfers Among Funds.   Transfers among funds have been properly separated from the revenues and expenditures sections of the statement. As will be seen in Figure 14–3, this is not so on the Statement of Current Funds Revenues, Expenditures, and Other Changes. On that statement "mandatory" transfers are reported as part of the caption "Expenditures and mandatory transfers." See the discussion on mandatory transfers below.

The transfer from the endowment fund of a portion of the quasi-endowment fund investment gains (under the total return concept) is properly shown as a transfer and not up in the revenues section (where many institutions would prefer to show such amounts). See Chapter 8 for a complete discussion of the total return concept, and the proper accounting thereof.

While a number of transfers are reported in this section of the statement, the use of a total-all-funds column greatly helps the reader to see that these transfers have no effect on the net results of activity for the institution as a whole. This is important; a reader who recognizes this is less likely to become hopelessly mired in confusing detail.

Net Increase (Decrease) for the Year.   The inclusion of this caption is quite important because, appropriately, it tells the reader what the net change was for the year in each fund and, where the total-all-funds column is also provided, for the institution as a whole.

The reason this caption reads as it does, instead of "Excess of revenues over expenditures," is that the various arbitrary transfers between funds essentially destroy the purity of such a caption. For this reason the authors of the Guide had to devise a caption which would not suggest to the reader that this "net change" in any given fund represented "Excess of revenues over expenditures." This was also necessary because, with the use of four separate plant funds, several of the nonrevenue and nonexpenditure transactions (retirement of indebtedness and expenditure for plant facilities) were transactions to which the caption "Excess of revenues over expenditures" would not be appropriate. However, the caption "Excess of revenues over expenditures" would be appropriate if it were associated only with the total-all-funds column. See pages 224–232 for a number of suggestions for simplifying the financial statements so that, among other things, the "Excess of revenues over expenditures" caption might then be appropriate.

Balance Sheet

Figure 14–2 shows the Balance Sheet for Mary and Isla College in a columnar format. The Balance Sheet, as illustrated in the Guide and prepared by most institutions, is set up in a typical format where the assets are on the left side of the page and the liabilities and fund balances are on the right side, with major fund groupings presented as separate Balance Sheets within the Balance Sheet. The illustrations on pages 38 and 236–237 are examples of this type of Balance Sheet. The Guide permits the use of a columnar presentation as an acceptable alternative, although it does caution against cross-footing the columns to a total "unless all necessary disclosures are made, including interfund borrowings." * While the columnar format used in Figure 14–2 is not used as widely, the authors prefer it because of the ease in seeing the overall picture of the institution. At the same time it must be recognized that the columnar format can be misleading if the reader does not recognize the restricted nature of most of the assets.

Statement of Current Funds Revenues, Expenditures, and Other Changes

Figure 14–3 shows the Statement of Current Funds Revenues, Expenditures, and Other Changes for Mary and Isla College. This is a very difficult statement for most readers to understand or to correctly interpret. It is an attempt to show on one statement all of the activity involving "current" funds—that is, the funds available for current use by the college in performing its primary objectives. Since the institution uses both restricted and unrestricted funds in carrying out its current objectives, it is necesary to include both types of funds in this statement.

It is important to note, however, that this statement "does not purport

* *Audits of Colleges and Universities,* AICPA, 1973, page 57.

to present the results of operations or the net income or loss for the period as would a Statement of Income or a Statement of Revenues and Expenses." * In fact it does not even purport to report all of the unrestricted activity for the year. Excluded from this statement are transactions involving board-designated funds (i.e., board-designated endowment funds) which have been set aside for purposes other than current operations, and restricted funds which are not directly for a "current" purpose. This statement attempts only to show the reader the revenues and expenditures used for current operations, and the amounts transferred to other funds either by board action or under agreement with outside parties. To further complicate matters (and thereby to confuse the reader) all of the amounts reported on this statement are also reported in total on the Statement of Changes in Fund Balances (Figure 14-1). For all of these reasons, it is not appropriate to look upon this statement as a Statement of Revenues and Expenditures; it is not, for it contains transactions which are extraneous to revenue and expenditure transactions in the conventional accounting sense. Since very few nonaccountant readers are likely to be aware of the limitations of this statement and what it purports to show, most readers are not able to properly interpret it. As is discussed later in this chapter, the authors would expect that eventually this statement will find so little acceptance that it will be replaced with a more meaningful statement.

Column Headings. Three column headings are used on this statement: current unrestricted, current restricted, and total. The amount shown in the current unrestricted column represents all of the current unrestricted fund activity for the year, including transfers in and out.

The major categories of revenues and expenditures on this statement can be seen also in the Statement of Changes in Fund Balances (Figure 14-1). For example, the total educational and general expenditures of $2,300,000 is the same amount shown in Figure 14-1. While there is no subtotal, thoughtful readers who are trying to learn what the net results were for the year are likely to subtract $2,300,000 from total current revenue of $3,385,000; if they do they will observe that there is an excess of revenue over expenses of $1,085,000.†

Restricted Fund Column. The restricted fund column is quite confusing because the amount *reported* as "revenue" is exactly the amount

---

* Page 55 of the Guide.

† This $1,085,000 is different from the $990,000 net increase before transfers discussed above because the $1,085,000 includes auxiliary enterprises revenues and excludes auxiliary enterprises expenditures.

MARY AND

BALANCE

June 30,

	Current Funds		Loan
	Unrestricted	Restricted	Funds
ASSETS			
Current assets:			
Cash	$ 910,000	$285,000	$16,000
Short-term investments	930,000		
Accounts receivable	18,000		80,000
Inventories	20,000		
Prepaid expenses	25,000		
Total	1,903,000	285,000	96,000
Long-term investments.			
Invested in plant			
Interfund receivable (payable)	(410,000)	(150,000)	
Total assets	$1,493,000	$135,000	$96,000
LIABILITIES AND FUND BALANCE			
Current liabilities:			
Accounts payable	$ 573,000		
Current portion of debt			
Tuition deposits	110,000		
Total	683,000		
Long-term debt			
Fund balances:			
Restricted		$135,000	$50,000
Unrestricted	810,000		46,000
Total	810,000	135,000	96,000
Total liabilities and fund balance	$1,493,000	$135,000	$96,000

Fig. 14–2. An example of a columnar presentation of a Balance the AICPA

ISLA COLLEGE
SHEET
19X1

Endowment and Similar Funds	Plant Funds				Total All Funds
	Unexpended	Renewal and Replacement	Retirement of Indebtedness	Investment in Plant	
$ 310,000	$ 20,000	$ 60,000			$ 1,601,000
	400,000	50,000	$100,000		1,480,000
					98,000
					20,000
					25,000
310,000	420,000	110,000	100,000		3,224,000
4,215,000					4,215,000
				$23,450,000	23,450,000
510,000	50,000				
$5,035,000	$ 470,000	$110,000	$100,000	$23,450,000	$30,889,000
	$ 35,000				$ 608,000
				$ 170,000	170,000
					110,000
	35,000			170,000	888,000
				580,000	580,000
$2,025,000	210,000	$110,000		22,700,000	25,230,000
3,010,000	225,000		$100,000		4,191,000
5,035,000	435,000	110,000	100,000	22,700,000	29,421,000
$5,035,000	$ 470,000	$110,000	$100,000	$23,450,000	$30,889,000

Sheet for a small college using fund accounting recommended in Audit Guide.

MARY AND ISLA COLLEGE

STATEMENT OF CURRENT FUNDS REVENUES, EXPENDITURES, AND OTHER CHANGES

For the Year Ending June 30, 19X1

	Current Fund		
	Unrestricted	Restricted	Total
Revenues:			
Educational and general:			
Student tuition and fees.	$1,610,000		$1,610,000
Governmental appropriations.	400,000		400,000
Governmental grants		$200,000	200,000
Gifts	900,000	340,000	1,240,000
Endowment income	350,000	10,000	360,000
Auxiliary enterprises	125,000		125,000
Total current revenues	3,385,000	550,000	3,935,000
Expenditures and mandatory transfers:			
Educational and general:			
Instruction	1,100,000		1,100,000
Research	300,000	550,000	850,000
Academic support	200,000		200,000
Student services	100,000		100,000
Operation and maintenance			
of plant	500,000		500,000
Institutional support.	100,000		100,000
	2,300,000	550,000	2,850,000
Mandatory transfers for:			
Principal and interest	200,000		200,000
Renewals and replacements	50,000		50,000
Total educational and general	2,550,000	550,000	3,100,000
Auxiliary enterprises:			
Expenditures	95,000		95,000
Mandatory transfer for principal			
and interest	20,000		20,000
Total expenditures and			
mandatory transfers	2,665,000	550,000	3,215,000
Other transfers and additions:			
Excess of restricted receipts over			
transfers to revenues		60,000	60,000
Refunded to grantors		(10,000)	(10,000)
Unrestricted gifts allocated to			
other funds	(600,000)		(600,000)
Portion of quasi-endowment			
gains appropriated	40,000		40,000
Net increase in fund balance	$ 160,000	$ 50,000	$ 210,000

Fig. 14–3. An example of a Statement of Current Funds Revenues, Expenditures, and Other Changes for a small college in the format recommended by the AICPA Audit Guide.

216

expended for the restricted purposes indicated. Note the $550,000 of revenue and the $550,000 of expenditures. Colleges follow the practice of reporting on this statement restricted revenues only to the extent expended for the restricted purposes. As is discussed above, this approach is very complicated and difficult for most readers to understand. For example, note that the amount reported as revenues in the Statement of Changes in Fund Balances is $610,000 rather than $550,000. The careful reader who tries to trace the figures back and forth between these two statements is bound to become confused.

Further complicating the figures shown in the restricted fund column is the need to report the "net increase" in fund balance for the restricted fund for the year, and the obvious necessity of having that net increase "agree" with the net increase reported on the Statement of Changes in Fund Balances. It will be noticed that the net increase shown in both statements for this restricted fund is $50,000. Yet, since the only revenue which is reportable in the Statement of Current Funds Revenues, Expenditures, and Other Changes is the amount actually expended (under the accounting principles followed), there has to be a "balancing figure" to reflect the net change in the restricted fund during the year. This can be seen at the bottom of Figure 14-3 where $60,000 has been indicated as the "Excess of restricted receipts over transfers to revenues." This figure plus the amount reported as "refunded to donors" net down to the "net increase" for the year. Obviously only the most knowledgeable accountant will comprehend these gymnastics.

The total column is required on the Statement of Current Funds Revenues, Expenditures, and Other Changes in order to show the reader the total current fund activity, i.e., the total activity for the year handled by funds which are available for current use.

Unrestricted Revenues.   Looking only at the unrestricted column, the reader is shown the complete revenue picture. *All* unrestricted contributions, bequests, investment income, and other revenue *must* be reported in this section. The only exception is capital gains, discussed below. If the institution receives a large unexpected gift on the last day of the year and it wishes to utilize these funds for board-designated endowment, it may do so but it must first report the receipt of this gift in the revenues section. Prior to the issuance of this Guide the board had the option of reporting such gifts directly in the Statement of Changes in Fund Balances, but this is no longer permitted.

It should also be observed that all unrestricted investment income (i.e., dividends and interest) must be reported in this section. The use of an "income stabilization reserve" is no longer permitted. All investment income that is unrestricted must be reported here, in the year in which it is earned.

Expenditures and Mandatory Transfers.   Included in this caption are mandatory transfers. Mandatory transfers are those transfers which are required under debt or under agreement with outside parties. The most typical mandatory transfer involves debt service, i.e., interest on indebtedness *and* repayment of debt principal. In Figure 14–3 the amount of such principal and interest was $220,000 ($200,000 under educational and $20,000 under auxiliary activities). Also, some institutions are required under contractual arrangements to put aside in a renewal and replacement fund certain amounts every year. Mary and Isla College is making a mandatory transfer of $50,000.

The important point to note here is that while these transfers are "required" the nature of these transactions is not that of an *expenditure* in a conventional accounting sense. Debt repayment, while requiring an expenditure of cash, is not considered an expenditure in an accounting sense any more than the proceeds from a bank borrowing is considered income. Thus, these mandatory transfers tend to frustrate the reader who is trying to learn what excess, if any, there was of revenues over expenditures in a traditional sense. This cannot be determined without some rearrangement of the figures shown in this statement.

Yet, keep in mind that it is not intended that this statement be looked at for purposes of determining an excess of income over expenditures. It is intended only to show the activity of the current funds, and these mandatory transfers obviously represent activity that reduced the available current funds.

Note also that there were mandatory transfers under the subcategory of "auxiliary enterprises." Auxiliary enterprises are those activities which are not central to the principal objectives of the institution, i.e., educating students. Typical auxiliary activities would be the dormitory system and the food service activities. The dormitory operation involves borrowing of funds on a long-term basis and often involves repayment through room charges. As can be seen in Figure 14–3, such auxiliary enterprises are reported separately within that statement.

Other Transfers and Additions.   In addition to mandatory transfers, the board obviously has the right to make transfers to its other funds. These "other transfers" are shown separately at the bottom of the Statement of Current Funds Revenues, Expenditures, and Other Changes, under this caption. The distinction between mandatory and other transfers is simply to indicate to the reader which transfers were required and which ones were truly a board decision. In the case of Mary and

Isla College there are two other transfers: the transfer of $600,000 of unrestricted gifts to other funds and the $40,000 transferred from the endowment and similar funds of gains on board-designated endowments under the total return concept.*

Excess of Revenues over Expenditures. It is important to observe that the reader is not shown a figure representing an excess of revenues over expenditures for the year, or, for that matter, the excess of revenues over expenditures and mandatory transfers for the year. The only total that is reported is the final figure on the statement, "Net increase in fund balance." Readers who try to draw some conclusion from this "net increase" amount will obviously be drawing an erroneous conclusion since this net amount can be controlled by the board. It has no significance other than being the amount the board has chosen to leave in this fund.

The Guide does not specifically prohibit a caption "Excess of revenues over expenditures and mandatory transfers" and this is one improvement that some institutions should perhaps consider. However, with the inclusion of mandatory transfers which are themselves a mixture of expenditures and nonexpenditures in an accounting sense, there is, of course, some question as to the significance of even that net amount. On the other hand, this net excess of revenues over expenditures and mandatory transfers would probably give the reader a little more accurate indication of what took place than does the final caption "Net increase in fund balance."

Significance of this Statement. As can undoubtedly be surmised by this point, this statement does not tell the readers what the results of activities were for the year. Certainly the readers should not focus on the net increase for the year and they must also be very careful if they focus on the total expenditures and mandatory transfers caption. For these reasons this statement probably serves relatively little purpose. It does serve a purpose at present, however, in that it provides some detail of the revenues and expenditures categories that go into the totals which are shown in the Statement of Changes in Fund Balances (Figure 14–1). As has been suggested, the authors feel that the Statement of Current Funds Revenues, Expenditures, and Other Changes will not survive too many years because of its limited usefulness. The authors of the Guide recognized this, too, and indicated that the information shown on this statement could be presented in other ways.

---

* See pages 88–95 for a discussion of this accounting approach to handling investment fund gains.

ACCOUNTING PRINCIPLES

Summarized below are the accounting principles prescribed by the Audit Guide for colleges and universities, a number of which were discussed above.

Accrual Basis

The Guide concludes that the accrual basis of accounting is normally necessary for financial statements prepared in accordance with generally accepted accounting principles. Investment income should be recorded on an accrual basis unless unrecorded amounts would not be material. Also, revenues and expenditures relating to a summer session should be reported in the fiscal year in which the summer session principally occurs.

Encumbrance Accounting

Implicit in the use of accrual basis accounting is the presumption that the only amounts to be recorded as expenditures will be those for which materials or services have been received and used as of the balance sheet date. Some institutions in the past have followed a governmental accounting approach in which expenditures were charged at the time purchase orders or other commitments were issued, without regard to the actual date of receipt. This is another form of "appropriation" accounting which is discussed in detail on pages 47–52.

The Guide states quite clearly that encumbrance accounting is not acceptable and that such amounts should not be reported either as expenditures or as liabilities in the Balance Sheet. If the institution wishes to designate or allocate a portion of the current unrestricted fund balance, it may do so but such designation would appear only in the fund balance section of the Balance Sheet.*

Unrestricted Gifts

All unrestricted gifts, donations, and bequests are recorded as revenue in the current unrestricted fund in the year received. While the board is free to designate any portions of such unrestricted gifts or bequests as "board-designated endowment," such gifts must nonetheless be reported initially in the current unrestricted fund. After being so reported, these

---

* See page 184 for a discussion of fund balance designations.

amounts may then be transferred by the board, as it wishes, to the endowment and similar funds.

Current Restricted Gifts

Restricted gifts for current purposes are reported in their entirety in the Statement of Changes in Fund Balances. However, as has been previously discussed, the amount of current restricted gifts reported as revenues in the Statement of Current Funds Revenues, Expenditures, and Other Changes would be only the amount which had been actually expended for such restricted purposes during the year. Thus, depending on the statement being looked at, the reader would see either the total amount received during the year or the total amount which had actually been expended.

Other Restricted Gifts

All other categories of legally restricted gifts would be reported directly in the fund to which they applied. If a donor made a contribution to the endowment fund it would be reported directly in that fund (assuming that the donor had made clear the intention, presumably in writing).

Pledges

The Guide is flexible with respect to handling pledges. The institution may record such amounts but if the institution elects not to do so, it must disclose in the footnotes the amount of uncollected pledges as of the financial statement date if they are material.

Investment Income from Unrestricted Funds

All investment income (dividends and interest) must be reported directly in the current unrestricted fund in the revenues section. Prior to the issuance of the Guide the use of an income stabilization reserve was permitted. This is no longer considered acceptable and all investment income must be reported in the year in which earned.

Endowment fund investment income is normally considered unrestricted income unless the donor has specified the restricted use for which the investment income is to be used. Accordingly, unrestricted endowment fund income should be reported directly in the current unrestricted fund.

Restricted Investment Income

All restricted investment income would be reported directly in the fund to which such investment income pertains. For example, the investment income from surplus plant funds temporarily invested would normally be reported in the plant fund.

Gains or Losses on Investments

Gains or losses (and appreciation or depreciation where investments are carried at market; see below) are normally considered adjustments of the carrying value of the investment and are reported in the Statement of Changes in Fund Balances in the fund holding the investment which gave rise to the gain. This means, therefore, that gains on board-designated endowment funds which are reported as part of the "endowment and similar funds" would be reported in that fund in the revenues and other additions section of the Statement of Changes in Fund Balances.

Where an organization carries its investments at market, the unrealized appreciation or depreciation would be reported in the same manner as the realized gains or losses.

Carrying Value of Investments

The Guide provides that a college or university can carry its investments at either market or cost. Previously investments could be carried only at cost or, in the case of donated securities, at the fair market value at the date of receipt. This is an important change which many institutions will want to consider carefully. If an institution so elects, however, it must carry all of its investments at market. It cannot carry some at market and some at cost.*

Total Return Concept

Where the board wishes to transfer some of the realized or unrealized gains on endowment and similar fund investments to the current unrestricted fund (and assuming the board has the legal right to do so)

---

* It should be noted that the Statement of Position discussed in Chapter 16 makes a distinction between marketable and nonmarketable investments. It provides that both marketable and nonmarketable investments may be carried at either market or lower of cost or market, and that the carrying value selected for one class of investments (i.e., marketable) need not be the same as the carrying value selected for another class of investments (i.e., nonmarketable).

the transfer must be shown in the nonmandatory transfer section of the Statement of Current Funds Revenues, Expenditures, and Other Changes. In the Statement of Changes in Fund Balances the transfer would also be shown in the transfer section. It is not permissible to treat this transfer as income in the revenue section in either statement. This can be seen in Figure 14–1 where a transfer of $40,000 from the endowment and similar funds has been reported in the current unrestricted fund. For a more complete discussion of the accounting under the total return concept, see pages 88–95.

Fixed Asset Accounting

The Guide follows the CUBA approach to handling fixed assets and requires that all fixed asset purchases be capitalized and carried on the Balance Sheet. This means that a college or university cannot "expense" its fixed asset purchases in the year in which acquired.

Depreciation Accounting

The Guide reaffirms the position historically taken by colleges and universities of not following depreciation accounting procedures. The Guide in discussing depreciation states:

Depreciation expense related to depreciable assets comprising the physical plant is reported neither in the statement of current funds revenues, expenditures, and other changes nor in the statemnt of changes in unrestricted current funds balance. The reason for this treatment is that these statements present expenditures and transfers of current funds rather than operating expenses in conformity with the reporting objectives of accounting for resources received and used rather than the determination of net income. Depreciation allowance, however, may be reported in the balance sheet and the provision for depreciation reported in the statement of changes in the balance of the investment-in-plant fund subsection of the plant funds group.*

This statement, of course, very succinctly states that it is not the Guide's intention to present financial statements that will show the cost of operations, and therefore there is no need to report depreciation. The authors disagree with this conclusion.

It should be observed, however, that in the last sentence quoted above provision has been made for reporting of depreciation in the plant fund column of the Statement of Changes in Fund Balances. Where depreciation is so reported and where a total-all-funds column is also presented,

* Pages 9–10 of the Guide.

effectively depreciation is presented in the financial statements as a whole. This can be seen in Figure 14–4.

SIMPLIFIED SET OF STATEMENTS

The principles of accounting and reporting presented so far in this chapter are those recommended by the Guide, and are followed by most colleges and universities. While the format is technically correct, in the authors' opinion these statements are deficient in that the average reader, not knowledgeable in either accounting or college reporting, will have considerable difficulty in understanding exactly what has taken place during the year. A large part of the difficulty arises because of the use of separate columns for each fund, normally without a total column, making it difficult for the reader to see an overall picture. This derives from the legal accountability such institutions have to see that funds entrusted to them for specific uses are expended in the manner designated by the donor. This legal accountability, however, does not mean that.the institution must report to the public on a detailed separate-statement basis for each fund grouping. There is no reason why financial statements cannot be presented in a format which will permit the reader to see the overall picture.*

The premise that a set of financial statements for a college should not show results of operations certainly has to be questioned. True, the college is not expected to make a "profit" in the commercial sense, but it is expected over a period of time to take in enough money to be able to sustain its operations. If it doesn't, clearly it is headed for serious trouble. It may very well be that the financial plight that many private institu-

---

* Other accountants have also indicated the need for an overall financial statement that shows the total operations of the entity in a meaningful manner. In a report of the Committee on Accounting Practice on Not-for-Profit Organizations of the American Accounting Association published in early 1971 that Committee stated on page 137:

"Another significant shortcoming of financial statements in the college and university and municipal areas, as measured against the standard of relevance, can be characterized as the lack of emphasis on organizational reporting. As noted in the preceding section, these organizations emphasize fund entity accountability in most instances almost to the complete exclusion of over-all accountability for the organization.

"A fundamental objective of accounting should be that of disclosing how a group of resources directed by a co-ordinated managerial group has been used to accomplish the goals of the entity. Since the upper level management group in all instances is responsible for the performance of the organization as a whole—and because externally interested groups must evaluate it as a whole—it seems imperative that these organizations develop reporting practices that would draw the elements of the financial data together in a meaningful manner for the total operating entity."

tions are presently in can be traced, at least in part, to financial reporting that really does not tell it "as it is."

Further, college financial statements as prescribed in the Guide give very little useful information to the reader or trustee as to the costs of operating the institution. Most institutions, for example, have a number of educational programs—different colleges within the university, different departments, etc. It would appear that the trustees should be told what the costs are for each type of major program of the institution; otherwise, though they are charged with the responsibility for the institution, they have no way of really making a judgment.*

An All-Inclusive Statement of Activities

Figure 14–4 shows an all-inclusive Statement of Revenues, Expenses, and Changes in Fund Balances for Mary and Isla College. A number of things should be noted about this statement.

Restricted versus Unrestricted.   Observe that we have included, on this all-inclusive statement, activities broken out in only two categories: unrestricted and restricted. Included in the restricted column are all funds which are restricted by outside persons. This includes current restricted funds, loan funds, true endowment funds, and plant funds which have been restricted by others (other than the investment in plant itself). Investment in plant has been included in the unrestricted fund column because these assets are available for the purposes for which the institution was formed—that is, for educational purposes. Whatever restrictions were originally attached to the contributions which were used to purchase these assets have been fulfilled by virtue of the purchase of these assets. Accordingly, fixed assets have been considered "unrestricted." †

The advantage of this simplified presentation with only two categories of funds—unrestricted and restricted—is that the reader quickly sees the total activity without a lot of potentially confusing detail. At the same time there is full disclosure that certain of the revenues and expenses during the year resulted from transactions over which the board had only partial control.

Total Column.   Another striking feature of this statement is that we have combined the unrestricted and restricted columns to show a total

* It is perhaps of interest that Price Waterhouse & Co., in a major policy paper in 1975 urged that colleges and universities prepare financial statements following the same approach recommended in this section. Further, Price Waterhouse & Co. indicated they would give an unqualified opinion on financial statements prepared in this format.

† This is the same position taken in the hospital Audit Guide. See Chapter 15.

MARY AND ISLA COLLEGE

STATEMENT OF REVENUES, EXPENSES, AND CHANGES IN FUND BALANCES

For the Year Ended June 30, 19X1

	Unrestricted	Restricted	Total
Operating revenues:			
Tuition and fees	$ 1,610,000		$ 1,610,000
Governmental appropriations . .	400,000		400,000
Research grants		$ 190,000	190,000
Auxiliary activities	125,000		125,000
Total operating revenues . .	2,135,000	190,000	2,325,000
Operating expenses:			
Educational:			
Engineering	930,000		930,000
Arts	410,000		410,000
Business	625,000		625,000
Research.	300,000	550,000	850,000
Supporting:			
Administrative	495,000		495,000
Fund raising.	90,000		90,000
Auxiliary activities	95,000		95,000
Total operating expenses . .	2,945,000	550,000	3,495,000
Excess of operating expenses over revenues . .	(810,000)	(360,000)	(1,170,000)
Other revenues:			
Gifts and bequests	900,000	635,000	1,535,000
Investment income	350,000	47,000	397,000
Realized and unrealized appreciation.		150,000	150,000
Total other revenues.	1,250,000	832,000	2,082,000
Excess of revenues over expenses	440,000	472,000	912,000
Fund balance, beginning of year. .	26,671,000	1,838,000	28,509,000
Transfer between funds	(220,000)	220,000	
Fund balance, end of year	$26,891,000	$2,530,000	$29,421,000

Fig. 14—4. An example of an all-inclusive Statement of Revenues, Expenses, and Changes in Fund Balances, in the format recommended by the authors.

column. This helps the reader to see total activity for the year. There are many valid arguments for not including such a total, but, as the authors have indicated elsewhere, these arguments are not as important as the need for the reader to see the total picture of the institution. In this instance, it is hard to imagine a reader not understanding that certain of the revenues and expenses shown are restricted and not available for unrestricted use.

Functional Reporting.   This statement is set up on a functional basis; that is, all expenses have been classified by the program or function which the funds have been used to accomplish. The principal purpose of a college is, of course, educational. Note that we have clearly indicated the amounts which have been spent directly for this purpose, and we have broken these amounts into three categories to represent the three individual programs offered by Mary and Isla College (i.e., engineering, arts, and business). Also, we have indicated the amounts spent on research, another major program of this institution. Certain expenses are related to the overall administration of the school and these are also shown separately, as are fund-raising expenses.

Depreciation.   Although it is not obvious from this statement, we have included $500,000 of depreciation as an expense and allocated this expense among the various programs. There are many arguments for and against depreciation but once it is concluded that a set of statements should attempt to reflect the "cost" of performing a particular service the question becomes basically moot. Depreciation is a cost and should be reflected. Otherwise the trustees are only kidding themselves if they think they know what each of the college's programs is costing.*

The college Audit Guide provides for institutions to record debt service (i.e., repayment of principal and interest) as a charge to the current unrestricted fund. Debt repayment is not an "expense" as generally thought of, and this has been eliminated in the simplified financial statements. Likewise, since we have included a depreciation charge of $500,000, the simplified statements exclude the "write off" of fixed assets of $85,000 reflected in Figure 14–1.

Excess of Revenues over Expenses.   Included on this statement is clear indication of what the excess of revenues over expenses was for the year. This is in keeping with the authors' strong belief that the trustees and other interested readers must know what the net results were for the year. Not to do so is sticking one's head in the sand and pretending that

---

* See Chapter 7 for a more complete treatment of the pros and cons of recording depreciation. Also, see page 181 for discussion of this topic in the Audit Guide for voluntary health and welfare organizations.

MARY AND

STATEMENT OF

For the Year

	Educational		
	Engineering	Arts	Business
Salaries and related benefits	$ 450,000	$ 180,000	$ 350,000
Scholarships	50,000	10,000	20,000
Operation of physical plant, exclusive			
of depreciation and salaries	150,000	100,000	100,000
Depreciation	200,000	70,000	95,000
Library books	30,000	10,000	10,000
Supplies	40,000	30,000	40,000
Interest			
Other	10,000	10,000	10,000
Total	$ 930,000	$ 410,000	$ 625,000
Student population	350	250	300
Cost per student	$ 2,657	$ 1,640	$ 2,083

*Excluding fund raising and research.

Fig. 14–5.   An example of a Functional Analysis of

the principles of survival applicable to all organizations somehow do not apply to a college or a university.

Operating Revenue Excludes Other Revenue.   In this statement we have reported gifts and investment income after reporting operating revenue and expenses, to assist the reader in seeing what the results of operations were, exclusive of such other, nonoperating revenue. Note that this "other revenue" is reported before the caption "Excess of revenues over expenses."

Restricted Grants Recorded in Year Received.   The college Audit Guide provides for reporting in the Statement of Current Funds Revenues, Expenditures, and Other Changes restricted revenues only to the extent expended during the year. This, of course, causes considerable confusion, as has been previously noted. In Figure 14–4 restricted income is reported in the year received unless the terms of the restriction are such that the funds could not have been expended during that year.*

Transfers Between Funds.   By including all unrestricted funds in a single column, the number of transfers between funds has been signifi-

* See Chapter 9 for a more complete description of the principles of recognizing revenues in the year in which they were received.

ISLA COLLEGE

FUNCTIONAL EXPENSES
Ended June 30, 19X1

| | | Supporting | | |
Research	Administrative	Fund Raising	Auxiliary Activities	Total Expenses
$720,000	$275,000	$40,000	$30,000	$2,045,000
				80,000
70,000	50,000	10,000	20,000	500,000
50,000	50,000	25,000	10,000	500,000
				50,000
10,000	40,000	15,000	25,000	200,000
	50,000			50,000
	30,000		10,000	70,000
$850,000	$495,000	$90,000	$95,000	$3,495,000
	900		900	900
	$ 550		$ 105	$ 2,839*

Expenses in the format recommended by the authors.

cantly reduced. In this instance the only transfer reported is the amount required to be set aside in a restricted fund under the debt agreement.

Functional Analysis of Expenses

Figure 14–5 provides an analysis of the natural expense categories going into the functional expenses reported on the Statement of Revenues, Expenses, and Changes in Fund Balances (Figure 14–4).

Note that each of the functional categories on the Statement of Revenues, Expenses, and Changes in Fund Balances appears also on the Statement of Functional Expenses and that the figures on both statements agree with each other in total.

For simplicity in presentation, the number of natural expense categories has been somewhat limited in this illustration. Nevertheless, the reader is given considerable information about the natural expenses which go into each of the functional categories. This gives the reader a chance to judge as to the appropriateness of these amounts.

Comparison with Prior Years. We have not shown a comparison with the previous year's figures but this could have been done. Typically there would have been a second "total expenses" column for the natural expense category comparison with the preceding year. Likewise, the unit cost information at the bottom of this report would also have been presented for the preceding year.

Unit Cost Information. Another important piece of information contained on this statement is a unit cost of providing educational and supporting services for each of the several functional categories. While one might argue whether these particular unit cost data are *the* appropriate data for this institution, they should give the reader an indication of the kinds of information which can be presented on a unit cost basis.°

Balance Sheet

Figure 14–6 shows the Balance Sheet for Mary and Isla College. It follows the basic presentation shown for the Statement of Revenues, Expenses, and Changes in Fund Balances.†

It should be observed that the fund balance section of this statement breaks out the unrestricted and restricted fund balances according to the purposes for which they are to be used. Note that in the unrestricted fund balance we have indicated the amount invested in plant assets ($23,450,000) and the amount in investment funds ($3,010,000). This aids the reader in seeing how the fund balance is being utilized. Observe, also, that the amount available for current use is only $431,000.

Again, many would take exception to the use of the total column reported on this statement. Nevertheless the authors feel that it is appropriate for the trustees or other interested readers to see the total resources available.

Statement of Changes in Financial Position

These simplified statements are deficient in one particular respect. They do not provide the reader with information on financial transactions

° In presenting unit cost information on this statement, the authors do not intend to imply that this suggestion is something new. Many studies have been made in the past to develop appropriate unit cost measurements.

† The reader is cautioned against trying to compare this Balance Sheet with the one shown in Figure 14–2. While the ending fund balance (for all funds) has been deliberately shown in both statements as $29,421,000, this has been merely for purposes of illustration, to make the reader's job somewhat easier. In reality the two amounts would not be the same because we are applying different accounting principles. For example, depreciation is being recorded in this revised format and this would result in a lower "fund balance." Also we have, again deliberately, shown our net plant assets as the same amount in both statements whereas in the earlier statement this amount was the gross amount; in Figure 14–6 it is the "net" amount after applying the accumulated depreciation.

MARY AND ISLA COLLEGE
BALANCE SHEET
June 30, 19X1

	Unrestricted	Restricted	Total
ASSETS			
Current assets:			
Cash	$ 1,220,000	$ 381,000	$ 1,601,000
Short-term investments	1,480,000		1,480,000
Accounts receivable	18,000		18,000
Student loans		80,000	80,000
Other current assets	45,000		45,000
Total current assets	2,763,000	461,000	3,224,000
Long-term investments			
(at market)	2,146,000	2,069,000	4,215,000
Plant assets:			
Land	500,000		500,000
Land improvements	2,900,000		2,900,000
Buildings	29,675,000		29,675,000
Equipment	4,660,000		4,660,000
	37,735,000		37,735,000
Accumulated depreciation. . . .	(14,285,000)		(14,285,000)
Net plant assets	23,450,000		23,450,000
Total assets	$28,359,000	$2,530,000	$30,889,000
LIABILITIES AND FUND BALANCES			
Current liabilities:			
Accounts payable.	$ 608,000		$ 608,000
Tuition deposits	110,000		110,000
Current portion of long-term			
debt	170,000		170,000
Total current liabilities . . .	888,000		888,000
Long-term debt, due 19X2-X5,	580,000		580,000
Total liabilities	1,468,000		1,468,000
Fund balances:			
Available for current use.	431,000		431,000
Invested in plant assets.	23,450,000		23,450,000
Endowment funds	3,010,000	$2,025,000	5,035,000
Other restricted funds		505,000	505,000
Total fund balances	26,891,000	2,530,000	29,421,000
Total liabilities and fund			
balances.	$28,359,000	$2,530,000	$30,889,000

Fig. 14–6. An example of a columnar Balance Sheet in the format recommended by the authors.

not affecting revenues, expenses, or the fund balance that took place during the year. For example, there is no information on resources used for acquisition of plant, or detail on how such acquisitions were financed. On the other hand, the AICPA Audit Guide Statement of Changes in Fund Balances (Figure 14–1) clearly provides this type of information.

Where significant nonrevenue or nonexpense transactions occur, consideration should be given to either including details of such transactions in a footnote or including a separate Statement of Changes in Financial Position. The Statement of Changes in Financial Position is not illustrated because it is a format widely used by profit-oriented organizations in their financial statements. Readers wishing more information on this format should refer to APB Opinion Number 19.

Conclusion

Undoubtedly these revised simplified statements have weaknesses, particularly when viewed from the perspective of traditional college financial statement presentations. However, the authors believe that present college financial statements are seriously deficient because most nonaccountant readers cannot understand them. Since the purpose of financial statements must be to communicate, thoughtful college trustees should encourage their business managers to experiment with simpler presentations, perhaps along the lines suggested above.

15

Hospitals

A very important nonprofit institution that has not been discussed so far is the hospital.* By and large hospitals tend to be more complex than other nonprofit organizations because they effectively operate a number of separate but related businesses all within the hospital framework. Yet in spite of their greater complexity, the financial and reporting problems of nonprofit hospitals are in very large measure similar to those of other large nonprofit organizations. Their similarity lies principally in their common problem of presenting meaningful financial statements, and in their need to communicate with the general public.† Fund accounting is normally used by voluntary nonprofit hospitals and as with most organizations using fund accounting, there is often difficulty in preparing statements in a straightforward manner that will allow readers to see the overall financial picture in a clear and concise manner. Unlike most nonprofit organizations, hospitals vitally affect the lives of the general public and are coming under increasing public pressure and governmental control. The fact that a hospital's activities are complex doesn't mean that the financial statements must be complex or hard to understand.

Hospitals are also faced with reporting to groups other than contributors because a substantial amount of their resources comes from

* Not all hospitals are nonprofit. There are about 850 proprietary hospitals out of a total of about 7,100. These proprietary hospitals are smaller in size with an average of about 70 beds each. About 2,650 hospitals are local, state, and federal institutions and the balance of 3,600 are nonprofit, nongovernmental.

† Hospitals also raise funds from the general public but a decreasing proportion of their total revenue comes from this source. About 90% of their revenue comes from patient revenue, including Blue Cross and governmental assistance.

third-party arrangements such as Blue Cross, Medicare, Medicaid, etc. This also influences financial reporting.

In 1972 the Committee on Health Care Institutions of the American Institute of Certified Public Accountants issued an Audit Guide recommending auditing and reporting standards to be followed by independent auditors in making examinations of the financial statements of hospitals.* Included in this Guide is a discussion of accounting principles and reporting standards that should be applied to all hospitals. While some hospitals were not following all of these principles at the time issued, this Guide represents an important pronouncement on hospital accounting and financial statements, and all hospitals that have audits made by certified public accountants will be expected to adopt these principles.† This chapter summarizes the accounting and reporting principles outlined in this Guide.

The principles of accounting and reporting presented in this Guide are, in the authors' opinion, applicable to most nonprofit organizations as well as to hospitals. Many of the principles of accounting recommended in earlier chapters are included in this Guide. Furthermore, while the form of reporting is not in the authors' recommended columnar format, it is relatively straightforward, particularly when compared to the form of reporting used by many nonprofit organizations. While there are still a few accounting and reporting principles that may be disagreed with,** this Guide goes a long way toward presenting the financial activities of a nonprofit organization in a meaningful and straightforward manner.

---

* In 1978, the AICPA issued a second edition of the Hospital Audit Guide; in addition to reproducing the first edition of the Guide, the second edition includes the Statements of Position *Clarification of Accounting, Auditing, and Reporting Practices Relating to Hospital Malpractice Loss Contingencies* (1978), and *Accounting by Hospitals for Certain Marketable Equity Securities* (1978).

† See page 304 for a discussion of the authority of an Audit Guide.

** The principal disputed area is the use of a separate Statement of Changes in Fund Balances in which all restricted fund activities are reported. The authors believe it preferable to show all such activity in a single Statement of Revenue, Expenses, and Changes in Fund Balances, in a columnar format. An example of this presentation is shown in Figure 15–5. As will be discussed, if this approach were followed the principle of recognizing restricted fund income only to the extent expended would, of course, not be appropriate since such unexpended income would be reported in the restricted fund column. Another change that the authors recommend is reporting contributed plant and equipment as nonoperating income in the Statement of Revenue and Expenses rather than as an addition to the unrestricted fund balance in the Statement of Changes in Fund Balances. Notwithstanding the above comments, the Guide on the whole represents an important step in defining accounting principles and reporting techniques that will go a long way toward strengthening nonprofit reporting.

FUND ACCOUNTING

Fund accounting is usually followed since hospitals receive restricted gifts and endowments. The fund groupings provided in the Guide differ somewhat from the fund groupings most nonprofit organizations have traditionally followed. The principal difference is that only two major fund groupings are permitted: the unrestricted fund and restricted funds. Here are the fund groupings:

Unrestricted Fund	Restricted Funds
Current	Specific Purposes
Board-Designated	Plant Replacement and Expansion
Plant	Endowment

While the unrestricted fund is divided into three parts, they are not individually considered separate funds. There is only one unrestricted fund and that is the total of the three parts. All reporting for the unrestricted fund is on the total of the three parts. The three restricted funds, however, are reported separately for each subgrouping. Here is a description of each of the funds.

Unrestricted Fund

All funds not restricted by donors or outside parties are included in this fund grouping. The unrestricted fund may be divided into the following three parts.

Current. The current portion represents the working capital of the hospital. The amounts included in this subgrouping are the unallocated general funds of the institution. Generally the current portion will consist of current assets, current liabilities, and any deferred credits.

Board-Designated. All board-designated assets are included in this subgrouping, including board-designated endowment or investment assets, board-designated assets for specific purposes and board-designated plant replacement assets.

Plant. The plant portion represents the actual investment in plant assets, land, building, leasehold improvements, and equipment. It should be particularly noted that the plant portion is included as part of the unrestricted fund grouping because the segregation of plant assets into a separate fund implies the existence of restrictions on their use or disposition. Also if plant assets were shown as part of the restricted fund grouping there would be mechanical problems of showing short- and

JOHNSTOWN

BALANCE SHEET
December 31

ASSETS

UNRESTRICTED

Current assets (in total)	$ 1,500,000
Board-designated funds:	
Cash	50,000
Investments	475,000
Property, plant and equipment	10,000,000
Less depreciation	(4,400,000)
Total	$ 7,625,000

RESTRICTED

Specific-purpose

Cash	$ 100,000

Plant replacement and

Cash	25,000
Investments	100,000
Pledges	75,000
	$ 200,000

Endowment

Cash	$ 25,000
Investments	5,000,000
	$ 5,025,000

Fig. 15–1. An example of a Balance Sheet in the

long-term liabilities related to such assets without distorting working capital. In addition, there is the usual problem of presenting depreciation when funds are separated.

Restricted Funds

All contributions, gifts or income which are restricted by the donor or grantor (as distinct from the board) are included in this fund grouping. Three subgroupings are used.

Specific Purposes Fund. All donor-restricted funds other than plant or endowment are placed in this fund until such time as the restrictions lapse, either through passage of time or by the expenditure for the

HOSPITAL

(CONDENSED)

19X2

LIABILITIES AND FUND BALANCES

FUNDS

Current liabilities (in total)	$1,200,000
Deferred third-party reimbursement	100,000
Long-term debt	400,000
Fund balance	5,925,000
Total	$7,625,000

FUNDS

<u>fund</u>

Fund balances.	$ 100,000

<u>expansion fund</u>

Fund balance	$ 200,000
	$ 200,000

<u>fund</u>

Fund balances:

Permanent	$4,500,000
Term	525,000
	$5,025,000

format recommended for hospitals by the Guide.

specified purpose. At that time such funds are transferred to the unrestricted fund. This is discussed under "restricted contributions" below.

Plant Replacement and Expansion Funds. All restricted cash and other assets given to the hospital for plant or fixed asset purchases are included in this fund. Revenue received from third parties who specify that part of the revenue is to be used for plant additions will also be transferred into this fund. Note that the plant assets themselves are not included in this fund; only cash and other assets that will eventually be used to purchase plant assets are included.

Endowment Funds. All donor-designated gifts that are to be held for the production of income are included in this fund. Such endowments may be permanent in nature or may be term endowments. Term endowments should be disclosed separately in the financial statements and taken into income when the term expires.

FINANCIAL STATEMENTS

Four primary financial statements are used by hospitals:

Balance Sheet
Statement of Revenue and Expenses
Statement of Changes in Fund Balances
Statement of Changes in Financial Position

In addition to these four statements, additional supplementary schedules may be appropriate for certain of the users of the statements. These schedules might include Patient Service Revenue, Expense by Functional Divisions, etc.

Balance Sheet

As previously noted, there are two principal fund groupings—unrestricted and restricted. The Balance Sheet of a hospital therefore shows these two groupings separately. Figure 15–1 shows an example of the layout of the Balance Sheet in somewhat abbreviated form.

It should be noted that on this Balance Sheet there is a single fund balance figure representing all unrestricted funds. The reader does not have to wonder what the total resources available to the board are. It is clearly shown. At the same time, the Guide suggests that the composition of the unrestricted fund be shown. On a less abbreviated balance sheet the composition could be shown right on the statement. For example, in our illustration this would look like this:

Fund balances:	
Unallocated	$ 200,000
Board-designated investment fund	300,000
Board-designated specific operating purposes	125,000
Board-designated equipment fund	100,000
Property, plant and equipment	5,200,000
	$5,925,000

Alternatively, this information could be shown at the bottom of the Statement of Changes in Fund Balances, or possibly in the notes to the financial statements. The important thing, however, is that the reader sees a total of all these unrestricted resources. Normally it is not necessary to include a separate statement showing the changes in these individual elements making up the total unrestricted fund balance since these internal actions have no significance except as they affect the balances at the end of the year.

The restricted funds are themselves broken down into three self-balancing subfund groupings. Notice that the "plant replacement and expansion fund" contains no plant assets. This fund merely accumulates restricted funds until such time as they are used for actual plant purchases. At that time the amount involved is transferred to the unrestricted fund.

Statement of Revenue and Expenses

Figure 15–2 shows an example of the Statement of Revenue and Expenses contemplated by the Guide. This statement is easy to read

---

JOHNSTOWN HOSPITAL
STATEMENT OF REVENUE AND EXPENSES
For the Year Ended December 31, 19X2

Patient service revenue	$5,000,000
Allowance and uncollectable accounts (after deduction of related gifts of $30,000)	(1,000,000)
Net patient service revenue	4,000,000
Other operating revenue (including $50,000 from specific-purpose funds)	100,000
Total operating revenue	4,100,000
Operating expenses:	
Nursing services	1,800,000
Other professional services	1,300,000
General services	1,000,000
Fiscal services	200,000
Administrative services (including interest of $18,000)	500,000
Provision for depreciation	200,000
Total operating expenses	5,000,000
Loss from operations	(900,000)
Nonoperating revenue:	
Unrestricted gifts and bequests	600,000
Unrestricted income from endowment funds	300,000
Income and gains from Board-designated funds	50,000
Total nonoperating revenue	950,000
Excess of Revenue over Expenses	$ 50,000

Fig. 15–2. An example of a Statement of Revenue and Expenses in the format recommended for hospitals by the Guide.

and understand because it shows all unrestricted income on one state-ment with a minimum of confusing detail. Notice the simplicity of the basic arrangement:

Patient Revenue	$ 4,000,000
Other Operating Revenue	100,000
Operating Expenses	(5,000,000)
Nonoperating Revenue	950,000
Excess of Revenues over Expenses	$ 50,000

Since this statement includes all unrestricted revenues and expenses there should be a minimum of reader confusion resulting from the use of fund accounting.*

Statement of Changes in Fund Balances

The third basic statement for hospitals shows the changes in fund balances for all fund groupings. Figure 15–3 shows an example of this statement in the format recommended in the Guide. Figure 15–4 shows the same statement in the format preferred by the authors, where a columnar format is used.

Some of the transfers on this statement may confuse the reader: first, the transfer from the plant replacement and expansion fund to the unrestricted fund of $100,000, and second, the transfer from the un-restricted fund to the plant replacement fund of $75,000. The basic concept is that all plant fund assets belong on the unrestricted fund statement, but cash and other assets restricted by others should be carried in a separate restricted fund until expended. At the time these funds are used to purchase fixed assets the amount must then be trans-ferred to the unrestricted fund balance. The reverse is true where por-tions of operating revenue have been restricted, usually by third-party payors, for fixed asset additions. An example would be where Blue Cross allowed in the rate reimbursement formula an amount which the hos-pital could expend only for certain types of medical equipment. The full amount received from Blue Cross is initially recorded in the unre-

---

* An alternative columnar format of the Statement of Revenue and Expenses is provided in the Guide. In this format, three columns and a total column are provided. The three columns are headed: "operations" "other," and "plant." The total column would show the same amounts as in Figure 15–2. The purpose of this alternative for-mat is to provide detail on these unrestricted funds. The authors do not recommend this alternative approach since these extra columns tend to complicate the statement presentation without providing meaningful information.

JOHNSTOWN HOSPITAL
STATEMENT OF CHANGES IN FUND BALANCES

	Year Ended December 31,	
	19X2	19X1

UNRESTRICTED FUNDS

Balance, beginning of the year	$5,750,000	$5,630,000
Excess of revenue over expenses	50,000	80,000
Donated medical equipment	100,000	10,000
Transferred from plant replacement and expansion fund to finance property, plant and equipment expenditures	100,000	80,000
Transfers to plant replacement and expansion fund to reflect third-party payor revenue	(75,000)	(50,000)
Balance, end of the year	$5,925,000	$5,750,000

RESTRICTED FUNDS

Specific-purpose fund:

Balance, beginning of the year	$ 80,000	$ 75,000
Restricted gifts and bequests	65,000	45,000
Net gain on sale of investments	5,000	—
Transferred to other operating revenue and to offset allowances	(50,000)	(40,000)
Balance, end of the year	$ 100,000	$ 80,000

Plant replacement and expansion fund:

Balance, beginning of the year	$ 95,000	$ 85,000
Restricted gifts and bequests	100,000	25,000
Income from investments	10,000	10,000
Net gain on sale of investments	20,000	5,000
Transferred to unrestricted funds	(100,000)	(80,000)
Transferred from unrestricted funds	75,000	50,000
Balance, end of the year	$ 200,000	$ 95,000

Endowment fund:

Balance, beginning of the year	$4,825,000	$4,645,000
Restricted gifts and bequests	100,000	150,000
Net gains on sale of investments	100,000	30,000
Balance, end of the year	$5,025,000	$4,825,000

Fig. 15–3. An example of a Statement of Changes in Fund Balances in the format recommended for hospitals by the Guide.

JOHNSTOWN HOSPITAL

STATEMENT OF CHANGES IN FUND BALANCES
For the Year Ended December 31, 19X2

	Unrestricted	Specific Purposes	Restricted Plant Replacement and Expansion	Endowment
Balance, beginning of the year	$5,750,000	$ 80,000	$ 95,000	$4,825,000
Excess of revenue over expenses	50,000			
Restricted gifts and bequests		65,000	100,000	100,000
Donated medical equipment	100,000		10,000	
Income from investments		5,000	20,000	100,000
Net gain on sale of investments				
Additions to plant fund from plant replacement and expansion fund	100,000		(100,000)	
Portion of reimbursement of third-party payors restricted to replacement of equipment	(75,000)		75,000	
Transferred to other operating revenue and to offset allowances		(50,000)		
Balance, end of the year	$5,925,000	$100,000	$200,000	$5,025,000

Fig. 15-4. An example of a columnar Statement of Changes in Fund Balances in the format preferred by the authors.

stricted fund as operating revenue since services have been provided which gave rise to the income. The portion of this revenue that is restricted by Blue Cross for medical equipment is then transferred to the restricted plant replacement and expansion fund until expended.

Statement of Changes in Financial Position

The fourth basic statement recommended by the Guide for hospitals is the Statement of Changes in Financial Position for the unrestricted fund.

The accounting profession requires that a Statement of Changes in Financial Position or its equivalent be included as a basic financial statement for profit-oriented entities. An illustration of a Statement of Changes in Financial Position is shown on page 278.

ACCOUNTING PRINCIPLES

Generally Accepted Accounting Principles

Generally accepted accounting principles are applicable to hospitals. As a result, the opinions of the Accounting Principles Board and its successor, the FASB, are also applicable to hospitals except where they are clearly inappropriate, and hospitals must conform their accounting practices to such opinions in order to receive unqualified opinions from their CPAs.

Accrual Basis

The accrual basis of accounting should be used by hospitals. This means that a number of valuation reserves must be established. Hospitals, for example, normally record all receivables for patient services at the gross amount of the billing. In a substantial number of instances the hospital will ultimately settle the bill for a lesser amount. Part of this lesser settlement will be because of charity cases, and part will be because of special arrangements with third-party payors such as Blue Cross, Medicare, etc. Traditionally hospitals have recorded their receivables at the gross amount and then recorded the actual allowance at the time of settlement. Accrual accounting requires that an estimate of this allowance be set up at the time of billing. Accrual accounting also requires that receivables be recorded at the time services are rendered and not at the time the patient is discharged.

Accrual accounting requires that much the same type of valuation judgments be made for those contracts which are subject to periodic adjustment. The hospital must make its best estimate of these adjustments on a current basis and reflect these amounts in the Statement of Revenue and Expenses. To the extent that the subsequent actual adjustment is more or less than the estimate, such amount should be reflected in the accounts of the period in which the final adjustment becomes known.

Investment income should also be recorded on an accrual basis. The same is true with investment income from trusts held by outside trustees. That amount can also be estimated and should be recorded.

Unrestricted Contributions

Unrestricted contributions and bequests must be included as non-operating revenue in the Statement of Revenue and Expenses in the year received. It is not permissible for the board to place restrictions on these amounts and then to include them as restricted fund income. The donor is the only person who can place restrictions on gifts. If no legally binding restrictions are placed on the gift it must be reported in the Statement of Revenue and Expenses.

Restricted Contributions

Contributions and bequests restricted by the donor must be shown on the Statement of Changes in Fund Balances in the year received in the appropriate subfund. If the gift is for a current but restricted purpose, it is recorded in the restricted fund and then, as expended for the designated purpose, is transferred to the Statement of Revenue and Expenses. The mechanics of this transfer can be seen in Figures 15–2 and 15–3. Notice that in the Statement of Changes in Fund Balances $65,000 of restricted gifts and bequests have been received and added to the specific purposes fund; $50,000 has then been transferred from the specific purposes fund to the Statement of Revenue and Expenses and is recorded in that statement as part of "other operating revenue," and the $50,000 is shown parenthetically.

Term endowment gifts should also be included in the Statement of Changes in Fund Balances. At the time such term endowments become legally unrestricted, the amount of the term endowment (plus any capital gains accumulated therewith) should be shown as nonoperating income on the Statement of Revenue and Expenses.

Pledges

Pledges should be recorded, less an appropriate estimate for the uncollectible portion. Pledges made for unrestricted purposes should be recorded in the accounts in the same manner as any other unrestricted gift. Restricted pledges should be handled as restricted gifts.

Grants

Restricted grants should be treated as restricted contributions and be recorded in the Statement of Changes in Fund Balances. Unrestricted grants, or grants that by their terms are fully expended within the year of receipt, would be shown directly in the Statement of Revenue and Expenses. If the purpose of the grant is to provide for charity cases, then the grant should be netted against the "allowances and uncollectible accounts" line. This can be seen in Figure 15–2. If the grant is for a specific activity or function other than payment for services provided to specific patients, the grant would be shown as part of "other operating income." If the gift is for the general operations of the hospital and is not restricted in any way, it should be included as a nonoperating revenue.

Donated Services

Donated services should be recorded only when an employer–employee relationship exists and when there is an objective basis for valuing the services rendered. Thus the services of most volunteers are not recorded. There are many hospitals, however, run by religious organizations where the majority of the employees are unpaid. In that instance it is appropriate to record the value of these donated services.

Donated Materials

Donated materials that are normally purchased by the hospital should be recorded as operating revenue in the Statement of Revenue and Expenses. The use of these materials would be accounted for in the same manner as any purchased material.

Donated Property and Plant

Donated property, plant, and equipment should be recorded at fair market value on the Statement of Changes in Fund Balances as a direct addition to the Unrestricted Fund balance. It would not be recorded as a gift on the Statement of Revenue and Expenses. There is an example of this on the Statement of Changes in Fund Balances shown in Figure 15–3.

The reason why the Guide recommends recording here rather than on the Statement of Revenue and Expenses is, apparently, that such gifts, not being in the form of cash, are a form of restricted gift. As such the board does not have the same use of the gift as it would if it were in the form of cash. Since donated medical equipment, for example, could be sizable in any one year, many are concerned that such gifts would distort the Statement of Revenue and Expenses.

Investments

Investments in marketable equity securities should be carried at the lower of aggregate cost or market value, and investments in marketable debt securities at cost.* The market value of all investments should be shown parenthetically on the Balance Sheet or in the notes. If the aggregate market value of equity securities is less than cost, then cost should be written down to market.

A Statement of Position was issued by the AICPA in 1978 and it provides that reporting changes resulting from the write-down from cost to market is a function of both the *type* of fund—for example, unrestricted or restricted—that carries the marketable equity securities, and the *status* —current or noncurrent—of the investment. The write-down on unrestricted investments classified as current assets is reflected in the nonoperating revenue section of the Statement of Revenue and Expenses. The write-down on unrestricted investments classified as noncurrent assets, and the write-down on both current and noncurrent restricted investments, are reflected in the respective Statement of Changes in Fund Balances.†

Where investment funds are pooled, gains or losses and income should be distributed to each fund on the basis of the number of units each fund holds, and not on a cost basis. If unrestricted fund investments are pooled with restricted funds, income and gains and losses should be

---

* The Audit Guide for hospitals is in direct conflict with the guides for colleges and for voluntary health and welfare organizations, and with the Statement of Position (discussed in Chapter 16). The authors believe it is only a matter of time before this conflict is resolved and hospitals are also permitted or required to carry their investments at market.

† Statement of Position, *Accounting by Hospitals for Certain Marketable Equity Securities*, issued by the AICPA Subcommittee on Health Care Matters. See Chapter 18 for a discussion of the significance of Statements of Position.

distributed currently in order to record such amounts in the Statement of Revenue and Expenses.

Investment Income

Investment income from all unrestricted funds should be included in the nonoperating revenues section of the Statement of Revenue and Expenses. Investment income from endowments, which is not restricted by the terms of the endowment, should also be added to nonoperating revenue. Endowment income, which is restricted for a specific purpose, should be added to the restricted funds for specific purposes. Investment income on restricted funds for specific purposes and on the plant replacement and expansion fund is normally added to the restricted fund balances.

Capital Gains and Losses

Capital gains or losses on unrestricted funds should be recognized as nonoperating revenue in the year in which such gains or losses are realized. Gains or losses on restricted investment funds normally would be added to the principal of such funds on the Statement of Changes in Fund Balances. If, however, such gains on restricted funds are legally unrestricted, they would also be shown on the Statement of Revenue and Expenses.

Related Organizations

In recent years many hospitals have set up legally separate "foundations" whose purpose is primarily to raise funds for and in the name of the hospital. The primary motivation of setting up these separate organizations has been to insure that third-party payors could not insist that unrestricted gifts be used to reduce hospital costs subject to third-party reimbursement.

The accounting question that arises is whether the hospital's financial statements should reflect in some manner the activity and assets of this separate foundation. Obviously from the standpoint of hospital management the strong preference is not to, because of a concern that this will defeat the purpose of setting up the separate foundation. Unfortunately, this view ignores the facts of the situation—that is, the separate foundation exists to benefit the hospital and represents a resource available to it. Further, most donors will not even be aware of the separate existence of the foundation and therefore may very well be misled by the hospital's financial statements.

In 1981, the AICPA issued a Statement of Position * which addresses the issue of financial statement presentation by hospitals and related organizations. Although presentation of combined financial statements for the hospital and related organizations is not required, the Statement of Position does mandate disclosure in the hospital's financial statement footnotes of the existence of related organizations meeting certain criteria, and summary financial data about the related organizations. The authors believe that more informative financial statements result from the combination of controlled related organizations, which exist only to support the hospital, with the hospital, and recommend that hospitals prepare their financial statements on this basis.

Funds Held in Trust by Others

Occasionally a donor will give to an outside trustee an endowment fund, the income from which is to be given by the trustee to the hospital. Should these funds be combined with the financial statements of the hospital? If the principal is not controlled by the hospital, the answer is usually no; these funds should not be included in the balance sheet, although their existence should be disclosed. If the trustee is obligated to make distributions to the hospital, these distributions should be reported as investment income. If the trustee has discretion over distributions they should be reported as gifts or in such other manner as specified by the trust or trustee.

Property, Plant, and Equipment

Property, plant, and equipment should be recorded in the Unrestricted Fund at cost, or at fair market value in the case of donated property. Where historical cost records are not available an appraisal at "historical cost" should be made and these amounts recorded.

Depreciation

Depreciation should be recognized in hospital financial statements, and the amount of depreciation should be shown separately in the Statement of Revenue and Expenses.

Provision for Replacement

Provisions for replacement or expansion of plant are not charges against the Statement of Revenue and Expenses but represent a board

* See page 305 for a discussion of the significance of a Statement of Position.

decision to set aside certain funds for this purpose. Such provisions should be treated as allocations of the unrestricted fund balance. On the Balance Sheet such amounts would be shown as part of the board-designated funds. See the example in Figure 15–1.

Appropriations

Appropriations of the unrestricted fund balance can be made by the board at its discretion since there are no restrictions on the use of this fund.* Appropriations are, however, only designations of the unrestricted fund balances and should not be reflected as an expense in the Statement of Revenue and Expenses. All expenditures in subsequent periods for the purpose of the appropriation are handled in exactly the same manner as all other expenditures and are reported in the Statement of Revenue and Expenses. The assets representing the appropriation are shown as part of the board-designated funds on the asset side of the Balance Sheet.

Third Party Reimbursement Timing Differences

For purposes of calculating rate reimbursement from third parties, accelerated depreciation may be used whereas for financial statement purposes the straight line method may be followed. The use of accelerated depreciation in this circumstance results in a larger reimbursement in the early years. In subsequent years, when accelerated depreciation is less than straight line depreciation, the reverse is true. The amount of additional revenue arising from this accelerated method of depreciation for rate reimbursement purposes should be "deferred" and not recognized as income in the year received. This deferred income should be subsequently recognized over the years when the allowable depreciation for reimbursement purposes will be less than that for book purposes on a straight line basis.

The accounting principles followed are similar to those generally used in following deferred tax accounting. Of course, if depreciation does not directly enter in the reimbursement formula, as for example in a negotiated contract in which a factor for depreciation not based on actual costs is used, then timing differences do not arise and no deferral is necessary. Other types of timing differences.should also be accounted for on a deferred basis. Examples are pension costs and vacation accruals.

* See Chapter 5 for a full discussion of accounting for appropriations.

For example, using a very simple illustration, assume that an asset is purchased having a cost of $10,000, and a life of five years. The hospital depreciates this asset over a five-year period, and assuming no salvage value, charges depreciation of $2,000 a year. In the rate reimbursement formula for third-party payors, however, depreciation is taken on the accelerated sum-of-the-year's digits method.* This results in larger depreciation in the first several years, offset by lower depreciation in the last several. Here is a comparison of the depreciation on both bases:

Year	Straight Line Method	Sum-of-the-Year's Digits Method	Difference Book Greater (less)
1	$ 2,000	$ 3,333	($1,333)
2	2,000	2,667	(667)
3	2,000	2,000	—
4	2,000	1,333	667
5	2,000	667	1,333
	$10,000	$10,000	$ —

Now if third-party payors were effectively reimbursing the hospital for 100 per cent of the cost of this equipment (which is normally not the case), the amount received in years 1 and 2 in excess of the straight line depreciaton should be deferred to years 4 and 5 when an amount less than straight line will be received. This is merely an attempt to match revenue and the related expenses.

In practice, third-party payors will not represent the only source of revenue, and therefore will not be reimbursing the hospital for 100 per cent of the cost of the equipment. Therefore, in calculating the amount to defer, the hospital should compare the amount received from third-party payors with the amount that would have been received if the rate reimbursement formula used depreciation calculated on a straight line basis.

---

* The sum-of-the-year's digits method of calculating depreciation is a method in which the amount of depreciation in a given year is calculated by multiplying a "fraction" times the cost of the asset (less salvage value, if any). This "fraction" is calculated by taking the number of years of remaining life as the numerator and the sum of the year's digits over the asset's total life as the denominator. The denominator remains constant from year to year, but the numerator decreases each year. In the illustration above, the fraction for the first year is 5/15. The numerator (5) is the number of remaining years of life. The denominator (15) is the sum of the numbers "5," "4," "3," "2," and "1," or 15. The fraction for the second year is 4/15, the fraction for the third year is 3/15 and so forth.

Patient Revenues

The amount of income shown as patient revenues should be the full amount at established rates regardless of whether the hospital expects to collect the full amount. The amount of allowance for charity and the amount of discount given third-party payors should be shown as part of "allowances and uncollectible accounts." In this way the reader is in a position to see what portion of the hospital's full rate structure is being collected.

Bad Debts

At the time of recording revenues (at full rates, as noted above) the hospital should estimate the portion that will not be collected, such as charity cases, etc. This amount would be shown as part of the "allowances and uncollectible accounts" and deducted from revenue in the Statement of Revenue and Expenses. Subsequent bad debts should also be shown as a further adjustment of the allowances and uncollectible accounts line.

RECOMMENDED SIMPLIFIED STATEMENT

In previous chapters we have shown how it is possible through the use of a columnar format to combine the activities of all funds on one statement. The same approach is possible with hospital financial statements. Figure 15-5 shows how the columnar format could be applied to the Johnstown Hospital.

As will be observed in this illustration, the reader can quickly see the total activity of the hospital, including all activity in the restricted funds. For example, there were substantial restricted gifts received during the year, as well as restricted investment income and gains. As has been noted in other chapters, many argue that there is a real danger that the reader will be misled by showing such restricted income on the same page as unrestricted income, particularly where a "total" or, as here, a "combined all funds" column is shown. Such persons believe that the reader is not likely to appreciate the significance of these restricted funds and will, mistakenly, assume that the board has available for general purposes all of the income shown on the statement, including restricted income. However, as has been discussed repeatedly throughout this book, the authors recognize these risks but feel that they are less important than the risk that the reader will not understand or grasp

JOHNSTOWN HOSPITAL

STATEMENT OF REVENUE, EXPENSES, AND CHANGES IN FUND BALANCES
For the Year Ended December 31, 19X2

	Unrestricted	Specific Purpose Fund	Restricted Plant Replacement and Expansion Fund	Endowment Fund	Combined All Funds
Patient service revenue	$5,000,000				$ 5,000,000
Allowances and uncollectible accounts	(1,030,000)				(1,030,000)
Net patient service revenue	3,970,000				3,970,000
Other operating revenue	50,000				50,000
Total operating revenue	4,020,000				4,020,000
Operating expenses:					
Nursing services	1,800,000				1,800,000
Other professional services	1,300,000				1,300,000
General services	1,000,000				1,000,000
Fiscal services	200,000				200,000
Administrative services (including interest of $18,000)	500,000				500,000
Provision for depreciation	200,000				200,000

Total operating expenses	5,000,000				5,000,000
Loss from operations	(980,000)				(980,000)
Nonoperating revenue:					
Gifts and bequests	680,000	$ 15,000	$100,000	$ 100,000	895,000
Investment income	320,000		10,000		330,000
Realized gains on sale of investments	30,000	5,000	20,000	100,000	155,000
Donated medical equipment	100,000				100,000
Total nonoperating revenue	1,130,000	20,000	130,000	200,000	1,480,000
Excess of revenue over expenses	150,000	20,000	130,000	200,000	500,000
Fund balance, beginning of the year	5,750,000	80,000	95,000	4,825,000	10,750,000
Interfund transfers, net	25,000		(25,000)		—
Fund balance, end of the year	$5,925,000	$100,000	$200,000	$5,025,000	$11,250,000

Fig. 15–5. An example of a Statement of Revenue, Expenses, and Changes in Fund Balances for all funds in the format recommended by the authors.

the total picture of the institution when separate statements are presented for each fund.

In this columnar format, several principles of reporting have been followed that differ from the Guide. Notice that donated medical equipment has been shown as nonoperating revenue rather than being added directly to the fund balance on a separate Statement of Changes in Fund Balances. Presumably the board accepted this equipment because it felt it would contribute to the hospital, and accordingly it should be reflected as nonoperating revenue.

Another change is that restricted gifts for specific purposes have been shown in the unrestricted fund column to the extent that such gifts were actually expended during the year. Likewise the amount reported as specific purpose gifts is only the net amount not expended during the year. By contrast, the Guide provides that such income will be shown in its entirety in the specific purposes fund and then transferred to the unrestricted fund and reported as "other operating revenue." This appears to be awkward and is difficult for the reader to understand, partly because gifts are reported in three different places in the Statement of Revenue and Expenses (gifts under "nonoperating revenue," gifts as a deduction from "allowances," and gifts transferred from specific purpose funds in the other operating revenue). In the suggested simplified format, all gifts are reported as nonoperating revenue.

In our illustration, the amount shown as unrestricted gifts and bequests is $680,000 compared to $600,000 shown in the Statement of Revenue and Expenses in Figure 15–2. Fifty thousand dollars of this difference is restricted fund gifts which were expended during the current year for operating purposes and the remaining $30,000 are gifts which were previously netted against "allowances and uncollectible accounts" in the operating revenue section.

Another change that has been made is that the two partially offsetting plant fund transfers have been netted and shown without explanation. If the details of such transfers are important they could be shown in a footnote where the risk of confusion would be minimized. Also, observe that the fund balances at the beginning and end of the year have been shown on this statement, thus eliminating the need for a separate Statement of Changes in Fund Balances. This should help the reader to understand the statements. Finally, in the process of combining the two statements, the caption "Excess of revenue over expenses" has been somewhat de-emphasized by not showing it as the last line on the statement. This is appropriate since emphasis on excess of revenue is relatively less important in nonprofit reporting.

CONCLUSION

The Hospital Guide published by the American Institute of Certified Public Accountants represents a significant step forward in establishing realistic accounting principles and reporting standards. The most important concept in this Guide is that there are only two types of funds —restricted and unrestricted, and that all unrestricted funds should be reported together. This is a very important principle. This Guide should be studied by all nonprofit organizations.

At the same time some suggestions have been offered by the authors to simplify the statements even further. The major recommendation is to combine the Statement of Revenue and Expenses and the Statement of Changes in Fund Balances in a columnar format and to modify certain of the accounting and reporting principles.

16

Accounting Standards for
Other Nonprofit
Organizations

In late 1978 the American Institute of Certified Public Accountants (AICPA) issued a "Statement of Position" applicable to all nonprofit organizations which are not covered by one of the three previously issued Industry Audit Guides, discussed in the three preceding chapters. This Statement of Position was addressed to the Financial Accounting Standards Board (FASB). As discussed more fully in Chapter 18, only the FASB presently has authority to issue accounting principles which are binding on organizations wishing to describe their financial statements as being in accordance with "generally accepted accounting principles." However, the AICPA can issue a Statement of Position which, in the absence of FASB comments to the contrary, represents the most authoritative pronouncement of the accounting profession on a given subject. Thus the Statement of Position has much the same authority as the Industry Audit Guides previously discussed.

The Statement of Position did not contain an effective date. It acknowledged that the FASB was presently developing a conceptual framework policy statement applicable to all nonbusiness entities (see Chapter 18) and was cognizant that differences, if any, between the principles outlined in the Statement of Position and those in the completed conceptual framework policy statement would have to be eliminated. In the interim, however, the Statement of Position represents the most authoritative literature concerning these other types of nonprofit organizations.*

* See pages 304–305 for a discussion of the rule-making procedures in the accounting profession and the level of authority inherent in a Statement of Position.

Applicable to Many Categories of Organizations

The Statement of Position is applicable to all nonprofit organizations not covered by one of the three Audit Guides, other than governmental units and such business-oriented entities as mutual savings banks, insurance companies, and employee benefit plans. Included in the many categories of organizations for which this Statement of Position is applicable are the following: cemetery organizations, civic organizations, fraternal organizations, labor unions, libraries, museums, other cultural institutions, performing arts organizations, political parties, private elementary and secondary schools, private and community foundations, professional associations, public broadcasting stations, religious organizations, research and scientific organizations, social and country clubs, trade associations, and zoological and botanical societies.

Once an effective date is established, use of the accounting principles and reporting practices discussed in the Statement of Position is mandatory only for organizations that want to describe their financial statements as being prepared in accordance with "generally accepted accounting principles." * For many smaller organizations adoption of some of the recommended accounting principles may be neither practical nor economical.

Unlike the earlier Industry Audit Guides, this Statement of Position deals primarily with underlying accounting principles, leaving financial statement format largely up to each organization to develop as best suits its needs. In fact, over 50 pages of illustrative financial statements are presented in the Statement of Position to document the wide differences in format which are possible. This is not to suggest that complete freedom has been granted in terms of statement format; in some instances the accounting principles prescribed effectively dictate format.

Most of the accounting principles in the Statement of Position are also covered in the earlier Industry Audit Guides. In most instances the principles are in agreement, but in some cases they are not and, as noted in Chapter 18, eventually these differences will have to be reconciled.

For the convenience of the reader, this chapter first discusses accounting principles and then financial statements. Where the principles have already been covered in earlier chapters, the treatment herein is abbreviated, and readers wanting further information should refer back to the earlier discussions.

* See page 372 for discussion of the concept of generally accepted accounting principles.

ACCOUNTING PRINCIPLES

Accrual Basis of Reporting

Probably the most far-reaching of the accounting principles addressed is the requirement that nonprofit organizations report on the accrual basis of accounting. As noted in Chapter 3, this conflicts with the reporting practices of a large number of small and medium-sized nonprofit organizations, which presently use cash basis accounting for purposes of reporting.

This accrual basis requirement specifically applies to financial *reporting* and does not necessarily apply to internal *bookkeeping*. Many nonprofit organizations find it more practical to keep their records on a cash basis throughout the period, and then prepare accrual basis financial statements through worksheet adjustments or formal journal entries.*

Fund Accounting

The Statement of Position indicates that the use of fund accounting for reporting purposes may be helpful, but is not required. Emphasis is on the clarity and usefulness of the information disclosed rather than on the use of fund accounting to disclose the information.

This subtle distinction cannot be overemphasized. As noted throughout this book, it is widely assumed that fund accounting is mandatory for nonprofit organizations, and that the use of fund accounting for record keeping dictates the use of detailed multifund reporting formats. Unfortunately, financial statements prepared on the basis of fund accounting are confusing to most readers. The Statement of Position has redirected emphasis from the form of disclosure to the appropriateness and clarity of the disclosure. While it reaffirms that financial statements utilizing traditional fund-by-fund disclosure may in many instances still be the most appropriate way to communicate certain information, it does not mandate the use of a fund accounting format.

Unrestricted Gifts, Grants, and Bequests

Unrestricted gifts, grants, and bequests are to be recorded as income at the time received (see the section on "pledges" below for a discussion of the timing of recording pledges, unrestricted gifts, and grants).

---

* See pages 20–22.

Current Restricted Gifts

The Statement of Position provides that current restricted gifts * be recorded as deferred income on the Balance Sheet until the organization has expended funds which meet the restriction imposed by the donor. Once expenditures have been made that meet the terms of the restriction, such gifts should be reflected as income in the Statement of Activity.

Observe carefully that current restricted gifts are deferred only so long as the organization has not expended funds, from whatever source, which meet the terms of the restriction. There is no requirement that the specific dollars represented by the restricted gift must be spent, only that the legal restrictions are met through the expenditure of whatever funds the organization chooses to utilize. For example, assume a donor gives $5,000 for a specific research project, and subsequent to the date of the receipt of the gift the organization uses $5,000 of its unrestricted funds to perform this same research project. In all probability the restriction has been met and, if so, the $5,000 restricted gift must be reflected as income in the period. In many cases the money is all commingled in a single bank account anyway, and the question of which money has been spent is irrelevant.

This approach differs significantly from that provided in the earlier Industry Audit Guides.

Current Restricted Fund.   Under the treatment discussed above, there will continue to be assets and liabilities in such a current restricted fund, but the "fund balance" will always be zero. Unspent amounts will be reflected as deferred income outside the fund balance section (as may be seen in the "Deferred gifts and dues" section in Figure 16–1, page 269). For this reason there is no need for a separate current restricted fund in the Balance Sheet, although it is not specifically prohibited by the Statement of Position.

For the same reason the need for a current restricted fund column in the Statement of Activity is also reduced. Once the restriction has been met, a current restricted gift effectively becomes unrestricted and can be shown with the other unrestricted income, separately disclosed. The organization could, however, still choose to show such a current restricted column, in which case the amount of current restricted income would be exactly offset by current restricted expenses, coming down to a zero net. There is no objection to this type of presentation, but it would serve little purpose.

---

* See pages 100 to 107 for a complete discussion of current restricted gifts.

Grants for Specific Projects

Grants given to a nonprofit organization by government, by a foundation, or by others to accomplish a particular purpose are accounted for in the same manner as current restricted funds; that is, they should be recorded as deferred income until the restrictions imposed by the grantor have been met, at which time they are recognized as income. Normally this occurs when expenses have been incurred.

Restricted Gifts for Fixed Assets

Restricted gifts for the purchase of fixed assets or plant expansion are also treated as deferred income in the Balance Sheet until such time as the restriction has been met, which is usually when the fixed asset has been purchased. This treatment is consistent with the treatment of current restricted gifts discussed above, but differs from the treatment outlined in the Industry Audit Guides issued earlier.

Pledges

Recorded as an Asset. Pledges which *can* be enforced are to be recorded as an asset. This represents a departure from previous Industry Audit Guides in that the determining criterion is now the ability of the organization to enforce collection. Note, however, that the criterion is the legal right to enforce collection of the pledge, not the willingness of the organization to actually exercise this right. Few organizations would, in fact, ever take legal action.

Those organizations wanting to avoid recording pledges can, therefore, include on their pledge card a statement to the effect that the pledgor can unilaterally withdraw the pledge at any time. As long as it is clear that the pledgor retains this right, the pledge would be unenforceable and therefore not recorded as an asset.

Unrestricted Pledges Recorded as Income. The timing of recording the pledge as income depends on the donor's intention. If the donor has clearly indicated the period for which the pledge is being made, that intention governs. In most instances, however, the donor is silent. The presumption then is that the donor intended the gift to be used in the period in which the pledge is payable. This is a different position from that taken by the Industry Audit Guides for voluntary health and welfare organizations and for hospitals. In those Guides the presumption is made that the gift is intended for the period in which the donor made the pledge.

This treatment also applies to unrestricted grants by foundations and others, which are payable over a several-year period. Unless there are indications to the contrary, the presumption is that the grant is intended for the period in which the grantor has indicated that payment would be made.

Observe that the period in which the pledge is to be recorded as income is the period in which the donor has said payment will be made, not the period in which payment is actually made. Thus, if a donor doesn't make payment in the specified period the pledge would still be recorded as income in that period, although the collectibility of the pledge might become a question.

For example, a donor who pledges a contribution of $500, payable $100 a year starting next year, is implying that the gift should be used during each of the five years at the rate of $100 a year. Thus, at the time the pledge is made, the pledge receivable of $500 would be recorded as an asset ($400 of which would be a long-term asset), and $500 would be shown as deferred income on the liability side of the Balance Sheet.

Pledges for Current Restricted Purposes.   Pledges for current restricted purposes should also be recorded as an asset. The recognition of the pledge as income would follow the rules for recognizing current restricted support; that is, the support would be recognized at the time expenditures are made which meet the terms of the restriction. Thus it is possible that a pledge for a current restricted purpose would be recognized as income prior to receipt of the pledge. The rationale here is that the organization has performed the services for which the pledge has been made and therefore should recognize the pledge as income.

Pledges for Fixed Assets.   Pledges for fixed assets should also be recorded in the Balance Sheet as an asset. However, the recognition of the pledge as income is dependent upon the date on which the restriction has been met, i.e., the date on which the fixed assets are purchased. Thus the recognition of income follows the rules for current restricted gifts.

Donated Services

The Statement of Position clearly indicates that donated services should be recorded only if four specific criteria are met. The first three of these criteria basically follow those specified in the Voluntary Health and Welfare Audit Guide, discussed on page 183. The fourth criterion is new:

The services of the reporting organization are not principally intended for the benefit of its members. Accordingly, donated and contributed services would not normally be recorded by organizations such as religious communities, professional and trade associations, labor unions, political parties, fraternal organizations, and social and country clubs.*

The intent is to limit the recording of contributed services to those organizations which are providing services for the benefit of the general public as distinct from providing services for the benefit of the organization's members. The authors expect that this new criterion will be liberally interpreted and widely applied, and that the recording of donated services will be limited to situations where the organization is clearly rendering a public service, and where the absence of recording would distort the financial statements. Note that once the four criteria are met, all appropriate donated services should be recorded including those of an administrative nature such as office work. The fourth criterion is not intended to restrict the types of services recorded, but merely to limit the types of organizations that can record any donated services.

The accounting profession is withdrawing from its earlier, more stringent rules which required a number of nonprofit organizations to record donated services. The whole tenor of the Statement of Position is that organizations normally do not record donated services, and therefore, before a nonprofit organization can do so, all four criteria must be clearly met.

Donated Materials

Donated materials, if significant in amount, should be recorded at their fair value at the date of receipt. The one proviso is that the organization must have a reasonable basis for valuation. Where the organization receives materials which are difficult to value, then no amount should be recorded. Examples of items which would be difficult to value include used clothing, furniture, and similar items. However, if a value can be reasonably determined, donated materials should be recorded. Essentially the position taken is similar to the Industry Audit Guide for voluntary health and welfare organizations.

Donated Facilities

Some nonprofit organizations receive rent-free or reduced-rent offices, warehousing, and similar facilities. The fair value of such facilities should be recorded as a contribution and as an expense in the period utilized.

The value recorded should be based on the use actually being made

* Paragraph 67 of the Statement of Position.

of the facility. Accordingly, if a donor makes available high-cost office space, but the organization would normally rent low-cost office space, the organization should record as a contribution an amount representing the rent which the organization would pay if the donated facilities were not available. If the donation is in the form of reduced rent, only the excess of what the organization would normally pay over the reduced rent would be recorded.

Donated facilities should be recorded as income in the period the facilities are actually used. Accordingly, if a donor gives the organization a five-year, rent-free lease, the value of the donated rent would be recorded in each of the five years as the facility is used. The organization would not record the full five-year rental as income in the year in which the donor gave the five-year lease, although footnote disclosure of the commitment would be appropriate if the amount is significant.

Investment Income

Unrestricted Investment Income. Unrestricted investment income is reported as income as earned. Unrestricted investment income includes income from endowment or other restricted funds where no restriction has been placed by the donor on the use to be made of the investment income.

For reporting purposes some organizations may choose to segregate investment income from other types of income, which is acceptable provided it appears above the caption "Excess of revenue and support over expenses before nonexpendable additions" (see the discussion on statement format below).

Restricted Investment Income. The reporting of restricted investment income depends on the use to be made of the restricted income. If the investment income is from investment of current restricted funds, or from endowment funds where the donor has specified that the income shall be used for a current restricted purpose, then such income would not be recognized as current investment income, but instead would be recorded as deferred income on the Balance Sheet until such time as the restrictions have been met. Once the restrictions are met, income is recognized on the Statement of Activity. This follows the treatment for current restricted gifts discussed above.

Where investment income arises from endowment funds containing a donor-imposed requirement that the income be accumulated as part of the endowment fund, such investment income would be reflected as income in the "nonexpendable additions" section of the Statement of Activity (see below).

Gains and Losses

Realized gains and losses on investments would generally be treated in a manner similar to the treatment of investment income, discussed above. Unrestricted gains and losses would be reflected as current income while gains and losses on restricted funds would be reported either as "nonexpendable additions" (in the Statement of Activity) or as deferred income (in the Balance Sheet) depending on the nature of the restrictions.

Unrealized Losses on Investments Carried at the Lower of Cost or Market. Where investments in marketable securities are carried at the lower of cost or market, recognition must be given to unrealized losses when the total market value of all marketable securities in a fund group is less than cost. When this occurs, the write-down of investments classified as current assets would be reflected as charges in the Statement of Activity in the same manner as realized losses. However, if the write-down is of investments classified as noncurrent assets, the charge would be reflected in the "changes in fund balances section" of the Statement of Activity as a direct deduction of the fund balance. This means unrealized losses from the noncurrent investments would be below the "excess" caption for the period. In future periods if the aggregate market value increases, similar adjustments, reported in this same section of the statement, should be made to increase the carrying value back to original cost, but no higher.

Investments at Market. As noted below, marketable investments may be reported at either the lower of cost or market (or amortized cost for certain marketable debt securities) or at market. If reported at market, no distinction is made between realized and unrealized gains. Rather, the amount of gain or loss reported each year will be equal to the change in carrying amount during the reporting period. As more fully discussed on page 88, it is not meaningful to separate the period's gains and losses into the realized and unrealized portions. Chapter 8 contains a full discussion of gains and losses of investments carried at market.

Nonmarketable investments such as real estate or mineral rights may continue to be reported at either the lower of cost or market or at market, and gains and losses would be handled in the same manner as discussed above.

Total Return Approach

The Statement of Position reaffirms the stand taken in the earlier Industry Audit Guides that transfers under the total return approach to investments should be reflected as a "transfer" and not as part of income. See the extended discussion in Chapter 8.

Membership and Subscription Income

Membership organizations receiving dues in advance of dispensing services to members are required to allocate the dues over the period of time in which the members will receive the services. This is a significant requirement.

Observe that under this requirement dues are recognized as income over the period to which they relate, but not necessarily on a pro rata basis. If the organization can show that the services being rendered are not performed ratably over time, another basis of income recognition can be used. For example, if an organization incurs substantial membership renewal costs, the portion of the membership dues applicable to these costs could be recorded currently with only the remainder deferred over the membership year.

Some membership organizations will find as a result of this requirement that their net worth (i.e., fund balance) will drop into a deficit position. This is likely to happen where the organization has little working capital and spends its dues as soon as it receives them.

Some organizations use the term "membership" as a fund-raising device, and no real economic benefit accrues to the member by virtue of membership. Such "dues" should be treated as contribution income. Alternatively, if the membership dues are really a combination of dues and contribution, the payment should be appropriately allocated between these two categories.

Subscription income should be prorated over the period to which the subscription applies. Where there are significant costs of obtaining the subscription, or renewal, only the net subscription income need be prorated.*

Life Membership and Initiation Fees

Some organizations offer life memberships which represent a prepayment of dues. These life membership dues should also be recognized as income in the periods during which the member will receive services.

---

* However, at a minimum, the deferred amount should at least equal the cost of fulfilling the subscription obligation. If the subscription is sold at a price insufficient to pay all costs, the subscription income which is deferred should be sufficient to cover the future period costs of fulfilling the subscription. The effect in this latter case will be to record a loss on subscriptions in the current period.

If the number of life memberships is significant, the amortization would probably be based on the collective life expectancy of the members.

Initiation fees which are not in fact a prepayment for services to be rendered in the future and which are not refundable should be reflected as income in the period in which the fees are payable. If the entire initiation fee is payable at the time a member joins, the entire fee would be recorded at that time. Some organizations provide for the payment of the initiation fee over a several-year period, in which case the fee should be recognized as it becomes due, i.e., it should be spread over the several-year period corresponding to the payment schedule. The theory behind this deferral is simply that very few membership organizations will collect unpaid initiation fees if the member withdraws before the due date of the second or subsequent installments.

Where the initiation fee is a prepayment for services to be rendered in the future, the fee should be amortized over the period in which the services are to be rendered. In some instances an initiation fee is charged and in addition a fee will be assessed in future years to cover all or part of the cost of the services to be rendered. Where the future year's fee can reasonably be expected to cover the cost of such future year's services, then the initiation fee should be reflected as income currently; otherwise all or part of the initiation fee should be amortized as appropriate.*

Grants to Others

Some nonprofit organizations such as foundations make grants to other organizations. Grantor organizations should record both as a liability and as an expense the amount of grants awarded at the time the grantee is "entitled" to the grant. Normally this is either at the time the board of trustees approves a specific grant or at the time the grantee is notified that it has been awarded the grant.

Some grants provide for payment over a several-year period. Where the grantee will routinely receive such payments without the necessity of more than a cursory subsequent review by the grantor, the full amount of the grant, including the amounts payable in future years, should be recorded at the time of the initial award. If, instead, the

---

* The members of the AICPA Subcommittee on Nonprofit Organizations which wrote the Statement of Position were particularly concerned with a situation which frequently arises with "retirement homes." That is, a large initial fee is charged and, in addition, monthly fees are assessed. If the monthly fees are insufficient to cover service costs, an appropriate portion of the initial fee should be allocated to future periods.

grantor indicates that the future payments are contingent upon an extensive review and formal decision process by the grantor prior to making payment, subsequent payments would not be recorded as a liability and expense until this subsequent decision process is completed. In these circumstances each subsequent payment would effectively be treated as a new grant. See pages 294–297 for a further discussion.

It should be observed that the accounting treatment of the grantor making a restricted grant is different from that of the grantee receiving the grant. In the case of the grantor, the grant is treated as an expense at the time the award is made, while from the grantee's standpoint the grant is recorded as deferred income until the restrictions have been met. While this may appear inconsistent, this differing treatment recognizes that there are two different perspectives to certain transactions.

Reported Valuation of Investments

Marketable securities may be reported at either the lower of cost or market (or amortized cost for certain marketable debt securities) or at market. Marketable securities include both stocks and bonds. Whichever election is made for stocks, this same basis must be used for all stocks of the organization, and similarly for bonds.

Other types of investments which are not readily marketable, such as oil and gas interests and real property, may also be reported at either the lower of cost or market or at market, but the basis selected does not have to be the same basis as that selected for marketable securities.

Fixed Assets

Consistent with all three Industry Audit Guides, the Statement of Position provides that fixed assets must be capitalized. However, it recognizes the implementation problem for organizations that have previously been writing off their fixed assets as expenses. It provides that if historical cost records are not reasonably available at the time of initial implementation, other bases may be used such as an appraisal, replacement costs, property tax assessments, etc.

The Statement of Position discusses the desirability of reporting a value for museum and similar collections, but concludes that this is not required because it is not practical to do so in most instances. Museums are nonetheless encouraged to value their collections if circumstances permit.

Depreciation Accounting

Depreciation accounting techniques are required, except for inexhaustible assets such as collections, landmarks, cathedrals, and houses of worship. This is controversial and readers should refer to Chapter 7 for a complete discussion of the arguments for depreciation accounting.

Life Income and Annuity Funds

The present value of the liability arising from life income and annuity gift contracts should be recorded as a liability at the time the gift is received. The excess of the gift over such liability is then recognized as income, also at the time the gift is received. Normally there would be no excess for life income funds since by definition the donor receives the income generated by the gift.

FINANCIAL STATEMENTS

Required Financial Statements

Three financial statements have been identified in the Statement of Position as usually required:

Balance Sheet
Statement of Activity
Statement of Changes in Financial Position

Even here, the Statement of Position makes clear that what is required is the disclosure of certain information, and not the specific format of the financial statements. Each organization is encouraged to develop a format suitable to its needs. The key is disclosure, not format.

Balance Sheet

The Balance Sheet should show the amount of the aggregate unrestricted funds and the balance of major types of restricted funds. However, the requirement is for disclosure of the balance of such funds in the fund balance section of the Balance Sheet, and not for disclosure of the specific assets and liabilities of each fund. Accordingly, a Balance Sheet in which all assets and liabilities are commingled would be acceptable provided the fund balance section clearly discloses the amounts of funds that are unrestricted and funds that are restricted. Figure 16–1 shows an example of such a Balance Sheet.

Unrestricted Fund Balance Subdivided. The requirement to disclose the aggregate of unrestricted fund balances does not preclude sub-

---

WAUWATOSA COMMUNITY SERVICE ORGANIZATION

BALANCE SHEET
June 30, 19X1

ASSETS

Current assets:

Cash	$ 79,000	
Pledges receivable	16,000	
Accounts receivable	48,000	
Inventory	25,000	
Total current assets		$168,000
Endowment fund investments, at market		320,000
Building and equipment, less depreciation of $151,000		211,000
Total assets		$699,000

LIABILITIES AND FUND BALANCES

Current liabilities:

Accounts payable		$ 24,000
Current portion of mortgage		7,000
Deferred gifts and dues:		
Membership fees	$ 18,000	
Plant fund gifts	25,000	
Restricted gifts	18,000	
Unrestricted gifts	3,000	64,000
Total current liabilities		95,000
Mortgage, 8%, due 1989		75,000
Total liabilities		170,000

Fund balances:

Unrestricted, available for current operations	80,000	
Invested in fixed assets, net	129,000	
Endowment fund	320,000	
Total fund balances		529,000
Total liabilities and fund balances		$699,000

Fig. 16–1. An example of a Balance Sheet that meets the requirements of the Statement of Position. Note that the Wauwatosa Community Service Organization elected to carry the marketable securities in its endowment fund at their fair market value.

dividing the unrestricted fund balance into several subcategories. However, where this is done these subcategories must be aggregated to show a total unrestricted fund balance. Figure 13–5 shows an example of such subdividing of the unrestricted fund.

Some nonprofit organizations choose to segregate their fixed assets in a separate fixed asset fund. The resources that are used to purchase such fixed assets can, of course, be both restricted and unrestricted. The Statement of Position indicates that where the organization chooses to report fixed assets as a separate fund it need not subdivide the fixed asset fund balance into its restricted and unrestricted components. Note that fixed assets need not be reported in a separate fund but may be included with either the unrestricted or restricted funds as appropriate.

Classified Balance Sheet.   Nonprofit organizations which have only unrestricted funds must classify their assets and liabilities as short-term and long-term. This will result in a so-called "classified" Balance Sheet in which current assets and current liabilities are clearly shown. This is a new requirement not provided for in the earlier Industry Audit Guides.

Many nonprofit organizations have, of course, both restricted and unrestricted funds. The requirement for a classified Balance Sheet is waived where the nature of the fund classifications clearly indicates the current and long-term nature of the assets and liabilities. However, where the nature of the fund classifications is such that this information is not readily apparent, a classified Balance Sheet probably will still be needed. In Figure 16–1 a classified Balance Sheet has been presented since the presentation would not otherwise clearly distinguish between current and long-term amounts.

Interfund Borrowings.   A significant interfund borrowing which is intended to be repaid must be disclosed even where the reporting is on a combined or consolidated basis. This can be done either on the face of the Balance Sheet or in the footnotes thereto. However, "borrowing" where there is no intention to repay or where the borrowing fund is unlikely to have the financial ability to repay is in effect an interfund transfer and should be reported as such.

Statement of Activity

"Statement of Activity" is the name given in the Statement of Position to a statement that shows all of the organization's activity from the beginning to the end of the year. The title of the statement could be any one of a number of different names, including "Statement of Revenue, Expenses, and Changes in Fund Balances," "Statement of Changes in Fund Balances," "Statement of Revenue, Expenses, Capital Additions, and Changes in Fund Balances," or "Statement of Income and Expenses." The title is not particularly important so long as the statement shows all relevant activity.

At the same time, the Statement of Activity could be broken into two sections. and each treated as a separate statement—that is, a section showing revenue, expenses, and nonexpendable additions, and a section showing changes in fund balances. However, there seems little purpose in creating a separate Statement of Changes in Fund Balances since the only types of transactions normally shown in the "changes in fund balance" section of the Statement of Activity are the addition of the excess for the year and the transfers between funds.* The authors would expect that most organizations will prepare a single all-inclusive Statement of Activity.

Required Disclosures.   The Statement of Position requires that a number of specific disclosures be made in the Statement of Activity:

1. The amount of unrestricted revenue by major category.
2. The amount of unrestricted support by major source.
3. The amount of current restricted revenue and support by major source.
4. The amount of gifts and other income restricted for nonexpendable purposes.
5. The excess of revenue and support over expenses.
6. The excess of revenue, support, and nonexpendable additions over expenses.

Note that there is no requirement that the aggregate of unrestricted support and unrestricted revenue be shown.

Figure 16–2 is an example of a Statement of Activity that illustrates these required disclosures.

Other Types of Fund Classifications.   Fund classifications other than the more traditional ones may be entirely appropriate. For example, "unrestricted/restricted" or "expendable/nonexpendable" could be used. The requirement is for appropriate disclosure, not the specifics of the classifications to be utilized.

Total of All Funds.   One of the more controversial issues in nonprofit accounting is the use of a "total of all funds" column in the financial

---

* Unrealized losses on noncurrent investments which are carried at the lower of cost or market would also be reflected as a change in the "change in fund balance" section. See the discussion above on unrealized losses on investments carried at the lower of cost or market.

WAUWATOSA COMMUNITY SERVICE ORGANIZATION

STATEMENT OF REVENUE, EXPENSES, CAPITAL ADDITIONS, AND CHANGES IN FUND BALANCES
For the Year Ending June 30, 19X1

	Operating	Plant	Endowment	Total
Revenue and support:				
Service fees	$155,000			$155,000
Grants, including $34,000 of				
restricted grants	61,000			61,000
Membership dues	53,000			53,000
Unrestricted contributions and				
bequests	35,000			35,000
Dividends and interest	16,000			16,000
Unrestricted realized and				
unrealized gains	18,000			18,000
Total revenue and support .	338,000			338,000
Expenses:				
Program:				
Project A	105,000	$ 10,000		115,000
Project B	95,000	13,000		108,000
Membership services	40,000	4,000		44,000
Total program.	240,000	27,000		267,000
Supporting:				
General management.	38,000	2,000		40,000
Fund raising.	6,000	1,000		7,000
Membership development . .	7,000	1,000		8,000
Total supporting	51,000	4,000		55,000
Total expenses	291,000	31,000		322,000
Excess of revenue and support				
over expenses	47,000	(31,000)	—	16,000
Nonexpendable additions:				
Restricted gifts		20,000	$ 39,000	59,000
Restricted interest		1,000		1,000
Restricted realized and				
unrealized gains			17,000	17,000
Excess of revenue, support,				
and nonexpendable addi-				
tions over expenses	47,000	(10,000)	56,000	93,000
Fund balances, beginning of				
period	64,000	108,000	264,000	436,000
Transfers.	(31,000)	31,000		—
Fund balances, end of period . . .	$ 80,000	$129,000	$320,000	$529,000

Fig. 16–2. An example of a Statement of Activity in which the nonexpendable additions are reported separately from current activities.

statements where a multicolumn presentation is shown. As noted earlier, many believe that the use of such totals is misleading since a total column may imply that interchanges and substitutions between assets are possible, despite restrictions on certain assets.

The Statement of Position, while not requiring a total column, clearly states that it is preferable to include one. This is another significant step toward recognizing that nonprofit organizations are single entities, and not a series of separate entities called funds. At the same time the document notes that care must be taken to assure that all appropriate disclosures are made either in the fund balance section or in the footnotes to the financial statements, to make certain the captions are not misleading.

Nonexpendable Additions. The Statement of Position distinguishes between support for current operations and support not intended directly for operations. It provides different reporting treatments for each category.

Nonexpendable additions—also referred to as capital additions—are defined as gifts and other income restricted for purposes other than current activities. The two most common types of nonexpendable additions are gifts for endowment and gifts for purchase of fixed assets. Neither type is available directly for current activities. The Statement of Position provides that these nonexpendable gifts be reported separately from expendable gifts, and shown after the "Excess of revenue and support over expenses" caption. This can be seen in Figure 16-2.

The Statement of Position requires that nonexpendable additions be segregated from other sources of support because the transactions resemble capital transactions; that is, they are similar to capital stock transactions in a commercial entity. In the past, some have advocated showing nonexpendable additions as direct additions to the fund balance to distinguish between the two types of transactions. Others have taken the position that such gifts increase the net worth of the organization and should be reflected as income along with other sources of current support. The approach taken in this Statement of Position is a compromise between these two extremes. The additions are shown before the final excess for the year, but after the excess from current activities. Thus the reader is shown two excesses, one with and one without these nonexpendable additions.

Observe that the timing of recognizing certain types of nonexpendable gifts is dependent on the nature of the restriction, as discussed earlier in this chapter. It is at the time of "income" recognition that such amounts are reflected as nonexpendable additions.

Two Excess Captions.   One unusual requirement of the Statement of Position is that the organization show the excess of revenue and support over expenses before and after nonexpendable additions. While at first this may seem awkward, both captions—the excess from current activities and the excess from all activities of the organization—provide useful information for the reader.

Transfers Between Funds.   Transfers between funds are shown after the "Fund balances, beginning of the period" caption in the Statement of Activity. It is not acceptable to reflect a transfer between funds above this line, either before or immediately after the second "excess" caption. Thus it is not acceptable to report a transfer after the caption "Excess of income and nonexpendable additions over expenses," but before the caption "Fund balances, beginning of the period."

Program Services.   The Statement of Position continues to emphasize the functional reporting advocated in the three Industry Audit Guides. It provides for two basic expense categories: program and supporting.

Nonprofit organizations exist to perform services either for the public or for the members of the organization. They do not exist to provide employment for their employees or to perpetuate themselves. They exist to serve a particular purpose. The Statement of Position re-emphasizes this obvious truth by requiring the organization that raises funds from the public to identify major program services and their related costs. Some organizations may have only one specific program category, but most will have several.

Organizations that do not raise funds from the general public or from federated fund-raising organizations are encouraged to prepare their statements on a functional basis, but are not required to do so. Funds raised from government sources, or from sources other than the general public such as private foundations, or from a bona fide membership organization would not constitute funds from the general public. It would appear that if an organization were to raise as little as 10% of its support from the general public it would clearly be required to use functional reporting.

Presentation of an analysis of the various types of expenses (rent, salaries, etc.) included in each function is optional in the Statement of Position. This is mandatory in the voluntary health and welfare Audit Guide.

Supporting Services.   Supporting services are those expenses which do not directly relate to performing the functions for which the organization was established, but which nevertheless are essential to the continued existence of the organization. Depending on the type of organization, the following are among the supporting services one would expect to find:

Management and general expenses
Fund-raising expenses
Membership development costs
Cost of obtaining grants

Management and General Expenses. This is probably the most difficult of the supporting categories to define because a major portion of the time of top management usually will relate more directly to program activities than to management and general. Yet many think, incorrectly, that top management should be considered only "management and general." The Statement of Position defines management and general expenses as follows:

Management and general costs are those that are not identifiable with a single program or fund-raising activity but are indispensable to the conduct of those activities and to an organization's existence, including expenses for the overall direction of the organization's general board activities, business management, general recordkeeping, budgeting, and related purposes. Costs of overall direction usually include the salary and expenses of the chief officer of the organization and his staff. However, if such staff spend a portion of their time directly supervising program services or categories of supporting services, their salaries and expenses should be prorated among those functions. The cost of disseminating information to inform the public of the organization's "stewardship" of contributed funds, the publication of announcements concerning appointments, the annual report, and so forth, should likewise be classified as management and general expenses.

Some suggested methods of computing the allocation of certain types of expenses to the various functions are described in the Statement of Position. Other methods may also be appropriate and could be used.

Fund-Raising Expenses. Fund-raising expenses are a very sensitive category of expense because a great deal of publicity has been associated with certain organizations that appear to have very high fund-raising costs. The cost of fund raising includes not only the direct costs associated with a particular effort, but a fair allocation of the overhead of the organization, including the time of top management.

Fund-raising expenses are normally recorded as an expense in the Statement of Activity at the time they are incurred. It is not appropriate to defer such amounts except under very specific circumstances, discussed in the next paragraph. Thus the cost of acquiring or developing a mailing list which clearly has value over more than one year would nevertheless be expensed in its entirety at the time the list was purchased or the costs incurred. The reason for this conservative approach is the difficulty accountants have in satisfying themselves that costs that might logically be deferred will in fact be recovered by future support related thereto. Further, if substantial amounts of deferred fund-raising costs were permitted, the credibility of the financial statements would be in jeopardy, particularly in view of the increased publicity surrounding fund-raising expenses.

Notwithstanding the above guidelines, there are certain very limited circumstances when fund-raising expenses can be deferred. If a donor has made a gift, or pledge, which is not reflected as income in the current period but is recorded as deferred income, *and* if the donor has specifically indicated that the contribution can be used for paying the fund-raising costs of obtaining the gift, then identifiable expenses associated with the gift may be deferred. All of these limitations must be met before expenses can be deferred. The authors expect it to be a fairly rare situation when all of these requirements are met, particularly the donor-consent requirement.

If fund raising is combined with a program function, such as educational literature which also solicits funds, the total cost should be allocated between the program and fund-raising functions on the basis of the use made of the literature, as determined from its content, reason for distribution, and audience.

Membership Development Costs. Membership organizations that incur significant expense obtaining new members and renewing existing memberships should report these costs as a separate category of support service, with a caption such as "Membership development expenses."

Observe carefully that this category is only for bona fide memberships and is not applicable for memberships which are in reality contributions. Members must be receiving services commensurate with their dues. It is, of course, possible for membership dues to represent both a fee for services and a contribution. If so, membership development costs should be allocated between the fund-raising and membership development categories.

Cost of Obtaining Grants. Organizations soliciting grants from governments or foundations have a cost which is somewhat different from fund-raising costs. Where such amounts are identifiable and material in amount they should be separately identified and reported as a supporting service.

Statement of Changes in Financial Position

The Statement of Changes in Financial Position is a summary of the resources made available to an organization during the year and the uses made of such resources. Until now this statement has not been required for nonprofit organizations, but commercial organizations have had to prepare it for many years.*

Figure 16–3 shows an example of a Statement of Changes in Financial Position. Several points should be observed. First, the statement begins by reporting the excess of revenue and support over expenses, both before and after capital additions, as reported on the Statement of Activity. By using this technique both "excesses" are emphasized. The statement then adds noncash transactions (e.g., depreciation) to arrive at resources available from the activities of the year.

The next section of the statement, showing asset and liability conversions, is most important. Asset and liability conversions are merely the exchange of one type of asset or liability for another and do not affect the net worth of the organization. For example, exchanging cash for a building, or borrowing funds from a bank, does not increase or decrease the net worth of the organization. It changes the liquidity but not the net worth. The types of transactions shown in this section are important to see.

The bottom section of the statement shows how the working capital changed during the period.

The Statement of Changes in Financial Position could present the changes in working capital, as shown in Figure 16–3, or it could merely present the changes in cash. The nature of the organization and its activities dictate the choice.

In many instances, and particularly for smaller organizations, the information in the Statement of Changes in Financial Position can be adequately disclosed in the footnotes to the financial statements. This is perfectly acceptable.

COMBINED FINANCIAL STATEMENTS

The Statement of Position discusses when it is appropriate to prepare combined (or consolidated) financial statements; the question of combined financial statements arises when the reporting organization is affiliated or has a close working relationship with other organizations. There are many types of affiliations between nonprofit organizations and the question of whether it is appropriate or necessary to present combined financial statements of legally separate organizations is a difficult one.

---

* See Accounting Principles Board Opinion No. 19.

WAUWATOSA COMMUNITY SERVICE ORGANIZATION

STATEMENT OF CHANGES IN FINANCIAL POSITION
For the Year Ending June 30, 19X1

Working capital was provided by:
Current activities:

Excess of revenue and support over expenses	$16,000	
Nonexpendable additions	77,000	
Excess of revenue, support, and nonexpendable additions over expenses	93,000	
Add—Expenses not requiring outlay of working capital—depreciation	31,000	
Less—Income not providing working capital—unrealized gains	(15,000)	
Net.		$109,000
Proceeds of mortgage		10,000
Sale of investments.		45,000
Deferred gifts and fees in excess of gifts and fees recognized as support		26,000
Total working capital provided		190,000

Working capital was utilized for:

Acquisition of fixed assets	(20,000)	
Acquisition of investments	(90,000)	
Repayment of bank loan	(7,000)	
Total working capital utilized		(117,000)
Net increase in working capital.		$ 73,000

Components of change in working capital:
Increases in current assets:

Cash	$43,000	
Pledges receivable	2,000	
Accounts receivable	6,000	
Inventory	1,000	
		$ 52,000

Decrease (increase) in current liabilities:

Accounts payable	(5,000)	
Deferred gifts and dues	26,000	
		21,000
		$ 73,000

Fig. 16–3. An example of a Statement of Changes in Financial Position in which all funds are combined.

The difficulty is compounded because the attribute which normally decides this question in commercial organizations is usually absent, namely the element of ownership. With the exception of membership organizations, "ownership" of nonprofit organizations typically rests with the state acting on behalf of the people of the state. Thus, even where one nonprofit organization establishes another, the two are legally separate and the establishing organization does not "own" the second organization even though the two may have the same board of directors.

Another attribute which is considered in determining whether consolidated financial statements are appropriate in the case of commercial entities is the element of control. Does one organization have effective legal control over the second such that it can dictate its actions? For nonprofit organizations control often exists through contractual arrangements such as the formal chartering of affiliates.*

The accounting question which the Statement of Position attempts to answer is whether two or more affiliated organizations should present combined financial statements where one organization controls the other, either directly or indirectly. The question is important because of two types of situations:

1. The first type of situation is where an organization establishes separate affiliates to insulate its own financial statements from showing certain financial activities, such as fund raising, endowment funds, etc. Those who are concerned believe that when a reporting organization sets up a separate affiliate to raise or hold funds which are for its benefit, the financial affairs of the affiliate are an integral part of the reporting organization and should be reported as such.

2. The second situation is where an affiliate has program activities similar to those of the reporting organization. Many believe that the only meaningful financial statements are those that show all of the activities of an organization, including those of the affiliates.

Criteria Requiring Combination

The Statement of Position attempts to respond to the first situation by requiring combined financial statements, but has carefully limited the instances where the second situation would require combined financial statements. If control, along with any of the following criteria exist, as

---

* The term affiliate is used to denote an organization which has a close relationship to another through comomn purpose, contractual arrangement, or common boards of directors.

expressed in the Statement of Position, combined financial statements are
required:

a. Separate entities solicit funds in the name of and with the expressed or implicit approval of the reporting organization, and substantially all of the
funds solicited are intended by the contributor or are otherwise required to
be transferred to the reporting organization or used at its discretion or direction, or

b. A reporting organization transfers some of its resources to another separate
entity whose resources are held for the benefit of the reporting organization,
or

c. A reporting organization assigns functions to a controlled entity whose funding is primarily derived from sources other than public contributions.

The first two criteria are fairly straightforward and need little further
explanation. The key words in the first criterion are: ". . . substantially
all of the funds . . . are intended . . . [for] . . . the reporting organization. . . ." Thus, an affiliate that raises funds in the reporting
organization's name but retains a substantial portion for its own use
would not be covered. Most national philanthropic organizations with
local affiliates that do not transmit all of the funds collected to the
national organization fall into this category.*

The second criterion attempts to cover the situation where an organization is embarrassed by its riches and sets up a separate organization to which it transfers some of its assets. Combined financial statements in this instance are clearly required.

The third criterion is less straightforward. There are three aspects to
this criterion:

1. The reporting organization assigns one of its functions to the
affiliate.
2. The affiliate is a controlled entity.
3. Public contributions are *not* involved.

Some examples:

> The McLean Center receives a government contract to do
> research in a particular area and establishes a separate legal

---

* In a few instances the affiliate will routinely pass to the national all of the funds
collected, but the national will routinely pass to the affiliate a stipulated portion of
the amounts collected. As long as the stipulated portion is a specified percentage of
the amount collected, effectively only a part of the funds raised by the affiliate is
for the benefit of the national. On the other hand, if the national establishes and
directs the specific local activities and finances those activities without regard to the
funds collected by the affiliate, then it would appear that the affiliate's relationship
is such that combined financial statements would be required.

entity, the McLean Research Center, to perform the contract. Combined financial statements are required.

The McLean Center decides that research should be performed in a particular area but does not have the funds to do it. It establishes a separate entity, the McLean Research Center, loaning it the funds to get started; the two organizations have the same board of directors. All of its funds come from government contracts entered into in the name of the McLean Research Center. Combined financial statements are required.

The facts are the same as in the above situation except that the McLean Research Center has an entirely separate board and there are no contractual arrangements which create "control." Combined financial statements are not required.

Alternatively, the boards are the same but all of the funding comes from the general public. Combined financial statements are not required.

The intent is clearly to limit the instances where combined financial statements are required. In part, the reason for this limitation is a very practical one—cost. It is expensive to prepare combined financial statements, particularly for organizations that have hundreds and in some cases thousands of affiliates. While combined financial statements in those instances would be interesting, and probably useful, the costs would not seem warranted.*

Religious Exemption.   Probably the most difficult question which the AICPA had to wrestle with is the question of combination of financially interrelated religious organizations. There are many complex and unique relationships among religious organizations, and after trying for almost two years to write words which made no specific reference to religious organizations, but which would clearly exempt them, the AICPA put in the following statement:

In view of the unique and complex organizational relationships and degrees of local autonomy common in religious organizations, there may be many circum-

---

* Some national organizations do prepare combined financial statements showing all of their affiliates, and at least one national rating bureau requires combined financial statements before it will give its highest rating to an organization. This suggests the possibility that combined financial statements may become more common in the future. The authors caution, however, against moving in this direction without a careful evaluation of the cost, both in actual dollars and personnel time.

stances in which application of this section on combination would not result in meaningful financial information. Thus, if a religious organization concludes that meaningful financial information would not result from the presentation of combined financial statements, the provisions of this section need not be applied.

Funds Held in Trust by Others

Some organizations are beneficiaries under trusts or other arrangements where the organization itself doesn't have direct control over the assets. The Statement of Position indicates that under these circumstances the assets should not be combined with those of the organization. The key is control. If the organization has no ability to control the investment of the assets, the timing of income distribution, and the like, the combination of assets is not appropriate.

17

Special Accounting Problems
of Specific Organizations

In the preceding chapter we discussed the Statement of Position issued by the AICPA in late 1978 for nonprofit organizations not covered by one of the three AICPA Industry Audit Guides discussed in Chapters 13 through 15. This chapter discusses some of the specialized accounting and reporting problems of specific types of organizations covered by this Statement of Position. It identifies the unique accounting problems of these organizations and gives the authors' views on how the Statement of Position applies. The specific types of organizations covered in this chapter are:

Associations and professional societies
Churches
Clubs
Libraries
Museums
Performing arts organizations
Private and community foundations
Religious organizations other than churches
Research and scientific organizations
Private elementary and secondary schools

The chapter does not attempt to examine in detail subjects covered earlier in the text. Accordingly, readers should use this chapter primarily as a reference to subjects which are more fully discussed in earlier chapters.

ASSOCIATIONS AND PROFESSIONAL SOCIETIES

Associations and professional societies are membership organizations that have been formed for other than a religious or social purpose. They include trade associations, engineering and academic societies,* business leagues, and the like. Dues or other fees charged to the membership and subscriptions to publications of the organization are the main sources of revenue for these organizations.

Reporting on a Functional Basis

Associations and professional societies can exist only so long as their membership is convinced that the services being rendered justify the dues and other payments being made. The members must see a benefit for their money. This means an association has a real need to communicate with its members. Functional reporting † is one of the most effective ways of communicating since it requires the board to identify the association's programs and then to report the cost of each of these programs. The Statement of Position encourages associations to use functional reporting, but does not require it.

Reporting of Sections or Groups

Many national and regional professional societies establish separate sections, groups, or local units which operate within certain geographical regions or within certain disciplines. These units often operate more or less autonomously, although they are legally part of the main organization. The board of directors of the main organization usually has final legal responsibility for both their activities and their financial affairs. The question often is asked: Should the financial affairs of these sections and groups be reported on a combined basis with those of the main organization? Generally the Statement of Position indicates that such combination would *not* be required.

The most typical situation is when the section or group receives part of its funds from the national organization as a dues rebate and part from local assessments and fees for local events. While technically the board of the national organization may have final legal responsibility with respect to this local section, the financial interrelationship is not analogous to that contemplated in the Statement of Position as warrant-

---

* Often referred to as "learned societies."
† Functional reporting is illustrated and discussed on pages 191–192.

ing consolidated financial statements. Accordingly combination is not required.

Some organizations are structured so that all of the activities of the local organization are financed entirely by the national organization, and on the surface it might appear that the financial interrelationship is such that combination is appropriate. Here is where the element of control becomes critical. If the local section is totally under control of the national organization, with its activities totally dependent on specific direction from the national organization, *and* if the activities being performed are a delegated function of the national organization, then—and only then—would combination be required. The key words in the Statement of Position are:

A reporting organization assigns functions to a controlled entity whose funding is primarily derived from sources other than public contributions.°

Before combination is required, therefore, the national organization must control and provide support to the local unit, and the local activities must be the responsibility of the national organization. Most local sections have their own boards, with considerable flexibility as to program activities and emphasis, and the authors can conceive of few situations where combination would be required, although combination is not prohibited in any case where some degree of affiliation exists.

Nevertheless, many associations would be well advised to consider the advantages of preparing combined financial statements. Many associations have substantial activity at the local level and a reader can see the total picture only by looking at combined statements.

The authors recognize that the major problem with preparing combined financial statements relates to the cost and difficulties of getting the local units to prepare financial statements on a uniform and timely basis. But the association anxious to present a comprehensive view of its activities should consider combined financial statements.

Use of Appropriation Accounting

Associations and professional societies often follow appropriation accounting techniques under which an expense is recorded at the time purchase orders are issued for goods or services to be received in future periods. This is not an acceptable method of accounting under the Statement of Position.

Some associations and professional societies incorrectly use the term

° Paragraph 44 of the Statement of Position.

"appropriation" when they really mean "expense." As is discussed in detail on pages 47–52, the use of the term "appropriation" is easily misunderstood and should be avoided.

Separate Charitable Organizations

Most associations are organized as noncharitable, tax-exempt organizations, usually under Section 501(c)6 of the Internal Revenue Code.* As such, contributions received are not tax-deductible by the donor. Often an association will set up a second, separate "501(c)3 organization" which is charitable in nature and can receive tax-deductible contributions. This charitable organization must then carefully conduct its affairs so that all of its activities are for "charitable" purposes. Usually the boards of both organizations are substantially the same and both organizations may occupy the same quarters (with appropriate interorganization charges).

The reporting question is: Should the financial statements of the two organizations be combined? The answer is "yes" because the distinction between the two organizations is basically a legal and tax distinction and effectively the combination of the two organizations is what most members think of when the association's name is mentioned. In fact, members will often be unaware that the second organization is a legally separate entity. Members have a right to see the total financial picture of both organizations.

There are two ways to present the financial affairs in such circumstances. The most common is to use columnar statements with a separate column for each organization, with a total or consolidated column. The other approach is to combine the two organizations and present only the combined figures disclosing the existence of the charitable organization in the footnotes. Either is acceptable although the authors prefer the second approach.

CHURCHES

In this section we are discussing individual parishes, churches, or synagogues as distinct from religious organizations discussed later in this chapter. Typically all support is received as contributions directly from the membership.

---

* See Chapter 25 for a discussion of federal tax aspects of nonprofit organizations.

Cash Basis Accounting

Most churches keep their records on a cash or modified cash basis of accounting, mainly for ease of record keeping. This is probably appropriate, at least for interim financial statement purposes. However, if there are any material amounts of unrecorded liabilities or assets at the end of the accounting period, these should be reflected on the financial statements. The key word is "material."

It is not suggested, for example, that uncollected dividends or interest be recorded where such amounts are not in the aggregate significant. Perhaps the easiest way to determine whether accruals are needed is to ask whether the board might make different decisions if it saw financial statements in which all accruals were reported. If the answer is "yes," then they are material and should be recorded.

Many churches will continue to present cash basis reports and there is no reason to change as long as the board recognizes the limitation of this type of reporting. At the same time it is important to recognize that if the financial statements of the church are audited, the independent accountant will not be able to say that the financial statements have been prepared in accordance with generally accepted accounting principles if they are prepared on a cash basis (unless, in the accountant's view, unrecorded amounts are immaterial).

Fixed Assets and Depreciation

Fixed asset and depreciation accounting is one of the more difficult areas for churches because of the complexity of the bookkeeping. Most churches do not capitalize fixed assets and even fewer follow depreciation accounting practices. Nevertheless, the Statement of Position makes clear that fixed assets should be recorded as assets and, except for "houses of worship," depreciation accounting techniques should be followed.

The exception provided to depreciation accounting for houses of worship does not apply to other church property. Thus community centers, residential property, and parish houses must be depreciated. At the same time, it should be observed that all assets including houses of worship must still be carried at cost as fixed assets on the Balance Sheet.

Adequacy of the Bookkeeping Staff

Another problem is that churches often have bookkeeping difficulties. Typically, the treasurer of a small church will be the person actually keeping the records. The quality of the record keeping and financial statements is directly related to that individual's competency and availability of time. Also, treasurers come and go and some are more skilled than others. Thus it is important that the system be kept simple or it is likely to fall apart at some time in the future.

CLUBS

Clubs include many types of organizations ranging from small social clubs that meet informally to much larger clubs that own buildings and property. Country clubs and city clubs are typical of this latter category.

Initiation Fees and Capital Shares

Most clubs charge a fee to new members—an initiation fee, or payment for capital shares, or sometimes a combination of the two. Should such amounts be treated as revenue and reported as part of the excess of revenue over expenses for the period? The answer depends on the nature of the payment.

Capital Shares.   Capital shares represent members' equity in the club. Normally there is provision for redemption of capital shares, or the right of direct transfer of ownership of the shares to others. Payment for capital shares is not revenue and should be reported as a direct addition to the fund balance of the organization.

Initiation Fees.   Initiation fees are nonrefundable charges which are usually considered a contribution and should be reported as revenue. Most clubs with significant turnover look upon initiation fees as additional, spendable income which should be reported as such.

Alternatively, some argue that initiation fees are similar to capital stock payments which should be reported as a direct addition to the fund balance as contributed capital. They argue that such fees represent the new member's share of equity.[*] The Statement of Position indicates that initiation fees should be reported as revenue in the Statement of Activity. In this way the reader sees all the "revenue" the club receives. Since initiation fees are not refundable, clearly such fees represent revenue to the club, albeit revenue of a different type than revenue from sale of goods.

Some clubs provide for installment payment of initiation fees over a

---

[*] This is the approach taken in *Uniform System of Accounts for Clubs*, published by Club Managers Association of America, 1967.

several-year period. The Statement of Position indicates that a club should report initiation fees as the installment payments are due. It is not necessary to record the entire initiation fee at the time the member joins the club. In most instances the club would not insist upon payment if the member resigns prior to the due date of the subsequent installments.

Fixed Asset Accounting

The Statement of Position requires that clubs having buildings and other major fixed assets capitalize these assets and follow depreciation accounting practices. This is appropriate since most clubs need to know the cost of particular services being rendered to insure that the pricing structure recovers all costs. Fixed assets wear out and depreciation represents the process of allocating the costs of the assets over their useful lives. To do otherwise is to leave the club membership with an inadequate understanding of the costs of providing particular services, with a possible need for a special assessment at the time new fixed assets are purchased. Further, if nonmembers are served by the club, with resulting "unrelated business income," depreciation is an expense which is deductible when arriving at taxable income.

"Unrelated Business Income"

Many clubs provide services not only to their membership but to guests of members and in some instances to the public at large. If "unrelated business income" becomes sizable it can jeopardize the club's tax-exempt status, as well as create taxable income (see Chapter 25). Accordingly, it is very important that clubs keep track of revenue from nonmembers and applicable expenses. This usually involves a fairly elaborate reporting and bookkeeping system, and most clubs are well advised to get competent advice from a CPA.

LIBRARIES

Libraries as contemplated are all nonprofit, nongovernmental libraries. Libraries run by a government usually follow fund accounting principles common to government entities.

Recording a Value for Books

There is no requirement that library books be recorded as an asset on the financial statements. A strong theoretical argument could be made that they should be recorded and there is no objection to doing so.

When library books are recorded as an asset, depreciation accounting practices are probably appropriate since most books are dated. While it is difficult to establish a composite life for all types of books, a three- to ten-year life is not unreasonable. Of course depreciation practices should not be followed where a library has a rare collection which is likely to maintain its value over a considerable period of time. Similarly, rare books which increase in value should continue to be recorded at the value at the original date of acquisition.

MUSEUMS

Museums include all nongovernmental, private institutions which maintain a collection exhibited to the public with or without a charge.

Valuing the Collection as an Asset

The most controversial question is whether to place a value on the "collection" and record it as an asset in the financial statements. With very few exceptions, museums do not record their collections as an asset.

There is no requirement in the Statement of Position to record a collection as an asset because it is recognized that establishing a value would often be very difficult, if not impossible. Nevertheless, the Statement of Position indicates that there seems to be little theoretical justification for not placing a value on the collection and that acceptance of the current practice is based solely upon pragmatic considerations.

At the same time the Statement of Position requires that the cost or contributed value of current accessions and the nature and proceeds from deaccessions be reported in the financial statements or notes thereto. In the case of donated accessions, there are two ways to report such gifts. The first would be to reflect the contribution as a gift in the revenue section of the Statement of Activity, offset by the same amount in the expense section. The second approach is to reflect the transaction solely in a footnote. Since purchased accessions will be reflected in the Statement of Activity because a disbursement is involved, it seems more natural and the authors consider it preferable to record donated accessions in a similar manner. However, either approach is acceptable.

Fixed Asset Accounting

Except for collections, museums should capitalize and depreciate their fixed assets.

Contributed Facilities

The Statement of Position indicates that museums receiving rent-free (or reduced-rent) facilities should reflect the value of such facilities both as a contribution and as an expense. This will be particularly applicable to museums that occupy city-owned buildings.

Museum Accounting Manual

In 1976 the Association of Science-Technology Centers published *Museum Accounting Guidelines* for the use of museums in preparing financial statements. Individuals from many museum associations participated in this project and it has been widely recognized as the accounting manual which museums should be following. For the most part this manual is in agreement with the Statement of Position. However, in a number of areas there are differences. Some of the major differences are outlined below:

1. *Museum Accounting Guidelines* provides that current restricted fund gifts be reported as income when available for expenditure, whereas the Statement of Position provides that such gifts be deferred until the restrictions have been met.
2. *Museum Accounting Guidelines* provides that recording pledges is "preferable" whereas the Statement of Position indicates that pledges which can be enforced *must* be recorded.
3. The Statement of Position provides that contributed facilities be recorded whereas *Museum Accounting Guidelines* does not require such recording.
4. *Museum Accounting Guidelines* discusses the total return concept of investment management but does not provide a clear prescription regarding its application. The Statement of Position is very specific.
5. *Museum Accounting Guidelines* does not require depreciation accounting whereas the Statement of Position does.
6. The Statement of Position provides that: "The nature and the cost or contributed value of current period accessions and the nature of and proceeds from deaccessions should be disclosed in the financial statements." * There is no such requirement in *Museum Accounting Guidelines*.
7. The Statement of Position provides for reporting nonexpendable additions separately from operating income. *Museum Accounting Guidelines* does not discuss this subject.
8. *Museum Accounting Guidelines* requires all transfers between funds

* Paragraph 114 of the Statement of Position.

to be reported after the "Excess or deficit of revenue and support over expenses," whereas the Statement of Position provides that transfers be reported after the "Fund balance, beginning of the year."

PERFORMING ARTS ORGANIZATIONS

Performing arts organizations include a wide variety of organizations: theatrical groups, ballet and opera companies, symphonies, and the like. In most instances they rely on ticket sales as their primary source of revenue but are usually heavily dependent on public support as well. They range in size from all-volunteer companies to such professional groups as the Metropolitan Opera and the New York Philharmonic.

Recognition of Expenses

A basic reporting problem for many performing arts organizations is the timing of expense recognition for particular productions which have not as yet been performed. Should a theatrical company which has incurred costs for the performance of a new play which will not be opening until the following period report such costs in the current period or should they be deferred until the following period?

The answer depends in part on the relationship of ticket income to the total cost of the production. The general rule is that costs should be deferred so as to match costs and revenues. However, if ticket revenue will not be sufficient to cover the total cost, including the costs yet to be incurred, then only the costs that will be recovered in the following period should be deferred. In other words, if a loss on the production is anticipated, the loss should be recorded in the current period.

The reporting period for most performing arts organizations should conclude immediately after the close of the season, to minimize this kind of issue as well as a good number of bookkeeping problems.

Recognition of Ticket Revenue

A related question is when to recognize ticket revenue—when the tickets are sold or on the date of the performance? Clearly ticket revenue income should be recorded when earned, i.e., on the date of the performance. This is particularly important for organizations having advance ticket sales for the following season.

The revenue from sales of "season" tickets and subscriptions should be prorated over the performances covered by the subscription. Sometimes ticket prices for special events such as "opening night" or "gala" performances will be higher than normal and include what is in effect an element of contribution. If the contribution element is disclosed separately to patrons (for tax-deduction purposes), the organization should record this amount under contributions. Otherwise the ticket amount should be allocated between ticket revenue and contribution based on the facts and circumstances.

Recording Costumes and Stage Scenery as Fixed Assets

The Statement of Position provides for recording fixed assets. Does this apply to costumes and scenery? In principle the answer is "yes," but in practice "no."

The Statement of Position does not specifically speak to this question and it would appear such assets should be recorded. However, the implication in recording a fixed asset is that it does have a future value and that there will be revenue which will absorb some of the costs of such assets. This is probably fine where a performing arts company has a production which is given season after season; in this instance the costumes and scenery should be recorded as an asset and depreciated over their expected useful life.

But most performing arts companies do not perform the same production on a regular schedule and effectively the costumes and scenery have assured value only for the initial season. If so, they should be expensed currently.

Financial Statement Presentation

Since contributions are usually an essential part of their income, performing arts organizations should consider a statement format that emphasizes the role these gifts play toward keeping the organization solvent. A recommended format is to show first the loss from operations and then the contribution income. Here in very abbreviated form is an example:

Ticket sales		$500,000
Less—Expenses:		
Production costs	($600,000)	
Administration and general	(50,000)	(650,000)
Loss from operations		(150,000)
Contribution income, net of		
fund-raising costs of $10,000		160,000
Excess for the year		$ 10,000

PRIVATE FOUNDATIONS

The term "private foundation" is used here as defined in the Tax Reform Act of 1969. The tax aspects of private foundations are discussed in considerable detail in Chapter 25. For the most part, such organizations do not solicit funds from the public but are supported mainly by endowment income. Occasionally private foundations receive new gifts but, by definition, these come from relatively few individuals.*

Timing of Recording Liability for Grants

There are several problems unique to private foundations. The most important deals with the reporting of unpaid grants. Often private foundations will make a grant award payable in several installments, often over a several-year period. Typically, subsequent payments are dependent upon satisfactory performance or compliance with the original grant agreement, and as such, the "liability" for future payments is somewhat "conditional." The accounting question relates to the timing of recording these grant liabilities by the private foundation.

Alternatives. Three possible approaches can be taken by private foundations. Some foundations prefer to treat payments to grantee institutions on a "cash" basis. That is, they will not record future grant obligations either as an expense or as a liability until they are paid. The second approach is for the foundation to record both as an expense and as a liability the full commitment at the time the grantee institution is informed of the foundation's intention to make such payments.

Still other foundations (but much fewer in number) record both as an expense and as a liability amounts which the board of trustees has "appropriated" for particular areas of interest. This board action usually occurs before grantees have been selected and is a nonbinding action indicating only where the trustees would like to see the foundation spend its money. Where such "appropriations" are recorded, the foundation effectively treats as an expense the amount which the board has concluded it will spend in a given area in the future. This recording is at the time of appropriation, as distinct from recording at the time the grantee is informed or the grant is awarded.

Statement of Position. While sound accounting arguments can be cited for both the first and second approaches and a sound business reason advanced for the last approach, the Statement of Position is fairly ex-

---

* Community foundations, another type of foundation, do receive gifts from the general public. See the last paragraph of this section.

plicit in saying that the second approach is appropriate for private foundations that wish to describe their financial statements as being prepared in accordance with generally accepted accounting principles. The Statement of Position provides:

> Organizations that make grants to others should record grants as expenses and liabilities at the time recipients are entitled to them. That normally occurs when the board approves a specific grant or when the grantee is notified.
>
> Some grants stipulate that payments are to be made over a period of several years. Grants payable in future periods subject only to routine performance requirements by the grantee and not requiring subsequent review and approval for continuance of payment should be recorded as expenses and liabilities when the grants are first made. . . .*

The real problem, of course, is determining when a grant is subject ". . . only to routine performance requirements . . . and not requiring subsequent review and approval. . . ." As noted above, most multipayment grant awards contain language that requires certain interim reporting by the grantee and review by the private foundation. When do these "routine performance requirements" stop being routine, and instead become a basis for re-evaluation of the foundation's grant commitment every time it receives a report by the grantee?

There is no easy answer to this question, and it is necessary to examine very carefully the wording in the grant notification document. If from the terms of that document it is clear that the foundation has made the decision to make future years' payments conditional only upon the grantee institution doing what it says it will do, and it is reasonably clear that the grantee has the capacity to do so, then the full amount of future payments should be recorded. On the other hand, if the grant document merely indicates the foundation's general intent to consider favorably future requests, subject to a full review at that time, future payments would not be recorded. This would not constitute the type of grant obligation which should be reported since the commitment is contingent on a future decision by the foundation. Footnote disclosure of significant unrecorded amounts should, of course, be made.

Perhaps key to this discussion is the phrase "subject only to routine performance." All private foundations reserve the right to revoke unpaid grants if the grantee institution fails to live up to its past performance, to submit routine financial reports of the use of such funds, and the like. Grants made subject to these routine performance requirements would not normally constitute language sufficiently restrictive to

---

* Paragraphs 101–102 of the Statement of Position.

avoid the recording of the future grant payments. On the other hand, grants containing language such as the following would not be recorded:

The D. E. Martin Foundation Board of Trustees hereby grants to the Karen J. Sylvestre Home for Unwed Mothers the sum of $100,000 to establish a program for runaway teenage girls in the Washington, DC area. The staff of the Foundation will review carefully the uses made of this money during the first twelve months, and based upon their evaluation of the effectiveness of the program will consider additional annual requests for $100,000 to fund the second and third years' programs.

From the above, it is clear that next year the Foundation will investigate the uses made of the money and will then make a decision as to future support. Yet on the basis of the Foundation's intent, this organization can plan its program on the assumption that it will get the additional support in the following two years.

On the other hand, wording such as the following would appear to require recording in full:

The D. E. Martin Foundation Board of Trustees hereby grants $300,000 to the Karen J. Sylvestre Home for Unwed Mothers, payable $100,000 by check herewith and additional payments of $100,000 in each of the next two years. The payment of these future amounts is contingent upon receipt by the Foundation of a report by the Home which details the uses made of the monies received in the preceding year, an evaluation of the results of the program, and detailed budgets at the beginning of each program year.

In this instance it appears fairly clear that the Foundation has, in fact, committed itself for a three-year period and that it should record the full $300,000 both as an expense and as a liability at the time the grant is made.

There are, of course, many gray-area grants where the answer will not be as clear as in the illustrations above. The intent of the Statement of Position is for the foundation to record the grant if in all likelihood future payments will be routinely made. However, if the foundation has not made a final judgment on future payments, they should not be recorded.

Rationale. Some question why the obligation should be recorded both as a liability and as an expense in the current year. They point out that foundations derive their revenue primarily from endowment income, and that the future years' payments should be recorded as an expense at the time the income that will be used to pay the grant obligation is generated. Also, they point out that the recipient institution will normally be recording its "income" in the year in which the payment is due, not at the time of the grant award.

The reason the Statement of Position takes the approach discussed above is that historically such amounts are in fact paid and are, therefore, obligations. If a foundation which had committed itself to making future payments were not to record such amounts as an obligation, it would be presenting a rosier financial picture than is in fact the case. For example, one use of the financial statements is for the board to be aware of how much money is available for future grants. Amounts already committed, even if to be paid in future years, are clearly not available for new grants.

Others express concern because the recipient organization is following a somewhat different accounting treatment, namely recording income at the time the restrictions lapse, which is normally as the grant is spent. The reason is simply the different perspectives of the two organizations. In one the principle is to record at the time committed, whereas in the other it is to record at the time restrictions have lapsed.

Investments at Market

Private foundations typically have large investment portfolios. Under the Statement of Position, investments in marketable securities may be carried at either the lower of cost or market or market value (or amortized cost for certain marketable debt securities). Nonmarketable investments, such as oil and gas interests, real estate, etc., can continue to be carried at either the lower of cost or market or at market. Reference should be made to pages 83–85 and 264–267 for a discussion of the appropriate accounting and reporting procedures for investments.

Distinction Between Principal and Income

One accounting distinction that private foundations often make is the distinction between principal and income in their fund balance. Where such a distinction is made, the original principal and usually all capital gains thereon are accounted for separately from the accumulated, unspent income arising from investment of this principal. This distinction appears to be arbitrary and except where legal restrictions are involved usually serves no purpose to the readers of the financial statements.

This distinction between principal and income seems even less meaningful since the Tax Reform Act of 1969, and its requirement that minimum distributions be made (which will have the effect of dipping into capital gains and principal if dividends and income are not sufficient). The authors recommend that in the absence of legal restrictions these two amounts be combined and reported as a single "fund balance."

If an organization wishes to maintain the distinction, then the only place where the distinction should be made is in the fund balance section of the Balance Sheet as illustrated in the following abbreviated example:

Unrestricted Fund Balance:
Accumulated undistributed income .... $ 200,000
Original donor contribution 1,000,000

Total unrestricted fund balance $1,200,000

Community Foundations

Community foundations differ from private foundations mainly in that their source of contributions is the community at large rather than one person or family. This gives rise to certain tax and legal considerations which do not really affect financial accounting or reporting. Thus, all of the accounting and reporting principles discussed above are applicable to community as well as private foundations.

RELIGIOUS ORGANIZATIONS OTHER THAN CHURCHES

The term "religious organization" as contemplated here excludes individual churches which were discussed earlier in this chapter. Organizations that exist to service the particular needs of organized religion on a regional or national basis are included, as are organizations involved in the national administration of churches or their foreign missionary activities.

Combined Financial Statements

One of the difficult questions for a religious organization is to determine which entities are so financially interrelated that combined financial statements should be prepared as required by the Statement of Position. See the discussion on pages 277–282 in Chapter 16.

The intent of the Statement of Position is that there would be very few instances where combined financial statements would be appropriate, even for entities which are controlled by the reporting organization under ecclesiastical law.

It should be observed that even where the criteria requiring combined financial statements in the Statement of Position are met, there is a general exception for religious organizations. They may prepare combined statements, but are not required to do so. The key to determining when combination would be appropriate rests not on the factor of control but on the financial interrelationship. There is no requirement for preparing combined financial statements unless substantially all of the funds collected by the secondary unit will be transferred to the reporting organization or used for its benefit. Thus, for example, a diocese would not be required to combine the financial statements of the individual church units within its jurisdiction for purposes of its reporting. While the individual church units may raise funds in the name of the church, such funds will largely be used for local purposes, and not transmitted to the diocese.

Allocations from Other Organizations

Religious organizations frequently receive allocations from affiliated local or regional organizations. Usually the allocation is established by the "parent" organization at the beginning of the fiscal year, but is paid by the local organization at varying times throughout the year. An accounting question often arises as to timing of income recognition. Should it be at the beginning of the year when the allocation is determined, at the time it is paid, or pro rata throughout the year?

Recognition normally should be on a pro rata basis throughout the year since the services are presumably being rendered throughout the year. Where experience shows that the full allocation or assessment will not be paid, only the amount which can reasonably be expected to be paid should be recorded on this pro rata basis. Of course, unpaid collections at the end of the year must be reviewed for collectibility.

RESEARCH AND SCIENTIFIC ORGANIZATIONS

Research and scientific organizations are those nonprofit organizations existing primarily to do research in particular areas, usually under contract with government agencies, private foundations, or third parties.

Timing of Recording Contract Revenue

The most difficult question most research and scientific organizations have relates to the timing of recording contract revenue. Under the Statement of Position, contract revenue should be recorded as revenue at the time the contract terms are met. In most instances this is as expenses are incurred which can be charged against the contract.

Some research and scientific organizations receive grants unrestricted as to use, to assist the organizations in meeting their general expenses. Usually these organizations submit budgets to the granting organization indicating the time.frame and the type of activities which will be carried out with these unrestricted funds. As a general rule, recognition of such unrestricted grants should be on a time-frame basis, that is, pro rata over the period which the grant specifies. Where the research or scientific organization has submitted a budget to the grantor indicating an uneven use of these unrestricted funds, the grant revenue should be recognized in the time period provided in the submitted budget.

The recognition of revenue is independent of the actual receipt of the grant funds. In some instances grantors pay all of the funds in advance, and in others, in arrears. Where the grant is paid in advance it would be reflected as "deferred grant revenue" on the Balance Sheet; where the grant is paid in arrears, a receivable would be set up at the time of revenue recognition.

Recording Future Grant Awards. A related question arises as to the appropriateness of recording as both a receivable and as deferred grant revenue the amounts which the organization has been told it will receive for future activities—either restricted or unrestricted. Should an organization reflect large future years' grants on the Balance Sheet?

This is a difficult question to answer, but the general answer is "no," unless there is a legal right of the organization to enforce payment. Clearly if the grant has language in it such that the grantor can change its mind, with or without cause, such future grants would not be recorded. On the other hand, where a grantor has made the grant unconditional and it is clear that the only condition is the passage of time, there is justification for recording the grant both as a receivable and as deferred grant income. The burden, however, is on showing that the grant is unconditional and could be legally enforced. In many ways such future grants are similar to "pledges." The Statement of Position provides that pledges which are enforceable should be recorded; otherwise, not. The same applies to future grants.

PRIVATE ELEMENTARY AND SECONDARY SCHOOLS

Private elementary and secondary schools are those institutions which provide education below the college and university level and which are supported by tuition and contributions from private sources. Excluded from this category are publicly supported school systems.

Competency of Bookkeeping Staff

The most difficult accounting problem many of these institutions have does not relate to accounting principles, but rather to not having adequate bookkeeping and accounting capability to prepare meaningful financial statements on a periodic basis. The boards of such organizations should consider carefully their need for timely financial information and whether their present staffing arrangements can realistically meet this need. Where it appears that this is not possible, the board will have to consider the financial risks involved in not receiving timely financial information. See Chapter 21 for a discussion of alternatives to having a full-time bookkeeper.

Depreciation Accounting

Traditionally private elementary and secondary schools have tended to follow the accounting principles in the College and University Audit Guide which prohibits depreciation accounting techniques.° However, the Statement of Position clearly indicates that private schools should be using depreciation accounting.

Unfortunately, most private elementary and secondary schools have not been following depreciation accounting techniques in the past. In the authors' opinion, one of the reasons many private schools have run into financial difficulties is that boards of trustees have not been fully aware of the true cost of their schools, and accordingly have set their tuition fees too low. Depreciation is a cost, albeit not a cash cost, and should be reported as an expense if financial statements are to accurately reflect the actual cost of operating a school.

Accounting Manual

The National Association of Independent Schools published the second edition of *Accounting for Independent Schools* in 1977. It is widely recognized as the accounting manual private elementary and secondary schools should follow. For the most part, this manual is in agreement with the Statement of Position; however, in a number of areas there are differences. Some of the major differences are outlined below:

1. The Statement of Position provides that current restricted gifts and plant fund gifts are reported as income when the restrictions

° The College and University Audit Guide does permit depreciation accounting, but only in the plant fund. A college is not permitted to report depreciation in the current funds.

are met, whereas *Accounting for Independent Schools* requires they be reported as income when received.

2. The Statement of Position provides that board-designated endowment be reported as part of the unrestricted fund and not combined with the endowment fund. *Accounting for Independent Schools* provides that board-designated endowments are reported as part of the endowment fund.

3. As noted above, depreciation accounting is required by the Statement of Position, whereas *Accounting for Independent Schools* states depreciation is not recommended.

4. The Statement of Position provides for pledges being recorded if enforceable, whereas *Accounting for Independent Schools* provides that pledges are not recorded.

5. The Statement of Position provides that investment income is recorded directly in the fund to which the income applies, whereas *Accounting for Independent Schools* provides that such income should initially be recorded in the fund having the investments.

6. The Statement of Position requires interfund transfers to be shown in the fund balance section after the caption "Fund balance, beginning of the year." *Accounting for Independent Schools* provides that interfund transfers are reported before the final caption, "Net change for the year."

7. A Statement of Changes in Financial Position is required by the Statement of Position, but is not discussed at all by *Accounting for Independent Schools*.

Presumably the National Association of Independent Schools will in due course revise its manual to incorporate the changes brought about by the Statement of Position. In the meantime, institutions following the second edition of *Accounting for Independent Schools* should be aware that CPAs making an examination of the financial statements will not be able to say that the statements are in accordance with generally accepted accounting principles.

18

The Financial Accounting
Standards Board and
Future Trends in
Nonprofit Accounting

So far the discussion of accounting principles and reporting practices has dealt with existing authoritative literature which accountants and CPAs refer to when determining appropriate treatment of accounting questions. This chapter will deal with probable future developments. The chapter first discusses the potential impact on nonprofit accounting of the introduction into the nonprofit accounting arena of the Financial Accounting Standards Board (FASB). The later portion deals with some of the trends and developments which the authors see as likely to take place during the next five to ten years. It should be emphasized that much of the discussion in this chapter is conjecture, based on the authors' close involvement with many of the recent developments in this field, and reasonable expectations as to future developments.

FINANCIAL ACCOUNTING STANDARDS BOARD

The most interesting recent development has been the involvement of the Financial Accounting Standards Board in rule making for nonprofit organizations. Ultimately the FASB will have a significant impact on nonprofit accounting. To put this development into perspective, it is first necessary to describe the accounting profession's existing rule-making machinery, and detail its enforcement.

Establishment of Accounting Rules

Until June 30, 1973, the senior rule-making body was the Accounting Principles Board of the American Institute of Certified Public Accountants (AICPA). Accounting principles formally established by the Accounting Principles Board or its successor, discussed below, represent "generally accepted accounting principles," and CPAs reporting on financial statements of their clients cannot indicate that their clients are following generally accepted accounting principles unless they are, in fact, following the principles established by this Board or its successor. CPAs who report on a contrary treatment without appropriate indication in their opinion can be disciplined by both the accounting profession and the state licensing boards, with a possible loss of their CPA certificates.

The Accounting Principles Board never formally established accounting principles for nonprofit organizations as such. However, the Board did authorize publication of the various Industry Audit Guides discussed in Chapters 13–15. These Guides have some authoritative status although they do *not* formally constitute generally accepted accounting principles. This means that accountants would not necessarily be disciplined for violating the principles in these Guides. However, they could be called on to justify a departure from the Guides, since they represent the most authoritative literature on the subject. Embarrassing as this could be, seldom would it result in loss of a CPA certificate. However, all of the major accounting firms and most conscientious CPAs look upon these Guides as authoritative and are reluctant to violate them. This means that in practice the Guides are closely followed.

It is important to recognize that technically there are two levels of accounting rules: those rules that formally constitute generally accepted accounting principles from which departures cannot occur without CPAs calling attention to them as such in their opinions, and those rules that represent the best thoughts of the accounting profession from which departures can occur without CPAs identifying them in their opinions, although they may later have to justify their failure to do so.

Formation of FASB. In June, 1973, the Accounting Principles Board turned over its rule-making authority to a new and totally independent organization, the Financial Accounting Standards Board, usually referred to as the FASB. The Accounting Principles Board was disbanded. Since then, only the FASB is empowered to issue accounting principles which formally constitute generally accepted accounting principles. However, the FASB has yet to issue any accounting principles specifically addressed to the nonprofit sector.

AICPA's Statement of Position.   At the time the FASB was established in 1973, the AICPA set up an ongoing committee to make recommendations to the FASB on accounting issues. This ongoing AICPA body is the Accounting Standards Executive Committee (AcSEC). Its recommendations are made in the form of "Statements of Position" addressed to the FASB for its consideration. These Statements of Position are widely publicized, so in no sense are they private communications. In the absence of FASB statements to the contrary, these Statements of Position represent the best thoughts of the accounting profession on a given subject.

Upon receipt of a Statement of Position, the FASB has two basic options. The FASB can conclude that the subject matter of the Statement is sufficiently important that the FASB will place the subject on its agenda and consider it in the near future. When this is done the Statement of Position has little authority pending the FASB's resolution.

Alternatively, the FASB can indicate that it does not intend to consider the matter covered in the Statement of Position in the near future. When this happens the Statement of Position becomes the "most authoritative" discussion of the accounting principles involved on that subject, and has much the same authority as the Industry Audit Guides discussed above. As with the Audit Guides, a violation of a Statement of Position by a CPA would not necessarily result in disciplinary action by the accounting profession or by state licensing boards. The FASB has not as of this writing placed on its agenda the consideration of formal accounting standards for nonprofit entities, nor has it disapproved the Statement of Position.* The Statement of Position will continue to be the most authoritative discussion of accounting principles for nonprofit organizations not covered by one of the Industry Audit Guides until the FASB issues specific accounting standards for nonprofit organizations or until the FASB issues a "Conceptual Framework" for nonprofit organizations which conflicts with the Statement of Position (see below).

---

* The FASB has announced a proposed procedure for ultimately transforming existing AICPA Audit Guides and Statements of Position into FASB standards, but no action has yet been taken with respect to any of the nonprofit Guides or the Statement of Position. The FASB has also issued an accounting standard (no. 32) which states that for purposes of making a change from one accounting principle to another, the principles contained in the Guides and Statements of Position are considered preferable. This standard does not require an organization to change the accounting principles it follows, but if it wishes to change, the new principle must be in conformity with the applicable Guide or Statement of Position.

FASB Conceptual Framework

In August, 1977, the FASB indicated that it was exploring the possibility of issuing a financial reporting "conceptual framework policy statement" applicable to nonprofit organizations. A conceptual framework policy statement is a document which attempts to establish the framework on which individual, specific accounting principles (referred to by the FASB as "standards") can be developed which will facilitate consistency among principles. The conceptual framework policy statement, however, would not represent detailed accounting standards as such; these would be adopted subsequently as a separate procedure. In an earlier document,* the FASB summarized the purposes of such a framework as follows:

To establish the objectives and concepts that the Financial Accounting Standards Board will use in developing standards of financial accounting and reporting.

To provide guidance in resolving problems of financial accounting and reporting that are not addressed in authoritative pronouncements.

To enhance the assessment by users of the content and limitations of information provided by financial accounting and reporting and thereby further their ability to use that information effectively.

The FASB commissioned Dr. Robert Anthony of Harvard to develop a Research Study that would identify the issues he believed should be considered by the FASB in such a conceptual framework policy statement. His assignment was not to discern specific answers but rather to identify the issues and the alternatives he felt the FASB should consider.

The FASB also decided to include within the scope of this Research Study all entities not organized on a for-profit basis, that is, all "nonbusiness" entities. Initially it was the intention of the FASB to include governmental units in the scope of the study. Later, at the request of various groups connected with governmental accounting, the FASB agreed to remove governmental units from this study and make them the subject of separate concepts and standard-setting processes, under the control of a separate Government Accounting Standards Board.

Dr. Anthony completed his study in May, 1978, and it was published under the title: "Financial Accounting in Nonbusiness Organizations— An Exploratory Study of Conceptual Issues."

Subsequent to the issuance of Dr. Anthony's research study, the FASB decided to put the conceptual framework policy statement on its

---

* Financial Accounting Standards Board, *Exposure Draft*, "Objectives of Financial Reporting and Elements of Financial Statements of Business Enterprises" (Stamford, Conn: FASB, 1977), p. 1.

formal agenda. In doing so, the FASB indicated in a formal Discussion Memorandum the issues it intended to cover. All interested parties were asked to submit comments on the issues identified in the Discussion Memorandum, public hearings were held in late 1978, and an exposure draft was issued for public comment in 1980. Late in 1980 the FASB published Statement of Financial Accounting Concepts No. 4, "Objectives of Financial Reporting by Nonbusiness Organizations."

It is important to note that, while a conceptual framework policy statement sets the framework under which formal financial accounting standards will be written, the conceptual framework policy statement itself is *not* a rule book. The development of specific financial accounting standards is a separate, formal process and could take several years.

Expected Future FASB Action

The FASB has committed itself to a long and involved schedule of activities which has as its culmination the issuance of not only the conceptual framework described above, but also detailed accounting standards. With the heavy pressures the FASB is under from the profit-oriented sector, it would be surprising if detailed standards for the private nonprofit sector became final much before the mid-1980's.

Relationship of the AICPA to the FASB

This, of course, raises the obvious question of the relationship of the AICPA Statement of Position discussed in Chapter 16, and the various Industry Audit Guides, to the FASB and its proposed conceptual framework policy statement and possible future actions.

Even before completion of the conceptual framework project, the AICPA and FASB have taken steps to identify the accounting issues which must be considered in writing accounting standards for nonprofit organizations. The AICPA Nonprofit Accounting Subcommittee prepared a list of fifteen issues for FASB consideration. For one of the issues, the allocation of joint costs of multipurpose informational materials, the AICPA committee also prepared an "issues paper" setting forth its views. This issues paper, together with the list of fourteen other issues, will be used by the FASB in its deliberations prior to preparing formal accounting standards.

Once formal accounting standards have been issued by the FASB they will supersede the Industry Audit Guides and the Statement of Position. However, until then, unless the FASB takes contrary action, the Industry Audit Guides and the Statement of Position will continue to represent the most authoritative pronouncements on the subject by the accounting profession. Thus for the immediate future they will continue to have great impact.

TRENDS IN NONPROFIT ACCOUNTING

The balance of this chapter is devoted to discussing some of the reporting and accounting trends which the authors see, with the hope that readers may find these observations useful as they explore ways to strengthen the reporting of organizations with which they are associated.

The Organization as a Reporting Entity

Perhaps the most significant reporting trend is toward reporting on the organization as a whole, and away from reporting on the individual funds of the organization. For too long, organizations have been reporting on a fund-by-fund basis either in multicolumn format or on separate statements; confusion has resulted for most readers. In the future, more and more emphasis will be placed on reporting on the organization as a single entity. The use of multicolumn, layered, or separate fund-by-fund financial statements will gradually give way to reporting on a combined basis where the individual funds making up the entity will not be separately shown.

Figures 13–4 and 13–5 illustrate the type of reporting which seems to make sense and which the authors believe will ultimately become fairly standard.

Readers should compare Figures 13–4 and 13–5 with Figures 13–1 and 13–3 to appreciate the changes being suggested. Observe that while the financial statement presentation is much simpler in appearance, all essential information in the statements shown in Figures 13–1 and 13–3 is included in these new statements. The only essential difference is the degree of detail of restricted resources.

This is not to suggest that monitoring the restrictions and limitations placed on resources by outside parties will not continue to be important. Of course it will. However, the use of fund accounting for bookkeeping purposes does not dictate the use of fund accounting for reporting purposes; this is the significance of the trend.

Use of a Bottom Line

Another trend is toward reporting a "bottom line," that is, reporting the excess of revenue and support over expenses. Some nonprofit organizations have resisted this, believing that there is no significance to the fact or size of such an excess. However, boards and other readers are recognizing with increasing frequency that one of the most important single indicators of financial health is the "bottom line." The axiom that over time you can't spend more than you receive applies to all organizations, including nonprofit organizations.

Further, many readers find they are able to get a better overall understanding of the organization's financial statements if they first see a clearly labeled bottom line. The bottom line pulls together financial details and helps the reader to focus on the overall results of activities. It is similar in effect to the perspective astronauts achieve when looking at the North American continent from space. Once the overview is comprehended it is much easier to focus on the specifics.

Similarity to Profit-Oriented Reporting

Another related trend is that nonprofit reporting will become more similar in appearance to reporting by profit-oriented entities. This is not to suggest that there aren't transactions unique to nonprofit organizations; rather, it reflects the fact that readers of financial statements of nonprofit-oriented entities feel more comfortable—that is, more confident in their interpretive ability—with reporting formats that closely parallel those of profit-oriented entities. As a result, except where unique transactions suggest contrary treatment, the trend will be toward profit-oriented reporting.

Emphasis on Functional Reporting

Consistent with the various accounting pronouncements, reporting for nonprofit organizations will continue to emphasize program or functional reporting. Nonprofit organizations exist to perform services, not to pay salaries. Thus there will be greater emphasis on appropriately reporting the cost of services being rendered. Cost accounting techniques will become a standard tool in nonprofit accounting.

A Single Set of Accounting Principles for All Nonprofit Organizations

With the entry of the FASB, and increased awareness on the part of CPAs of the awkwardness of applying different principles to the same transaction for different types of organizations, we will see a gradual reconciliation of existing accounting pronouncements and the evolution of a single set of basic underlying accounting principles and reporting practices for all nonprofit organizations.

As with the Statement of Position discussed in Chapter 16, this does not mean that there will be a single reporting format applicable for all nonprofit organizations. This is neither practical nor appropriate, and it can reasonably be expected that there will continue to be many different reporting formats. But there will be greater uniformity in the basic information disclosed in the statements.

Development of "Industry" Accounting Manuals

The development of a single set of accounting principles will not decrease the need for individual manuals for each of the various types of nonprofit organizations; rather, it will increase the need. Just as the development of accounting principles in the nonprofit sector was initiated by industry groups, so too it can be expected that the various industry associations of different types of nonprofit organizations will continue to develop detailed accounting manuals to assist their own membership. Recent examples such as *Museum Accounting Guidelines,* developed by the museum world, and *Mission Accounting Guidelines,* developed for overseas missions, will be emulated by most other industry groups.

Uniform State Reporting

As is more fully discussed in Chapter 27, many states have reporting requirements for charitable organizations soliciting funds within their jurisdiction. Unfortunately, the reporting requirements differ from state to state, as have some of the reporting formats which must be used. This constituted a great expense for a national charity which may have had to file different reports in each of the various states. It was also awkward since the accounting principles applicable in one state often differed from those of another state.

In the past several years there has been increased recognition of these problems by various state regulatory bodies. As a result of efforts on the part of the Internal Revenue Service, state regulators, charities, the accounting profession, and others, starting in 1982, almost all the states have agreed to accept a copy of a (slightly revised) Form 990 in satisfaction of the basic financial statement reporting requirements. Most states require additional schedules and some an auditor's opinion; but using a single set of financial statements will be a major cost saving for national charities.

Federal Reporting Requirements

As discussed in Chapter 26, present federal reporting requirements relate primarily to filing information with the IRS to enable it to determine the tax status of activities of nonprofit organizations. The present IRS form (990) is largely a statistical report and is not particularly useful from a financial analysis perspective. Contributors and other interested parties get relatively little information from this tax report.

With the increased emphasis on full disclosure and accountability in recent years and an occasional newspaper headline about a charity that has abused its public trust, legislation has been introduced in the last several sessions of Congress which would, if adopted, require additional reporting by charitable organizations soliciting funds from the public. The legislation proposed has fallen basically into two alternative categories: regulatory and disclosure. Since each is distinctively different they are discussed separately below.

Regulatory-Type Legislation.   The regulatory-type legislation basically provides for filing financial statements and other information with a regulatory body to allow that body to determine the organization's conformity to certain standards established either by the legislation or by the regulatory body. Typically, the regulatory body is given authority to discipline the organization if transgressions occur which are deemed to be not in the public interest. The financial statements filed with the regulatory agency are usually open for public inspection, although often only at the agency's offices with the result that they are not really publicly available.

Disclosure-Type Legislation.   This alternative type of legislation basically provides that certain information be disclosed on the face of all fund-raising literature, including a statement that financial statements will be sent directly to the contributor upon request. Typically such legislation does not require the routine filing of a financial statement with a regulatory body, or the passing of judgment on these statements or on the charity by a regulatory body. The presumption is that, with access to financial information, the contributor can make a wiser decision than a regulatory body on which charity to support.

As can be seen, these two approaches are quite different. In the one, the presumption is that a regulatory body can better make the judgment as to the worthiness of an organization. In the other, the presumption is that the contributor can make the better judgment.

The authors believe that the *disclosure* approach would eliminate 95% of the credibility problems currently experienced by charitable organizations simply because charities will know that their financial affairs will routinely become public. Few will abuse public trust if they know with certainty they will be found out. In addition, the authors endorse recognition of the individual contributor, equipped with adequate information, as the best arbiter of worthiness among organizations competing for funds.

The authors expect that in the coming years our lawmakers in Washington will pay increased attention to charitable organizations and their reporting practices, and that some federal legislation will be passed. Unfortunately, it is far from clear which type of legislation will be enacted; in large measure the climate at the time of passage will be the determining factor. If legislation is passed as a result of newspaper headlines about the abuse of public trust by charities, an emotional outcry will likely produce a regulatory-type bill. Philanthropic organizations would be well advised to anticipate the problem by working toward passage of a disclosure-type bill.

CONCLUSION

With the introduction of the Financial Accounting Standards Board into the nonprofit accounting sector, and with increased attention directed at all of our public institutions, it appears that financial reporting by nonprofit organizations is bound to undergo increasing scrutiny. Perhaps foremost among the changes that will emerge is a re-assessment of the appropriateness of different accounting treatments for the same transaction by different types of organizations.

This trend toward greater openness and accountability is desirable and will continue to accelerate in the coming years. By the early 1980's financial statements will increasingly report on the organization as a whole rather than on a fund-by-fund basis. Our nonprofit institutions will increasingly find themselves in the "sunshine" environment of the post-Watergate era, and will increasingly recognize their responsibility to provide the public with meaningful financial information.

PART IV

CONTROLLING
THE NONPROFIT
ORGANIZATION

19

The Importance of Budgeting

A budget, like motherhood, is something very few would argue against. Yet, the art of preparing *and* *using* budgets in a meaningful manner is completely foreign to many nonprofit organizations. It is not that the treasurer or board is unaware of their importance, but more that they are uncertain of their skills in budgeting techniques, and often are reluctant to use a budget as a tool to control the financial activities. The purpose of this chapter is to discuss the importance of budgeting, the art of skillfully preparing a useful budget, and equally important, the art of actually using the budget to control.

THE BUDGET: A PLAN OF ACTION

A budget is a "plan of action." It represents the organization's blueprint for the coming months, or years, expressed in monetary terms. This means the organization must know what its goals are before it can prepare a budget. If it doesn't know where it is going, obviously it is going to be very difficult for the organization to do any meaningful planning. All too often the process is reversed and it is in the process of preparing the budget that the goals are determined.

So the first function of a budget is to record, in monetary terms, what the realistic goals or objectives of the organization are for the coming year (or years). The budget is the financial plan of action which results from the board's decisions as to the program for the future.

The second function of a budget is to provide a tool to monitor the financial activities throughout the year. Properly used, the budget can provide a bench mark or comparison point which will alert the board to the first indication that their financial goals won't be met. For a budget to provide this type of information and control four elements must be present:

1. The budget must be well-conceived, and have been prepared or approved by the board.
2. The budget must be broken down into periods corresponding to the periodic financial statements.
3. Financial statements must be prepared on a timely basis throughout the year and a comparison made to the budget, right on the statements.
4. The board must be prepared to take action where the comparison with the budget indicates a significant deviation.

Each of these four elements will be discussed in this chapter.

Steps for Preparation

It was noted above that a budget should represent the end result of a periodic review by the board or by the membership of the organization's objectives or goals, expressed in monetary terms. Often the budget process is a routine "chore" handled by the treasurer to satisfy the board that the organization has a budget, which the board, in turn, routinely ratifies. Frequently, such budgets are not looked at again until the following year, at the time next year's budget is prepared. This type of budgeting serves little purpose and is worth little more than the paper it is written on. A budget, to be effective, must be a joint effort of many people. It must be a working document which forms the basis for action.

Here are the basic steps that, in one form or another, should be followed by an organization in order to prepare a well-conceived budget:

1. A list of objectives or goals of the organization for the following year should be prepared. For many organizations this process will be essentially a re-evaluation of the relative priority of the existing programs. Care should be taken, however, to avoid concluding too hastily that an existing program should continue unchanged. Our society is not static and the organization that does not constantly re-evaluate and update its program is in danger of being left behind.
2. The cost of each objective or goal listed above should be estimated. For continuing programs, last year's actual expense and last year's budget will be the starting point. For new programs or modifica-

tions of existing programs, a substantial amount of work may be necessary to accurately estimate the costs involved. This estimating process should be done in detail since elements of a particular goal or objective may involve many categories of expenses and salaries.

3. The expected income of the organization should be estimated. With many organizations, contributions from members or the general public will be the principal income and careful consideration must be given to the expected economic climate in the community. A year when unemployment is high or the stock market is down is a poor year to expect "increased" contributions. With other organizations the amount of income will be dependent on how successful they are in selling their program. Possibly some of the programs can be expanded if they are financially viable, or contracted if they are not. Organizations are often overly optimistic in estimating income. This can prove to be the organization's downfall if there is no margin for error, and realism must be used or the budget will have little meaning.

4. The total expected income should be compared to the expense of achieving the objectives or goals. Usually the expected expenses will exceed income, and this is where some value judgments will have to take place. What programs are most important? Where can expected costs be reduced? This process of reconciling expected income and expenses is probably the most important step taken during the year because it is here that the program's blue-print for the coming year is fixed.

It is important that consideration be given to the reliability of the estimated income and expense figures. Is it possible that expenses have been underestimated or that income has been overestimated? If expenses have been underestimated by 15 per cent and income has been overestimated by 10 per cent, there will be a deficit of 25 per cent, and unless the organization has substantial cash reserves it could be in serious difficulty. If the organization has small cash reserves or has little likelihood of getting additional funds quickly, then a realistic safety margin should be built into the budget.

5. The final proposed budget should be submitted to the appropriate body for ratification. This may be the full board or it may be the entire membership. This should not be just a formality but should be carefully presented to the ratifying body so that, once ratified, all persons will be firmly committed to the resulting plan of action.

The steps listed above may seem so elementary that there is no need to emphasize them here. But elementary as they are, they are often not followed and the resulting budget is of very little value to the organization.

Responsibility for Preparation

There has been very little said about who should follow these steps in preparing the budget. The preparation of a budget involves policy decisions. The treasurer may be the person best qualified to handle the figures, but may or may not be the person to make policy decisions. For this reason, a "budget committee" should consist of persons responsible for policy decisions. Usually this means that either the board should itself act as the budget committee, or it should appoint a subcommittee of board members.

This doesn't mean that the detailed estimated cost studies for various programs can't be delegated to staff members. But the decision as to what are the goals and their relative priority has to be a board-level function.

Take, for example, a private independent school. At first glance there might not appear to be many board-level decisions to make. The purpose of a school is to teach and it might seem that the budget would be a most routine matter. But there are many decisions that have to be made. For example:

1. Should more emphasis be placed on science courses?
2. Should the school get a small computer to help teach computer science?
3. Should the school hire a language teacher for grades 2–4?
4. Should the school increase salaries in the coming year and try to upgrade the staff?
5. Should the athletic field be resodded this year?
6. Should a fund raiser be hired?
7. Should the music program be expanded?
8. Should tuition be increased?

These questions and many more face the board. Undoubtedly they may rely on the paid staff to make recommendations, but the board is responsible for policy and the budget represents "policy." This responsibility cannot be delegated.

MONTHLY AND QUARTERLY BUDGETS

Many organizations have no real difficulty in preparing an annual budget. The real problem comes in trying to divide the budget into meaningful segments that can be compared to interim financial statements prepared on a monthly or quarterly basis. Some organizations attempt to do this by dividing the total budget by twelve and showing the resulting amounts as a monthly budget, which is then compared to actual monthly income and expenses. While this is better than not making any budget comparison, it can produce misleading results when the income or expenses do not occur on a uniform basis throughout the year. Consider the following abbreviated statement of a small church:

	Annual Budget	Three Months Ending March 31	
		Annual Budget ÷ 4	Actual
Contributions	$ 120,000	$ 30,000	$ 35,000
Less Expenses	(120,000)	(30,000)	(30,000)
Excess	—	—	$ 5,000

The logical conclusion that might be drawn is that the chun h will have a surplus at the end of 12 months of approximately $20,000—four times the quarterly excess of $5,000. If this conclusion were reached the temptation would be to slacken off on unpaid pledge collection efforts and to be a little less careful in making purchases. This would be a very serious mistake if, in fact, the normal pattern of pledge collections were such that $36,000 should have been collected in the first quarter instead of the $35,000 actually received. A monthly or quarterly budget can produce misleading conclusions unless considerable care is taken in preparing it.

Allocating an Annual Budget to Monthly or Quarterly Periods

One of the best and easiest ways to allocate an annual budget into shorter periods is to first analyze the actual income and expense for the prior year, and then allocate this year's budget based on last year's actual expenses.

To illustrate, assume the church's income last year was $100,000 but is expected to be $120,000 this year. A budget for the new year could be prepared as follows:

Income:	Actual Last Year	Percent of Last Year's Total	New Budget
First quarter	$ 30,000	30%	$ 36,000
Second quarter	25,000	25%	30,000
Third quarter	25,000	25%	30,000
Fourth quarter	20,000	20%	24,000
	$100,000	100%	$120,000

In this illustration we have assumed that the increase in income of $20,000 will be received in the same pattern as the prior year's income was received. If this assumption is not correct, then adjustment must be made for the anticipated income which will depart from past experience. For example, if it is anticipated that a single gift of $10,000 will be received in the first quarter and the other $10,000 will be received in about the same pattern as last year's income, the calculations to arrive at a new budget would be somewhat different, as shown below:

	Actual Last Year	Percent of Last Year's Total	New Budget Other Than Special	Special Gifts	Total Budget
First quarter	$ 30,000	30%	$ 33,000	$10,000	$ 43,000
Second quarter	25,000	25%	27,500	—	27,500
Third quarter	25,000	25%	27,500	—	27,500
Fourth quarter	20,000	20%	22,000	—	22,000
	$100,000	100%	$110,000	$10,000	$120,000

If at the end of the first quarter income of only $35,000 had been received compared to a budget of $43,000, it would be apparent that steps should be taken to increase contributions or the church will fall short of meeting its budget for the year.

The expense side of the budget should be handled in the same way. Generally, expenses tend to occur at a more uniform rate, although this is not always so. In many ways the expense side of the budget is more important than the income side since it is easier to increase expenditures for things that weren't budgeted than to raise additional contributions. If the budget is regularly compared to actual expenditures for deviations, it can be an effective tool to highlight unbudgeted expenditures.

The budget should probably be prepared on a monthly rather than on a quarterly basis to reduce the time lag before effective action can be taken. If a monthly basis appears to be too cumbersome, consideration could be given to bimonthly budgets and statements. However, if the organization's cash position is tight, monthly statements become almost a necessity.

ILLUSTRATIVE EXPENSE BUDGET

The Valley Country Club is a good example of an organization that has to be very careful to budget its income and expenses. While the club has a beautiful clubhouse and a fine golf course, all of its money is tied up in these fixed assets and there is no spare cash to cover a deficit. Accordingly each fall when the board starts to wrestle with the budget for the following year it is aware that it cannot afford the luxury of a deficit. Since the budget is so important, the entire board sits as a budget committee to work out the plans for the following year. The treasurer, with the help of the club manager, prepares a worksheet in advance of the budget meeting. This worksheet indicates the actual expenses for the current year to date, the estimate of the final figures for the year, and the current year's budget to show how close the club will come. The board through discussion and debate attempts to work out a budget for the coming year. Figure 19–1 shows the worksheet for the expense budget.

In looking at this worksheet notice first that the expenses are grouped by major function so that the board can focus attention on the activities of the club. The alternative presentation would have been to list expenses by type—salaries, supplies, food, etc.—but this doesn't tell the board how much each of the major activities is costing.

There are three columns for the proposed budget—the minimum, the maximum, and the final amount. As the board considers each item it records both the minimum and the maximum it feels is appropriate. No attempt is made at the beginning to fix a "final" budget amount. Instead all budget items are considered, listed as to the minimum and maximum cost, and totals arrived at. It is only after all items have been considered, and only after a preliminary review of potential income has been made, that the board is in a position to make a judgment.

After the board has completed this worksheet showing final figures for the year, the next step is to break down the budget into monthly budgets. As with many organizations, the Valley Country Club's expenses (and income) are seasonal. In this case, the budget is broken down into monthly segments assuming that the expenses will be incurred

THE VALLEY COUNTRY CLUB

WORKSHEET FOR PREPARING 19X1 EXPENSE BUDGET
(in thousands)

	Actual Current Year			Budget Current Year	Budget for New Year		
	To Date (10 Months)	Estimate Balance Of Year	Estimate For Year		Proposed Minimum	Proposed Maximum	Final
Maintenance of greens and grounds:							
Salaries and wages	$ 47	$ 3	$ 50	$ 46	$ 50	$ 65	$ 55
Seeds, fertilizer and supplies	14		14	13	14	14	14
Repairs, maintenance and other	12	2	14	10	10	15	15
Maintenance of clubhouse:							
Salaries and wages	20	4	24	23	24	28	26
Supplies, maintenance and repair	10	1	11	12	11	11	11
Golf activities:							
Salaries and wages	10		10	11	12	20	20
Tournament costs	14		14	15	15	15	15
Golf cart maintenance	8		8	5	5	5	5

Swimming pool expenses:							
Salaries and wages	4		4	4	5	10	5
Supplies and maintenance	2		2	1	2	2	2
General and administrative salaries	35	6	41	40	44	51	44
Property taxes	33	7	40	38	42	42	42
Other expenses	41	7	48	40	40	50	50
Total, excluding restaurant	250	30	280	258	274	328	304
Restaurant expenses:							
Food and beverages	96	13	109	67	110	150	130
Salaries and wages:							
Kitchen	32	6	38	30	45	60	50
Dining room	20	4	24	19	26	39	32
Bartender	11	2	13	10	14	19	16
Supplies, repairs and maintenance	13	4	17	8	15	25	18
Total restaurant	172	29	201	134	210	293	246
Total expenses	$422	$59	$481	$392	$484	$621	$550

Fig. 19—1.   Worksheet used in preparing an expense budget for a country club.

in the same pattern as they were for the current year, in the manner discussed earlier.

TIMELY INTERIM STATEMENTS

The most carefully thought out budget will be of little value if it is not compared throughout the year with the actual results of operations. This means that the interim financial statements must be prepared on a timely basis.

What is timely? This largely depends on the organization and how much "slippage" or deviation from budget the organization can afford before serious consequences take place. If the cash balance is low an organization can't afford the luxury of not knowing where it stands on a timely basis. Guidelines are dangerous, but if an organization is unable to produce some form of abbreviated monthly or quarterly financial statement within 20 days of the end of the period the likelihood is that the information is "stale" by the time it is prepared. If 20 days is the length of time it takes then the board should plan to meet shortly after the twentieth of the month so as to be able to act on deviations while there is still time to act.

This is not to suggest that monthly financial statements are always appropriate for nonprofit organizations. But even if prepared on a bi-monthly or quarterly basis, they should still be prepared on a timely basis.

Importance of Budget Comparison

The financial statement should also show the budget, and for the same period of time. Interim figures for the three months cannot easily be compared to budget figures for twelve months. The budget must also be for three months. Last year's actual figures for the same period may also be shown, although this added information could detract from the reader's seeing the deviation from the current year's budget.

Figure 19–2 shows the Valley Country Club Statement of Income and Expenses for both the month of June and for the six months, with budget comparisons to highlight deviations from the budget.

This financial statement gives the reader a great deal of information about the club's activities for the two periods. It should have the effect of alerting the reader to the fact that unless something happens, there may be a deficit for the year. For instead of having a small excess for June, there was a deficit of $6,240, and instead of having an excess of $7,500 for the six months, there was a deficit of almost $5,000. The board member reading the statement should be concerned about these devia-

VALLEY COUNTRY CLUB

STATEMENT OF INCOME AND EXPENSES, AND COMPARISON WITH BUDGET
For the Month of June and the 6 Months Ending June 30, 19X1

	Month			6 Months		
	Actual	Budget	Deviation Favorable (Unfavorable)	Actual	Budget	Deviation Favorable (Unfavorable)
Income:						
Annual dues	$15,650	$17,000	($1,350)	$ 81,900	$ 90,000	($ 8,100)
Initiation fees	2,100	2,000	100	6,600	4,500	2,100
Greens fees	4,750	4,000	750	11,000	8,000	3,000
Swimming	3,300	3,000	300	2,300	2,000	300
Other	6,710	8,000	(1,290)	18,250	14,000	4,250
Total, excluding restaurant	32,510	34,000	(1,490)	120,050	118,500	1,550
Restaurant	37,850	34,000	3,850	168,500	180,000	(11,500)
Total income	70,360	68,000	2,360	288,550	298,500	(9,950)
Expenses:						
Maintenance of greens and grounds	14,650	12,000	(2,650)	37,650	36,000	(1,650)
Maintenance of clubhouse	3,450	3,000	(450)	18,100	19,000	900
Golf activities	13,500	10,000	(3,500)	19,500	16,000	(3,500)
Swimming pool	3,400	3,000	(400)	5,100	4,000	(1,100)
General and administrative	4,200	3,700	(500)	24,150	22,000	(2,150)
Payroll taxes	3,700	3,500	(200)	23,500	21,000	(2,500)
Other expenses	4,150	5,000	850	19,560	20,000	440
Total, excluding restaurant	47,050	40,200	(6,850)	147,560	138,000	(9,560)
Restaurant	29,550	27,000	(2,550)	145,650	153,000	7,350
Total expenses	76,600	67,200	(9,400)	293,210	291,000	(2,210)
Excess of income over (under) expenses	($ 6,240)	$ 800	($7,040)	($ 4,660)	$ 7,500	($12,160)

Fig. 19–2. Statement of Income and Expenses for both the month and year to date, showing a comparison to budget.

tions from the budget. This form of presentation makes it easy to see deviations. All unfavorable deviations can be quickly pinpointed and the reasons for them can be explored to determine the action that must be taken to prevent their recurrence.

Notice that both the current month and the year-to-date figures are shown on this statement. Both are important. The monthly figures give a current picture of what is happening, which cannot be learned from the six-month figures. If only the six-month figures were shown the reader would have to refer to the previous month's statements showing the first five months to see what happened in June. Likewise, to show only the month, with no year-to-date figures, puts a burden on the reader. Some calculating using previous monthly statements would be required to get a total and see where the club stood cumulatively. Year-to-date budget comparisons are often more revealing than monthly comparisons because minor fluctuations in income and expenses tend to offset over a period of months. These fluctuations can appear rather large in any one month.

Restaurant Operation

Restaurant income and expenses have been shown "gross" in the statements. It would be equally proper for the club to show net income for the club before the restaurant operation was considered. Here is how this would look:

Income (excluding restaurant)	$ 120,050
Expenses (excluding restaurant)	147,560
Excess of expenses over income excluding restaurant	(27,510)
Restaurant	
Gross income	168,500
Expenses	(145,650)
Net restaurant income	22,850
Excess of expenses over income	$ (4,660)

Another possibility is to show only the net income of the restaurant in the statements, perhaps in the income section. In condensed form here is how the statements would look:

Income	
Other than restaurant	$ 120,050
Restaurant net income	22,850
Total income	142,900
Expenses (other than restaurant)	(147,560)
Excess of expenses over income	$ (4,660)

Either presentation, or the one in Figure 19–2, is acceptable. The appropriate presentation depends on the importance of highlighting the restaurant activities.

Variable Budget

One technique that is often used in budgeting an operation where costs increase as the volume of activity increases is to relate the budgeted costs to income. For example, the final expense budget (Figure 19–1) and the relationship to budgeted income for the restaurant operation is as follows:

	Amount	Percent of Income
Income	$290,000	100%
Food and beverages	$130,000	45%
Salaries and wages		
Kitchen	50,000	17
Dining room	32,000	11
Bartender	16,000	6
Supplies, repairs and maintenance	18,000	6
	$246,000	85%

If all costs increase proportionately as income increases, it is a simple matter to create new budget figures each month based on actual income. Using the six-month figures shown in Figure 19–2, our budget comparison for the restaurant activity for the six-month period would look like this:

	Actual	Variable Budget	Deviation from Variable Budget	Deviation from Original Budget Shown in Figure 19–2
Income	$168,500	$180,000 *	$(11,500)	$(11,500)
Expenses (in total)	145,650	143,225 †	(2,425)	7,350
Net	$ 22,850	$ 36,775	$(13,925)	$ (4,150)

* Original budget for six months.

† 85% of actual income for the six months, based on the relationship of budgeted expenses to budgeted income as shown above.

The significant observation here is that while the original budget comparison in Figure 19–2 showed an unfavorable deviation from budget of only $4,150, the unfavorable deviation using this variable budget is significantly higher, $13,925. Obviously if the variable budget is accurate, the club manager has not been watching costs carefully enough.

The financial statements would show only the variable expense budget. The original expense budget would not be used. This kind of budget is more difficult to work with because each month the treasurer or bookkeeper has to recalculate the expense figures to be used based on actual income. At the same time by doing so, a meaningful budget comparison can then be made. It is very difficult otherwise for the board to judge the restaurant's results.

One final observation about this variable budget. Certain costs are not proportional to income. For example, the club cannot have less than one bartender or one chef. Accordingly, in preparing a variable budget sometimes the relationships that are developed will not be simple percentage relationships. For example, perhaps the relationship of bartender salary will be, say, $5,000 plus 5 per cent of total income over $75,000. If so, then if restaurant income is $350,000, the budget will be $18,750 ($5,000 + 5 per cent of $275,000).

Narrative Report on Deviations from Budget

It will be noted that much of the detail shown in the budget (Figure 19–1) has not been shown on the interim financial statement (Figure 19–2). If the board felt it appropriate, supporting schedules could be prepared giving as much detail as desired. Care should be taken, however, not to request details that won't be used since it obviously takes time and costs money to prepare detailed supporting schedules.

It may be that a more meaningful supporting schedule would be a narrative summary of the reasons for the deviations from budget for the major income and expense categories. The club manager, in the case of the Valley Country Club, would probably be the one to prepare this summary. The amount of detail and description that might be put in this summary would vary from account to account. Clearly the report should only discuss reasons for the major deviations. This report should accompany the financial statement so that questions raised by the statement are answered immediately. Figure 19–3 shows an example of the type of summary that might be prepared to explain the expense deviations from budget (in part).

This type of report can be as informal as you want to make it as long as it conveys why there have been deviations from the original budget. But it should be in writing, both to ensure that the board knows the reasons, and to force the club manager to face squarely the responsibility

VALLEY COUNTRY CLUB

CLUB MANAGER'S REPORT TO THE BOARD
EXPENSE DEVIATIONS FROM BUDGET, JUNE 19X1

Maintenance of greens and grounds ($2,650)

As you will recall, April and May were fairly wet months. This coupled
with other unfavorable soil conditions required that we treat about 25%
of the course with a fungicide which had not been budgeted ($1,850). We
also had some unexpected repairs to the sprinkler system ($1,500). For
the six months to date we have exceeded budget by only $1,650 and I am
confident that our annual budget will not be exceeded.

Maintenance of clubhouse ($450)

We had scheduled painting the Clubhouse for May but because of the
rains were not able to get it done until this month. Year-to-date expenses
are $900 under budget.

Golf activities ($3,500)

After the budget had been approved the Board decided to have an
open tournament with a view toward attracting new membership. With
promotion and prizes this came to $2,850. So far the membership com-
mittee has received thirteen new applications for membership.

**Fig. 19–3. An example of a narrative report prepared by the manager of a
country club explaining why certain major deviations have occurred from budget.**

to meet the projected budget. This report is a form of discipline for the
manager.

Action by the Board

The best-prepared budget serves little purpose if the board is un-
willing to take action once it becomes apparent that expenses are exceed-
ing budget or that income has not been as high as anticipated. To be
useful, the budget must be a planning device that everyone takes seriously; otherwise its usefulness is truly limited. There must be follow-up
action.

The type of reporting discussed in this chapter will give the board
information on where the plan is not being followed. But the board must
be prepared to take action when the deviations are serious. Perhaps all
that will be appropriate is for the board to discuss the budget deviations
with the club manager. A club manager who knows that the board fully
expects performance within the budget will take appropriate action. If
some matters are beyond the control of the manager, he or she may suggest alternatives to the board for its action.

The board must be prepared to take action to modify its plans if it becomes apparent that the budget cannot be met. If the organization has substantial resources to fall back on, it can afford to accept some deviations from the original budget without serious financial consequences. For most organizations, this is not the case. The board must be willing to face unpleasant facts once it becomes apparent from interim financial statements that corrective action must be taken. Many budgets fail, not because there is not enough information available to the board, but because the board fails to take aggressive, corrective action. In these instances, the board is not fulfilling its responsibilities and the budget is a meaningless formality.

A FIVE-YEAR MASTER PLAN

So far our discussion has centered on budgeting techniques for the current year. Almost as important, and quite related, are the techniques for planning even further into the future than the twelve-month period most budgets use. As will be discussed more fully in the next chapter, organizations must be constantly alert to changing conditions which may alter their goals or objectives and thus their sources of income. Otherwise they may find themselves in unexpected financial difficulty. One of the more effective ways organizations can avoid the unexpected is to prepare, and periodically update, a five-year master plan. The purpose of this five-year plan is to force the board to look ahead and anticipate not only problems but goals and objectives that it wants to work toward achieving.

The development of a five-year plan requires considerable effort. The treasurer can be the person who initiates and pushes the board toward developing such a plan but cannot single-handedly prepare it. As was discussed earlier on budget preparation, to be effective any plan of action involving the organization's program and allocation of resources must be developed by all of the people who will have to live with the resulting plans. To unilaterally prepare a five-year plan risks the strong possibility that the treasurer's conceptions of the important objectives are not truly representative of the conceptions of the rest of the board.

Suggested Procedures

There is no "standard" way to go about preparing a five-year plan. Probably the best way to start is to set up a committee of, say, three persons. As with the budget committee discussed earlier in this chapter, the persons chosen for this five-year planning committee should be persons who are in policy-making roles within the organization. There is little point in putting a person on this committee who is not both knowledgeable and influential within the organization. Otherwise the resulting document will be of relatively little value to the organization.

Setting Goals.   Before meeting as a committee, each member should be instructed to take five sheets of paper, each representing one of the five years. On each sheet the member should list all of the goals or objectives that are considered important for that year. The list can be specific or general. The important thing is to get down some thoughts as to what the organization should be doing during each year, particularly as they might be different from what is being done currently. No consideration should be given at this point to dollar costs—only goals or objectives.

Once each member of the committee has independently prepared this conception of the future goals or objectives of the organization, the committee should meet and discuss these projections jointly. There may or may not be initial agreement among the three, and if not, there should be extended discussions to try to establish a plan of objectives that all members can agree on as being reasonable. If, after extended discussions, the committee cannot agree on these broad objectives, they should go back to the board for direction. All of this is *before* any figures have been associated with each specific objective or goal. The organization must decide what its goals or objectives are before it starts worrying about costs.

Estimating Costs.   Once the committee has agreed upon objectives for each of the five years, then it is appropriate to start to estimate the costs involved in reaching each of these goals. This can be difficult because there are always many unknowns and uncertainties as to the details of how each goal will be accomplished. Nevertheless, it is important that the best estimate be made by the committee. Clearly the treasurer is a key person in this estimating process. Among other things, it is up to the treasurer to try to factor inflation and realism as to costs into these figures.

After the committee has associated dollar costs with each objective for the five years, the next step is to add up the total to see how much income will have to be raised. Notice that until this point, no real consideration has been given to how the goals will be financed. This is important because in long-range planning an organization should sets its objectives and then look for the means to reach them. If the objectives are good ones which the membership or public will agree should be accomplished, the financial support should follow. An organization gets into difficulty when it does not periodically re-evaluate its direction and thus finds itself out of step with our rapidly changing society. So the procedure to follow is first to define the objectives and goals, then to associate dollar amounts with each, and finally to determine how to raise the necessary income. It must be in this order.

Plan for Income.   This final step of determining how the income will be raised is usually not as difficult as it may sound provided the goals and objectives are ones that the board and the membership believe are sound. It is possible that as a result of this five-year plan new sources of income may be required. Perhaps a foundation will be approached, or perhaps a major capital improvement fund drive will be started. There are many possibilities. The important thing is that the organization has no right to exist except as it serves societal or members' interests. So if the organization keeps up with the times it should be able to get sufficient support to achieve its objectives; if it does not, this is clear evidence that the objectives or goals are not sufficiently important to justify support. At that point the organization should either change its goals or should seriously consider the desirability of discontinuing its existence.

Illustrative Master Plan

The result of this whole process is a master plan that should guide the board in its planning. It should be reviewed at least every year or two and should be updated and extended so that it represents, at all times, a five-year plan for the future. Figure 19–4 shows an example of a simple master plan for the Center for the Development of Human Resources. The Center for the Development of Human Resources is one of many organizations that has come into existence in the last few years to help individuals "grow" through interaction in study groups. The center has a professional staff organizing and running programs, which are held in a rented building.

Note that on this master plan the center has indicated future expenses not in terms of the type of expenses (salaries, rent, supplies, etc.) but in terms of the goals or objectives of the organization. This distinction is important because the center pays salaries and other costs only to further some goal or objective. Thus, in a master plan it is entirely appropriate to associate costs with each goal or objective. This means that a certain amount of allocation of salaries between goals will be necessary.

Another observation is that the format of this master plan did not start off with the traditional approach of showing income and then deducting expenses. Instead, the goals or objectives were stated first and only after the organization agreed on what it wanted to do did it start to work on

CENTER FOR THE DEVELOPMENT OF HUMAN RESOURCES
MASTER PLAN—19X2 THROUGH 19X6

	19X2	19X3	19X4	19X5	19X6
Goals or objectives:					
Develop and run management program	$ 17,000	$ 22,000	$ 25,000	$ 27,000	$ 30,000
Reprogram receptive listening program	12,000	–	–	–	–
Continue receptive listening program	35,000	35,000	45,000	45,000	45,000
Work with other "centers" across country	–	12,000	15,000	15,000	15,000
Develop and run child day care training centers	8,000	15,000	20,000	20,000	20,000
Explore Project "A"	20,000	10,000	–	–	–
Run other programs	40,000	45,000	50,000	55,000	55,000
Purchase building for center	–	150,000	–	–	–
Total	132,000	289,000	155,000	162,000	165,000
Sources of income:					
Contributions from members	60,000	45,000	60,000	60,000	60,000
Special gifts and legacies	10,000	10,000	–	–	–
Building fund drive	–	100,000	–	–	–
Program fees:					
Management	10,000	15,000	18,000	20,000	22,000
Receptive listening	30,000	35,000	45,000	45,000	45,000
Child care	–	5,000	10,000	10,000	10,000
Other	38,000	40,000	45,000	45,000	45,000
Foundation grants:					
Child care	10,000	–	–	–	–
Building fund	–	50,000	–	–	–
Total	158,000	300,000	178,000	180,000	182,000
Projected surplus	$ 26,000	$ 11,000	$ 23,000	$ 18,000	$ 17,000

Fig. 19–4. An example of a five-year master plan which emphasizes the objectives and goals of the organization.

how to raise the necessary income. This point has been emphasized because the organization does not exist to raise money and pay expenses; it exists to accomplish certain objectives, and unless these are spelled out clearly and are constantly kept in mind the organization may lose sight of the reason for its existence.

No attempt was made in this master plan to balance the amounts of income and expense except in a general way. In each year there is an indicated surplus. This recognizes that while the board has made its best guess as to how it will raise its income, there are a great many unknowns when working with a five-year budget. As each year passes and this five-year plan is updated (and extended) the sources of income will become more certain, as will costs, and these figures will be refined and adjusted. The important thing, however, is that the board has set down what it plans to do in the future, and how it now expects to be able to finance such plans.

CONCLUSION

A budget can be an extremely important and effective tool for the board in managing the affairs of the organization. However, to prepare a meaningful budget the organization must know where it is heading and its goals and objectives. Priorities change, and this means that many people should be involved in the budget preparation and approval process to insure the resulting budget is fully supported. Once prepared, the budget must be compared to actual results on a timely basis throughout the year to insure that the board knows where deviations are occurring. Equally important, the board must promptly take corrective action if unfavorable deviations occur. The foundations of a sound financial structure are a well-conceived budget, a timely reporting system, and a willingness by the board to take corrective action.

The importance of planning into the future cannot be overemphasized. In this fast-moving age, worthy nonprofit organizations can quickly get out of step with the times, and when this happens contributions and income quickly disappear. A five-year master plan is one technique to help ensure this won't happen.

20

Avoiding Bankruptcy

"Bankruptcy?" "It can't happen to us!" These are famous last words. Of course it can. Don't think that your organization is immune to all of the ills that can befall any organization whether it is a commercial or a nonprofit one. Insolvency will be the fate of many organizations that are today vigorous and healthy. An organization's importance and reputation will not by themselves protect it. Avoiding bankruptcy takes effort and real skill.

EARLY RECOGNITION OF PROBLEMS

While the final responsibility for the financial health of the organization is the board's, the treasurer is the person charged with watching both the day-to-day and long-term financial picture. Without doubt one of the most important functions of the treasurer is to recognize potential problems while there is still time to act. While it might seem like a simple task to recognize that the organization is in, or is headed for financial trouble, the fact is that many organizations hide their heads in the sand like ostriches and fail to recognize the symptoms at a time when they might be able to do something.

The reason why recognizing that there is a problem on a timely basis is so important, is that most nonprofit organizations have so little cash. They cannot afford the luxury of waiting until after the problem has fully manifested itself, because if they do, they may run out of cash. If there are substantial reserves in the bank, most small organizations can afford several years of deficits before they really have to become concerned about the future. But few organizations have this amount of cash reserves. Organizations usually have enough cash for only three or four months' operations if all income ceased.

A balanced budget, based on conservative revenue estimates, is an effective means to avoid financial calamity. A balanced budget requires that difficult decisions, such as program curtailment or elimination, be made during each budget cycle, rather than deferring them until a future date, at which time a genuine crisis may have developed and the future of the organization itself may be imperiled.

There is no perpetual life for nonprofit organizations. And this is as it should be. Nonprofit organizations have a privileged place in our society. Most have been granted certain tax privileges which means that society as a whole has a right to demand that they perform their function in the public interest. If the organization fails to be responsive, no matter how "worthwhile" its program may be when viewed objectively from afar, the organization will have a short life. This is as true of churches and religious organizations as it is of other types. The organization must be responsive, and the contributor is the final judge of whether it is or not. This means the treasurer must be alert to indications that the health of the organization may be declining either as shown in historical financial statements, or as projected into the future.

Historical Statements as a Guide

Many look upon past financial statements only as an historical book-keeping record that has little significance for the future. This is a mistake. Often there is a clear indication in these statements of potential problems for the future. This can often be seen by comparing several years' statements, because relationships may become obvious that were not apparent when looking at only one year's statements.

An example can best illustrate this point. The five-year master plan of the Center for World Peace is shown in Figure 20–1.

This statement offers a great deal of information to the observant treasurer and should help in anticipating problems. The obvious and most serious problem revealed is that there has been a large deficit in 19X5 which, if repeated, would wipe out the organization. But beyond this obvious observation, a number of other important clues can be seen. Note first the relationship between expenses and program fees over the years. From 19X1 to 19X5 expenses have gone up almost 40 per cent, but program fees have gone up only 13 per cent. Either the organization is not charging enough for its programs, or the programs are not responsive to the membership and therefore attendance is down. Alternatively, perhaps the center has gotten too sophisticated in its program-

CENTER FOR WORLD PEACE

SUMMARY OF INCOME, EXPENSES, AND CASH BALANCES
RESULTING FROM CASH TRANSACTIONS
For the Five Years Ended December 31, 19X5

	19X1	19X2	19X3	19X4	19X5
Income:					
Contributions	$ 53,000	$ 65,000	$ 56,000	$ 66,000	$ 49,000
Program fees	46,000	48,000	48,000	50,000	52,000
Other	3,000	3,000	2,000	3,000	2,000
Total income	102,000	116,000	106,000	119,000	103,000
Expenses:					
Salaries	68,000	72,000	76,000	78,000	80,000
Rent	14,000	16,000	18,000	20,000	24,000
Supplies	9,000	10,000	14,000	18,000	22,000
Other	3,000	3,000	4,000	5,000	6,000
Total expenses	94,000	101,000	112,000	121,000	132,000
Excess of income over (under) expenses	8,000	15,000	(6,000)	(2,000)	(29,000)
Cash balance, beginning of the year	34,000	42,000	57,000	51,000	49,000
Cash balance, end of the year	$ 42,000	$ 57,000	$ 51,000	$ 49,000	$ 20,000

Fig. 20–1.　An example of a five-year Statement of Income, Expenses, and Cash Balances which can assist the reader in spotting trends.

ming, with too many paid staff for the size of fees that can be charged. These are the kinds of questions that have to be asked.

Another question that should concern the treasurer is why contributions have fluctuated so much from year to year. Is there significance in the decline in contributions received, from $66,000 in 19X4 to $49,000 in 19X5? Does this represent a strong "vote" by the membership that they are not interested in the programs of the center, or that something is wrong? This question concerned the treasurer and after some digging, these facts were found:

Year	Recurring Contributions	Special or One-Time Gifts	Total
19X1	$43,000	$10,000	$53,000
19X2	45,000	20,000	65,000
19X3	47,000	9,000	56,000
19X4	55,000	11,000	66,000
19X5	49,000	—	49,000

CENTER FOR WORLD PEACE

SUMMARY OF INCOME AND EXPENSES
For the Five Years Ended December 31, 19X5

	19X1	19X2	19X3	19X4	19X5
Recurring income:					
Contributions	$43,000	$ 45,000	$ 47,000	$ 55,000	$ 49,000
Program fees	46,000	48,000	48,000	50,000	52,000
Other	3,000	3,000	2,000	3,000	2,000
Total	92,000	96,000	97,000	108,000	103,000
Expenses (total)	94,000	101,000	112,000	121,000	132,000
Excess of expenses over recurring income	(2,000)	(5,000)	(15,000)	(13,000)	(29,000)
Special nonrecurring gifts	10,000	20,000	9,000	11,000	–
Excess of income over (under) expenses	$ 8,000	$ 15,000	($ 6,000)	($ 2,000)	($ 29,000)

Fig. 20–2. A five-year Statement of Income and Expenses in which nonre-curring special gifts are shown separately to highlight continuing income.

From this analysis it is easy to see what happened. The center had been living off special or one-time gifts and these gifts were not received in 19X5. Most of the special gifts had come from half a dozen people, some now deceased. It is obvious that the earlier five-year summary did not tell the whole story, and the treasurer recast this statement showing these special gifts separately. Figure 20–2 shows in condensed form these revised statements.

From this statement it is easy for the treasurer and the board to see that they had been living off special gifts in every year except 19X5. Obviously hard decisions had to be made as to whether the center should count on receiving such special gifts in the future and, if not, how expenses could be cut or additional income gained.

Analysis of Interim Statements

It is not necessary (or wise) to wait for the completion of a full year's activities before starting to draw conclusions from the trends that should be obvious to the careful analyst. Figure 20–3 illustrates a worksheet showing a comparison of actual with budget for three months, and a projection for the entire year based on the assumption that the experience for the first three months compared to budget is a good indication of what can be expected for the next nine months.

CENTER FOR WORLD PEACE

WORKSHEET SHOWING CALCULATION OF PROJECTED INCOME AND EXPENSES
For the Year 19X6

| | 3 Months to March 31 | | | 9 Months April to December | | 12 Months | |
	Actual	Budget	Percentage Actual to Budget	Budget	Projected Based on Actual*	Budget	Projected
Recurring income:							
Contributions	$18,000	$20,000	90%	$38,000	$ 34,200	$ 58,000	$ 52,200
Program fees	17,000	18,000	95%	42,000	39,900	60,000	56,900
Other	500	500	100%	1,500	1,500	2,000	2,000
Total	35,500	38,500	92%	81,500	75,600	120,000	111,100
Expenses:							
Salaries	22,000	21,000	105%	63,000	66,100	84,000	88,100
Rent	6,000	6,000	100%	18,000	18,000	24,000	24,000
Supplies	4,500	2,500	180%	7,500	13,500	10,000	18,000
Other	1,000	500	200%	1,500	3,000	2,000	4,000
Total	33,500	30,000	111%	90,000	100,600	120,000	134,100
Excess of income over (under) expenses	$ 2,000	$ 8,500		($ 8,500)	($ 25,000)	—	($ 23,000)

*I.e.: percentage actual to budget for three months times budget for nine months (90% x 38,000 = $34,200).

Fig. 20—3. An example of a worksheet projecting income and expenses for the year based on only the first three months' actual experience.

Based on this worksheet it is obvious that unless something happens to change the pattern, instead of being ahead of budget the center is headed for a deficit of $23,000. As will be recalled, the center had only $20,000 in cash at the beginning of the year, and obviously cannot afford to have a deficit of $23,000! The board can hardly spend money it does not have, and yet it appears that some time during the fourth quarter this is exactly what is going to happen.

The point should be obvious. If the treasurer does not stay on top of the finances of an organization, serious trouble may be discovered after it is too late to do anything about it.

Treasurer's Duty To Sound the Alarm

With all of these warning signs, the treasurer must call for help—loudly! The treasurer's job is to call the situation to the attention of the board, and perhaps to offer suggestions. The real responsibility of solving the problem, however, is the board's. Of course, the treasurer should be prepared to offer recommendations on how to solve the problem. As the person closest to the finances the treasurer will probably have some sound ideas. But under the laws of most states, it is the board itself that is responsible for the continuation of the organization.

There is another very practical reason for calling for help as loudly as possible. Sometimes calling attention to a problem is all that is really necessary to start the wheels in motion to solve it. Perhaps some of the members who have been lax in making contributions or attending programs will start doing so.

REMEDIAL ACTION

Once the board has been forced to recognize the problem, what are the alternatives or courses of action that can be taken? There are perhaps six or seven, some of which may not be available to all organizations.

Increasing Contributions

The most obvious solution to most organizations' financial problems is to raise additional contributions. This is usually much easier said than done. If there are many small donors, it is not realistic to expect that the organization will be able to increase contributions by a very large amount. Unless the organization really motivates the donors, contributions tend to remain fairly constant from year to year except for small increases attributable to general cost of living increases, increased personal income, etc.

This is not as true with donors making large contributions. If the organization can sell its program, often these larger donors will make additional special contributions. The key is that the organization must convince these large donors that the extra amount it needs to solve this year's crisis will not be needed again next year. This means that in presenting its case, the organization must be able to show how it can and will avoid a similar difficulty next year. Otherwise, to the donor it will appear that a contribution is not really helping to solve the problem but only to postpone it.

Credibility is an important aspect of the ability to raise additional funds. The board will have a greater chance of success if over the years it has presented meaningful financial statements to all donors and has not created doubts about the true financial condition. But even with good statements, an organization that is in serious difficulty will probably find that the first place to look is not at contributions. Contributions can be increased but usually the response rate is too slow and the amounts too modest.

Increasing Fees

Another source of increased income is raising fees charged for services being rendered. Modest increases usually can be "sold" if there has not been a recent increase. Most people recognize the effect of inflation. At the same time, increasing fees may decrease the number of persons using the services.

For example, in the case of the Center for World Peace, if the board were to increase charges by only 10 per cent effective April 1, almost $4,000 would be added to income assuming nobody dropped out as a result of the increase. This represents almost 20 per cent of the projected deficit for the year. If the programs are worthwhile, the board should be able to convince the membership that the alternative to increasing fees is discontinuing the organization's activities. If the board is unable to "sell" this, then perhaps it should question the need for these programs.

Cutting Expenses

If it appears that there will be a deficit, and this deficit cannot be covered by increasing income, then it must be covered by reducing expenses. This is always difficult for the board of a nonprofit organization to accept. Somehow the board finds it difficult to accept the fact that sometimes an organization cannot do all that it wants to do, no matter how worthy.

Whatever the reason, nonprofit organizations seem to have particular difficulty in recognizing that as with any individual, they must spend within their means. This is one reason why the treasurer can offer only suggestions but not final solutions. The board has to wrestle with the policy question of which programs are in fact most "indispensable." The treasurer may have suggestions, but if these are forced upon the organization without the board's full concurrence, the suggestions either will not "stick" or the treasurer's efforts will be sabotaged. Remember that nonprofit organizations, unlike commercial ones, are heavily dependent on volunteer help and these volunteers must be in agreement with what is going on or they will stop volunteering their time and effort.

The conclusion is obvious. When the organization is threatened with insolvency the board must either raise income or cut expenses. Cutting expenses, however unpleasant, is often the only practical solution to an immediate crisis.

Borrowing

One source of emergency funds that many organizations use is the bank. They will borrow to cover short-term emergency needs, particularly when they have fluctuations in their income. Short-term borrowing is fine if used only to cover fluctuating income, and if the treasurer is sure that there will be income from which to pay these monies back. On the other hand, what should not be done without some serious thought is to mortgage the organization's physical property to raise money to pay current operations. It is one thing to borrow money for capital additions but it is an entirely different thing to borrow money which will be used for the day-to-day operations of the organization. If this becomes necessary, the treasurer and board should consider very carefully how they can reasonably expect to repay these loans. If repayment is in doubt, the board must seriously consider the future of the organization, and why it is prolonging the organization's life.

Keep in mind that the board of a nonprofit organization has a responsibility to act prudently on all matters. If it mortgages the "cow" to pay for its fodder with the full knowledge that it is going to have to sell the "cow" to pay the bank back, perhaps it should sell the "cow" to start with.

Many times a bank will lend funds to an organization on the basis of the members of the board being well known and influential in the business community. This often means an organization will be able to borrow money when the banker may have some doubts about repayment. The banker knows, however, that the board members will not let the organization default. The board members should carefully consider the repayment problem. They will not want their personal reputations tarnished by subsequent difficulties with the bank.

Applying for Foundation Grants

Other sources of financial help that many organizations should consider are grants from foundations. There are approximately 25,000 foundations in the United States and under the Tax Reform Act of 1969 these foundations are required to distribute a minimum of 5 per cent of their assets every year. While there are limitations regarding to whom such money can be given, generally any nonprofit organization that is itself a tax-exempt organization (which excludes social clubs) and is not a "private foundation" can receive grants from foundations. Most people think of foundations as being only the large ones—the Ford Foundation, the Carnegie Foundation, etc. While these giant foundations are giving millions of dollars to worthwhile organizations every year, there are thousands of lesser known foundations that are also granting millions.*

In trying to find foundations to approach, an advantage may be gained where members of the board already know one or more of the trustees of the foundation. There is no question that the chances are improved if the board's message can be informally presented to individual members of the foundation's board of trustees in advance of their considering the formal request. This does not mean that such personal contacts can assure success, but it certainly will improve the chances.

Obviously each foundation receives many more requests than it can possibly handle, so it is important that application be made only to those whose stated interests coincide with the organization's. There is no point in wasting time in submitting a request for funds that will not receive serious consideration because it is outside of the foundation's scope of interest.

The formal application itself is very important. There are no standard forms as such to fill out. Instead, the application should outline suc-

* *The Foundation Directory,* published by The Foundation Center, is a good source of information. Included in the 1977 edition were listings on over 2,800 foundations. They are listed geographically by state. Included in each listing is a brief description of the foundation, the size of its assets, the amount of grants made, and the purposes for which the foundation will consider making a grant.

cinctly and with feeling what the objectives of the organization are. It should document why the foundation's gift would be of significant help *and* how it would further the foundation's stated objectives. Keep both of these points in mind—*why* the grant would be significant, and *how* it would further the foundation's stated objectives. An application which cannot answer both of these points is defective.

The application should contain evidence that the board is effective and that the foundation won't be wasting its money if it makes a grant. Obviously the application should contain complete financial information in a format that clearly indicates that the board has financial control of the organization. In the case of the Center for World Peace, the application would include the five-year summary of income and expenses, the budget for the current year, the projections based on the first quarter's results, and a projection for five years. This five-year projection is important to show that the crisis is truly under control, or will be under control, and that the foundation's grant will not necessarily have to be a continuing one.

The application should specify quite explicitly how the money will be used. Most foundations will not consider requests for money that will be merely added to the "pot" and used for general purposes. In the 1971 edition of *The Foundation Directory* this point is emphasized:

> Fund-raisers need to be warned that at least the larger foundations do not usually make grants toward the operating budgets of agencies, whether national or local, or for individual need. Many foundations have accepted the doctrine that their limited funds should be used chiefly as the venture capital of philanthropy, to be spent in enterprises requiring risk and foresight, not likely to be supported by government or private individuals. In their fields of special interest they prefer to aid research, designed to push forward the frontiers of knowledge, or pilot demonstrations, resulting in improved procedures apt to be widely copied.
>
> Support for current programs, if it comes at all from foundations, must usually be sought from the smaller organizations, and especially those located in the area of the agency, well acquainted with its personnel and its needs. Most small foundations, and some larger ones, restrict their grants to the local community or state. Immense variety exists; the interests and limitations of each foundation need to be examined before it is approached.

Care must be taken to plan exactly how these funds will be used. This should not be done hastily. It takes many months to get foundation help and an organization that has not carefully thought out its needs may find that when it receives the grant it really would have preferred to spend the money in some other way. Foundations look with disfavor on organizations that ask that their grants be used for different purposes than originally specified.

Another thing to keep in mind is that many foundations like to make grants on a matching basis. That is, they will make the grant at such time as the organization has raised an equal or greater amount from other sources. This is in line with many foundations' concern that recipients not become dependent on foundation help.

Timing is important. Many foundations will make grants only once or twice a year. This means that unless the application is received on a timely basis there may be a long delay before there is an answer. Foundation grants are not very likely to get an organization out of an immediate cash bind. But foundations can be very helpful to the organization that truly plans for its future and knows what it wants and how to accomplish its objectives. For these organizations, foundation help should be carefully considered because there are monies available.

Merging With Another Organization

One of the alternatives that the board must consider if bankruptcy looms on the horizon is the possibility that the organization should merge with another organization having similar or at least compatible objectives. This, obviously, is not a course of action that is appealing but if the alternative is bankruptcy, then the only real question is how the objectives and programs of the organization can best be salvaged. It is probably better to have a combined program with another organization than to have no program at all. If the board doubts that this is true, then clearly the reason for the continued existence of the organization is in doubt and perhaps bankruptcy is the appropriate answer.

Where do you look for other candidates for merger? There is no easy answer. Basically you have to know the field that your organization is working in, and then you have to approach all possible candidates. Do not hesitate to do so, for it may turn out that there are other organizations in similar financial straits, which if combined with yours would make the resulting organization stronger than either was before. Keep in mind that unless you personally know the board members of the other organization you are not likely to know of their problems before you approach them. Perhaps they are also looking for a merger candidate.

There are other considerations which must be taken into account. One of the more important is to determine whether any of your donor-restricted funds contain restrictions that would prohibit use by a combined organization. Ideally the board could find a compatible organization with similar enough goals and objectives so that any restricted funds could be effectively used. If there are problems in this area, ask the original donor for permission to change the restrictions.

Another consideration is, of course, whether the merged organization can accomplish the organization's objectives more effectively and at less cost than if it remained a separate entity. The merger may provide more resources which will probably make possible economies of scale. The chances are that there will be some opportunity for cost saving, perhaps through sharing staff, or facilities, or a combination of both. The board, however, should be sure that it looks very carefully before it leaps. It must analyze the other organization's financial statements and five-year plan very carefully. It serves very little purpose to trade one set of problems for another if several years from now the combined organization will again be on the verge of bankruptcy.

CONFRONTING BANKRUPTCY

Another possibility is that the board will conclude that the organization has accomplished the purposes for which it was set up, or that times have changed and the original objectives are no longer appropriate. If so, perhaps the humane thing to do is to let the organization "die," but in a controlled manner so as not to leave a trail of debts behind it. Although this may not seem like a very practical suggestion at first, it is one that must be considered by every thoughtful board member. If the members are not supporting the organization, then why not? If it is only a temporary problem of a poor economy, it is perhaps appropriate to try to wait for better times. But the board must be cautious in drawing this conclusion. It must not get so emotionally involved in the mechanics of the organization's programs that it loses sight of the need to respond to today's conditions, which are different from yesterday's. In this "throw away" society that we are in, nonprofit organizations are not exempt, and those that do not serve society's current needs will find that bankruptcy will always be close by.

As the board gets closer and closer to a decision to curtail operations, the individual members of the board, as well as the treasurer, have to consider carefully the steps that should be taken to ensure that actual bankruptcy as such does not take place. No board wants to incur financial obligations that cannot be met. This includes salary obligations. As the time for going out of existence looms nearer, consideration must be given to an orderly dismissal of the staff with appropriate termination benefits to help them over the period of relocation. This is expensive, because once the decision to terminate operations is made, sources of income will dry up promptly. This means that the board members cannot wait until the bank account is empty to face these difficult decisions. If they do, either the board members themselves are going to personally face the prospects of making sizable contributions to cover their moral obligations, or they are going to leave unpaid debts and recriminations. Most board members have personal reputations at stake and this last alternative is not very attractive.

One area that must be carefully watched as cash gets low is the payment of withholding taxes to the various levels of government. Usually the federal government can sue the treasurer and all other persons responsible for nonpayment of such withholding taxes. These amounts are not usable funds of the organization as such, but are held in escrow until paid to the government. To use these funds to pay other bills is a very serious offense that can result not only in recovery from the treasurer, but also in subjection to fine and/or imprisonment.

Another consideration, if it is decided to discontinue operations, is that any funds or other assets that remain must either be given to another exempt organization or to the state. This is true for all tax-exempt organizations except social clubs. Obviously when thinking about discontinuing operations, competent legal help is needed to consider all ramifications. Timing is of major importance. The point at which operations will be discontinued must be anticipated and this must be before the bank account is empty. Very few board members want the stigma of having been on a board of an organization that actually went bankrupt and could not pay its bills.

CONCLUSION

This chapter has discussed the ever present threat of bankruptcy almost all nonprofit organizations face at one time or another. It was noted that one of the characteristics of such organizations is that they receive support only so long as they serve the needs of the public or their members. Since most organizations find it difficult to build up large cash reserves, they must be responsive.

If they are not, support will drop and unless the organization responds quickly, it could very well find itself on the verge of actual bankruptcy.

The treasurer's role of eliminating the unexpected was discussed, and several techniques reviewed to help the treasurer stay on top of the current financial situation. It was emphasized that when trouble looms the treasurer's first and most important responsibility is to call "loud and clear" so that the board can take appropriate action. It is the board that must take action.

Most organizations in financial trouble find that it is difficult to increase income by any substantial amount in a short period of time. Accordingly, when financial troubles loom, one of the first things the board must do is to cut back on its rate of expenditures. If some of the budgeting techniques discussed in the previous chapters have been followed, the board will have plenty of warning that it must cut expenses and should be able to avoid actual bankruptcy.

It may very well be that the board will find, however, that the organization is not viable, and that the reason for its continuation no longer exists. When this occurs, it is important that the board take action on a timely basis to either merge it into another more viable organization, or to actually discontinue operations and dissolve the organization in a controlled manner. It is also important to constantly remember that a nonprofit organization does not have a perpetual life. It can continue to exist only so long as it serves a worthwhile purpose which its members or the public will support.

21

Small Organizations—Obtaining the Right Bookkeeper

Obtaining and keeping the right bookkeeper is the key to making life easy and routine for the treasurers of small organizations.° For, unless the treasurer wants to spend substantial time and effort in keeping the records, a good bookkeeper is essential. There is nothing difficult about bookkeeping as such, but the details can become most wearisome to the busy volunteer treasurer. The time they consume can detract from the treasurer's other responsibilities, particularly that of planning. For most nonprofit organizations, a part- or full-time bookkeeper will be hired.

The problem of finding the right bookkeeper is compounded for nonprofit organizations because traditionally such organizations pay low salaries to all of their staff, including the bookkeeper. The salary level frequently results in the organization's getting someone with only minimum qualifications. This appears to be false economy. A good bookkeeper can help the organization save money and can free the time of the volunteer treasurer.

Often the other staff in the organization are extremely dedicated individuals interested in the particular program of the organization and willing to accept a lower than normal salary. Bookkeepers are seldom dedicated to the programs of the organization as such. They have been hired to provide bookkeeping services and often have no special interest in the program of the organization.

° This chapter deals only with the bookkeeping problems of relatively small organizations. Larger organizations are not discussed because to a very large extent they are run like commercial organizations.

LEVEL OF BOOKKEEPING SERVICES NEEDED

The first step in obtaining a bookkeeper is to determine what book-keeping services are needed. Depending on the size of the organization, there are a number of possibilities. If the organization is very small and only 15–25 checks are issued a month, the treasurer will probably find that a "checkbook" type set of records will be all that is required or appropriate. If so, the treasurer may very well keep the records and not try to find someone to help. In this case the "bookkeeping problem" is merely one of finding enough time to keep the checkbook up-to-date and to prepare financial statements on a timely basis. While the prob-lem of finding this time is not to be underestimated, still the bookkeep-ing problems are largely under control.

Secretary as Bookkeeper

For many organizations, the number of transactions is too large for the treasurer to handle but not large enough to justify a full-time book-keeper. If the organization has a paid full- or part-time secretary, often some of the bookkeeping duties are delegated to the secretary. Usually this means keeping the "checkbook" or perhaps a simple cash receipts and cash disbursements ledger.° At the end of the month the treasurer will summarize these cash records and prepare the financial statements. While this means the treasurer will still have a lot of work to do, the work has been reduced significantly by having the secretary keep the basic records. This is a very practical approach for small organizations with very limited staff and not too many transactions.

Volunteer as Bookkeeper

Another possibility for the small organization is to find a volunteer within the organization who will help keep the records. While this can occasionally be effective it often turns out to be less than satisfactory. There is less control over the activities of a volunteer bookkeeper and it is difficult for the treasurer to insist that the records be kept on a timely basis. After all, volunteer bookkeepers are just that—volunteers —with all the rights and privileges that go with volunteers. Volunteers have to work around their own schedules and it is difficult to insist that they perform their duties on as strict a basis as with full-time em-

---

° Chapter 28 discusses both a checkbook system of bookkeeping and a simple cash basis bookkeeping system. A secretary could probably keep most of the records in these two systems with a minimum of instruction.

ployees. Another problem with volunteers is that their tenure tends to be short. Keeping a set of books is hard work, and while a volunteer bookkeeper's enthusiasm may be great at the beginning, it tends to diminish in time. The result is that there are often delays, clerical errors, and eventually the need to get another bookkeeper. The volunteer bookkeeper is not a good solution. A treasurer who cannot handle the bookkeeping should use a paid secretary or consider hiring a part-time bookkeeper.

Part-Time Bookkeepers

In considering a part-time bookkeeper, the first question is how much time is required. Is the job one that can be handled on a one-day-a-month basis, two-days-a-month, two-days-a-week? For most small organizations the answer will probably be only a day or two a month, or at the most, a day a week. Where do you go to find a good part-time bookkeeper? This can be difficult.

Some of the best potential may be found among mothers with school children who were full-time bookkeepers at one time. Since a part-time bookkeeping job can easily fit into a flexible schedule, permitting the mother to be home before and after school, this can be a very good arrangement if the bookkeeping needs are not more than 15–20 hours a week.

If the organization wants someone at its office for a full day each week or during hours not suitable for a mother with school children, then perhaps a retired bookkeeper or accountant will be the next best bet. However, it is difficult to find a suitable retired person. Many persons will apply who have an impressive background but very little practical bookkeeping experience. An example might be a retired assistant treasurer of a large and well known organization. Typically, he had bookkeeping back in school forty years ago, but never used his bookkeeping. While he may have a sophisticated knowledge of business, he is not competent as a bookkeeper, often finds the detail boring, and his interest is short-lived. Also, the hourly rate such persons may demand will probably be higher than that commanded by a competent bookkeeper. An ad in a local newspaper is probably the best place to start to look for a qualified person.

Full-Time Bookkeepers

For larger or growing organizations, there is a point when a full-time bookkeeper is needed.

An advertisement in the newspaper is probably the best approach. The ad should be explicit and should indicate salary, and the type of experience and competence this person will need. It should also indicate the type of organization since some applicants will not be interested in working for a nonprofit organization.

Alternatively, an employment agency can be used. The principal advantage of a good agency is a saving of time and effort of the treasurer. The agency will place the ad in the paper and will do the initial weeding out of the obvious misfits before forwarding the potential candidates to the organization for review. Agencies also know the job market and will probably be in a good position to advise on the "going" salary. They should also be able to help in checking references.

These agencies charge a fee which usually the organization ends up paying, and this can be from two to six weeks' pay. The question that the treasurer must ask is, is it worth this amount for the help an agency can give? There is no sure answer to this question. In many instances their help is most valuable. On the other hand some agencies do very little screening and the organization ends up with almost the same work that it would have had without the agency.

Often a friend of the treasurer knows of someone who is looking for a job and while there is no reason not to consider such a person, the treasurer should also interview others.

If the organization has outside auditors, they may be able to help. Get their advice, and before actually hiring a bookkeeper, let them talk with the candidates. While there is no guarantee that the right person will be hired, the auditors are more likely to be able to judge the candidate's technical skills and background than the treasurer is.

PERSONALITY CHARACTERISTICS

There are several personality characteristics that good bookkeepers often have that the treasurer should be aware of. Obviously a good bookkeeper is usually a very meticulous and well organized person. This often means that the bookkeeper will become impatient with other members of the staff who are slow in providing the required information or who are sloppy in providing all of the necessary details. To the rest of the staff the bookkeeper often appears to be a "nit picker." Obviously if the bookkeeper is not diplomatic, this can be annoying to the rest of the staff, but these are desirable qualities that the treasurer should not discourage.

Another desirable characteristic is that the bookkeeper will often be critical of the spending patterns of the organization, particularly if the organization is apparently not being frugal. This tendency to be critical of spending habits can be a very helpful trait which the treasurer should not discourage. The bookkeeper sees all of the spending of the organization and is bound to have an opinion about how wisely expenditures are made. The conclusion may not be correct because the vantage point is quite limited. Yet, from the treasurer's standpoint, the bookkeeper acts as a watchdog and will often have some good ideas. The treasurer should act on them.

ALTERNATIVES TO BOOKKEEPERS

Outside Preparation of Payroll

One thing that can be done either to relieve the burden on the bookkeeper or to minimize the time requirements is to let a bank or a service bureau handle the payroll. This is particularly effective where employees are paid the same amount each payroll period.

There are many ways to delegate actual bookkeeping to sources external to the organization. Responsibility for bookkeeping, however, cannot be delegated outside the organization. The treasurer or another employee of the organization must continuously monitor and review the work of an outside bookkeeper.

Some banks will handle the complete payroll function and will use their own bank checks. This eliminates the need for the organization to prepare a bank reconciliation. Others will prepare the payroll but use the organization's checks, which after being cashed are returned to the organization. Some will prepare the payroll tax reports, others will not. Banks usually have a minimum fee which ranges from $40 to $50 for each payroll. If there are more than about 20 employees, this amount increases. While the charge may seem high, the time saved can be considerable. Remember that in addition to the payroll preparation the bank will also keep cumulative records of salary paid to each employee and will prepare the various payroll tax returns, W-2 forms, etc.

The use of a bank or service bureau works best where the payroll is regular and routine in amount, that is, where there are not a lot of hourly employees, or changes in rates between periods. While a bank can handle such changes, the "input" to the bank is such that the organization would be faced with the need to have someone act as a payroll clerk to assemble the information for the bank, and this takes time. If there are a lot of changes each period, it may be just as easy for the bookkeeper to handle the complete job and not use an outside service bureau or bank.

Service Bureau Bookkeeping Records

Another possibility is to have a service bureau keep all the bookkeeping records. If there is any volume of activity, a service bureau can often keep the records at less cost than an organization can hire a bookkeeper. For example, there are some service bureaus that will keypunch information from original documents such as the check stubs, invoices, etc. They can then prepare a cash receipts book, cash disbursement book, general ledger, financial statements, etc., all automatically. All the organization has to provide is the basic information. The costs for such services vary widely depending on the volume and type of records and the geographic area in which the organization is located.

A treasurer starting to think about going to a service bureau should get some outside professional advice on whether it is practical. While talking to the service bureau will provide information on costs, etc., the treasurer must keep in mind that the service bureau will be trying to sell its services and will not describe all the problems that will be encountered or the other alternatives that could be considered. A treasurer who wants to study these alternatives should seek the advice of a CPA. If the organization has no CPA, it should hire one for the express purpose of getting advice on this one area.

Accounting Service

Another alternative is to hire an outside accounting service to perform the actual bookkeeping. Many CPAs and public accountants provide bookkeeping services for their clients. Under this arrangement the accountant has one of the staff do all of the bookkeeping but takes the responsibility for reviewing the work and seeing that it is properly done. The accountant usually prepares financial statements monthly or quarterly.

There are still some functions the organization itself usually must perform. The organization will normally still have to prepare its own checks, vouchers, payroll, depositing of receipts, and billings. This means that normally it cannot delegate 100 per cent of the bookkeeping to an outside accounting service.

The cost of this type of service is its principal disadvantage. The accountant is in business and has overhead and salaries to pay, including salaries for employees when they are not busy. All of these costs are considered in establishing hourly rates. These rates are generally about twice what it costs to hire a competent bookkeeper on a full-time basis; they will range from $15–30 an hour. Nevertheless, it may still be cheaper to hire an accountant than to have someone on the payroll. The outside accountant is paid only for work performed. If the work totals 10 hours a month, the pay is for 10 hours. Also, these services are performed by experienced staff, and there is no problem of competency.

One of the problems with this type of service is that the accountant cannot be in two places at the same time. The chances are that at the time the books are ready, several other clients will also be ready. This can result in some delay, although usually not an excessive amount.

TIMING IN HIRING A REPLACEMENT

One question that is frequently asked is when should a replacement be hired if the present bookkeeper is leaving. Should there be an overlap in employment so that the retiring bookkeeper can indoctrinate the new one and if so, how long a period of overlap is appropriate? Or is it better to have no overlap at all?

It is appropriate to have some overlap, but it should be fairly short. While the present bookkeeper may not agree, a good bookkeeper can pick up another bookkeeper's set of books and procedures fairly quickly. A bookkeeper can usually get oriented to the broad outlines of the procedures within a few days. Most of these details are learned by experience and not from having the former bookkeeper tell about them. Also, the new bookkeeper will tend to be confident of an ability to do things better than the last bookkeeper. This means that too long an overlap period will grate on the nerves of the new bookkeeper.

For most organizations, it is probably best to keep the overlap short and recognize that things will not be entirely smooth for a month or two. Unless the organization is willing to have an overlap period of at least a month, it must expect that it will take some time for the new bookkeeper to get firmly established.

SUMMARY

The bookkeeping needs of nonprofit organizations vary widely. At the one extreme is the small organization which has so few transactions that the treasurer is able to handle all the bookkeeping. On the other extreme is the large national organization that has an accounting or bookkeeping staff of many persons which is run exactly like a commercial organization., In between these two extremes is every conceivable combination of full- and part-time bookkeeping need.

A number of sources for bookkeepers were discussed. Often in small organizations, a paid secretary will keep some simple records for the treasurer. Until the records get voluminous, this can be quite satisfactory. On the other hand, "volunteer" bookkeepers are seldom satisfactory because of rapid turnover and the problem of control. It was suggested that part-time bookkeeping jobs could be particularly attractive to mothers with children in school who might want to earn some extra money. This, of course, assumes previous bookkeeping experience. The procedures to follow in looking for both part- and full-time bookkeepers were discussed and the importance of paying the going salary was emphasized. The use of banks or service bureaus was also suggested as one way to reduce the work load for the bookkeeper. Finally, it was suggested that while some overlap in bookkeepers is necessary, this overlap period should be relatively short.

22

Small Organizations—Providing
Internal Control

"EMPLOYEE ADMITS EMBEZZLEMENT OF TEN THOUSAND DOL-
LARS." "TRUSTED CLERK STEALS $50,000." These headlines are all too com-
mon and many tell a similar story—a trusted and respected employee in
a position of financial responsibility is overcome by temptation and
"borrows" a few dollars until payday to meet some unexpected cash
need. When payday comes, some other cash need prevents repayment.
Somehow the employee just never catches up, and borrows a few more
dollars, and a few more and a few more.

The reader's reaction may be, "Thank goodness, this kind of thing
could never happen to my organization. After all, I know everyone and
they are all honest, and besides who would think of stealing from a
nonprofit organization?" This is not the point. Very few who end up as
embezzlers start out with this intent in mind. Rather they find themselves
in a position of trust and opportunity and when personal crises arise,
the temptation is too much. Nonprofit organizations are not exempt,
regardless of size. There is always a risk when a person is put in a position
where there is an opportunity to be tempted.

The purpose of this chapter is to outline some of the practical procedures that a small organization can establish to help minimize this
risk and thus safeguard the organization's physical assets. For purposes
of this discussion the emphasis is on smaller organizations where one
or two persons handle all the bookkeeping. This would include many
churches, country clubs, local fund-raising groups, YMCAs, etc. Internal
control for larger organizations is not discussed here because controls

for such organizations can become very complicated and would require many chapters. The principles, however, are essentially the same. Setting up a set of internal controls requires an understanding of the basic principles plus a great deal of common sense. Larger organizations will probably want professional help in setting up a strong set of controls. Readers who are interested in this subject should refer to the Bibliography (pages 543–548).

REASONS FOR INTERNAL CONTROL

Internal control is a system of procedures and cross checking which in the absence of collusion minimizes the likelihood of misappropriation of assets or misstatement of the accounts and maximizes the likelihood of detection if it occurs. For the most part internal control does not prevent embezzlement but should insure that, if committed, it will be promptly discovered. This likelihood of discovery usually persuades most not to allow temptation to get the better of them. Very few first-time embezzlers are so desperate that they would steal if they really expected to be promptly caught.

There are several reasons for having a good system of internal controls. The first, obviously, is to prevent the loss through theft of some of the assets. A second reason, equally important, is to prevent "honest" employees from making a mistake that could ruin their lives. An employer has a moral responsibility to avoid putting undue temptation in front of employees. Internal controls are designed to help remove the temptation.

Aside from this moral responsibility of the employer there is also a responsibility of the board to the membership and to the general public to safeguard the assets of the organization. The board has an obligation to use prudence in protecting the assets. If a large sum were stolen and not recovered it could jeopardize the program of the organization. Furthermore if only a small amount were stolen it would be embarrassing to the members of the board. In either case, the membership or the public would certainly want to know why internal control procedures had not been followed by the board.

FUNDAMENTALS OF INTERNAL CONTROL

The very simple definition of the purpose of internal control noted above relates to small organizations and emphasizes the fraud aspects.

For larger organizations this definition would have to be expanded to include a system of checks and balances over all paperwork to insure that there was no intentional or unintentional misstatement of the accounts.* For purposes of this discussion, however, the emphasis is on the physical controls over the organization's assets, principally cash.

One of the most effective internal controls is the use of a budget which is compared to actual figures on a monthly basis. If deviations from the budget are carefully followed up by the treasurer or executive director, the likelihood of a large misappropriation taking place without being detected fairly quickly is reduced considerably.† This type of overall review of the financial statements is very important, and every member of the board should ask questions about any item that appears out of line either with the budget or with what would have been expected to be the actual figures. Many times this type of probing for reasons for deviations from the expected has uncovered problems.

SOME BASIC CONTROLS

There are a number of other basic internal controls that are probably applicable to many, if not most, small nonprofit organizations and these are discussed below. However, it must be emphasized that these are only basic controls and should not be considered all-inclusive. Establishing an effective system of internal control requires knowledge of the particular organization and its operations. The controls discussed below should give the reader, however, some indication of the nature of internal control and act as a starting point for establishing an appropriate system.

In this discussion we will be considering the division of duties for a small organization, The Center for World Peace, whose financial statements were discussed in Chapter 20. As will be recalled, this organiza-

---

* The American Institute of Certified Public Accountants in an official pronouncement, Statement on Auditing Standards No. 1, has defined internal control as follows:

"Internal control comprises the plan of organization and all of the co-ordinate methods and measures adopted within a business to safeguard its assets, check the accuracy and reliability of its accounting data, promote operational efficiency, and encourage adherence to prescribed managerial policies. This definition possibly is broader than the meaning sometimes attributed to the term. It recognizes that a system of internal control extends beyond those matters which relate directly to the functions of the accounting and financial departments." Copyright 1973 by the American Institute of Certified Public Accountants, Inc.

† Chapter 19 discusses budgeting techniques.

tion sponsors seminars and retreats and has a paid staff to run its affairs. The office staff consists of:

An executive director
The executive director's secretary
A program director
A bookkeeper

The officers of the Center are all volunteers and usually are at the Center at irregular times. The executive director, treasurer, president, and vice president are check signers. With this background let us now look at each of eleven controls in detail and see how each applies to this organization.

Control Over Receipts

The basic objective in establishing internal control over receipts is to obtain control over the amounts received at the time of receipt. Once this control is established, procedures must be followed to ensure that these amounts get deposited in the organization's bank account. Establishing this control is particularly difficult for small organizations because of the small number of persons usually involved.

1. *Prenumbered receipts should be issued for all money at the time first received. A duplicate copy should be accounted for and a comparison eventually made between the aggregate of the receipts issued and the amount deposited in the bank.*

The purpose of this control is to create a written record of the cash received. The original of the receipt should be given to the person from whom the money was received; the duplicate copy should be kept permanently. Periodically, a comparison should be made of the aggregate receipts issued, with the amount deposited. The receipts can be issued at the organization's office, or if door-to-door collections are made, a prenumbered receipt can be issued as amounts are received by the collector. It is hoped that all contributors will learn to expect a receipt for cash payments.

It is important that both the duplicate copy and the original be prenumbered in order to provide control over the receipts issued. If a receipt is "voided" by mistake both the original and the duplicate should be kept and accounted for. In this way there will be complete accountability over all receipts that have been issued.

In our illustration, the Center receives a fair amount of cash at its seminars and retreats on weekends when the bookkeeper and treasurer are not available. One of the participants is designated as the fee collector for that session and he in turn collects the fees and issues the receipts. After he has collected all of the fees he turns over the duplicate copy of the receipts (along with all unused receipt forms) and the cash collected to the program director. He also prepares and signs a summary report of the cash collected, in duplicate. He mails one copy of this report directly to the treasurer at his home in an envelope provided, and the duplicate is turned over to the program director. The program director in turn counts the money, agreeing the total received with the total of the duplicate receipts, and with the summary report. The program director puts the money in the safe for the weekend and on Monday morning gives the money, the duplicate receipts, and the copy of the summary report to the bookkeeper for depositing. The bookkeeper in turn deposits the money from each program separately, and files the duplicate receipts and summary report for future reference. Once a month the treasurer compares his copy of each summary report with the deposits shown on the bank statement.

2. *Cash collections should be under the control of two people wherever possible, particularly where it is not practicable to issue receipts.*

In the illustration in the previous paragraph, control was established over cash collections by having the person collecting at each seminar issue receipts and a summary report. The program director, in turn, also had some control since he knew how many persons attended and was able to compare the amount collected with the amount that should be collected. This provided dual control.

There are many instances, however, where cash collections are received when it is not appropriate to give a receipt. Two examples are church "plate" collections on Sundays, and coin canisters placed in stores and public places throughout the community for public support. To the extent that only one person handles this money, there is always a risk. The risk is not only that some of it will be misappropriated, but also that someone may erroneously think it has been. This is why it is recommended that two people be involved.

With respect to church plate collections, as soon as the money has been collected, it should be locked up until it can be counted by two people together. Perhaps the head usher and a vestryman will count it after the last service. Once the counting is completed, both should sign a cash collection report. This report should be given to the treasurer for subsequent comparison with the deposit on the bank statement. The cash should be turned over to the bookkeeper for depositing intact.

This procedure will not guard against an usher's dipping a hand into the "plate" before it is initially locked up or counted, but the ushers' duties are usually rotated and the cumulative risk is low. But the bookkeeper and treasurer normally have access to such funds on a regular and recurring basis. This is why their function of counting these cash receipts should be controlled by having a second person involved. It is not because they are not trusted; it is to insure that no one can think of accusing one of them.

Canisters containing cash which are placed in public places should be sealed so that the only way to get access to the cash is to break the canister open. Of course, someone could take the entire canister, but if the canister is placed in a conspicuous place—near the cash register, for example—this risk is fairly low. These canisters should be serially numbered so that all canisters can be accounted for. When the canisters are eventually opened, they should be counted by two people using the same procedures as with plate collections.

3. *Two persons should open all mail and make a list of all receipts for each day. This list should subsequently be compared to the bank deposit by someone not handling the money. Receipts in the form of checks should be restrictively endorsed promptly upon receipt.*

Two persons should open the mail; otherwise there is a risk that the mail opener may misappropriate part of the receipts. This imposes a heavy burden on the small organization with only a few employees but it is necessary if good internal control is desired.° One alternative is to have mail receipts go to a bank lock box and let the bank do the actual opening of the mail.

The purpose of making a list of all checks received is to ensure that a record is made of the amount that was received. This makes it possible for the treasurer to later check to see whether the bookkeeper has deposited all amounts promptly.

Checks should be promptly endorsed since once endorsed there is less likelihood of misappropriation. The endorsement should be placed on the check by the person first opening the mail.

In theory if the check has been made out in the name of the organization, no one can cash it. But experience has shown that a clever enough person could probably find a way to cash it. On the other hand, once the check is endorsed with the name of the bank and account number it is very difficult for the embezzler to convert the check to personal use.

In our illustration at the Center, the secretary to the executive director together with the bookkeeper jointly open all mail and place the rubber stamp endorsement on the check. They then make a list, in duplicate, of all checks received, with one copy of the list going to the bookkeeper

---

° Organizations that have their financial statements audited by CPAs will find that the CPA cannot give an unqualified opinion if internal control is considered inadequate. See page 373.

with the checks for depositing. They both sign the original of the list, which goes to the executive director. The executive director obtains this copy to see what amounts have been received. At the end of the month, he turns over all of these lists to the treasurer who then compares each day's lists with the respective credit on the bank statement.

4. *All receipts should be deposited in the bank, intact and on a timely basis.*

The purpose of this control is to insure that there is a complete record of all receipts and disbursements. If an organization receives "cash" receipts, no part of this cash should be used to pay its bills. The receipts should be deposited, and checks issued to pay expenses. In this way there will be a record of the total receipts and expenses of the organization on the bank statements.

This procedure does not prevent someone from stealing money but it does mean that a check must be used to get access to the money. This leaves a record of the theft and makes it more difficult for a person to cover up.

In our illustration, it should be noted that the bookkeeper deposits each day's mail receipts intact, and also deposits, separately, the receipts from each seminar. On some days she has two or three deposits. Making the deposits separately enables the treasurer at the end of the month to compare his copy of the summary of seminar receipts and the daily mail receipts to the bank statement. This comparison by the treasurer does not take more than a few minutes each month but it provides excellent internal control over receipts and it also gives him assurance that the bookkeeper is depositing all receipts daily.

Control Over Disbursements

The basic objective in establishing internal controls over disbursements is to ensure that a record of all disbursements is made and that only authorized persons are in a position to withdraw funds. The risk of misappropriation can be significantly reduced if procedures are established to minimize the possibility that an expenditure can be made without leaving a trail or that an unauthorized person can withdraw money.

5. *All disbursements should be made by check and supporting documentation kept for each disbursement.*

This control is to insure that there will be a permanent record of how much and to whom money was paid. No amounts should be paid by cash, with the exception of minor petty cash items. For the same reason no checks should be made payable to "cash." Checks should always be payable to a specific person, including checks for petty cash reimbursement. This makes it more difficult to fraudulently disburse funds.

At the Center, the bookkeeper is the one who prepares all checks for payment of bills. Before she will prepare a check, however, the vendor's invoice must be approved by the executive director. If the purchases involved goods that have been received at the Center she also insists that the person who received the goods indicate their receipt, right on the vendor's invoice.

The bookkeeper is not a check signer since, if she were, she could fraudulently disburse funds to herself and then cover them up in the books. The check signers are the executive director, the treasurer, the president, and the vice president. Normally the executive director signs all checks. Checks of more than $1,000 require two signatures, but these are very infrequent. The executive director carefully examines all supporting invoices, making sure that someone has signed for receipt of the goods before he signs the check. After he has signed the check, he personally marks each invoice "paid" so that he won't inadvertently pay the same invoice twice. His secretary mails all checks to the vendors as an added control over the bookkeeper. By not letting the bookkeeper have access to the signed checks, the bookkeeper is not in a position to profit from preparing a fraudulent check to a nonexistent vendor.

6. *If the treasurer or check signer is also the bookkeeper, two signatures should be required on all checks.*

The purpose of this control is to insure that no one person is in a position to disburse funds and then cover up the disbursement in the records. In part, this recommendation is designed to protect the organization, and in part, to protect the treasurer.

Two signatures on a check provide additional control only so long as the second check signer also examines the invoices or supporting bills behind the disbursement before signing the check. The real risk of having dual signatures is that both check signers will rely on the other and will review the supporting bills in such a perfunctory manner that there is less control than if only one person signed but assumed full responsibility.

Even when the treasurer is not the bookkeeper, two signatures should also be required on checks of very large amounts and for transfers out of a savings account. This gives some added protection that the treasurer won't be able to abscond with the entire assets of the organization.

As was noted before, the bookkeeper at the Center is not a check signer. This reduces the need for a second signature on checks under $1,000. Where .the second signature is required for large checks the treasurer is usually the second signer. He very carefully inspects all bills involving such payments although he is usually well aware of the purchase in advance because of the size. The Center has a safe deposit box at the bank, and two signatures are also required for access. The same persons who are authorized to sign checks have access to this box.

7. *A person other than the bookkeeper should receive bank statements directly from the bank and should reconcile them.*

This control is to prevent the bookkeeper from fraudulently issuing a check for personal use and, as bookkeeper, covering up this disbursement in the books. While the bookkeeper may not be a check signer, experience has shown that banks often do not catch forged check signatures. The bookkeeper usually has access to blank checks and could forge the check signer's signature. If the bookkeeper were to receive the bank statements the fraudulent and forged cancelled checks could be removed and then destroyed, with the fraud covered up through the books.

In most smaller organizations the bank statement and cancelled checks should go directly to the treasurer, who should prepare the bank reconciliation.° In those situations where the treasurer is also the bookkeeper the bank statements should go directly to another officer to reconcile. The treasurer should insist on this procedure as a protection from any suspicions of wrongdoing.†

In the Center's case, the bank statement and cancelled checks are mailed directly to the treasurer's home each month. He usually spends

---

° In large organizations the control can be even more effective where the division of duties is such that an employee who is not a check signer *or* bookkeeper can prepare the bank reconciliation. Obviously, it is possible for check signers to fraudulently make out a check to themselves and then, if they have access to the returned checks, to remove the cancelled check. However, if they don't also have a means of covering up the disbursement, sooner or later the shortage will come out. The person reconciling the bank account is not in a position to permanently "cover up" a shortage although it could be hidden for several months. For this reason, it is preferable to have neither a check signer nor the bookkeeper prepare the reconciliation.

† In those situations where the treasurer or other officer does not have the time to prepare the reconciliation, then, as a minimum procedure, the treasurer should receive the unopened bank statement directly from the bank. Each check returned by the bank should be checked for both the payee and the purpose of the check. If a check is not recognized a question should be raised about it. After this review, which usually doesn't take very much time, the bank statement and checks are turned over to the bookkeeper (or treasurer) to reconcile. The completed bank reconciliation should be returned to the treasurer (or other officer) for review. The review of the completed reconciliation should consist of reviewing the reconciling items, comparing the balance "per bank" to the bank statement, and the balance "per books" to the general ledger.

This alternative procedure should be used only where it is not practical for the treasurer or other officer to actually prepare the bank reconciliation. While this alternative procedure can be effective, it does not offer the protection that comes from having someone independent of the bookkeeper actually perform all of the steps of a bank reconciliation.

half a day at the Center's offices on the Saturday after receiving the bank statement. He prepares the complete bank reconciliation. At this time he also compares the lists of mail and program receipts he has received throughout the month to the deposits shown on the bank statement.

Other Areas of Control

8. *Someone other than the bookkeeper should authorize all write-offs of accounts receivable or other assets.*

This control is to insure that a bookkeeper who has embezzled accounts receivable or some other assets will not also be in a position to cover up the theft by writing off the receivable or asset. If the bookkeeper is unable to write such amounts off, someone will eventually ask why the "receivable" has not been paid and this should trigger correspondence that would result in the fraud's being discovered.

Generally, write-offs of small receivables should be approved by the treasurer (provided the treasurer is not also the bookkeeper), but if they are large in amount they should be submitted to the board for approval. Before any amount is written off, the treasurer should make certain that all appropriate efforts have been made, including, possibly, legal action. The treasurer must constantly keep in mind the fiduciary responsibility to take all reasonable steps to make collection.

The Center only very rarely has accounts receivable. It does have, however, many pledges receivable. Although the Center would not think of taking legal action to enforce collection * it does record those pledges as though they were receivables. Very occasionally the bookkeeper has to call the treasurer's attention to a delinquent pledge. He, in turn, usually calls the delinquent pledgor in an effort to evaluate the likelihood of future collection. Once a year he submits a written report to the board advising it of delinquent pledges, and requesting formal approval to write them off. The board discusses each such delinquent pledge before giving its approval.

9. *Marketable securities should be kept in a bank safe deposit box or held by a bank as custodian.*

This control is to insure that securities are protected against loss by fire or theft or from bankruptcy of a brokerage house. For most organizations, marketable securities represent long-term rather than short-term investments and they should not be kept in a safe in the organization's office or at the broker's office. The organization should provide the maximum protection for these assets. Either a bank should keep these securities as custodian or they should be kept in the bank safe deposit box

---

* Pledges are discussed more fully in Chapter 9.

under dual signature control. Safeguarding investments is discussed more fully on pages 390 to 392.

In our illustration, the Center does not have very much in the way of investment funds. What endowments the Center has it keeps in a bank common stock fund. This is a form of mutual fund which the bank set up to handle investments on a pooled basis for a number of nonprofit organizations. All decisions at the Center to put money into or take money out of this bank fund are made by the executive committee of the board. The bank insists that the executive committee's minutes accompany any request for withdrawals of or additions to the Center's shares in this fund. There are no share certificates as such although the bank sends quarterly statements to the treasurer showing the number of shares the Center has.

10. *Fixed asset records should be maintained and an inventory taken periodically.*

These procedures insure that the organization has a complete record of its assets. The permanent record should contain a description of the asset, cost, date acquired, location, serial number, and similar information. Such information will provide a record of the assets that the employees are responsible for. This is particularly important in nonprofit organizations where turnover of employees and officers is often high. It also provides fire insurance records. An example of the type of fixed asset record that should be kept is shown in Chapter 29 (Figure 29-3).

11. *Excess cash should be maintained in a separate bank account. Withdrawals from this account should require two signatures.*

Where an organization has excess cash which will not be needed for current operations in the immediate future, it should be placed in a separate bank account to provide an added safeguard. Frequently this separate account will be an interest-bearing savings account. The bank should be advised that the signatures of two officers are required for all withdrawals. Normally in such situations withdrawals are infrequent, and when they are made the funds withdrawn are deposited intact in the regular current checking account. In this way all disbursements are made from the regular checking account.

Obviously in this situation the officers involved in authorizing a withdrawal should not do so without being fully aware of the reasons for the need of these funds. Approval should not be perfunctorily given.

FIDELITY INSURANCE

One final recommendation. Fidelity insurance should be carried. The purpose of fidelity insurance is to insure that if a loss from embezzlement occurs the organization will recover the loss. This insurance does not cover theft or burglary by an outside person. It provides protection only against an employee's dishonesty. Having fidelity insurance also acts as a deterrent because the employees know that the insurance company is more likely to press charges against a dishonest employee than would a "soft hearted" and embarrassed employer.

There is only one "catch" to this type of coverage. The organization has to have good enough records to prove that an embezzlement has taken place. This means that this coverage is not a substitute for other internal controls. If the theft occurs but the employer doesn't know it or if there is no proof of the loss, fidelity insurance will not help.

This protection is not expensive since the risk is usually low. Of course, the risk varies from one organization to another, and thus the premium will vary. In the case of the Center, a fidelity policy covering losses of up to $100,000 costs about $200 annually. In any case the cost is relatively so little that prudence dictates that all nonprofit organizations, except possibly the very smallest, have this coverage.

Sometimes employees feel that a lack of confidence is being expressed in them if the organization has fidelity insurance. The treasurer should assure them that this is not the case, and that fidelity insurance is similar to fire insurance. All prudent organizations carry such coverage.

CONCLUSION

Internal control as discussed in this chapter for small organizations is a system of procedures which in the absence of collusion minimizes the likelihood of misappropriation of assets or misstatement of the accounts, and if it has occurred maximizes the likelihood of detection. These controls largely depend on a division of duties such that no one person is in a position to both misappropriate assets and to cover up the theft in the records. These controls are very important even in a smaller organization where it is difficult to provide for this division of duties. One of the principal reasons often overlooked for having good internal control is to remove temptation from normally honest employees.

Even the smallest organization should be able to apply the eleven internal controls that have been recommended in this chapter. The board should insist that these and similar controls be established. It has a responsibility to insist that all practical measures be taken to protect the organization's assets. Otherwise the board is subject to severe criticism if an embezzlement were to occur. Fidelity insurance was also recommended.

The controls discussed in this chapter are basic ones and should not be considered all-inclusive. A complete system of internal control encompasses all of the procedures of the organization. If the organization is a large or complex one, or if it has peculiar problems or procedures, the board will want to retain the services of a professional to help set up and monitor the effectiveness of internal control. The next chapter discusses the services that the certified public accountant can provide, including assistance in establishing internal controls.

23

Independent Audits

Related to the internal controls discussed in Chapter 22 is the question whether the books and records should be audited, and if so, by whom. Like many other decisions the board has to make, this is a value judgment for which there are no absolute answers. Audits cost money, and therefore the values to be derived must be considered carefully.

FUNCTIONS AND LIMITATIONS

An audit is a series of procedures followed by an experienced professional accountant to test, on a selective basis, transactions and internal controls in effect, all with a view to forming an opinion on the fairness of the presentation of the financial statements for the period. An audit is not an examination of every transaction that has been recorded; it is a series of tests designed to give the accountant a basis for judging how effectively the records were kept and the degree of reliance that can be placed on the internal controls. The end result of an audit is the expression of an opinion.

Several things should be underscored. Auditors do not examine all transactions. If they were to do so the cost would probably be prohibitive. They do look at what they believe is a representative sample of the transactions. In looking at these selected transactions, they are as concerned with the internal control and procedures that were followed as they are with the legitimacy of the transaction itself. If internal controls are good, the extent of the testing can be limited. If controls are weak, the auditors will have to examine many more transactions to be satisfied.

In smaller organizations where internal controls are often less effective, they must examine proportionately more transactions.

Another point that should be made is that for the most part the auditors can only examine and test transactions that have been recorded. If a contribution has been received but not deposited in the bank or recorded in the books, there is little likelihood that it will be discovered. This is why Chapter 22 emphasized that controls should be established over all receipts at the point of receipt and all disbursements should be made by check. In this way a record is made and the auditor has a chance of testing the transaction.

The end product of the audit is not a "certificate" that every transaction has been properly recorded, but an expression of an opinion by the auditor on the fairness of the presentation of the financial statements. The auditor does not guarantee accuracy; the bookkeeper may have stolen $100, but unless this $100 is material in relation to the financial statements as a whole, the auditor is not likely to discover it.

Auditor's Opinion Explained

Here is a typical opinion prepared by a certified public accountant which in this case is on the financial statements of the National Environmental Society.

In my opinion, the accompanying balance sheet and the related statement of income and expense present fairly the financial position of National Environmental Society at December 31, 19X1, and the results of its operations for the year, in conformity with generally accepted accounting principles applied on a basis consistent with that of the preceding year. My examination of these statements was made in accordance with generally accepted auditing standards and accordingly included such tests of the accounting records and such other auditing procedures as I considered necessary in the circumstances.

This opinion is very carefully worded, and each phrase has significance. The wording has evolved over a period of time and is designed to tell the knowledgeable reader what responsibility the auditor takes and does not take. Since this opinion is the end product of an audit it is important to know exactly what the opinion means. Let us look at the opinion phrase by phrase to see what is being said.

Identification of Statements. "In my opinion the accompanying balance sheet and the related statement of income and expense . . ."

The auditor is carefully identifying the statements covered by the opinion—the "accompanying" balance sheet and statement of income and expense. These statements and only these statements are the ones referred to.

Statements Present Fairly. "In my opinion . . . present fairly the financial position . . . at December 31 and the results of its operations for the year . . ."

Here the auditor is saying the statements "present fairly"—not that they are correct or that they are accurate, but that they present "fairly." What does "fairly" mean? It means that there is no *material* misstatement of these figures. The statements may not be 100 per cent accurate, but they are not materially inaccurate. The question of what is "material" cannot really be answered with any definitiveness since this is largely a subjective question, and in part depends on what figures you are looking at.*

Accounting Principles Followed. ". . . in conformity with generally accepted accounting principles . . ."

Here the auditor is defining the principles of accounting which have been followed—"generally accepted accounting principles." These words have specific meaning and refer to published pronouncements by the American Institute of Certified Public Accountants and the Financial Accounting Standards Board and to general usage by organizations similar to the one being audited. Where there have been pronouncements of accounting principles by the AICPA or the FASB, the auditor is saying here that these principles have been followed. Where there have been no pronouncements, the auditor is saying that the principles followed are those generally used by similar organizations. Chapters 2–9 discuss some of the principles generally accepted as they relate to nonprofit organizations. If an opinion is issued without these specific words "in accordance with generally accepted accounting principles" the reader should be certain the principles used are clearly explained and understood.

Principles Consistently Followed. ". . . applied on a basis consistent with that of the preceding year . . ."

The auditor is saying here that there have been no changes in accounting principles or in the application of these principles during the current year and the reader can compare last year's statements to this year's statements and know that they are comparable in this respect. If there have been changes, the auditor always has to spell out or make reference to these changes in the opinion.

Audit Standards Followed. "My examination was made in accordance with generally accepted auditing standards . . ."

---

* The SEC in referring to reporting requirements for SEC filings defines "material" as ". . . the information . . . [about] which an average prudent investor ought reasonably to be informed before purchasing the security registered."

Here the auditor is spelling out in technical language how the examination was conducted. There is a whole body of literature and pronouncements which define "generally accepted auditing standards." These include standards of training, proficiency, independence, planning, supervision of staff, evaluation of internal control, and obtaining evidential matter to support the audit conclusions. They also provide that the auditor must perform certain specific tests where applicable.

Essential Tests.   There are two specific tests which cannot be omitted by the auditor: confirmation of accounts receivable, and observation of physical inventories. Confirmation of accounts receivable involves writing to those owing money (or making pledges) to the organization and asking them to confirm that they do, in fact, owe the organization. Observation of physical inventories involves going out and physically verifying the existence of the inventory. Both of these tests can require substantial amounts of the auditor's time, and often an organization will ask the auditor to eliminate these tests to save time and cost. If omitted, however, and if receivables or inventories are material, the auditor will not be able to say that the examination has been made in accordance with generally accepted auditing standards. An opinion cannot be expressed on the financial statements "taken as a whole."

Extent of Audit Tests.   ". . . and accordingly included such tests of the accounting records and such other auditing procedures as I considered necessary in the circumstances."

This phrase says that in addition to all other auditing requirements spelled out in official pronouncements, the auditor has performed whatever additional tests he or she believes should be performed.

Adequacy of Internal Control Over Contributions

The auditor must be satisfied that internal control over contributions is such as to ensure that all contributions received have been recorded. Internal control was discussed in the previous chapter, but one control in particular should again be noted. Normally two persons should open all mail to prevent misappropriation. In the absence of adequate internal control, the CPA is required to qualify the opinion.

Qualified Opinions

A "qualified" opinion is an opinion in which the independent auditor takes exception to some specific aspect of the financial statements as presented, or is unable to form an unqualified opinion because of some contingency which might affect the financial statements. The independent auditor will spell out in the opinion exactly what the nature of the qualification is. A qualification with respect to presentation can result because generally accepted accounting principles were not followed, or because they were not consistently followed. A qualification because of a material uncertainty results when neither the auditor nor anyone else is in a position to know the ultimate outcome of a pending transaction which affects the financial statements. A lawsuit against the organization is a good example.

Adverse Opinion. An "adverse" opinion results when, in the opinion of the auditor, the financial statements taken as a whole do not present fairly the financial position in conformity with generally accepted accounting principles. The distinction between a "qualified" opinion and an "adverse" opinion is primarily one of materiality.

Disclaimer. A "disclaimer" of opinion results when the auditor is unable to form an opinion on the financial statements. This could be the result of limitations on scope of the examination, uncertainties about the outcome of some event that would affect the financial statements in a very material way, or because the records were inadequate and it was not possible to form an opinion. When an auditor gives a disclaimer the reasons for it are spelled out in the opinion.

Any qualification detracts from the credibility of the financial statements. Since one of the functions of an auditor's opinion is to add credibility to the financial statements, an opinion other than a "clean" or unqualified opinion will detract and raise questions about the statements. Wherever it is possible for an organization to take corrective action to eliminate the qualification, it should do so.

BENEFITS OF AN INDEPENDENT AUDIT

Audits are not free. This means that the board has to evaluate the benefits to be derived from an audit and the cost of this professional service. What are the benefits that can be expected from an audit? There are four: credibility of the financial statements; professional assistance in developing meaningful financial statements; professional advice on internal control, administrative efficiency, and other business matters; and assistance in tax reporting and compliance requirements.

Credibility of the Financial Statements

We have already touched on credibility. This is the principal benefit of having an independent CPA express an opinion on the financial statements. Unfortunately, over the years, there have been many instances where nonprofit organizations have been mismanaged and the results buried in the financial statements in a manner that made it difficult, if not impossible, for the reader of the statements to discern.

It has been noted that the purpose of financial statements is to communicate in a straightforward and direct manner what has happened. The presence of an auditor's opinion helps in this communication process because an independent expert, after an examination, tells the reader that the financial statements present fairly what has happened. Nonprofit organizations are competing with other organizations for the money of their members or of the general public. If an organization can tell its financial story accurately and completely and it is accepted at face value, the potential contributor is more likely to feel that the organization is well managed.

Meaningful Statements

Another benefit of having professional help is that the auditor is an expert at preparing financial statements in a format that will be most clear to the reader. All too often financial statements are poorly organized and hard to understand. The CPA has had years of experience in helping organizations prepare financial statements in clear and understandable language.

Advice on Internal Control and Other Matters

Another benefit is that the CPA will be in a position to advise the board on how to strengthen internal controls and simplify the bookkeeping procedures. As an expert, the CPA can also assist the board in evaluating the competency of the organization's bookkeeper or accountant and be able to help the organization when it comes time to hire someone for these positions.

The CPA has had experience in dealing with many different types of organizations and is likely to have a number of general business suggestions. Typically, periodic meetings with the treasurer or executive director will be held to discuss the problems of the organization and business conditions in general. Many boards arrange annual meetings to ask questions and to be sure that the organization has picked the CPA's brain. This meeting also provides the CPA with an opportunity to call any potential problems to the board's attention.

Assistance in Tax Reporting and Compliance Requirements

As is discussed in Chapters 25–27, almost all nonprofit organizations are required to submit some form of report to one or more agencies of a state government and the IRS. These reports are almost always technical in format and unless the treasurer is an accountant, the assistance of an expert will probably be required. The CPA is an expert, and can either offer advice on how to prepare the returns or can actually prepare them.

SELECTING A CERTIFIED PUBLIC ACCOUNTANT

Like doctors and lawyers, certified public accountants seldom advertise. They depend on word of mouth to spread their reputation. Accordingly when it comes time to choose a CPA, talk with your banker, attorney, and fellow members of the board. The chances are that collectively they will know many CPAs practicing in your locality and will know of their reputations. Talk also with officers of other nonprofit organizations. They will probably have had some experience which may be of help.

In any professional relationship, the interest and willingness of the CPA to serve the organization is one of the most important factors to consider in making a selection. It is always difficult to judge which of several CPAs have the greatest interest in helping the organization. In large part the treasurer will have to make the decision from impressions formed in personal interviews.

One of the more effective ways to gain an impression is to send the CPA financial statements before an interview. Then, at the time of the interview, ask for comments on the statements. The amount of homework done will be obvious in the response.

During this personal interview, let the CPA take a look at the records to get a general impression of the amount of time that will be necessary, and thus the fee. For the most part the treasurer's judgment should not be swayed significantly by the fee range estimated unless it is out of line with other CPA fees. Like a doctor or lawyer, the accountant expects to receive a fair fee for services. The organization is largely dependent on the honesty and professional reputation of the accountant to charge a fair fee.

Cost of an Audit

What does it cost to have an audit? This is a difficult question to answer because most CPAs charge on an hourly basis. If the organization's records are in good shape and up to date the time will be less. There is no way to know how much time will be involved without looking at the records and knowing something about the organization.

The hourly rates vary, depending on the individual assigned and his or her experience. Most examinations involve a combination of experienced and inexperienced staff members. In 1982 the hourly rates ranged from $30 to $170, with an overall average effective rate of between $50 and $60 an hour. This average rate is a composite. Most of the time spent on any audit will be by less experienced staff members whose billing rates will be lower than for the CPA in charge.

The only accurate way to find out what it will cost to have an audit is to call a CPA and ask for an estimate. Even then it will be difficult to know all the problems that may be encountered and the CPA will probably hedge on the estimate by indicating that while it is a best estimate the final amount might be more or less. Keep in mind that the CPA is providing a professional service just as does a doctor or a lawyer.

Sometimes an organization will shop around in an effort to find the CPA that will charge it the least. While understandable, this makes about as much sense as choosing a doctor based on the rate charged for an office visit. You get what you pay for. Since the salaries paid by the various firms are pretty much the same at any given level of competence, each CPA firm will charge about the same amount per hour for a staff member's services. The variable is the length of time it will take to perform the examination. Since the treasurer is not likely to be in a position to judge the quality of the work, there is a risk in choosing a professional accountant solely on the basis of an estimated fee. Choosing a CPA should be on the basis of reputation and willingness to serve the organization.

Review Services

A possible alternative to an audit, for an organization which does not have to submit audited financial statements to a state, a funding source, or another organization, is to have its financial statements "reviewed" by a CPA. A review requires less time, hence incurs less cost; however, it results in a lesser degree of assurance by the CPA. Instead of saying that the financial statements "present fairly," the CPA does only enough work to be able to say, "I am not aware of any material modifications that should be made in order for the financial statements to be in conformity." This is called "negative assurance" and does not give as much credibility to the financial statements as an audit does. Nevertheless, a review may meet the needs of some smaller organizations.

The "Big Eight" Accounting Firms

Many smaller organizations tend to feel that the major accounting firms, including the "big eight," won't be interested in serving a smaller nonprofit organization. This is not the case with most of these firms. There should be no hesitation in soliciting their interest, as well as that of smaller firms.

PUBLIC ACCOUNTANTS

So far we have talked about the advantages of bringing in a "certified public accountant." There are also "public accountants" in many states. What does the difference in title mean?

Certified public accountants are the "professionals." They have been licensed by the state after proving their competency by passing a rigorous two-and-a-half-day examination, meeting certain educational requirements, and in most states, working for another CPA for a period of time. The CPA is continually accountable to the state. Only a CPA can join the American Institute of Certified Public Accountants.

Public accountants may or may not be licensed by the state. Where they are licensed, there are usually no examinations to pass or educational requirements to meet, and for the most part they can practice without experience. Nevertheless, public accountants are often quite competent and can provide good and effective service to clients, particularly in keeping the records or preparing financial statements. If an organization is going to hire an accountant to help keep the records, the public accountant may well be the right person to hire. But, as a general rule, it should retain a certified public accountant if it wants an audit to be made.

THE INTERNAL AUDIT COMMITTEE

Many smaller organizations do not feel they can afford a CPA (or a public accountant) and yet want some assurance that all disbursements have been made for properly approved purposes. One solution to this is to set up an "internal audit committee" consisting of several members of the board or of the membership. The purpose of this internal audit committee is usually to review all disbursements "after the fact" to make sure that all have been properly approved and documented. The review can take place at any time, but for convenience it is usually done some time after the payment has been made. The committee may meet on a monthly or bimonthly basis and review all transactions since the last meeting. It may also review bank reconciliations, marketable securities bought, sold, and on hand, and any other matter which could be "sensitive."

The advantage of an internal audit committee is that it strengthens internal control significantly with little cost. This is particularly important where internal control is weak because it is not practical to segregate duties as much as might be desired.

The weakness of an internal audit committee is that it can become so routine and perfunctory that the committee does little effective auditing and is merely a rubber stamp. Probably the best way to see that this doesn't happen is to rotate committee membership. Perhaps the past president, past treasurer, and a member chosen from the board would constitute an effective and knowledgeable internal audit committee. Since both the president and treasurer have limited tenure, the composition of the committee would automatically change with time.

There is also a risk that the board will get a false sense of security with an internal audit committee. The committee members are usually not trained accountants and might very well miss clues that a CPA would see. Also, this committee is essentially looking at only disbursements and is making no test of receipts. All of this means that an internal audit committee has some limitations although it clearly is better to have such a committee than to have no control at all.

CONCLUSION

We have discussed the principal advantages of retaining a certified public accountant to make an audit of nonprofit organizations. In addition to providing "credibility" to the financial statements, the CPA can provide advice for improving the format of the financial statements to make them more effective in communicating to the reader, and can offer suggestions to improve internal controls and administrative efficiency. In addition, in this increasingly complex society of rules and reports, the CPA is an expert and can help an organization comply with the many reporting requirements.

The importance of hiring the right CPA was discussed and some suggested procedures to follow were outlined. As with any professional, it is important to find a CPA who is interested in serving your organization. This is largely a personal judgment and one that each organization has to make based on interviews and the reputation of the accountant. The difference between a "public accountant" and a "certified public accountant" was discussed. While there are many competent public accountants, the CPA is the professional and therefore is the accountant that should be hired if an audit is needed. The use of an internal audit committee was suggested as one way in which internal control could be strengthened.

24

Investments

Some nonprofit organizations have an investment program to manage resulting from receipt of endowment funds and other restricted gifts. In addition, some organizations also have excess cash in their unrestricted general fund which can be invested. Together all of these investment funds can be very sizable. They are usually invested in publicly traded securities, although occasionally part may be invested in real estate or in mortgages.

One of the practical problems faced by the nonprofit organization is how to handle its investment program where there are a number of separate funds, each with amounts available for investment. The question that arises is whether investments should be made on a separate fund-by-fund basis or whether all investments should be pooled together in one pot. This chapter discusses the concept of pooling of investments and shows how to keep the appropriate records. Some sources of investment advice are given, along with the considerations a treasurer must take into account in providing physical safeguards over the securities themselves.

POOLING VERSUS INDIVIDUAL INVESTMENTS

Typically, most organizations have a number of different individual funds, each having cash that can be invested. These individual funds may include board-designated endowment funds, as well as donor-designated endowment funds. Within these fund groupings there are frequently many individual "name" funds. All of this means that a nonprofit organization can have a number of separate accounting entities which have assets invested in marketable securities. This is where some practical problems arise.

The organization can, of course, invest the money of each individual fund in specific securities and keep track of the actual income and gain or loss associated with these specific investments. If it does so, there is no question about the amount of income, or the gain or loss associated with each separate fund.

But for many organizations, the cash available for investment in each fund is not large enough to make individual purchases. If purchases were made on an individual fund basis there probably would be little diversification. Yet the aggregate of the available assets of all individual funds could be sizable enough to provide a well diversified portfolio if all of the assets were invested together as an investment pool.

This is what many organizations do. They pool all of their investment funds together and prorate the resulting income and gains or losses.

Example of Individual Investments for Each Fund

An example will illustrate the difference in these two approaches. The Johnstown Museum has investments aggregating about $200,000. It follows the approach of making specific investments for each fund. What the portfolio looked like at December 31, 19X1, is shown at the top of the next page.

As is typical, some of the individual investments have done better than others but on an overall basis, market value is a third above cost. Since the museum keeps track of its portfolio by individual fund, the gain or loss and the income for each of these funds are based on the actual investments in each fund. As can be seen the board-designated endowment fund had income of $3,900, and if the organization were to sell all of these investments there would be a capital gain of $55,000. On the other hand, the R. A. Adler Fund has had a decline in value of $25,000.

One of the problems of making investments on an individual fund basis is that there are usually some amounts of cash which are too small to be individually invested. In this case the Johnstown Museum has a total of $18,500 of uninvested cash in all of its funds, which is large enough to be put to work.

Example of Pooled Investments

A fair amount of paperwork is involved in keeping track of specific investments by individual funds. Pooling all investments and putting

	Cost	Market 12/31/X1	Income Year 19X1
Board-designated endowment fund			
1,000 shares of Stock A	$ 20,000	$ 45,000	$1,400
500 shares of Stock B	20,000	40,000	1,500
1,000 shares of Stock C	40,000	50,000	1,000
Uninvested cash	15,000	15,000	
	95,000	150,000	3,900
Endowment fund—W. H. Miller			
1,000 shares of Stock D	9,000	31,000	1,500
100 shares of Stock E	5,000	3,000	100
Uninvested cash	1,000	1,000	
	15,000	35,000	1,600
Endowment fund—R. A. Adler			
500 shares of Stock F	37,500	12,500	500
Uninvested cash	2,500	2,500	
	40,000	15,000	500
Total all funds	$150,000	$200,000	$6,000

them into one pot eliminates the need to keep track of the individual purchases by specific fund. It also provides a larger investment fund which helps to cushion the effect of any single poor investment decision. In the case of the 500 shares of stock F, which has declined in value, the effect on the R. A. Adler Fund is devastating. It is worth a fraction of its original $40,000. On the other hand, if stock F had been pooled with the other stocks, the effect on the Adler Fund would have been only a pro rata portion. Likewise, the large gain on stock D in the Miller Fund would have been spread over all of the funds. The principal advantage of pooling is that it spreads the risk uniformly over all of the pooled funds. A second advantage is that the total uninvested cash is usually lower. And, as noted above, a third advantage is simplified record keeping.

Let us now examine how these funds would have looked if the museum had been on a pooled basis. For the sake of simplicity it is assumed that no investments have been sold since the original principal was established in each fund and that all funds were established on the same date. Accordingly, each fund has been assigned "shares" on the basis of one share for each dollar transferred to the investment pool. Shown on the next page is how the individual funds would look at December 31, 19X1.

The number of shares in each fund represents the original amount pooled as, in this example, $1.00 per share. The market value per share is simply the aggregate portfolio market value (including uninvested

	Number of Shares	Cost	Market 12/31/X1	Income for 19X1
Board-designated fund	95,000	$ 95,000	$126,666	$3,800
Endowment fund				
W. H. Miller	15,000	15,000	20,000	600
R. A. Adler	40,000	40,000	53,334	1,600
	150,000	$150,000	$200,000	$6,000
Per share		$1.00	$1.33	$.04

cash) divided by the number of shares (i.e., $200,000 ÷ 150,000 shares = $1.33). The market value for each individual fund is the value per share of $1.33 times the number of shares in each fund. Likewise, the overall per-share income of $.04 is first calculated ($6,000 ÷ 150,000 shares) and then the individual fund income amounts are arrived at by multiplying $.04 times the number of shares.

When a comparison is made of the market value of each fund on a pooled basis to the market value on an individual investment basis, it will be seen that there are significant differences. The Adler Fund is the most conspicuous example because the market on the pooled basis is now $53,334 compared to only $15,000 before.

Distribution of the income on a pooled basis is also based on shares, and as can be seen the Adler Fund is again a beneficiary of this method.

CALCULATING SHARE VALUES IN POOLED INVESTMENTS

The discussion above has been centered on a relatively simple illustration showing the principles involved in pooling. It was assumed that all of the funds pooled their money on the same date, and accordingly each fund received shares with a "cost" of the same amount per share. In practice this doesn't happen except for the single date when the pool is set up. At subsequent dates the market value per share will be higher or lower, and additions or withdrawals to and from the pool must obviously be at the then existing per-share market value.

Let us look at the transactions that took place in the Johnstown Museum portfolio in 19X2:

March 31: The board transferred $40,500 from the unrestricted general fund to the board-designated fund.

August 10: The board found it had transferred more than it should have and needed to redeem some of its shares. It transferred $14,300 from the board-designated fund back to the unrestricted general fund as of the end of the calendar quarter.

December 31: The board received a large contribution for addition to the R. A. Adler Fund.

Figure 24–1 shows a calculation of the share values at the end of each of the calendar quarters. The market value of the portfolio is determined, based on actual market values on these dates plus all uninvested cash.

Generally, organizations calculate share values only at the end of the calendar quarter. If the board wants to buy or redeem shares during a period between quarters, the value of the shares purchased or redeemed is based on the value at the end of the quarter in which the request to purchase or redeem is made. Thus, if the board decides to redeem some of the shares in the board-designated fund on August 10, the transaction does not take place until the next date on which share values are calculated. In this case, this would be the end of the quarter, September 30. If the board wanted to calculate share values on August 10, the transaction could be effected on that date.

Cost Basis Accounting

Different types of nonprofit organizations have different bases for carrying their investments.* For organizations on a cost basis, marketable securities cannot be "written up" to reflect the market value of the portfolio. However, when a stock is sold, the realized gain or loss should be recorded.

There is no difficulty in determining the amount of gain or loss when individual stocks are purchased for a specific fund. It is quite clear which fund realized the gain or loss. On pooled investments, however, each fund shares in all realized gains or losses on a prorata basis. This presents a mechanical problem of allocation. From a practical standpoint, this allocation is usually not made each time a stock is sold unless such sales are made very infrequently. Instead, these gains or losses are accumulated and allocated at the end of the quarter, or at the end of the year if there has been no change in the number of shares outstanding.

* The Audit Guide for voluntary health and welfare organizations, the Audit Guide for colleges and universities, and the Statement of Position applicable to many other nonprofit organizations permit the carrying of investments on a market value basis. In 1978, hospitals were required to carry marketable equity investments at the lower of aggregate cost or market. See pages 80–88 for a more complete discussion.

JOHNSTOWN MUSEUM

CALCULATION OF SHARE VALUES FOR PURPOSES
OF PURCHASING AND REDEEMING SHARES
By Quarter for 19X2

Date	Shares Outstanding Before Purchase or Redemption	Market Value Before Purchase or Redemption	Value Per Share	Shares Purchased (Redeemed) This Date		Shares Outstanding After Purchase or Redemption	Market Value After Purchase or Redemption
				Shares*	Amount		
12/31/X1	150,000	$200,000	$1.33	—	—	150,000	$200,000
3/31/X2	150,000	202,500	1.35	30,000	$40,500	180,000	243,000
6/30/X2	180,000	252,000	1.40	—	—	180,000	252,000
9/30/X2	180,000	257,400	1.43	(10,000)	(14,300)	170,000	243,100
12/31/X2	170,000	238,000	1.40	10,000	14,000	180,000	252,000

*The number of shares purchased or redeemed is determined by dividing the amount invested or withdrawn by the value per share.

Fig. 24—1. A worksheet showing how to calculate share values for a pooled investment fund.

An illustration may be helpful. Assume the following transactions took place during 19X2:

March 10: 500 shares of Stock F were sold for $12,500 with a cost of $37,500, and a loss of $25,000.

August 15: 500 shares of Stock C were sold for $30,000 with a cost of $20,000, and a gain of $10,000.

September 15: 100 shares of Stock E were sold for $4,000 with a cost of $5,000, and a loss of $1,000.

At the end of the first and third quarters the loss of $25,000 and net gain of $9,000 are allocated on the basis of shares as shown in the following statement.

	March 31		September 30	
	Shares Outstanding *	Gain/(Loss) Allocated	Shares Outstanding *	Gain/(Loss) Allocated
Board-designated fund	95,000	($15,833)	125,000	$6,250
Endowment fund:				
W. H. Miller	15,000	(2,500)	15,000	750
R. A. Adler	40,000	(6,667)	40,000	2,000
	150,000	($25,000)	180,000	$9,000
Gain (loss)		($25,000)	$9,000	
Per share		($.16666)	$.05	

* The purchase and redemption of shares in Figure 24–1 have also been reflected here, but notice that the allocation is based on the number of shares before purchases or redemptions on that date.

Here is the balance in each of the individual funds at December 31, 19X2, taking into consideration both gains and losses and purchases and redemptions shown in Figure 24–1:

	Number of Shares	Book Cost	Market Value (i.e. Share Value Times Number of Shares)
Board-designated fund	115,000	$111,617	$161,000
Endowment fund:			
W. H. Miller	15,000	13,250	21,000
R. A. Adler	50,000	49,333	70,000
	180,000	$174,200	$252,000

Each of these amounts was calculated at December 31, 19X2, as follows:

	Shares	Book Cost
Board-designated fund		
December 31, 19X1 balance	95,000	$ 95,000
March 31, allocation of loss	—	(15,833)
March 31, purchase of shares	30,000	40,500
September 30, allocation of gain (net)	—	6,250
September 30, redemption of shares	(10,000)	(14,300)
December 31, 19X2 balance	115,000	$111,617
W. H. Miller		
December 31, 19X1 balance	15,000	$ 15,000
March 31, allocation of loss	—	(2,500)
September 30, allocation of gain (net)	—	750
December 31, 19X2 balance	15,000	$ 13,250
R. A. Adler		
December 31, 19X1 balance	40,000	$ 40,000
March 31, allocation of loss	—	(6,667)
September 30, allocation of gain (net)	—	2,000
December 31, purchase of shares	10,000	14,000
December 31, 19X2 balance	50,000	$ 49,333

It should be emphasized that while the calculation of share values for purposes of purchases and redemptions of shares is based on the market value of the portfolio at date of valuation, this calculation is only for purposes of this purchase or redemption and is not recorded in the books. The books are kept on a cost basis adjusted only for realized gains or losses.*

ALLOCATION OF POOLED INCOME

There has been no discussion of the handling of income and interest received on pooled funds, but the mechanics of allocation are exactly the same as with the allocation of gains or losses. Generally, allocation of income is also made on a quarterly basis, although some organizations allocate on an annual basis. Investment income is usually not added back to the principal of the fund and reinvested. It is expended for the purposes specified by the donor or added to the unrestricted general

---

* Of course if an organization carries its investments at market, then the books would be periodically adjusted to reflect unrealized gains and losses.

fund in the case of board-designated endowment funds. This means that as income is received it is put into a separate account. At the end of each quarter, it is allocated to each fund on a share basis. An organization could, of course, allocate more often than quarterly but this would complicate the bookkeeping.

Once the mechanics of these calculations are established they should not cause difficulty. It is important to formalize these calculations in worksheets which become part of the records of the organization.

PROFESSIONAL INVESTMENT ADVICE

Let us turn now to a practical nonaccounting question. Where should an organization go to get good investment advice? The answer is clear: to a professional, to someone who knows the market, and is in the business of advising others.

You may feel that this skirts the question. Yet many medium and some large organizations try to outguess the market on their own and they usually don't succeed. They make all of the investment mistakes that many individuals do. They tend to rely on their own intuition and try to outguess the professionals. This doesn't make sense when an individual's own money is involved and it makes even less sense when the money belongs to a nonprofit organization.

Sometimes the board, recognizing its fiduciary responsibilities, will tend to be too conservative in its investment policy, and will purchase high-grade, low-interest-bearing bonds. This conservatism can be almost as risky as purchasing a highly volatile stock, as many holders of bonds discovered in recent years when high interest rates depressed bond prices. This is why professional advice is needed.

Investment Funds.   There are a number of places to go for professional advice. If the total investments are relatively small in size (say, under $100,000), many organizations find that a no-load mutual fund or a bank common stock fund is the answer.* In both cases the organization is purchasing expertise while it pools its funds with those of many other people. Mutual funds offer a convenient way to obtain investment management when the organization has a minimum amount to invest.

---

* If an organization has under $100,000 to invest, the board should carefully con-.ider the nature of the funds being invested before buying common stocks. If the funds available are to be invested for only a short period of time, or if investment income is essential, then the organization should not be investing in common stocks. Instead, a savings account or money-market instrument is probably more appropriate.

There are several hundred mutual funds with different investment goals and varying degrees of risk. A good place to start looking for a mutual fund is the Forbes Magazine annual review of mutual funds published each August. This review gives a great deal of comparative information which should help pinpoint several funds to study.

Bank-commingled or common stock investment funds are a form of mutual fund. One of the advantages of using a bank fund is that the reputation of the bank is involved and the bank will pay close attention to the investments made. Banks are often more conservative than mutual funds in their investment decisions, but this may be appropriate when one considers the fiduciary responsibility of nonprofit organizations.

If the investment fund is large in size (over $100,000) the organization may prefer to select a professional to advise on specific stocks and bonds to purchase for its own portfolio. Most brokers are pleased to offer this service. On the other hand many nonprofit organizations are reluctant to entrust investment decisions to the brokers who handle the actual purchasing, because they are "wearing two hats." This can be avoided by going to one of the many available investment advisory services that does not handle the actual purchasing or selling.

Short-Term Investments. Investment professionals can also offer advice on a type of investment which is frequently not given the attention it warrants by nonprofit organizations—short-term investments. Short-term investments are investments in interest-bearing instruments of that portion of an organization's cash balances which is currently inactive but will be needed to fund programs and activities in the near future.

An ordinary savings account is one type of short-term investment of cash balances that are temporarily not deployed. Often, however, it is possible to improve on the interest rate available in savings accounts, without substantially increasing risk, by purchasing "money-market" instruments. These vary in interest rate, risk, minimum denomination available, time to maturity, and marketability prior to redemption; included are U.S. Treasury Bills, "agencies," certificates of deposit, and repurchase agreements.

Treasury Bills are the most marketable money-market instrument. The smallest denomination currently available is $10,000 and the shortest maturity is 13 weeks.

"Agencies" are federally sponsored debt instruments issued by federal agencies or quasi-governmental organizations. Some are explicitly guaranteed by the full faith and credit of the United States government while others are not.

Certificates of deposit (CDs) are available directly from commercial or savings banks, or through securities dealers. Only large CDs (over $100,000) are negotiable, and all bear substantial penalties for redemption prior to maturity.

Repurchase agreements are agreements under which a bank or securities dealer agrees to repurchase at a specific date and at a specific premium securities sold earlier to an investor. Interest rates on repurchase agreements are often attractive, and a wide range of maturities is usually available.

Selecting an Investment Advisor. A list of investment advisory services can usually be found in the classified telephone directory. Bear in mind that, as with all professionals, the investment advisor's reputation should be carefully checked. The bank's trust department is usually also happy to give advice on investment decisions. The point to emphasize is that investment decisions should be made by professionals in the investment business and not by amateurs (this is as true of investments as it is of medicine!). And remember, too, that even professionals make errors in judgment.

The professional advisor will charge a fee which is generally calculated on the basis of a percentage of the monies invested. The larger the investment fund, the lower the rate charged. This rate will vary depending on the size of the fund, but frequently is in the range of ½ to 1 per cent annually. The rate structure follows pretty closely the structure that investment advisors charge mutual funds.

SAFEGUARDING INVESTMENT SECURITIES

The physical safeguarding of an organization's investment securities is as important as making the right decision as to which stocks to buy or sell. This is often overlooked. The board of directors or the finance committee of the board has general responsibility for all investment instruments owned by the organization. Periodic verification of the existence of the securities should be made, either by independent accountants or the board itself. Verification usually involves a physical counting of the securities at the location where they are deposited. Three areas warrant special attention. The first is that stock certificates aren't lost or misplaced through carelessness or poor handling. The second is that they are not lost through misappropriation by an employee. The third is that the stockbroker doesn't lose the certificates or, worse yet, go bankrupt. Let's look at the risks in each of these three areas.

Careless Handling.   If the organization keeps the certificates in its possession, the certificates should be kept in a bank safe deposit box. They should be registered in the name of the organization. The organization should also maintain an investment register which shows the certificate number as well as cost and other financial information.* There should be limited access to the safe deposit box and it is wise to require the presence of two persons (preferably officers) whenever the box is opened.†

Some organizations become careless in handling the certificates because they are registered in their name. They know they can "stop transfer" if the certificates are lost. While this is usually true, most transfer agents will require the registered owner to post a bond before a replacement certificate is issued. The purpose of the bond is to protect the agent from any loss that might result from misuse of the lost certificate. The bond can be purchased from an insurance company, but it is expensive, ranging between 1 and 4 per cent of the market value of the lost certificate on the date the replacement certificate is issued. This is a high price to pay for carelessness.

Embezzlement.   An organization must always be concerned that someone having access to stock certificates may be tempted to steal them. While the certificates may be registered in the organization's name, there is an underworld market for stolen certificates. Furthermore, if the loss is not discovered promptly and the transfer agent advised to "stop transfer," the organization's rights may be jeopardized.

The best control is to have the broker deliver the stock certificate directly to a custodian bank for safekeeping. When the stock is sold, the bank is then instructed to deliver the certificate to the broker. In this way, the organization never handles the certificate. The use of a custodian bank provides excellent internal control. There is, of course, a charge for this custodian service which usually ranges from $15–20 per year per issue held, plus a transaction charge of $12–20 for each purchase or sale. There is usually a minimum annual charge of $250–500.

Leaving Certificates With Brokers.   Some organizations leave their certificates in the custody of their broker. This has certain risks. One is that the broker will temporarily lose track of the certificates if the back office falls behind in its paperwork or incorrectly records the certificates.

---

* An example of an investment register is shown on page 504.

† It is also wise for the board to establish an investment committee charged with the responsibility for authorizing all investment transactions. If an outside advisor is retained, this committee should still review the outside advisor's recommendations before they are accepted. It is not wise to delegate complete authority to an outside advisor to act without prior review by the investment committee.

If this happens there might be some delay before the broker straightens out the records. This is a risk that cannot be completely avoided since the broker must buy or sell the stock. But it increases if the organization also has the broker hold the certificate in safekeeping. As long as the broker doesn't go bankrupt, the worst that is likely to happen is that there will be a delay in getting the certificates when the organization wants them. This risk can be minimized by making inquiries as to the broker's reputation for handling back office problems.

The other risk is the broker's going bankrupt while holding the stock. Provided the broker has not fraudulently hypothecated the stock, bankruptcy should not result in a loss to an organization. However, there could be considerable delay before the stock is released by a court. On the other hand, if the broker has, without the consent of the organization, pledged the stock for personal borrowings, there is a possibility of actual loss. While the organization might be able to take both civil and criminal action against the broker, this would be of little consolation in bankruptcy. The first $50,000 of such losses, however, would be recovered from the federally chartered Securities Investor Protection Corporation.

While these risks might be relatively small, a nonprofit organization has a fiduciary responsibility to act with more than ordinary care and judgment. Accordingly, it would be prudent for an organization to have the broker deliver the stock certificates in the organization's name, either to a custodian bank or to the organization.

CONCLUSION

The board of a nonprofit organization has an obligation to act prudently in all of its actions. When it comes to handling investments, very few boards are competent to make informed professional decisions. Accordingly, professional advice should be obtained to ensure that the organization's investments are wisely made. For very small organizations often this can be accomplished by choosing a mutual fund or bank common stock fund. For larger organizations a professional advisor should be retained. Investment counsel should also be sought for short-term investments.

The board should not overlook its responsibility for security of its stock certificates. The most effective arrangement is to have the broker deliver all certificates to a custodian bank. In this way neither the employees of the organization or the broker have access to the certificates.

PART V

TAX AND COMPLIANCE REPORTING REQUIREMENTS

25

Principal Federal Tax and Compliance Requirements

Congress has imposed an income tax on all individuals and organizations with few exceptions. Those organizations that are exempt from such tax are known as "exempt" organizations. Generally nonprofit organizations are "exempt" organizations if they meet certain specific criteria as to purpose for which formed and if their source of income is related to that purpose. But even "exempt" organizations can be subject to tax on certain portions of their income, and if they are a "private foundation" they are subject to a number of very specific rules as well as certain "excise taxes." The purpose of this chapter is to discuss generally the types of organizations that are exempt and the general provisions of the rules governing such organizations from a tax standpoint.

This discussion is intended only to give the reader a general understanding of the tax rules and is not intended to be a complete discussion of the law and the tax regulations. Each organization should consult with its own tax accountant or attorney about its own status and any specific problems it may have.

ORGANIZATIONS "EXEMPT" FROM TAX

The Internal Revenue Code provides exemption from tax for certain very specific organizations. The most widely applicable of these exemptions are:

1. "Corporations, and any community chest, fund or foundation, organized and operated exclusively for religious, charitable, scien-

tific, testing for public safety, literary, or educational purposes, or to foster national or international amateur sports competition . . . or for the prevention of cruelty to children or animals, no part of the net earnings of which inures to the benefit of any private shareholder or individual, no substantial part of the activities of which is carrying on propaganda, or otherwise attempting to influence legislation * (except as otherwise provided in subsection (h)), and which does not participate in, or intervene in (including the publishing or distributing of statements), any political campaign on behalf of any candidate for public office." 501(c)3 †

2. "Clubs organized for pleasure, recreation, and other nonprofitable purposes, substantially all of the activities of which are for such purposes and no part of the net earnings of which inures to the benefit of any private shareholder." 501(c)7

3. "Business leagues, chambers of commerce, . . . not organized for profit . . ." 501(c)6

4. "Corporations organized for the exclusive purpose of holding title to property, collecting income therefrom, and turning over the entire amount thereof, less expenses, to an organization which itself is exempt . . ." 501(c)2

There are other exempt organizations, but the exemptions listed above are primarily applicable to nonprofit organizations. Most organizations fall under the first exemption, the "501(c)3" exemption. It should be noted that there are basically four purposes that organizations exempt under Section 501(c)3 can have: religious, charitable, scientific, or educational. This covers organizations such as churches, hospitals, schools, community funds, museums, medical research organizations, YMCAs, etc.

The other exemption most applicable to this discussion is the second one pertaining to social clubs, "501(c)7." This would include country clubs, swim clubs, women's clubs, and any social clubs organized for pleasure and recreation.

Further Categories of Exempt Organizations

The Tax Reform Act of 1969 created two general categories of "exempt" organizations with different rules and benefits for each: "private

---

* The Tax Reform Act of 1976 provides an election that, if made, applies certain percentage limitations to permissible lobbying activities in lieu of the subjective "no substantial part" test.

† References are to specific sections of the Internal Revenue Code from which the quotation was taken. Exempt organizations often refer to their type of exemption by reference to this section.

foundations," and "other than a private foundation." For purposes of this discussion, organizations other than a private foundation are referred to as "publicly supported organizations."

"Publicly supported organizations"—these are organizations that receive public support and there are a minimum of rules that apply to these organizations. An individual donor can normally deduct contributions to such organizations up to 50 per cent of adjusted gross income.

"Private foundations"—these are organizations that do not receive broad public support. Private foundations are subject to many restrictions on their activities and are subject to certain taxes including a tax on failure to distribute income. Normally an individual donor can only deduct contributions up to 20 per cent of adjusted gross income unless the private foundation makes qualifying distributions within $2\frac{1}{2}$ months after the end of the taxable year.

Publicly Supported Organizations

A "publicly supported organization" is defined for this discussion as a "501(c)3" * organization that is not a private foundation.† There are three principal categories of organizations that are not private foundations. These three categories are as follows:

1. Organizations formed exclusively for religious, charitable, scientific, literary, or educational purposes, or to foster national or international amateur sports, that normally receive a substantial portion of their receipts from direct or indirect contributions from the general public or from a governmental unit. Also excluded are churches, educational institutions with a faculty and student body, hospitals and medical research organizations related to a hospital.
2. Organizations that meet both of the following "mechanical" tests, based on actual "support" during the previous four years:
   a. The organization receives not more than one third of its support from gross investment income, and

* Organizations exempt under another section of the law, such as social clubs, business leagues, etc., are not private foundations.

† Some organizations that are not private foundations do not receive broad public support. However, these organizations are subject to the same rules that organizations receiving broad public support are subject to; accordingly, in order to assist the reader in distinguishing between private foundations and other than private foundations, the title "publicly supported" organizations will be used throughout this discussion to refer to all "501(c)(3)" organizations which are not private foundations.

   b. The organization receives more than one third of its support
      from a combination of:
      (1) Contributions, gifts, grants, membership fees, except from
          "disqualified persons," ° and
      (2) gross receipts from admissions, sale of merchandise, per-
          formance of services, or furnishing facilities, all of which
          must be in an activity related to the organization's exempt
          purpose. Excluded from gross receipts are any amounts
          from any one person, governmental unit, or company in
          excess of $5,000 or 1 per cent of total support (whichever is
          greater).
3. Organizations organized and operated exclusively for the benefit
   of an exempt publicly supported organization.

Mechanical Test.   Most organizations that receive broad public support will qualify under the first category. † There are many other organizations, however, that do not receive broad public support which will
nevertheless qualify for the non-private foundation status under the so-
called "mechanical" test. This mechanical test is complicated because
of the limitation on support from "disqualified" persons and receipts from
individual sources. Here are several examples that show how these
mechanical tests work.

Example 1:

Contributions:		
Individual gifts of less than $5,000	$75,000	
Gift from Mrs. Stanneck	50,000	$125,000
Investment income		55,000
Total income (support)		$180,000

Test 1: Investment income must be less than one third of total support.

$$\text{Investment income} \quad\ldots\ldots\ldots\ldots\ldots\ldots \quad \frac{55,000}{180,000} = 30.6\%$$
$$\text{Total support} \quad\ldots\ldots\ldots\ldots\ldots\ldots$$

° A disqualified person is basically a substantial contributor, or a foundation manager, or a person having a sizable interest in a corporation which is itself a substantial
contributor. A substantial contributor is a person who has contributed in either the
current or a prior year $5,000, if that amount at the time of the contribution was 2
per cent or more of total contributions received since formation of the foundation. A
foundation manager is any officer, director, or trustee of the foundation.
   † There is a specific mathematical test for determining whether an organization receives broad public support. For the sake of clarity it has been omitted here.

Investment income is less than 33.3 per cent and therefore this test is met.

Test 2: Total qualified support must be more than one third of total support.

$$\frac{\text{Individual gifts}}{\text{Total support}} \quad \frac{75,000}{180,000} = 41.6\%$$

Qualified support is more than 33.3 per cent and therefore this test is met. Since the organization meets both of these tests, it is not considered a private foundation; therefore it is a "publicly supported organization."

Example 2:

Contributions:		
Individual gifts of less than $5,000	$110,000	
Gifts from "disqualified" persons	140,000	$250,000
Gross receipts from services:		
Receipts of less than $6,600 per donor *	90,000	
Receipts of more than $6,600 per donor	160,000	250,000
Investment income		160,000
Total income (support)		$660,000

* $6,600 is 1 percent of total support of $660,000. The limitation is the greater of 1% of total support or $5,000.

Test 1: Investment income must be less than one third of total support.

$$\frac{\text{Investment income}}{\text{Total support}} \quad \frac{160,000}{660,000} = 24.2\%$$

Investment income is less than 33.3 per cent and therefore this test is met.

Test 2: Total qualified support must be more than one third of total support.

$$\frac{\text{Qualified support (\$110,000 + \$90,000)}}{\text{Total support}} \quad \frac{200,000}{660,000} = 30.3\%$$

Qualified support is less than 33.3 per cent and therefore this test is not met. Accordingly this organization is a "private foundation."

These examples are presented only to show generally how these rules are applied. There are a number of exceptions to these rules and each organization should consult with legal or tax counsel to determine exactly how these rules affect it. Also, keep in mind that this mechanical test is applied only to organizations with four years' experience. Younger organizations having at least one year's experience can obtain a "temporary" exemption until they have four years' experience, at which time the above tests are applied.

Facts and Circumstances Test.   For newly formed organizations, or for organizations that do not fit one of the three categories of publicly supported organizations listed above, the Internal Revenue Service is allowed to apply a "facts and circumstances" test. If all the "facts and circumstances" indicate that the organization is, in fact, a publicly supported organization, the IRS can classify it as a publicly supported organization. However, even here the IRS requires that an organization show it can reasonably expect to obtain at least 10 per cent of its support from qualified public sources.

REGISTRATION AND REPORTING

Initial Registration

All charitable organizations except churches and certain organizations having annual gross receipts of less than $5,000 must comply with Internal Revenue Service notification requirements before they are considered "exempt" from tax. After reviewing the "notification" received from the organization, the IRS sends an "exemption" letter confirming the tax-exempt status of the organization.

For charitable organizations the "notification" should be on Form 1023. Other categories of exempt organizations (social clubs, business leagues, etc.) must also file a notification but different forms are used.

Form 1023 also serves as a notice that an organization is claiming to be "not a private foundation." If a charitable organization fails to provide such notice it will be presumed to be a private foundation. Churches are exempt from this second notification requirement as are charitable organizations with annual gross receipts of less than $5,000.

Annual Information Returns

Almost all exempt organizations are required to file annual information returns. The principal exceptions to this reporting requirement are churches and their integrated auxiliaries, and certain organizations normally having gross receipts of $25,000 or less.

This annual information return includes information on income, receipts, contributions, disbursements, assets and liabilities, and names and addresses of substantial contributors.

These information returns must be filed by the fifteenth day of the fifth month after the end of the fiscal year (May 15 for calendar year organizations). There is a penalty of $10 a day on an organization that fails to file this return. Extensions of time for filing can usually be obtained if there is good reason why the return cannot be filed on a timely basis, but application for extension must be made before the filing deadline. These returns do not require certification by an outside auditor.

In addition to this return, all exempt organizations having unrelated business income of $1,000 or more must file a separate tax return and pay taxes at regular corporate rates on all taxable income over $1,000. Unrelated business income is discussed later in this chapter. Chapter 26 discusses the annual reporting forms principally used by exempt nonprofit organizations.

PRIVATE FOUNDATIONS

Many specific rules and taxes that apply to private foundations are not applicable to publicly supported organizations. The most important are:

1. An excise tax on investment income.
2. At least a minimum amount of income (as defined) must be distributed.
3. Excess business holdings must be disposed of.
4. Certain transactions are prohibited, and if made, are considered "taxable expenditures."
5. A different and more complex annual information return must be filed.

Excise Tax on Investment Income

The Tax Reform Act of 1969 established an excise tax on net investment income.* Net investment income includes not only dividends, interest, and royalties but also net capital gains and losses. † For purposes

---

* This excise tax was originally established at the rate of 4% but was reduced to 2% in 1977.

† Capital losses can be offset only against capital gains and not against investment income.

of calculating gain on investments acquired prior to December 31, 1969, the fair market value at December 31, 1969, is considered the tax basis or "cost." In calculating net investment income, reasonable expenses can be deducted. An example of the excise tax applied to a private foundation that had stocks and bonds which were acquired both before and after December 31, 1969, follows:

		Taxable Income
Dividends and interest		$ 10,000
Sale of stock A for $45,000 purchased in 1967, at a cost of $20,000, but having a market value at December 31, 1969 of $30,000		
Proceeds	$ 45,000	
December 31, 1969 value	(30,000)	
Gain		15,000
Sale of stock B for $20,000 purchased in 1968 at a cost of $15,000, but having a market value at December 31, 1969 of $25,000		
Proceeds	$ 20,000	
December 31, 1969 value	(25,000)	
Difference, not recognized for tax purposes. No loss is recognized if using the December 31, 1969 market value creates a loss	$ (5,000)	
Sale of stock C for $15,000 purchased in 1970 at a cost of $20,000		
Proceeds of sale	$ 15,000	
Cost	(20,000)	
Loss		(5,000) *
Net		20,000
Less investment advisory fees and other expenses		(2,000)
Net investment income		$ 18,000
Tax at 2%		$ 360

* The amount of capital loss deductible from taxable income is limited to the amount of capital gain included therein.

It is obviously important to keep accurate accounting records of the cost basis for all investments as well as an accurate segregation of any expenses applicable to investment income. With respect to investments acquired prior to December 31, 1969, it is obviously also important to keep a record of the fair market value as of December 31, 1969.

Tax Consequences of Gifts of Securities

On investments received by gift subsequent to December 31, 1969, the contributor's tax basis is the "cost" basis which must be used when the investment is ultimately sold for purposes of calculating taxable gain. For investments received prior to December 31, 1969, the basis is the higher of fair market value at December 31, 1969, or contributor's tax basis. In most instances the fair market value would be higher. Thus a private foundation must obtain from the donor, at the time a gift of securities is received, a statement of tax basis.* This is very important and great care should be taken to obtain this information promptly upon receipt of the gift. At a later date the donor may be difficult to locate or may have lost the necessary tax records. Since donated securities are recorded for accounting purposes at fair market value at date of receipt, the foundation must keep supplementary memo records of the donor's tax basis.

Here is an illustration of how two gifts of the same marketable security can have different tax consequences to the private foundation. Both gifts made in 1980 involve 100 shares of stock A.

Gift 1—very low basis:
Mr. Jones acquired his 100 shares of stock A in 1933 when the company was founded. His cost was only 10 cents a share, and therefore his basis for these 100 shares was only $10. Market value on the date of gift was $90 a share, or a total of $9,000. The tax basis to Mr. Jones of $10 carries over to the private foundation. If the foundation later sells the stock for $10,000 it will pay a 2 per cent tax on $9,990 ($10,000 sales proceeds less $10 tax basis), or a tax of $199.80.

Gift 2—very high basis:
Mr. Smith acquired his 100 shares of stock A in 1970 at a cost of $110 a share or a total of $11,000. The market value on the date of his gift was also $90 a share, or a total of $9,000. If the private foundation later sells this stock for $10,000 it will have neither a taxable gain or loss. In this instance the donor's basis of $110 a share carries over to the foundation for purposes of calculating taxable gain, but for purposes of calculating *loss*, the fair market value at date of gift ($90 a share) becomes the tax basis. Since the sales price ($100) is more than the fair market value at the

---

* When a gift of $50,000 or more is contributed to an exempt organization, the donor is required to file a statement within 90 days with the IRS on Form 4629 stating the fair market value of such a gift. Form 4629 does not provide for reporting the tax-payer's basis. It should be noted that this Form is filed with the IRS, and not with the exempt organization.

date of gift ($90), but less than the donor's cost ($110), there is no gain or loss recognized.

As can be seen from this example, in one instance the private foundation had to pay a tax of $199.80 and in the other instance had no tax. To the extent a private foundation has capital losses, they can be offset against capital gains in the same year. If there are no capital gains to offset such losses, the losses cannot be offset against investment income. Capital losses cannot be carried over to another year.

Distribution of Income

A private foundation is required to make "qualifying distributions" of at least the "distributable amount" by the end of the year following the year of receipt. Qualifying distributions are those amounts paid to accomplish the exempt purposes of the foundation. If this is not done, taxes are imposed which ultimately have the effect of taxing 100 per cent of any amount not so distributed.

Starting in 1982, the "distributable amount" is defined as minimum investment return, less the excise tax and, where applicable, the unrelated business income tax.

Minimum investment return is 5 per cent of the fair market value of all the foundation's assets which are not used in directly carrying out the exempt purpose. Cash equal to 1½ per cent of the total foundation's assets is deemed to be used in carrying out the exempt purpose, and is deducted for this calculation. This means that if a foundation has marketable securities and cash with a market value of $1,000,000 it must make minimum qualifying distributions of 5 per cent of $985,000 ($1,000,000 less 1½ per cent of $1,000,000) or $49,250 regardless of its actual income. If, for example, actual investment income were only $30,000, the foundation would still have to make qualifying distributions of $49,250.

It should be emphasized that contributions or gifts are not included in the calculation of "distributable amount." This means that the private foundation will not have to make qualifying distributions out of principal provided its investment income plus contributions and gifts equal the distributable amount. In the illustration in the preceding paragraph, if contributions to the foundation were, say, $50,000, the distributable amount would still be $49,250. It would appear that these requirements will have little effect on private foundations that receive continuing contribution support and have a continuing program.

Here is an illustration showing how these calculations work. Using the condensed financial statements of the A. C. Williams Foundation shown on the next page, the distributable amount is calculated as follows:

Investment income	$ 50,000
	$ 50,000
Minimum investment return:	
Average fair market value of securities and cash	$1,000,000
Less 1½% of above amount for cash deemed to be used in carrying out the exempt purpose	(15,000)
Net, subject to stipulated minimum investment return	985,000
Stipulated rate of return	5%
	$ 49,250
Distributable amount:	
Minimum investment return	$ 49,250
Less—Excise tax	(1,000)
	$ 48,250

Thus the distributable amount is $48,250. Qualifying distributions were $70,000, which exceeds the distributable amount by $21,750, and the requirement has thus been met. This excess can be carried over for five years to meet the requirements of a year in which there is a deficiency. Where there is such a carryover, the order of application of the amounts distributed would be: current year, carryover from earliest year, carryover from next earliest year, and so forth.

Excess Business Holdings

A private foundation is not allowed to own a stock interest in a corporation if the stock it owns together with the stock owned by "disqualified" persons * would exceed 20 per cent of the voting stock.

* A "disqualified person" is defined in the footnote on page 398.

A. C. WILLIAMS FOUNDATION
SUMMARY OF RECEIPTS AND EXPENDITURES

Receipts:

Contributions	$140,000	
Investment income	50,000	$ 190,000

Expenditures:

For exempt purposes	70,000	
Excise tax	1,000	71,000
Net		$ 119,000

ASSETS

Cash	$ 30,000
Marketable securities	970,000
Fund balance	$1,000,000

Here is an example. Mr. Scotty owns together with his family 15 per cent of the voting stock in the A. M. Scotty Company, and he is a "substantial" contributor to the "Scotty Foundation" and thus is a "disqualified person." The maximum amount of stock that the Scotty Foundation can own is 5 per cent (20 per cent maximum less 15 per cent). There are several minor exceptions to this general rule, and there is a transitional period for foundations to dispose of their pre-1969 "excess" holdings. Failure to comply with these rules will result in taxes which can be as high as 200 per cent of the value of the excess stock held.

Prohibited Transactions

There are several categories of transactions that private foundations may not engage in. They cannot engage in "self-dealing," make investments that jeopardize their exempt function, or make expenditures for certain prohibited purposes (so-called "taxable expenditures"). There is an excise tax on both the foundation and the foundation manager who engages in these prohibited transactions. For example, the tax on taxable expenditures is initially 10 per cent and 2½ per cent on the foundation and foundation manager respectively, but is increased to 100 per cent and 50 per cent if corrective action is not taken.

Self-Dealing. The law prohibits private foundations from having certain transactions with "disqualified" persons, or foundation managers. These prohibited "self-dealing" transactions include the sale, leasing, or lending of property or money, the furnishing of goods or services on a basis more favorable than to the general public, or the payment of unreasonable compensation. All transactions involving one of these persons should be examined very closely to make absolutely certain they do not involve "self-dealing."

Investments That Jeopardize Exempt Function.   The law provides that the foundation may not make investments that jeopardize the exempt function of the foundation. Thus, the foundation is expected to use a "prudent trustee's approach" in making investments. Examples of investments that probably would not be prudent would be investments made on margin, commodity future transactions, trading in warrants, etc.

Prohibited Expenditures.   The law provides that a foundation may not make expenditures to carry on propaganda to influence legislation or the outcome of a public election. It also prohibits making a grant to an individual for travel or study unless it can be shown the grant was a tax-exempt scholarship to be used at an educational institution, or was a tax-exempt prize in recognition of a specific achievement, or was a grant for the purpose of achieving a specific product or report. The law also provides no grant shall be made to another *private* foundation unless the granting foundation exercises expenditure control over the grant to see that it is expended solely for the purposes granted. Finally, the law prohibits a private foundation from making any grant for any purpose other than a charitable purpose.

Annual Information Return

The annual information return (Form 990–PF) filed with the IRS is considerably longer and more complex than the Form 990 filed by most other nonprofit organizations. Chapter 26 discusses this annual return and illustrates a completed form.

A private foundation must also publish a notice in a newspaper broadly circulated in the county where its principal office is located stating that a copy of this annual return is available for inspection by anyone desiring to see it at the organization's office within six months of date of publication.

PRIVATE "OPERATING" FOUNDATION

Private "operating" foundations are private foundations that actively carry out program activities which are the exempt function for which the organization was founded. This is in contrast to private foundations that act only as a conduit for funds and have no operating programs as such. These private operating foundations have most of the characteristics of publicly supported organizations but do not meet the tests outlined for such organizations, discussed earlier in this chapter.

Qualifying Tests

In addition to expending substantially all (85 per cent) of its income directly for the active conduct of its exempt function, a private foundation, to be a private "operating" foundation, must meet one or more of the following tests:

1. It devotes 65 per cent or more of its assets to its exempt function.
2. Two thirds of its "minimum investment return" (see page 404) is devoted to its exempt function.
3. It derives 85 per cent or more of its support other than investment income from the general public and from five or more exempt organizations, no one of which provides more than 25 per cent. In addition not more than 50 per cent of its total support is from investment income.

Advantages

The advantage of being a private operating foundation is that the minimum distribution rules which private foundations are subject to do not apply, and the contributor receives the same tax treatment for a contribution as would be received if the foundation were a publicly supported organization. See page 397.

UNRELATED BUSINESS INCOME

Virtually every exempt organization, including churches and clubs, is subject to normal corporate taxes on its unrelated business income.

Definition

There is always difficulty in knowing exactly what is unrelated business income. Here is the way the law reads:

The term "unrelated trade or business" means . . . any trade or business the conduct of which is not substantially related . . . to the exercise or performance by such organization of its charitable, educational, or other purpose or function constituting the basis for its exemption . . . [Sec. 513(a) of the Internal Revenue Code].

. . . the term "unrelated business income" means the gross income derived by any organization from any unrelated trade or business . . . regularly carried on by it, less the deductions . . . which are directly connected . . . [Sec. 512(a)(1) of the Internal Revenue Code].

There are two key phrases in these definitions. The first is "unrelated" trade or business, and the second is "regularly carried on." Both must be present. It is not difficult to determine whether the business in question is "regularly carried on," but it is difficult to know what is truly unrelated. The burden, however, is on the exempt organization to justify exclusion of any income from this tax.

Exclusions. There are a few exemptions to this tax. They include, among others, income from research activities in a hospital, college, or university, income from a business in which substantially all the people working for the business do so without compensation, and income from the sale of merchandise donated to the organization. There are special rules for social clubs which are discussed on page 416.

Also excluded from unrelated business income is passive investment income such as dividends, interest, royalties, rents from real property, and gains on sale of property. However, rents which are based on a percentage of the net income of the property are considered "unrelated." Private foundations must still pay the excise tax on these items of passive income.

Advertising Income. One of the categories of unrelated business income which was clearly spelled out in the 1969 Act was income from advertising. Many exempt organizations publish magazines that contain advertising. While this advertising helps to pay the cost of the publication, which may itself be an exempt function, this advertising is nevertheless considered to be "unrelated business income." The advertising is not directly part of the exempt function, and therefore is taxable. The fact that the activity helps pay for exempt functions is not enough. It must be itself part of the exempt function. This is the distinction that must be made.

The IRS has adopted tough rules with respect to the taxability of advertising income. These rules limit the extent to which an organization can reduce its net advertising income by the allocation of member dues to income of the organization's publication. The rules are complex and professional advice should be sought concerning their application.

Trade Shows.   The Tax Reform Act of 1976 provided an exclusion from unrelated business income for certain organizations such as business leagues who hold conventions or trade shows as a regular part of their exempt activities. In order for the exclusion to apply the convention or trade show must stimulate interest in, and demand for, an industry's product in general. The show must promote that purpose through the character of the exhibits and the extent of the industry products displayed.

Foreign Conventions.   Many exempt organizations hold conventions in foreign countries. Often individuals attend these conventions as part of their business or profession. A taxpayer can deduct the costs of attending no more than two foreign conventions in one year. The deduction for transportation cost cannot exceed the cost of economy or coach fare. In addition, there are limitations on the deductibility of meals and lodging.

Caveats.   As is indicated in the above quotation from the tax law, the organization is allowed to deduct the costs normally associated with the .unrelated business. This places a burden on the organization to keep its records in a manner that will support its business deductions. Overhead can be applied, but the organization must be able to justify both the method of allocation and the reasonableness of the resulting amount. Also keep in mind that if after all expenses and allocation of overhead, the organization ends up with a loss, it will have to be able to convincingly explain why it engages in an activity that loses money. Logically no one goes into business to lose money and if there is a loss the allocation of expenses to that business is immediately suspect.

Tax Rates on Unrelated Business Income

Unrelated business income is taxed at the same rates as net income for corporations. This means that after a special $1,000 exemption, the first $25,000 of net income will be taxed at 15 per cent, the next $25,000 at 18 per cent, the next $25,000 at 30 per cent, the next $25,000 at 40 per cent, and the balance at 46 per cent (1983 rates). All exempt organizations having gross income from unrelated business activities of $1,000 or more are required to file Form 990-T within $4\frac{1}{2}$ months of the end of the fiscal year (May 15 for calendar year organizations). Extensions can be obtained if applied for before the due date of the return.

Need for Competent Tax Advice

From the above discussion, it should be obvious that taxes on unrelated business income are sizable and can apply to most organizations. It must be emphasized that every organization contemplating an income-producing activity should consult with competent tax counsel to determine the potential tax implications of that activity.

SUMMARY OF INDIVIDUAL TAX DEDUCTIONS

Nonprofit organizations depend to a very large extent on individual contributions for support. To the extent that a contributor receives a tax deduction for a contribution, there is more inclination to be generous in the contribution. Accordingly the tax deductibility of a contribution is of real importance. Figure 25–1 summarizes the general rules applicable to common types of contributions. There are many involved rules and exceptions and the figure should be used only as an overall guide.

SOCIAL AND RECREATION CLUBS

One of the types of organizations which are granted exemption from tax are "clubs organized for pleasure, recreation, and other nonprofitable purposes, substantially all of the activities of which are for such purposes and no part of the net earnings of which inures to the benefit of any private shareholder." The key words when considering tax implications for social clubs are the phrase "no part of the net earnings of which inures to the benefit of any private shareholder."

The members are the shareholders. If they operate the club in such a way that part of the fixed costs are paid for by non-members or the general public, then clearly there is a benefit to the members even though there may be no "net profit" as such. Thus a country club that rents out its facilities to non-members for an amount greater than its out-of-pocket costs is receiving income which benefits the membership by reducing the charges the members would have to pay to maintain the facilities.

This jeopardizes the tax-exempt status of the club, and also subjects the club to corporate income tax on this income from non-members as unrelated business income. Both have serious implications for social

DEDUCTIBILITY OF GIFT FOR INDIVIDUALS

Type of Property Contributed	Publicly Supported Organization*	Private Foundation†
Cash	100% up to total limitation	Same
Property held less than one year	Cost only	Same
Securities and real property held more than one year	Fair market value	
Tangible personal property not created or produced by donor	Fair market value if used by the charity in its exempt function	Fair market value less 1/2 of the appreciation
	Fair market value less 1/2 of the appreciation if not used by the charity in its exempt function	
Tangible personal property created or produced by donor (including inventory, art, books, etc.)	Cost	Same
Total limitation	50% of contribution base (which is usually adjusted gross income) except that long-term capital gain property is limited to 30%	20% of contribution base
Carry-over limitations	5 years	No carryover

*Including a private operating foundation. See pages 407–408 for definition.
†For purposes of donor's deductibility, the private foundation would be considered a publicly supported organization if the private foundation makes qualifying distributions of 100% of its contributions and 100% of its "distributable" income (see page 404), both within 2-1/2 months of the end of its fiscal year.

Fig. 25–1. Tax deductibility by individual donors of gifts to charitable organizations.

clubs. In the first instance, the club could lose its tax-exempt status and find all of its net income was subject to tax as well as finding limitations on accumulation of retained earnings. In the second instance, the club could find it had substantial tax to pay even though it had an overall loss for the year. While to some extent these problems have always been present, the Tax Reform Act of 1969 tightened up the rules under which all social clubs must live if they want to maintain tax-exempt status.

Exempt Status

The first concern that a social club must have if it intends to receive income from non-members is what implications such income will have for the organization's tax-exempt status. Significant use of the club by non-members can result in loss of the club's tax exemption. The congressional committee reports of the Tax Reform Act of 1976 indicate that a social club will not lose its exempt status if no more than 35 per cent of its gross receipts are from investments *and* non-member use of facilities. Within this 35 per cent, no more than 15 per cent can be derived from non-member use of facilities.

"Gross receipts" include receipts from normal and usual activities of the club, including charges, admissions, membership fees, dues, assessments, investment income, and normal recurring gains on investments, but exclude initiation fees and capital contributions.

Receipts from Non-Members. Gross receipts from non-members are the amounts not paid by members and amounts paid by members involving non-bona fide guests. Amounts paid by a member's employer can, depending on the situation, be considered as paid by a member or as paid by a non-member. See the discussion below.

The problem of determining whether someone using the club is a bona fide guest of a member has proved troublesome. Most clubs take the position that under club rules the facilities may be used only by members and their guests and that these rules are rigidly adhered to. The Internal Revenue Service has taken the position that, in many situations, the member's participation in, or connection with, a function is so limited that the member is merely using the membership to make the club facilities available to an outside group. In effect, they hold that in many instances the member merely acts as a sponsor.

If a member's charges are reimbursed by an employer, the income will be member income provided that the guests are in attendance due to a personal or social purpose of the member, or due to a direct business objective or relationship of the member in work for the employer. If there is no direct relationship between the business objective or purpose of the activities of the particular employee-member, the reimbursement will be considered non-member income. The distinction is where the member has a direct interest in the company function as contrasted with a situation where the member is merely serving as a sponsor to permit the company to use the facilities.

There are also guidelines to help determine whether group functions hosted by members at which guests are present constitute member or non-member receipts. In groups of eight or fewer individuals it is assumed that all non-members are guests. In larger groups, it is assumed that all non-members are bona fide guests provided 75 per cent of the group are members. In all other situations the club must substantiate that the non-member was a bona fide guest. In the absence of adequate substantiation it will be assumed such receipts are non-member receipts, even though paid for by the members.

Substantiation Requirements.   In order to rely upon the above assumptions regarding group functions, clubs must maintain certain records. Where the "8 or fewer" rule or the "75 per cent member rule" noted above is used, it is necessary to document only the number in the party, the number of members, and the source of the payments. For all other group occasions involving club use by non-members, even where a member pays for the use, the club must maintain records containing the following information if it wishes to substantiate that such receipts are not "non-member" receipts:

1. Date
2. Total number in the party
3. Number of non-members in the party
4. Total charges
5. Charges attributable to non-members
6. Charges paid by non-members

In addition, the club must obtain a statement signed by the member indicating whether there has been or will be reimbursement for such non-member use and, if so, the amount of the reimbursement. Where the member will be reimbursed, or where the member's employer makes direct payment to the club for the charges, the club must also obtain a statement signed by the member indicating (a) name of the employer, (b) amount of the payment attributable to the non-member use, (c) non-member's name and business or other relationship to the member

Member's Statement on Use of Private Dining Room

Income tax regulations require the following information to be furnished with respect to each use of a private dining room by more than 8 persons unless at least 75% of those present are Club members.

....
(Name and account number of member reserving room)   (Date of use)

1. Do you expect to be reimbursed by any person or organization, including your own employer (or partnership), for the charges for the party or function for which you are reserving this room?   Yes ☐   No ☐

   If your answer to Question 1 is "Yes", and it is your employer or partnership which will reimburse you, please answer Question 2 below. If your answer to Question 1 is "No", **or** if you will be reimbursed by a person or organization other than your employer or partnership, please disregard Question 2 entirely, and merely sign this form in the space provided below.

2. If you expect to be reimbursed by your **employer or partnership**, please enter below the name of your employer or partnership and complete **either** A or B below:

   Name of employer or partnership ....

   A. Is the room to be used for your own direct business objectives?   Yes ☐   No ☐

      If your answer is "Yes"

      (i) What is the business relationship of your guests to you? (Check applicable items.)

         ☐ Customers or clients, or prospective customers or clients.
         ☐ Suppliers of goods or services.
         ☐ Fellow employees or partners.
         ☐ Other (describe)* ....

         ....

      (ii) Is entertainment of persons of the above class one of your duties as an employee or partner?   Yes ☐   No ☐

   B. Is the room to be used merely for the accommodation of your employer or partnership (as distinguished from your own direct business objectives)?   Yes ☐   No ☐

....
(Signature of Member)   (Date)

*If the guests cannot be readily classified, please list on the back of this form their names and the business relationship of each to you.

_____

The items below this line are to be completed by the Club.

Number served   ....   Total Charges $...............

Number of Non-Members   ....   Charges for Non-Members $...............

Fig. 25–2. Typical statement completed by club members when they entertain guests at their club.

(or if readily identifiable, the class of individuals—e.g., sales managers), and (d) business, personal, or other purpose of the member served by the non-member use. Figure 25–2 shows the type of form used by some clubs.

Record-keeping requirements for other activities such as providing guest rooms, parking facilities; steam rooms, etc., have not been specifically set forth. Clubs must be careful to see, however, that their record-keeping procedures provide information regarding member and non-member use of these facilities.

A careful study of the implications of these rules will show that all social clubs must be extremely careful not to receive, even inadvertently, very much non-member income.

Unrelated Business Income

In addition to jeopardizing its exempt status, receipts from non-members have other tax implications for a social club since such receipts constitute unrelated business income. Social clubs are subject to tax at regular corporate tax rates on their unrelated business income. This is calculated on a somewhat different basis than for other types of exempt organizations. The total income of the club from all sources except for exempt function income (dues, fees, etc., paid by the members) is subject to tax. This means that income from non-members, as well as investment and other types of income, is subject to tax. Deductions are allowed for expenses directly connected with such income, including a reasonable allocation of overhead. As with other exempt organizations, there is a specific deduction of $1,000 allowed.

It is possible for a social club to have an overall loss but still have a substantial amount of unrelated business income. Here is an example of a country club where this is the case:

	Exempt	Unrelated	Total
Interest on taxable bonds	—	$ 10,000	$ 10,000
Membership fees	$ 100,000	—	100,000
Golf and other fees	40,000	20,000	60,000
Restaurant and bar	200,000	50,000	250,000
Total income	340,000	80,000	420,000
Direct expenses	(320,000)	(30,000)	(350,000)
Overhead	(60,000)	(20,000)	(80,000)
Net income (loss)	$ (40,000)	$ 30,000	$ (10,000)

As can be seen, this club will have taxes to pay on $30,000 of income, which at the 1983 corporate tax rates would be approximately $4,470.*

One of the real burdens for social clubs is to keep their bookkeeping records in such a manner that it is possible to not only determine direct expenses associated with non-member income, but also to provide a reasonable basis of allocation between member and non-member activities. Even the largest of corporations has difficulty in making allocation of overhead between functions, so the problems of allocation for social clubs should not be passed over lightly.

---

* $30,000 less $1,000 special exclusion, taxed at 15 per cent on first $25,000 of taxable income, plus 18 per cent on the remaining $4,000, or a total tax of $4,470.

26

Principal Federal Tax
Forms Filed

In the previous chapter it was noted that while nonprofit organizations may be exempt from most federal taxes, they must file annual information returns with the Internal Revenue Service. With few exceptions, all exempt organizations other than private foundations are required to file Form 990 annually. Private foundations are required to file Form 990–PF. Most nonprofit organizations having "unrelated business" income must file Form 990–T. Both private foundations and organizations having unrelated business income will probably have taxes to pay at the time of filing. This chapter discusses these three principal returns and comments on some of the less obvious points that the preparer must be aware of in filling out these forms.

FORM 990—RETURN OF ORGANIZATION EXEMPT FROM INCOME TAX

Who Must File

All nonprofit organizations exempt from income tax must file Form 990 except the following:

1. Churches, and certain other religious organizations
2. Organizations which are part of a federal, state, or local governmental unit
3. Employee benefit plans (they file other forms)

4. Organizations other than private foundations with gross receipts normally $25,000 or less (this limit was $10,000 in 1981)

5. Private foundations (they file Form 990–PF)

Gross receipts means the total amount received during the year, including contributions, investment income, proceeds from the sale of investments, and sale of goods, before the deduction of any expenses or costs including the cost of investments or goods sold. This means that if an organization received contributions of $15,000 and had gross receipts from the sale of marketable securities of $10,100 it would have to complete the form, even though the cost (or other basis) of these marketable securities might have been $10,000, leaving a net profit on the sale of only $100.

This means that most nonprofit organizations must file this return, including social clubs, educational institutions, and membership organizations. The return is due not later than the fifteenth day of the fifth month after the end of the fiscal year (May 15 for calendar year organizations), and there is a penalty of $10 a day for failure to file unless it can be shown that there was a reasonable cause for not doing so.

Contents of Form 990

This return consists of two parts:

Form 990   Completed by all filing organizations, except that smaller organizations may omit certain sections.

Schedule A   Completed by all 501(c)(3) filing organizations (see page 395) except private foundations.

Form 990—Illustration and Comments

Figures 26–1 through 26–3 show an example of a Form 990 * filled out with typical figures of a small public charity. The circled numbers on this form refer to the comments below. Figure 26–8 shows supplementary information where required by the instructions.

1. The first fiscal year must end within 12 months of date of inception. The organization can choose any month as the end of its fiscal year, but once the election is made it cannot easily be changed in future years. Thus it is important during the first year to select the "year

---

* The 1982 form was not available at the time this book went to press. It will differ slightly from the 1981 form, specifically with regard to the dollar limit for filing.

OMB No. 1545-0047

Form 990
Department of the Treasury
Internal Revenue Service

Return of Organization Exempt from Income Tax
Under section 501(c) (except black lung benefit trust or private foundation),
of the Internal Revenue Code or section 4947(a)(1) trust

1981

For the calendar year 1981, or fiscal year beginning (1)   1981, and ending   19

		A Employer identification number (see instruction L)
Use IRS label. Other- wise, please print or type.	Name of organization Nelle Plains Community Service Society	13 ¦ 6213564 (2)
	Address (number and street) 1400 Diamond Ave.	B State registration number (see instruction D) (3)
	City or town, State, and ZIP code Nelle Plains, New York 10977 (4)	C If address changed, check here . . ▶

D Check applicable box—Exempt under section ▶ ☐ 501(c) (   ) (insert number), OR ▶ ☐ section 4947(a)(1) trust
E Accounting method: ☐ Cash ☒ Accrual ☐ Other (specify) ▶
F Section 4947(a)(1) trusts filing this form in lieu of Form 1041, check here ▶ ☐ (see instruction C 10).
G Is this a group return (see instruction J) filed for affiliates? . . ☐ Yes ☒ No   If "Yes" to either, give four-digit group exemption
   Is this a separate return filed by a group affiliate? . . . . . ☐ Yes ☒ No   number (GEN) ▶

Note: You may be able to use a copy of this return to satisfy State reporting requirements. See instruction D.   (5)
☐ Check here if gross receipts are normally not more than $10,000. Do not complete the rest of this return (see instruction B11).
☐ Check here if gross receipts are normally more than $10,000 and line 12 is $25,000 or less. Complete Parts I (except lines 13–15), III, IV, VI, and VII and only the
indicated items in Parts II and V (see instruction I). If line 12 is more than $25,000, complete the entire return.

All section 501(c)(3) organizations and 4947(a)(1) trusts must also complete and attach Schedule A (Form 990).

These columns are optional— (6)
see Instructions

Part I Statement of Support, Revenue, and Expenses and Changes in Fund Balances

	(A) Total	(B) Unrestricted/ Expendable	(C) Restricted/ Nonexpendable
1 Contributions, gifts, grants, and similar amounts received:			
(a) Direct public support . . (7) 56,649		46,649	10,000
(b) Indirect public support . . . . . -0-		-0-	-0-
(c) Government grants . . . . . . -0-		-0-	-0-
(d) Total (add lines 1(a) through 1(c)) (attach schedule—see instructions)	56,649 (8)	46,649	10,000
2 Program service revenue (from Part IV, line (f)) (9)	-0-	-0-	-0-
3 Membership dues and assessments	10,500	10,500	-0-
4 Interest on savings and temporary cash Investments	3,875	3,875	-0-
5 Dividends and interest from securities	11,316	11,316	-0-
6 (a) Gross rents . . . . -0-			
(b) Minus: Rental expenses . . . . -0-			
(c) Net rental income (loss)	-0-	-0-	-0-
7 Other investment income (Describe ▶	-0-	-0-	-0-
8 (a) Gross amount from sale of assets other than inventory .			
(b) Minus: Cost or other basis and sales expenses (10)			
(c) Gain (loss) (attach schedule) (11)	5,000	-0-	5,000
9 Special fundraising events and activities (attach schedule—see instructions):			
(a) Gross revenue (not including $300 (12) of contributions reported on line 1(a)).			
(b) Minus: Direct expenses	600	600	-0-
(c) Net income (line 9(a) minus line 9(b)) (9) . . . . . -0-			
10 (a) Gross sales minus returns and allowances . -0-			
(b) Minus: Cost of goods sold (attach schedule) (13)	-0-	-0-	-0-
(c) Gross profit (loss)	-0-	-0-	-0-
11 Other revenue (from Part IV, line (g))	87,940	72,940	15,000
12 Total revenue (add lines 1(d), 2, 3, 4, 5, 6(c), 7, 8(c), 9(c), 10(c), and 11) . .	66,640	66,640	-0-
13 Program services (from line 44(B)) . . (14)	6,200	6,200	-0-
14 Management and general (from line 44(C)) . (15) .	1,700	1,700	-0-
15 Fundraising (from line 44(D)) . . . . . . (16) .	-0-	-0-	-0-
16 Payments to affiliates (attach schedule—see Instructions) .	74,540	74,540	-0-
17 Total expenses (add lines 13, 14, 15, and 16)	13,400	<1,600>	15,000
18 Excess (deficit) for the year (subtract line 17 from line 12) . . (17)	229,000	121,000	108,000
19 Fund balances or net worth at beginning of year (from line 74(A))	-0-	-0-	-0-
20 Other changes in fund balances or net worth (attach explanation) (18)	242,400	119,400	123,000
21 Fund balances or net worth at end of year (add lines 18, 19, and 20)			

Left margin labels: Support and Revenue / Expenses / Fund Balances

Line 8: Securities 7,000 Other -0- ; Cost basis 2,000 / -0- ; Gain 5,000 / -0-
Line 9: Gross revenue 1,300 ; Direct expenses 700

For Paperwork Reduction Act Notice, see page 1 of the Instructions.

Fig. 26–1. Page 1 of Form 990.

Form 990 (1981)   Page **2**

Part II Statement of Functional Expenses   If line 12, Part I, is $25,000 or less, you should complete only column (A). If line 12 is more than $25,000, complete columns (A), (B), (C), and (D).

Do not include amounts reported on line 6(b), 8(b), 9(b), 10(b), or 16 of Part I.	(A) Total	(B) Program services	(C) Management and general	(D) Fundraising
22 Grants and allocations (attach schedule)	7,000	7,000		
23 Specific assistance to individuals				
24 Benefits paid to or for members				
25 Compensation of officers, directors, etc.	15,130	10,000	4,930	200
26 Other salaries and wages	27,000	26,000		1,000
27 Pension plan contributions				
28 Other employee benefits	1,655	1,400	210	45
29 Payroll taxes	2,940	2,495	375	70
30 Professional fundraising fees				
31 Accounting fees	200		200	
32 Legal fees				
33 Supplies	2,580	2,470	110	
34 Telephone	555	485	50	20
35 Postage and shipping	785	460	25	300
36 Occupancy				
37 Equipment rental and maintenance . . .	305	305		
38 Printing and publications	2,495	2,200	230	65
39 Travel	210	210		
40 Conferences, conventions and meetings . .				
41 Interest				
42 Depreciation, depletion, etc. (attach schedule)				
43 Other expenses (itemize): (a)				
(b) Gas, oil, repairs for				
(c) bookmobile	8,855	8,855		
(d) City band-3 concerts	3,600	3,600		
(e) Miscellaneous	390	360	30	
(f) Insurance	840	800	40	
44 Total functional expenses (add lines 22 through 43)	74,540	66,640	6,200	1,700

Part III Statement of Program Service Activities

Describe each significant program service activity and indicate the total expenses attributable to each. Include relevant statistical information, such as the number of clients, patients, students, or members served. Also indicate the amount of grants and allocations that are included in the total expenses reported for that program.

	Expenses

(a) Awards for outstanding community service. Each year, awards are given to as many as three citizens of Nelle Plains who are judged to have contributed substantially to the community.

(Grants and allocations $ 4,000)   4,175

(b) Operation of bookmobile. Bookmobile contains approximately 1,000 books. In 1981, 7,200 books were borrowed.

(Grants and allocations $ -0-)   18,590

(c) Cultural activities. Historical exhibit in the town hall. 3 outdoor band concerts in River Park. Grant towards rehabilitation of old firehouse as a museum.

(Grants and allocations $ 3,000)   43,875

(d)

(Grants and allocations $)

(e) Other program service activities (attach schedule)   (Grants and allocations $)

(f) Total (add lines (a) through (e)) (should equal line 44(B))   66,640

Fig. 26—2.   Page 2 of Form 990.

Form 990 (1981)   Page **3**

Part IV Program Service Revenue and Other Revenue (State Nature)	Program service revenue	Other revenue
(a) Fees from government agencies		
(b) _____		
(c) _____		
(d) _____		
(e) _____		
(f) Total program service revenue (Enter here and on line 2)	–0–	/////////////
(g) Total other revenue (Enter here and on line 11)		–0–

Part V   Balance Sheets   If line 12, Part I, and line 59 are $25,000 or less, you should complete only lines 59, 66, and 74 and, if you do not use fund accounting, line 73. If line 12 or line 59 is more than $25,000, complete the entire balance sheet. See instructions.

Note: Columns (C) and (D) are optional. Columns (A) and (B) must be completed to the extent applicable. Where required, attached schedules should be for end-of-year amounts only.	(A) Beginning of year	End of year (6)		
		(B) Total	(C) Unrestricted/ Expendable	(D) Restricted/ Nonexpendable
Assets				
45 Cash—non-interest bearing	3,500	2,250	2,250	–0–
46 Savings and temporary cash investments	30,000	28,000	28,000	–0–
47 Accounts receivable ▶ 1,000 (24)				
minus allowance for doubtful accounts ▶ –0–	1,250	1,000	1,000	–0–
48 Pledges receivable ▶ 1,000				
minus allowance for doubtful accounts ▶ –0–	–0–	1,000	1,000	–0–
49 Grants receivable				
50 Receivables due from officers, directors, trustees and key employees (attach schedule) . (24)				
51 Other notes and loans receivable ▶_____				
minus allowance for doubtful accounts ▶_____				
52 Inventories for sale or use				
53 Prepaid expenses and deferred charges				
54 Investments—securities (attach schedule)	196,750	212,900	89,900	123,000
55 Investments—land, buildings and equipment: basis ▶_____				
minus accumulated depreciation ▶_____(attach schedule)				
56 Investments—other (attach schedule)				
57 Land, buildings and equipment: basis ▶_____				
minus accumulated depreciation ▶_____(attach schedule)				
58 Other assets: _____				
59 Total assets (add lines 45 through 58)	231,500	245,150	122,150	123,000
Liabilities				
60 Accounts payable and accrued expenses	2,500	1,250	1,250	–0–
61 Grants payable	–0–	1,500	1,500	–0–
62 Support and revenue designated for future periods (attach sched.) (25)				
63 Loans from officers, directors, trustees and key employees (attach schedule)				
64 Mortgages and other notes payable (attach schedule)				
65 Other liabilities: _____				
66 Total liabilities (add lines 60 through 65)	2,500	2,750	2,750	–0–
Fund Balances or Net Worth				
Organizations that use fund accounting, check here ▶ ☒ and complete lines 67 through 70 and lines 74 and 75. (26)				
67 Current funds	121,000	119,400	119,400	–0–
68 Land, buildings and equipment fund				
69 Endowment fund	108,000	123,000	–0–	123,000
70 Other funds (Describe ▶_____)				
Organizations that do not use fund accounting, check here ▶ ☐ and complete lines 71 through 75.				
71 Capital stock or trust principal				
72 Paid-in or capital surplus				
73 Retained earnings or accumulated income				
74 Total fund balances or net worth (see instructions)	229,000	242,400	119,400	123,000
75 Total liabilities and fund balances/net worth (see instructions) . .	231,500	245,150	122,150	123,000

Fig. 26–3.   Page 3 of Form 990.

Form 990 (1981)   **Page 4**

Part VI   List of Officers, Directors, and Trustees (See Instructions)

(A) Name and address	(B) Title and average hours per week devoted to position	(C) Compensation (if any)	(D) Contributions to employee benefit plans	(E) Expense account and other allowances
W. Jonathan Stephens Nelle Plains, New York	Executive Director 40	15,130	550	-0- (27)
Sean Fessenden, Jr. Waverly, New York	Trustee 2	-0-	-0-	-0-
Phyllis Kolowski Nelle Plains, N.Y.	Trustee 2	-0-	-0-	-0-

Part VII   Other Information

	Yes	No
76 Has the organization engaged in any activities not previously reported to the Internal Revenue Service?		X
If "Yes," attach a detailed description of the activities.		
77 Have any changes been made in the organizing or governing documents, but not reported to IRS?		X
If "Yes," attach a conformed copy of the changes.		
78 (a) Did the organization have unrelated business gross income of $1,000 or more during the year covered by this return? .		X
(b) If "Yes," have you filed a tax return on Form 990-T, Exempt Organization Business Income Tax Return, for this year? .		(9)
(c) If the organization has gross sales or receipts from business activities not reported on Form 990-T, attach a statement explaining your reason for not reporting them on Form 990-T.		
79 Was there a liquidation, dissolution, termination, or substantial contraction during the year (see instructions)?		X
If "Yes," attach a statement as described in the Instructions.		
80 Is the organization related (other than by association with a statewide or nationwide organization) through common membership, governing bodies, trustees, officers, etc., to any other exempt or nonexempt organization (see instructions)? . . .		X
If "Yes," enter the name of organization ▶		
. . . . and check whether it is ☐ exempt OR ☐ nonexempt.		
81 (a) Enter amount of political expenditures, direct or indirect, as described in the instructions . (28) . -0-		
(b) Did you file Form 1120-POL, U.S. Income Tax Return for Certain Political Organizations, for this year?		X
82 Did your organization receive donated services or the use of materials, equipment or facilities at no charge or at substantially less than fair rental value? . . . . (29) . . .	X	
If "Yes," you may indicate the value of these items here. Do not include this amount as support in Part I or as an expense in Part II. See instructions for reporting in Part III . . . . ▶ 8,600		
83 Section 501(c)(5) or (6) organizations.—Did the organization spend any amounts in attempt to influence public opinion about legislative matters or referendums (see instructions and Regulations section 1.162-20(c))?		
If "Yes," enter the total amount spent for this purpose		
84 Section 501(c)(7) organizations.—Enter amount of:		
(a) Initiation fees and capital contributions included on line 12		
(b) Gross receipts, included in line 12, for public use of club facilities (see instructions) . (30) . .		
(c) Does the club's governing instrument or any written policy statement provide for discrimination against any person because of race, color, or religion (see instructions)?		
85 Section 501(c)(12) organizations.—Enter amount of:		
(a) Gross income received from members or shareholders		
(b) Gross income received from other sources (do not net amounts due or paid to other sources against amounts due or received from them)		
86 Public interest law firms.—Attach information described in instructions.		
87 List the States with which a copy of this return is filed ▶ New York		
88 The books are in care of ▶ W. Jonathan Stephens . . . . . Telephone No. ▶ 914-521-6790		
Located at ▶ above address		

Please Sign Here	Under penalties of perjury, I declare that I have examined this return, including accompanying schedules and statements, and to the best of my knowledge and belief it is true, correct, and complete. Declaration of preparer (other than taxpayer) is based on all information of which preparer has any knowledge.		
	Signature of officer	May 6, 1982 Executive Director Date ▶ Title	
Paid Preparer's Use Only	Preparer's signature ▶	Date Check if self-employed ▶ ☐	
	Firm's name (or yours, if self-employed) and address ▶	ZIP code ▶	

☆ U.S. GOVERNMENT PRINTING OFFICE: 1981—O-343-046 58-040-1110

Fig. 26-4.   Page 4 of Form 990.

SCHEDULE A
(Form 990)
Department of the Treasury
Internal Revenue Service

Organization Exempt Under 501(c)(3)
(Except Private Foundation), 501(e), 501(f) or Section 4947(a)(1) Trust
Supplementary Information ▶ Attach to Form 990.

OMB No. 1545–0047

1981

Name: Nelle Plains Community Service Society

Employer identification number: 13 6213564

Part I — Compensation of Five Highest Paid Employees
(Other than Officers, Directors, and Trustees—see specific instructions)

Name and address of employees paid more than $30,000	Title and average hours per week devoted to position	Compensation	Contributions to employee benefit plans	Expense account and other allowances
None				

Total number of other employees paid over $30,000 . ▶

Part II — Compensation of Five Highest Paid Persons for Professional Services
(See specific instructions)

Name and address of persons paid more than $30,000	Type of service	Compensation
None		

Total number of others receiving over $30,000 for professional services . . . . ▶

Part III — Statements About Activities   (31)

	Yes	No
1 During the year have you attempted to influence national, State or local legislation, including any attempt to influence public opinion on a legislative matter or referendum? . . . . If "Yes," enter the total of the expenses paid or incurred in connection with the legislative activities $................................. Complete Part VI of this form for organizations that made an election under section 501(h) on Form 5768 or other statement. For other organizations checking "Yes," attach a statement giving a detailed description of the legislative activities and a classified schedule of the expenses paid or incurred.		X
2 During the year have you, either directly or indirectly, engaged in any of the following acts with a trustee, director, principal officer or creator of your organization, or any organization or corporation with which such person is affiliated as an officer, director, trustee, majority owner or principal beneficiary:		
(a) Sale, exchange, or leasing of property?		X
(b) Lending of money or other extension of credit?		X
(c) Furnishing of goods, services, or facilities?		X
(d) Payment of compensation (or payment or reimbursement of expenses if more than $1,000)? See Part VI Form 990 . . .	X	
(e) Transfer of any part of your income or assets?		X
If the answer to any question is "Yes," attach a detailed statement explaining the transactions.		
3 Attach a statement explaining how you determine that individuals or organizations receiving disbursements from you in furtherance of your charitable programs qualify to receive payments. (See specific instructions.) (32)		
4 Do you make grants for scholarships, fellowships, student loans, etc.?		X
5 During the year did you receive any qualified conservation contribution whose value was more than $5,000? . . . . . If "Yes," attach a schedule as described in the instructions.		X

For Paperwork Reduction Act Notice, see page 1 of the separate instructions to this form.

Fig. 26–5. Page 1 of Schedule A to Form 990, which must be completed by all 501(c)(3) organizations required to file Form 990.

Schedule A (Form 990) 1981   Page 2

Part IV   Reason for Non-Private Foundation Status (See instructions for definitions)   (33)

The organization is not a private foundation because it is (check applicable box; please check only ONE box):

6 ☐ ¹ A church. Section 170(b)(1)(A)(i).

7 ☐ ² A school. Section 170(b)(1)(A)(ii). (Also complete Part V, page 3.)

8 ☐ ³ A hospital. Section 170(b)(1)(A)(iii).

9 ☐ ⁴ A governmental unit. Section 170(b)(1)(A)(v).

10 ☐ ⁵ A medical research organization operated in conjunction with a hospital. Section 170(b)(1)(A)(iii). Enter name and address of

hospital ▶ ....

....

11 ☐ ⁶ An organization operated for the benefit of a college or university owned or operated by a governmental unit. Section 170(b)(1)(A)
        (iv). (Also complete Support Schedule.)

12 ☒ ⁷ An organization that normally receives a substantial part of its support from a governmental unit or from the general public. Sec-
        tion 170(b)(1)(A)(vi). (Also complete Support Schedule.)   (34)

13 ☐ ⁸ An organization that normally receives: (a) no more than ⅓ of support from gross investment income and unrelated business
        taxable income (less section 511 tax) from businesses acquired by the organization after June 30, 1975, and (b) more than ⅓ of
 (35)   its support from contributions, membership fees, and gross receipts from activities related to its charitable, etc. functions—subject
        to certain exceptions. See section 509(a)(2). (Use cash receipts and disbursements method of accounting; also complete Support
        Schedule.)

14 ☐ ⁹ An organization that is not controlled by any disqualified persons (other than foundation managers) and supports organizations
        described in (1) boxes 6 through 13 above or (2) section 501(c)(4), (5), or (6) if they meet the test of section 509(a)(2). See sec-
        tion 509(a)(3).

Provide the following information about the supported organizations. (See instructions for Part IV, box 14.)

(a) Name of supported organizations	(b) Box number from above

(c) Relationship of supported organizations to your organization:

(1) Check here ▶ ☐ if the supported organizations appoint a majority of your governing board.

(2) Check here ▶ ☐ if a majority of your governing board belong to governing boards of the supported organizations.

(3) Check here ▶ ☐ if (1) or (2) above does not apply. (See Regulations 1.509(a)–4.)

(d) If applicable, enter the number of supported organizations exempt under:

(1) Section 501(c)(4) . . . . _____

(2) Section 501(c)(5) . . . . _____

(3) Section 501(c)(6) . . . . _____

(e) Check here ▶ ☐ if your organization's main function is to provide funds to the supported organizations.

15 ☐ ⁰ An organization organized and operated to test for public safety. Section 509(a)(4). (See specific instructions.)

Support Schedule (Complete only if you checked box 11, 12, or 13 above)					
Calendar year (or fiscal year beginning in) ▶	(a) 1980	(b) 1979	(c) 1978	(d) 1977	(e) Total
16 Gifts, grants, and contributions received. (Do not include unusual grants. See line 29 below.) . . .	48,000	42,000	35,000	28,000	153,000
17 Membership fees received	8,700	8,000	6,500	5,000	28,200
18 Gross receipts from admissions, merchandise sold or services performed, or furnishing of facilities in any activity that is not a business unrelated to the organization's charitable, etc. purpose	1,100	900	750	500	3,250
19 Gross income from interest, dividends, amounts received from payments on securities loans (section 512(a)(5)), rents, royalties, and unrelated business taxable income (less section 511 taxes) from businesses acquired by the organization after June 30, 1975	11,500	9,500	7,950	5,500	34,450
20 Net income from unrelated business activities not included in line 19 . .	–0–	–0–	–0–	–0–	–0–

Fig. 26–6.   Page 2 of Schedule A to Form 990.

Part IV Support Schedule (continued) (Complete only if you checked box 11, 12, or 13 on page 2)

Calendar year (or fiscal year beginning in) ▶	(a) 1980	(b) 1979	(c) 1978	(d) 1977	(e) Total
21 Tax revenues levied for your benefit and either paid to you or expended on your behalf	–0–	–0–	–0–	–0–	–0–
22 The value of services or facilities furnished to you by a governmental unit without charge. Do not include the value of services or facilities generally furnished to the public without charge	8,500	7,500	3,500	3,500	23,000
23 Other income. Attach schedule. Do not include gain (or loss) from sale of capital assets	–0–	–0–	–0–	–0–	–0–
24 Total of lines 16 through 23 . . .	77,800	67,900	53,700	42,500	241,900
25 Line 24 minus line 18	76,700	67,000	52,950	42,000	238,650
26 Enter 1% of line 24	778	679	537	425	

27 Organizations described in box 11 or 12, page 2:

   (a) Enter 2% of amount in column (e), line 25 . . . . | 4,773

   (b) Attach a list (not open to public inspection) showing the name of and amount contributed by each person (other
36   than a governmental unit or publicly supported organization) whose total gifts for 1977 through 1980 exceeded
   the amount shown in 27(a). Enter the sum of all excess amounts here . . . . | 35,227

28 Organizations described in box 13, page 2:

   (a) Attach a list, for amounts shown on lines 16, 17, and 18, showing the name of, and total amounts received in each year from each
37   "disqualified person," and enter the sum of such amounts for each year:

   (1980)................................ (1979)........ .... (1978)............................ (1977)......... ....

   (b) Attach a list showing, for 1977 through 1980, the name and amount included in line 18 for each person (other than "disqualified
   persons") from whom the organization received more, during that year, than the larger of: the amount on line 26 for the year
   or $5,000. Include organizations described in boxes 6 through 12 as well as individuals. Enter the sum of these excess amounts for
38   each year:
   (1980) (1979) (1978) (1977)

29 For an organization described in boxes 11, 12, or 13, page 2, that received any unusual grants during 1977 through 1980, attach a list (not open to public inspection) for each year showing the name of the contributor, the date and amount of the grant, and a brief description of the nature of the grant. Do not include these grants in line 16 above. (See specific instructions.)

Part V Private School Questionnaire
To Be Completed ONLY by Schools that Checked Box 7 in Part IV

	Yes	No
30 Do you have a racially nondiscriminatory policy toward students by statement in your charter, bylaws, other governing instrument, or in a resolution of your governing body?		
31 Do you include a statement of your racially nondiscriminatory policy toward students in all your brochures, catalogues, and other written communications with the public dealing with student admissions, programs, and scholarships?		
32 Have you publicized your racially nondiscriminatory policy by newspaper or broadcast media during the period of solicitation for students or during the registration period if you have no solicitation program, in a way that makes the policy known to all parts of the general community you serve?		
If "Yes," please describe; if "No," please explain. (If you need more space, attach a separate statement.)		
33 Do you maintain the following:		
(a) Records indicating the racial composition of the student body, faculty, and administrative staff?		
(b) Records documenting that scholarships and other financial assistance are awarded on a racially nondiscriminatory basis? (See instructions.)		
(c) Copies of all catalogues, brochures, announcements, and other written communications to the public dealing with student admissions, programs, and scholarships?		
(d) Copies of all material used by you or on your behalf to solicit contributions?		
If you answered "No," to any of the above, please explain. (If you need more space, attach a separate statement.)		

Fig. 26–7. Page 3 of Schedule A to Form 990.

13–6213564
THE NELLE PLAINS COMMUNITY SERVICE SOCIETY
1400 DIAMOND AVENUE
NELLE PLAINS, NEW YORK

1981 Form 990–Supplementary Schedules

Part I, Line 1(d) and   Contributions in excess of $5,000:
Schedule A, Part IV,   B. Leonard Schultz Jr.
Line 27(b)   2 Butler Road
                               Scarswood, New York
                               $10,000 cash September 11, 1981
                               Total gifts received from Mr. Schultz during 1977–1980 in excess
                               of 2% of support: $35,227

Part I, Line 8   Gross amount received from sale of assets:
                               Sale of common stock to unknown parties through
                               Merrill Lynch.

Description	Number of Shares	How Acquired	Date Acquired	Date Sold	Basis	Selling Price	Gain
U.S. Lock-wood, common ..	1,000	Purchased	3/1/70	10/15/81	$2,000	$7,000	$5,000

Part I, Line 9   Special fundraising events:
                               Annual awards dinner

Gross Receipts	Contributions	Gross Revenue	Direct Expenses	Net Income
$1,600	$300	$1,300	$700	$600

Fig. 26–8.   An example of a supplementary schedule providing information requested by the instructions for Form 990.

Part II, Line 22

Grants and allocations paid (none of
recipients is a related person):
Awards for outstanding community service:
  Mrs. Mary Joe Philips, 18 Birch St.,
    Nelle Plains, New York $2,500
  Mr. Jack Anderson, 50 Chimney Ave.,
    Nelle Plains, New York   1,000
  Mr. L. A. Soben, Deerwood Rd.,
    Nelle Plains, New York   500
                                                                    4,000
Grant for rehabilitation of old firehouse:
  To Nelle Plains Volunteer Fire
  Department, Main St., Nelle Plains,
  New York   3,000
                                                                   $7,000

Part V, Line 54

Investments—securities (at end-of-year market value):
Corporate stocks:
  Non-publicly traded:
    J. J. Faraway Co., common . . . . $ 750
    The Lesch Corp., common   1,800
  Total publicly traded   210,350
                                                                  $212,900

Schedule A, Part III,
Line 3

Determination of qualifying recipients:
  An independent board headed by the Honorable
  George Burns, Mayor of Nelle Plains, makes the
  selection of the individuals who will receive the
  annual awards. These individuals are selected
  for public recognition based upon their outstanding contributions to Nelle Plains. The basis
  for the Nelle Plains Community Service Society's
  tax exemption is its attempt to further, encourage,
  and recognize outstanding achievements of its
  citizens. There are no organizations to which
  funds are expended in furtherance of its exempt
  function, except in the case of purely
  administrative matters.

Fig. 26–8.   Continued.

end" carefully, keeping in mind the "natural" year end for the organization. The election is made automatically when the first return is filed, which must be on a "timely" basis. This means the return must be filed within four and a half months after the chosen year end. The first return can cover a period as short as one month (or even a fraction of a month) or as long as twelve months. It cannot cover a period longer than twelve months, even though the first part of the period may have been a period of no activity.

2. The "employer identification number" is a number assigned by the Internal Revenue Service upon request by any organization. This number will be used on all payroll tax returns and on all communications with the IRS. It serves the same identification function that the social security number serves for an individual. The preparer of a return should always be careful to use the correct number. An employer identification number should be requested by an organization on Form SS-4 as soon as it is formed even if it has no employees. It takes the IRS a period of time to assign the number and if the organization must file a return before the number is received, it should put "applied for" in this space.

3. The "state registration number" is assigned by state charity registration or taxing authorities and will differ from state to state. Therefore, organizations which plan to use copies of Form 990 to meet state reporting requirements* should complete all parts of the form except this item and make as many copies of the form as will be needed. Then the appropriate state registration numbers can be inserted on the copies to be filed with each state. No number is needed on the IRS copy.

4. This refers to the section of the Internal Revenue Code under which the organization was granted exemption. This reference will be in the "exemption letter." A list of the principal types of nonprofit exempt organizations and their Internal Revenue Code references is given on pages 395–396. Request for exemption should be made as soon as the organization is incorporated and is made on Form 1023 (for organizations which believe they are exempt under Section 501(c)(3)) or Form 1024 (for other organizations). If an organization has applied for but not yet received exempt status, the preparer should write "Application Pending" at the top of Page 1 of Form 990.

5. "Gross receipts" means total receipts, including total proceeds from the sales of securities, investments, and other assets before deducting cost of goods sold or the cost of the securities or other assets. It is computed as the sum of lines 1(d), 2, 3, 4, 5, 6(a), 7, 8(a) (both columns), 9(a), 10(a), and 11. Gross receipts for filing requirements tests is not the same as "total income." Total income

---

* Use of Form 990 for this purpose is discussed on pages 310 and 452.

normally would not include the gross proceeds from the sale of assets, but only the profit or loss on such sale. The concept of gross receipts used in this return is a tax and not an accounting concept. Essentially gross receipts represents total cash received during the year as shown on the bank statement. If gross receipts are normally under $25,000, the rest of the return need not be completed.

6. An organization which will not use Form 990 to meet state reporting requirements will probably not complete columns B and C on page 1 or columns C and D on page 3. However, many states require that these columns be completed. Also, if the form is to be reported on by a CPA, as required by some states, the information in these columns may·be necessary for fair presentation of the financial data.

7. "Indirect public support" includes amounts received from United Way or similar federated fund-raising organizations, and from organizations affiliated with the reporting organization where the original source of the money is public contributions.

8. A schedule must be attached to the return listing all gifts aggregating $5,000 or more from any one person during the year. This schedule must show the name, address, date received, and value of all gifts received from each such person. For "publicly supported" organizations, this information is required only if the amount of such gifts from each person is 2 per cent or more of the total contributions received during the year (in addition to being over $5,000). There are some specific rules involved, and if the organization had contributions from any one person of $5,000 or more the instructions should be carefully read and followed. In our illustration here a schedule is included in Figure 26–8, which shows that Mr. Schultz donated $10,000 during the year.

9. Amounts reported as "Program service revenue" (Line 2) and "Gross sales" (Line 10) should be reviewed to determine if the organization has received income from an unrelated trade or business. If the organization had "unrelated business income" during the year it will have to file form 990–T and should answer Question 78(a) "yes." Form 990 should not be filed before Form 990–T is filed because this question would have to be answered "no" and this would only lead to further questions and correspondence.

10. "The cost or other basis and sales expenses" of assets sold includes the original cost of securities or other assets. The original cost of donated securities will be the fair market value at the date received.

11. A detailed schedule is required showing the type of asset sold, cost, to whom sold, etc. The instructions must be carefully followed to be sure that all the required information is shown. An example is presented in Figure 26–8.

12. Amounts reported in this blank will be those resulting from fund-

raising events such as dinners, dances, concerts, and sales of merchandise (e.g., cookies, candy), where the attendee or buyer pays more than a fair market price for the item received. For example, an organization may sponsor a benefit concert and sell tickets at $50. A normal price for such a concert ticket might be $10. The organization pays the performing group an amount which equals $8 per ticket, and incurs publicity, printing, and other "overhead" costs equal to $3 per ticket. Assuming, for purposes of illustration, that one ticket is sold, these amounts would be reported as follows:

$40   (the $50 selling price of the ticket, less $10, a normal price for such a ticket) will be included with other contributions on line 1(a), and also shown in the blank in the caption for line 9(a).

$10   (the normal price for a concert ticket) on line 9(a).

$ 8   (the direct cost to the organization of providing the benefit received by the ticket buyer) on line 9(b).

$ 2   ($10 on line 9(a) less $8 on line 9(b)) on line 9(c).

$ 3   (indirect costs of the event) included in fund-raising costs in Column D of Part II.

The $40 reported on Line 1(a) is included with other contributions, and will not normally be separately identifiable on that line.

It will be important for organizations which sponsor such fund-raising events to keep records which will allow completion of Form 990 in the above manner.

Although not affecting the sponsoring organization's accounting or financial reporting, such organizations should be prepared to inform those who buy tickets or merchandise what portion of the selling price is allowable as a tax deduction on the buyer's personal income tax return. In the above example, this amount is also $40, the "extra" amount paid over the fair value of the ticket. Since a person who wants merely to attend a concert can do so for $10, the presumption is that the extra $40 is intended as a contribution to the sponsoring charitable organization.

13. "Cost of goods sold" refers to the cost of actual merchandise or goods that were sold, but not selling expenses. Selling expenses are shown in Part II. In the case of a country club, cost of goods sold would include the direct cost of food and drink sold and direct labor.

14. Expenses incurred for the exempt purpose other than for soliciting contributions should be shown on this line, including applicable overhead expenses. It is important to remember that the Internal Revenue Service will look at this line to determine whether it appears that a substantial enough portion of contributions and dues is being expended to justify continuation of the organization's exempt status.

15. All expenses associated with the soliciting of contributions should be shown on this line. A typical example would be the salary of a fund raiser.

16. This line is used by organizations which are affiliated with other charitable organizations to report amounts remitted to or paid on behalf of the affiliated organization. For example, a local branch of a national charity may be required to pass through to the national office a certain percentage of all contributions, or the national office may allocate certain amounts to its local chapters. This line is not intended to be used for reporting allocations by a federated fund-raising organization such as United Way to its member agencies. These allocations should go on Line 22.

17. Line 20 will be used to report three main types of transaction:
    a. Interfund transfers between a fund included in Column B and one included in Column C (such transfers will always net to zero in Column A)
    b. Unrealized changes in the market value of investments reported at market value (only realized gains may be reported on Line 8)
    c. "Capital·additions" as defined in Statement of Position No. 78-10 (see discussion on page 273)

18. The amounts shown as fund balances or net worth at end of year should correspond to Line 74 on the Balance Sheet in Part V.

19. This part showing allocation of expenses among "Program services," "Management and general," and "Fundraising" is also very important because the method and amounts of allocation among these three categories become fixed once the return has been filed, and it is very difficult to go back and subsequently change it. The risk is that the Internal Revenue Service could challenge the conclusion that certain gross receipts are related to the exempt purpose. If they were successful in this challenge, the organization would want to be certain that it had already allocated a fair proportion of expenses to this gross income in order to minimize (or even eliminate) the resulting tax. It would be very awkward to go back and claim that a fair allocation of expenses had not been made at the time of initially filing this return.

20. A detailed schedule is required showing, among other things, to whom paid, relationship, purpose, and amount. The instructions should be carefully followed to be sure that all of the required information is shown. An example is shown in the schedule in Figure 26–8.

21. Details of the information requested here are shown in Part VI on page 4 of Form 990.

22. A schedule must be attached showing details of depreciation. Form 4562 can be used (this is a schedule giving the details requested) or the required information can be presented on a supplementary schedule.

23. Part III requires a brief description of the activities carried out by

the organization which form the basis for the organization's exempt status. Extensive details need not be given, but the descriptions should be informative enough that a person who knows nothing about the organization will obtain a basic understanding of the organization's programs.

24. Where required, information reported in blanks that are part of item captions or on supplementary schedules should be end-of-year information only.

25. Two kinds of amounts are reported on this line:
   a. Gifts and grants specified by the donor or grantor for use in future accounting periods are reported as deferred revenue until the intended period of use.
   b. Gifts and grants specified by the donor or grantor for a current, but restricted, purpose may be reported as deferred revenue until the organization carries out the intended purpose. This method of accounting is used by organizations which follow the AICPA Statement of Position, Accounting Principles and Reporting Practices for Certain Nonprofit Organizations. (This method of accounting is discussed on pp. 105–107 and 259–260.) Some state regulatory agencies have stated that this method of accounting for current restricted gifts is not acceptable for use on forms filed with those states. Organization managers should read carefully the instructions provided by each state with which a copy of the form will be filed.

26. "Net worth" has the same meaning as "fund balance," which is the term used throughout this book to represent excess of assets over liabilities of the organization. This section allows an organization to report its net worth in whatever way its records are kept. Most nonprofit organizations use fund accounting and will complete lines 67–70. Social clubs will probably have capital stock, and perhaps capital surplus. Foundations often keep their fund balance segregated between principal and unexpended income.

27. Not all expense allowances are reported here, rather only those for which the recipient did *not* account to the organization, or which exceeded the expense incurred by the recipient. Such amounts are taxable income to the recipient.

28. Membership organizations should enter the total amount of direct and indirect expenses for political purposes. Charitable organizations are also allowed to engage in political activities, but these expenses may be subject to very stringent limitations (see Chapter 25).

29. The value of donated services may not be reported as revenue or expense in Parts I and II, but may, if the organization wishes, be reported on Line 82.

30. Clubs may be challenged on their exempt status if receipts from the general public, including investment income, exceed 35 per

cent of gross receipts. However, within this 35 per cent limitation is a 15 per cent limitation on receipts from the general public.

Schedule A

Schedule A is prepared by all 501(c)(3) organizations that must file Form 990. This will include most exempt organizations except private foundations, clubs, business leagues, and similar noncharitable organizations. Schedule A, which consists of four pages, is broken down into six parts. Parts I–IV must be completed, while Part V applies only to schools and Part VI is used to compute the "lobbying limitation" (see Chapter 25).

Figures 26–5, 6, and 7 show pages 1–3 of Schedule A which have been completed for The Nelle Plains Community Service Society.

Comments on Schedule A

The information requested in Parts I and II is straightforward and does not require comment.

31. Part III attempts to determine whether the organization is engaging in any number of activities which, in certain circumstances, are improper. A detailed explanation of these transactions must be attached to the return. For example, most organizations compensate their officers or directors for their work. Problems can arise where the compensation is deemed excessive.
32. See Figure 26–8 for an example of the type of statement that would be required.
33. This section is the place where an organization states specifically why it is not a private foundation. Pages 395 to 400 discuss the various categories of publicly supported organizations (i.e., non-private foundation status).
34. This category is the one most publicly supported organizations will qualify under. See page 397 (category 1). Where an organization can qualify under this category, it should do so.
35. This category is the one resulting from the application of the "mechanical" test referred to on   pages 397–398 (category 2).
36. Lines 27(a) and 27(b) are designed to determine the amount of gifts, grants, and membership fees that must be excluded for purposes of the "substantial support from the public" test. Only the excess above the amount on line 27(a) is excluded.
37. Line 28(a) is asking for the year-by-year details of gifts, grants, gross receipts, and membership fees from disqualified persons. Such amounts are excluded from the "mechanical tests" discussed

on page 398, category 2(b) (1). See the footnote on page 398 for a definition of a "disqualified person."

38. Line 28(b) is asking for the year-by-year details of gross receipts from admissions, sales of services, etc., from any one person or company in excess of $5,000 or 1 per cent of total support, whichever is greater. The amounts in excess of that base amount are excluded from the mechanical test discussed on page 398, category 2(b) (2).

The final page of Schedule A containing the remainder of Part V and Part VI is not illustrated because relatively few organizations are affected. Part V is filled out only by schools. Part VI is filled out by organizations that have elected certain permissible levels of lobbying activities.

FORM 990–PF—RETURN OF PRIVATE FOUNDATION

All private foundations must file Form 990–PF by the fifteenth day of the fifth month after the end of the fiscal year (May 15th for calendar year private foundations) and there is a penalty of $10 a day for failure to file, unless it can be shown that there was a reasonable cause for not doing so.

This return consists of eight pages and to the uninitiated appears to be a difficult form to fill out. Most private foundations would be well advised to get competent tax counsel to prepare this form for them. The comments indicated below—while undoubtedly helpful—cannot substitute for the direct assistance of a tax lawyer or accountant knowledgeable in the foundation's particular circumstances.

Form 990–PF—Illustration and Comments

Figure 26–9 shows the first page of this form. Again, the numbers on the form refer to the comments below:

1. The fair market value of assets at the end of the year can differ from the net worth as shown in the Balance Sheet on page 2 of Form 990–PF (Figure 26–10) because most foundations carry their investments at cost rather than at fair market value. However, in the attached illustration, investments are carried at market since the Statement of Position discussed in Chapter 16 permits this treatment by private foundations.

Form 990-PF

Department of the Treasury
Internal Revenue Service

Return of Private Foundation
or Section 4947(a)(1) Trust Treated as a Private Foundation
Note: You may be able to use a copy of this return to satisfy State reporting requirements.

OMB No. 1545-0052

1981

For the calendar year 1981, or tax year beginning _____, 1981, and ending _____, 19__

Please type, print, or attach label. See Specific Instructions	**Name of organization** The Christiansen Foundation
	Address (number and street) 60 Broad Street
	City or town, State, and ZIP code New York, New York 10017

Employer identification number 13 : 5326271

State registration number (see instructions)

If the foundation is in a 60-month termination under section 507(b)(1)(B) check here ▶ ☐

If address changed, check here ▶ ☐   Foreign organizations, check here ▶ ☐

Check type of organization
☒ Exempt private foundation   ☐ 4947(a)(1) trust   ☐ Other taxable private foundation
Check this box if your private foundation status terminated under section 507(b)(1)(A) ▶ ☐

The books are in care of ▶ J. Steven Kreutz
Located at ▶ Above address   Telephone no. ▶ 212-422-6000

Fair market value of assets at end of year 2,900,461 ①

Section 4947(a)(1) trusts filing this form in lieu of Form 1041, check here and see general instructions . . . . . ▶ ☐

Part I   Analysis of Revenue and Expenses ②
(See instructions for Part I)

		(A) Revenue and expenses per books ③	(B) Computation of net investment income ⑥	(C) Computation of adjusted net income ⑧	(D) Disbursements for charitable purpose ⑨
	1 Contributions, gifts, grants, etc. (attach schedule)	-0-			
	2 Contributions from split-interest trusts . . .		-0-		
	3 Membership dues and assessments . . .	-0-			
	4 Interest on savings and temporary cash investments . .	8,330	8,330	8,330	
	5 Dividends and interest from securities . . .	226,483	226,483	226,483	
	6 Gross rents	-0-	-0-	-0-	
Revenue	7 Net gain or (loss) from sale of assets not on line 11 . ④	20,000			
	8 Capital gain net income		⑦ 2,274		
	9 Net short-term capital gain			-0-	
	10 Income modifications			-0-	
	11 Gross profit from any business activities: (Gross receipts ▶ $ -0- minus cost of sales ▶ $ -0- .)	-0-		-0-	
	12 Other income (attach schedule)	-0-	-0-	-0-	
	13 Total—add lines 1 through 12	254,813	237,087	234,813	
	14 Compensation of officers, etc.	20,395	4,046	4,046	16,349
	15 Other salaries and wages	13,211	-0-	-0-	13,211
	16 (a) Pension plan contributions	-0-	-0-	-0-	-0-
	(b) Other employee benefits	966	-0-	-0-	966
Expenses	17 Investment, legal, and other professional services	19,138	6,363	6,363	12,775
	18 Interest	-0-	-0-	-0-	-0-
	19 Taxes (attach schedule)	4,519	-0-	-0-	-0-
	20 Depreciation, amortization, and depletion . . .	-0-	-0-	-0-	
	21 Occupancy	10,507	722	722	9,785
	22 Other expenses (attach schedule)	11,340	-0-	-0-	11,340
	23 Contributions, gifts, grants (from Part XIII) . .	790,059			790,059
	24 Total—add lines 14 through 23	870,135	11,131	11,131	854,485 ⑩
	25 (a) Excess of revenue over expenses: Line 13 minus line 24 ⑤	<615,322>			
	(b) Net investment income (if negative, enter –0–) . .		225,956		
	(c) Adjusted net income (if negative, enter –0–) . . .			223,682	

Part II   Excise Tax On Investment Income (Section 4940(a), 4940(b), or 4948—See Instructions)

1 Domestic organizations enter 2% of line 25(b). Exempt foreign organizations enter 4% of line 25(b) . ⑪	4,519
2 Tax under section 511 (exempt foundations and exempt foreign organizations enter –0–)	-0-
3 Add lines 1 and 2	4,519
4 Tax under subtitle A (exempt foundations and exempt foreign organizations enter –0–)	-0-
5 Tax on investment income (line 3 minus line 4 (but not less than –0–))	4,519
6 Credits: (a) Exempt foreign organizations—tax withheld at source . . . . . -0-	
(b) Tax paid with application for extension of time to file (Form 2758) . . . . -0-	-0-
7 Tax due (line 5 minus line 6) . Pay in full with return. Make check or money order payable to Internal Revenue Service (Write employer identification number on check or money order) ▶	4,519
8 Overpayment—(line 6 minus line 5)	-0-

For Paperwork Reduction Act Notice, see page 1 of the instructions.

Fig. 26–9.   Page 1 of Form 990-PF.

Form 990–PF (1981)　　　　　　　　　　　　　　　　　　　　　　　　　　Page **2**

Part III　Balance Sheets Any required schedules should be for end of year amounts only. ⑫	(A) Beginning of year	(B) End of year
1 Cash—non-interest bearing	4,021	5,087
2 Savings and temporary cash investments	39,400	227,000
3 Accounts receivable ▶ –0–		
minus allowance for doubtful accounts ▶ –0–	47,438	–0–
4 Pledges receivable ▶ –0–		
minus allowance for doubtful accounts ▶ –0–	–0–	–0–
5 Grants receivable	–0–	–0–
6 Receivables due from officers, directors, trustees, and other disqualified persons (see instructions)	–0–	–0–
7 Other notes and loans receivable ▶ –0–		
minus allowance for doubtful accounts ▶ –0–	–0–	–0–
8 Inventories for sale or use		
9 Prepaid expenses and deferred charges		
10 Investments—securities (attach schedule)	3,554,409	2,668,374
11 Investments—land, buildings, and equipment: basis ▶ –0–		
minus accumulated depreciation ▶ –0– (attach schedule)	–0–	–0–
12 Investments—mortgage loans	–0–	–0–
13 Investments—other (attach schedule)	–0–	–0–
14 Land, buildings, and equipment: basis ▶ –0–		
minus accumulated depreciation ▶ –0– (attach schedule)	–0–	–0–
15 Other assets:	–0–	–0–
16 Total assets (add lines 1 through 15)	3,645,268	2,900,461
17 Accounts payable and accrued expenses	33,691	7,175
18 Grants payable	–0–	–0–
19 Support and revenue designated for future periods (attach schedule)	–0–	–0–
20 Loans from officers, directors, trustees, and other disqualified persons	–0–	–0–
21 Mortgages and other notes payable (attach schedule)	–0–	–0–
22 Other liabilities: Excise tax payable	10,926	4,519
23 Total liabilities (add lines 17 through 22)	44,617	11,694
Organizations that use fund accounting, check here ▶ ☒ and complete lines 24 through 27 and lines 31 and 32.		
24 (a) Current unrestricted fund	1,520,029	808,145
(b) Current restricted funds	–0–	–0–
25 Land, buildings, and equipment fund	–0–	–0–
26 Endowment fund	2,080,622	2,080,622
27 Other funds (Describe ▶ ....)	–0–	–0–
Organizations not using fund accounting, check here ▶ ☐ and complete lines 28–32.		
28 Capital stock or trust principal		
29 Paid-in or capital surplus		
30 Retained earnings or accumulated income		
31 Total fund balances or net worth (see instructions)	3,600,651	2,888,767
32 Total liabilities and fund balances/net worth (see instructions)	3,645,268	2,900,461

Part IV　Analysis of Changes in Net Worth or Fund Balances ⑬

1 Total net worth or fund balances at beginning of year—Part III, Column A, line 31	3,600,651
2 Enter amount from Part I, line 25(a)	615,322
3 Other increases not included in line 2 (itemize) ▶	–0–
4 Add lines 1, 2, and 3	2,985,329
5 Decreases not included in line 2 (itemize) ▶ Change in market value of securities	96,562
6 Total net worth or fund balances at end of year (line 4 minus line 5)—Part III, Column B, line 31	2,888,767

Part V　Statements Regarding Activities ⑭

File Form 4720 if you answer "No" to question 10(b), 11(b), or 14(b) or "Yes" to question 10(c), 12(b), 13(a), or 13(b).

	Yes	No
1 (a) During the tax year, did you attempt to influence any national, State, or local legislation?		X
(b) During the year did you participate or intervene in any political campaign?		X
(c) Did you spend more than $100 during the year (either directly or indirectly) for political purposes (see instructions for definition)?		X
If you answered "Yes" to 1(a), (b), or (c), attach a detailed description of the activities and copies of any materials published or distributed by the organization in connection with the activities.		
(d) Did you file Form 1120–POL?		X

Fig. 26–10.

Form 990–PF (1981)   Page **3**

Part V	**Statements Regarding Activities (continued)**	Yes	No

2 Have you engaged in any activities which have not previously been reported to the Internal Revenue Service? . . . → No: X

If "Yes," attach a detailed description of the activities.

3 Have you made any changes, not previously reported to the IRS, in your governing instrument, articles of incorporation, or bylaws, or other similar instruments? . . . . → No: X

If "Yes," attach a conformed copy of the changes.

4 (a) Did you have unrelated business gross income of $1,000 or more during the year? . . . . → No: X

(b) If "Yes," have you filed a tax return on Form 990–T for this year? . . . . (15) . .

5 Was there a liquidation, termination, dissolution, or substantial contraction during the year? . . . . → No: X

If "Yes," attach a schedule for each asset disposed of showing: the type of asset, the date of disposition, its cost or other basis, its fair market value on date of disposition, and the name and address of each recipient to whom assets were distributed.

6 Did you have at least $5,000 in assets at any time during the year? . . . . → Yes: X

If "Yes," complete Parts XIII and XIV.

7 Are the requirements of section 508(e) (relating to governing instruments) satisfied? (See instructions) . . . → Yes: X

If "Yes," are the requirements satisfied by:

(a) Language in the governing instrument (original or as amended), or . . . . (16) . . → No: X

(b) Enactment of State legislation that effectively amends the governing instrument with no mandatory directions in the governing instrument that conflict with the State law? . . . . → Yes: X

8 (a) Enter States to which the foundation reports or with which it is registered (see instructions) ▶
New York

(b) If you answered 6(a) "Yes," have you furnished a copy of Form 990–PF to the Attorney General (or his or her designate) of each State as required by General Instruction K.1? . . . . (17) . → Yes: X
If "No," attach explanation.

9 Are you claiming status as an operating foundation within the meaning of sections 4942(j)(3) or 4942(j)(5) for calendar year 1981 or fiscal year beginning in 1981 (see instructions for Part XII)? . . . . (18) → No: X
If "Yes," complete Part XII.

10 Self-dealing (section 4941):

(a) During the year did you (either directly or indirectly): (19)

(1) Engage in the sale, or exchange, or leasing of property with a disqualified person? . . . . . . → No: X

(2) Borrow money from, lend money to, or otherwise extend credit to (or accept it from) a disqualified person? . → No: X

(3) Furnish goods, services, or facilities to (or accept them from) a disqualified person? . . . . (20) . . → No: X

(4) Pay compensation to or pay or reimburse the expenses of a disqualified person? . . . . . → Yes: X

(5) Transfer any of your income or assets to a disqualified person (or make any of either available for the benefit or use of a disqualified person)? . . . . → No: X

(6) Agree to pay money or property to a government official? (Exception: check "No" if you agreed to make a grant to or to employ the official for a period after he or she terminates government service if he or she is terminating within 90 days.) . . . . → No: X

(b) If you answered "Yes" to any of the questions 10(a)(1) through (6), were the acts you engaged in excepted acts as described in regulations section 53.4941(d)–3 and 4? . . . . . (20) . . . . . . → Yes: X

(c) Did you engage in a prior year in any of the acts described in 10(a), other than excepted acts, that were acts of self-dealing that were not corrected by the first day of your tax year beginning in 1981? . . . . . . → No: X

11 Taxes on failure to distribute income (section 4942) (does not apply for years you were an operating foundation as defined in section 4942(j)(3) or 4942(j)(5)):

(a) Did you at the end of tax year 1981 have any undistributed income (lines 6(b) and (c), Part XI) for tax year(s) beginning before 1981? . . . . → No: X

If "Yes," list the years ▶................, ..., ..., ...

(b) If "Yes," to (a) above, are you applying the provisions of section 4942(a)(2) (relating to incorrect valuation of assets) to the undistributed income for ALL such years? . . . .

(c) If the provisions of section 4942(a)(2) are being applied to ANY of the years listed in (a) above, list the years here and see the instructions ▶................, ..., ..., ...

12 Taxes on excess business holdings (section 4943):

(a) Did you hold more than 2% direct or indirect interest in any business enterprise at any time during the year? . . → No: X

(b) If "Yes," did you have excess business holdings in 1981 as a result of any purchase by you or disqualified persons after May 26, 1969; after the lapse of the 5-year period to dispose of holdings acquired by gift or bequest; or after the lapse of the 10-year first phase holding period? . . . .

Note: You may use Schedule C, Form 4720, to determine if you had excess business holdings in 1981.

13 Taxes on investments which jeopardize charitable purposes (section 4944):

(a) Did you invest during the year any amount in a manner that would jeopardize the carrying out of any of your charitable purposes? . . . . (21) . → No: X

(b) Did you make any investment in a prior year (but after December 31, 1969) that could jeopardize your charitable purpose that you had not removed from jeopardy on the first day of your tax year beginning in 1981? . . . . → No: X

Fig. 26–11.

Form 990–PF (1981)   Page **4**

Part V	Statements Regarding Activities (continued)

	Yes	No
14 Taxes on taxable expenditures (section 4945):		
(a) During the year did you pay or incur any amount to:		
(1) Carry on propaganda, or otherwise attempt to influence legislation by attempting to affect the opinion of the general public or any segment thereof, or by communicating with any member or employee of a legislative body, or by communicating with any other government official or employee who may participate in the formulation of legislation?		X
(2) Influence the outcome of any specific public election, or to carry on, directly or indirectly, any voter registration drive?		X
(3) Provide a grant to an individual for travel, study, or other similar purposes?		X
(4) Provide a grant to an organization, other than a charitable, etc., organization described in paragraph (1), (2), or (3) of section 509(a)? . . . . ㉒ .		X
(5) Provide for any purpose other than religious, charitable, scientific, literary, or educational purposes, or for the prevention of cruelty to children or animals?		X
(b) If you answered "Yes" to any of questions (a)(1) through (a)(5), were all such transactions excepted transactions as described in regulations section 53.4945?		
(c) If you answered "Yes" to question 14(a)(4), do you claim exemption from the tax because you maintained expenditure responsibility for the grant? . . . . If "Yes," attach the statement required.		
15 Did any persons become substantial contributors during the tax year? . . . . ㉓ . If "Yes," attach a schedule listing their names and addresses.		X

Part VI	Statement Regarding Officers, Compensation, etc.

1 Officers, directors, trustees, foundation managers and their compensation, if any, for 1981:

Name and address	Title, and average hours per week devoted to position	Contributions to employee benefit plans	Expense account, other allowances	Compensation
Jane Cornell 60 Broad St., New York, N.Y. 10017	President 40	None	None	17,395
W.H. Larkin III 60 Broad St., New York, N.Y. 10017	Trustee 2	None	None	1,000
Robert A. Peron 60 Broad St., New York, N.Y. 10017	Trustee 2	None	None	1,000
Louis F. Reinhardt 60 Broad St., New York, N.Y. 10017	Trustee 2	None	None	1,000
Total . . . . ▶				20,395

2 Compensation of five highest paid employees for 1981 (other than included in 1 above—see instructions):

Name and address of employees paid more than $30,000	Title, and time devoted to position	Contributions to employee benefit plans	Expense account, other allowances	Compensation
No employee is paid over $30,000				

Total number of other employees paid over $30,000 ▶

3 Five highest paid persons for professional services for 1981 (see instructions):

Name and address of persons paid more than $30,000	Type of service	Compensation
No person is paid over $30,000 for professional services		

Total number of others receiving over $30,000 for professional services ▶

Fig. 26–12.

Form 990–PF (1981)

Part VII   Capital Gains and Losses for Tax on Investment Income (24)

a. Kind of property. Indicate security, real estate, or other (specify)	b. Description (examples: 100 sh. of "Z" Co., 2 story brick, etc.)	c. How acquired P—Purchase D—Donation	d. Date acquired (mo., day, yr.)	e. Date sold (mo., day, yr.)
1 Security	1000 sh. AT&T	P	11/1/58	12/11/81
Security	1200 sh. Xerox	D	7/11/67	12/1/81
Security	7500 sh. ITT	D	6/1/53	6/1/81
Security	2000 sh. G.M.	P	8/3/71	3/27/81

f. Gross sales price minus expense of sale	g. Depreciation allowed (or allowable)	h. Cost or other basis (25)	i. Gain or (loss) (f plus g minus h) (27)
46,000	–0–	22,000 (26)	24,000
144,000	–0–	176,000	⟨32,000⟩
350,000	–0–	300,000	50,000
135,000	–0–	117,000	18,000

Complete only for assets showing gain in column i and owned by the foundation on 12/31/69

J. F.M.V. as of 12/31/69 (28)	k. Adjusted basis as of 12/31/69 (29)	l. Excess of col. j over col. k, if any	m. Losses (from col. I) Gains (excess of col. i gain over col. l, but not less than zero)
29,726	22,000	7,726	16,274
			⟨32,000⟩
			–0–
365,000	300,000	65,000	18,000

2 Capital gain net income or (net capital loss) . { If gain, also enter in Part I, line 8 } . . . { 2,274 (30)
If (loss) enter –0– in Part I, line 8 }

3 Net short-term capital gain (loss) as defined in section 1222(5) and (6)
{ If gain, also enter in Part I, column (C), line 9 (see instructions for line 9) } . . . .   –0–
{ If loss, enter –0– in Part I, column (C), line 9

Part VIII   Minimum Investment Return for 1981 (31)

1 Fair market value of assets not used (or held for use) directly in carrying out charitable, etc., purposes:

(a) Average monthly fair market value of securities	2,757,412
(b) Average of monthly cash balances	79,830
(c) Fair market value of all other assets (see instructions)	23,720
(d) Total (add lines (a), (b), and (c))	2,860,962
2 Acquisition indebtedness applicable to line 1 assets	–0–
3 Line 1(d) minus line 2	2,860,962
4 Cash deemed held for charitable activities—enter 1½% of line 3 (for greater amount, see instructions) . .	42,914
5 Line 3 minus line 4	2,818,048
6 Enter 5% of line 5	140,902

Part IX   Computation of Distributable Amount for 1981 (See instructions) (31)

1 Adjusted net income from Part I, line 25(c)		223,682
2 Minimum investment return from Part VIII, line 6		140,902
3 Enter the larger of line 1 or line 2		223,682
4 Total of:		
(a) Tax on investment income for 1981 from Part II, line 5	4,519	
(b) Income tax under this subtitle A, for 1981	–0–	4,519
5 Distributable amount (line 3 minus line 4)		219,163
6 Adjustments to distributable amount		–0–
7 Distributable amount as adjusted (line 5 plus or minus line 6)—also enter in Part XI, line 1		219,163

Fig. 26–13.

Form 990-PF (1981)   Page **6**

Part X   **Qualifying Distributions in 1981 (See instructions)**   (32)

1 Amounts paid (including administrative expenses) to accomplish charitable, etc., purposes:
- (a) Expenses, contributions, gifts, etc.—total from Part I, column D, line 24   854,485
- (b) Program-related investments . . . .   -0-

2 Amounts paid to acquire assets used (or held for use) directly in carrying out charitable, etc., purposes . . .   -0-

3 Amounts set aside for specific charitable projects that satisfy the:
- (a) Suitability test (prior IRS approval required) . . . . . . (33) . . . .   -0-
- (b) Cash distribution test (attach the required schedule) . . . .   -0-

4 Total qualifying distributions made in 1981 (add lines 1, 2, and 3)—also enter in Part XI, line 4   854,485

Part XI **Computation of Undistributed Income (See instructions)** (34)	(a) Corpus	(b) Years prior to 1980	(c) 1980	(d) 1981 (35)
1 Distributable amount for 1981 from Part IX . .				219,163
2 Undistributed income, if any, as of the end of 1980				
(a) Enter amount for 1980			-0-	
(b) Total for prior years: ...., ..., ...		-0-		
3 Excess distributions carryover, if any, to 1981:				
(a) From 1976 . . (36) .	109,357			
(b) From 1977 . .	208,751			
(c) From 1978	<51,964>			
(d) From 1979	79,147			
(e) From 1980	101,101			
(f) Total of 3(a) through (e)	446,392			
4 Qualifying distributions for 1981 (854,485)				
(a) Applied to 1980, but not more than line 2(a) .			(-0-)	
(b) Applied to undistributed income of prior years (Election required)		(-0-)		
(c) Treated as distributions out of corpus (Election required)	-0-			
(d) Applied to 1981 distributable amount (37) .				(219,163)
(e) Remaining amount distributed out of corpus .	635,322			
5 Excess distributions carryover applied to 1981 . (If an amount appears in column (d), the same amount must be shown in column (a))	(-0-)			(-0-)
6 Enter the net total of each column as indicated below:				
(a) Corpus. Add lines 3(f), 4(c), and 4(e). Subtract line 5 . . . . (38)(b)	1,081,714			
(b) Prior years' undistributed income. Line 2(b) minus line 4(b)		(b) -0-		
(c) Enter the amount of prior year's undistributed income for which a notice of deficiency has been issued, or on which the section 4942(a) tax has been previously assessed . . .		(c) -0-		
(d) Subtract line 6(c) from line 6(b). This amount is taxable—File Form 4720		(d) -0-		
(e) Undistributed income for 1980. Line 2(a) minus line 4(a). This amount is taxable—File Form 4720	*		-0-	
(f) Undistributed income for 1981. Line 1 minus lines 4(d) and 5. This amount must be distributed in 1982				-0-
7 Amounts treated as distributions out of corpus to satisfy requirements imposed by section 170(b)(1)(D) or 4942(g)(3) (see instructions) . . .	(-0-)			
8 Excess distributions carryover from 1976 not applied on line 5 or line 7 (see instructions) . . .	(109,357)			
9 Excess distributions carryover to 1982. (Line 6(a) minus lines 7 and 8.) (38)	972,357			
10 Analysis of line 9:				
(a) Excess from 1977 . . .	208,751			
(b) Excess from 1978 . . .	<51,964>			
(c) Excess from 1979 . . .	<79,147>			
(d) Excess from 1980 . . .	101,101			
(e) Excess from 1981 . . .	635,322			

Fig. 26-14.

Form 990–PF (1981)   Page **8**

Part XIII Supplementary Information (continued)

3 If you award grants, scholarships, fellowships, loans, prizes or similar benefits, attach a statement giving: (a) the name, address, and telephone number of the person to whom applications should be addressed; (b) the form in which applications should be submitted and information and materials they should include; (c) any submission deadlines; and (d) any restrictions or limitations on awards such as by geographical areas, charitable fields, kinds of institutions, or other factors.

4 Grants and Contributions Paid During the Year or Approved for Future Payment

Recipient Name and address (home or business)	If recipient is an individual, show any relationship to any foundation manager or substantial contributor	Foundation Status of Recipient	Purpose of grant or contribution	Amount
(a) Paid during year See attached schedule	(39)			
Total (Enter this amount on line 23, Part I, also.) . . . . ▶				790,059
(b) Approved for future payment None				
Total . . . . ▶				–0–

Part XIV Itemized Statement of Securities and All Other Assets Held at the Close of the Tax Year (see instructions)

Asset	Book value	Market value
Cash	232,087	232,087
Securities: (40)		
USA Treasury Bill 9%, 11/1/92	568,024	568,024
AT&T Debenture 7½%, 8/1/95	387,666	387,666
G.M. Debenture 7%, 5/1/84	400,000	400,000
Common stock: AT&T	410,000	410,000
Xerox	176,000	176,000
G.M.	175,500	175,500
Polaroid	551,184	551,184
Total . . . . ▶	2,900,461	2,900,461

Part XV Public Inspection (41)

1 Enter the date the notice of availability of the annual return appeared in a newspaper ▶ May 9, 1982

2 Enter the name of the newspaper ▶ New York Times

3 Check here ▶ ☒ if you have attached a copy of the newspaper notice as required by the instructions. (If the notice is not attached, the return will be considered incomplete.)

Under penalties of perjury, I declare that I have examined this return, including accompanying schedules and statements, and to the best of my knowledge and belief it is true, correct, and complete. Declaration of preparer (other than taxpayer or fiduciary) is based on all information of which preparer has any knowledge.

Please Sign Here	Signature of officer or trustee	May 10, 1982 Date	▶ President Title	

Paid Preparer's Use Only	Preparer's signature ▶	Date	Check if self-employed ▶ ☐	Preparer's social security no.
	Firm's name (or yours, if self-employed) and address ▶		E.I. No. ▶	
			ZIP code ▶	

U.S. GOVERNMENT PRINTING OFFICE : 1981—O-343-053

Fig. 26–15.

2. Part I ("Analysis of Revenue and Expenses") looks more complicated than it actually is. In this section the foundation reports its revenue and expenses as recorded in its books. Then, through the use of a columnar arrangement, the figures are put in the appropriate columns to arrive at certain key amounts that the foundation must use to determine the amount of its excise tax and distributable income.

3. Column (A) ("Revenue and expenses per books") is exactly what it says it is, and the foundation should record its revenue and expenses (or receipts and expenditures for cash basis foundations) in this column. Record all the figures in column (A) before attempting to fill in the figures in the other three columns.

The foundation can keep its records on either the cash or the accrual basis of accounting and the amounts shown in column (A) will be the amounts on whichever basis is used. However, the amounts included in column (D) must be the amounts actually disbursed during the year (i.e., the cash basis).

4. The net gain or loss from sale of assets will be the book amount of the capital gains or losses from sale of investments. As noted on page 403, book gain or loss may or may not be the same as taxable gain or loss. The taxable gain will be reported only in column (B), on line 8 (see comment 7 below).

5. Line 25(a) will be the excess of all revenue over expenses (or vice versa) as shown by the foundation's books.

6. Column (B) looks complicated but it really is not. The amounts shown in the top section are merely those amounts which are subject to the excise tax on investment income. The amounts in the bottom half of this schedule are the allocated expenses which can be deducted in arriving at the amount of this taxable income. It is for this reason that there are a number of shaded areas in this column in the income section. (No figures should be put in these shaded areas.) For example, contributions, gifts, and grants are not taxable and therefore the appropriate areas in column (B) have been shaded.

The allocation of expenses should be made on the basis of the nature of the expense. See comment 19 on page 432.

The last line in this column ($225,956) is the amount of net investment income subject to the excise tax. The tax is calculated in Part II.

7. Taxable gain on sale of investments is calculated on page 5 (Figure 26–13) and the calculation on that page must be completed before a figure can be entered on line 8, in column (B).

8. Column (C) provides for the computation of "adjusted net income." As will be noted, net investment income and adjusted net income are not the same. The net capital gain of the foundation is included in the computation of net investment income, but only

the net short-term capital gain is included in the adjusted net income computation. The reason a calculation of adjusted net income is made is to help determine the "distributable amount" which is computed in Part IX on page 5.

9. Column (D) is used to report the amount of expenditures made for the exempt purpose. If the organization is on a cash basis (see note below), the amounts reported in column (D) on lines 14 through 22 are usually the amounts reported in column (A) less the amounts reported in column (C). One exception to this is line 19, taxes. Column (A) will probably include the excise tax on investment income. This tax is not deductible for purposes of the calculations being made here.

10. The amounts reported in column (D) are those that were actually *disbursed* during the current year (i.e., on a cash basis). Therefore, if a foundation keeps its books on an accrual basis, the amounts shown in columns (A) and (D) would differ.

11. This section is merely a calculation of the amount of excise tax on investment income.

12. See comments no. 24-26 on Form 990 (on p. 433) which are also relevant to Form 990–PF.

13. Part IV reconciles the net worth (fund balance) at the beginning of the year to the net worth at the end of the year. In many instances the amount reported on the first page as the excess of revenue over expenses will be the only reconciling item, except when the foundation carries its securities at market value, in which case the unrealized change in market value during the year will be shown on either line 3 or line 5.

14. Part V must be answered very carefully because it attempts to determine whether any of the many rules affecting private foundations have been violated (see pages 404–407). If the answer to any of the questions results in the filing of Form 4720, the foundation should consult with tax counsel because the foundation and the foundation managers may be subject to escalating taxes.

15. A substantial "contraction" has been defined as disposition of more than 25 per cent of the fair market value of the foundation's assets. Note we are talking of fair market value as distinct from book value.

16. The 1969 Tax Reform Act required foundations to put certain restrictive language in their governing instruments, or, alternatively, the state legislature could effectively amend these governing instruments for all foundations within the state through legislation. Many states did so, thus eliminating the need for individual foundations to amend their governing instruments. Question 7 is designed to make sure that either legislation was passed or the foundation individually amended its governing instruments as appropriate.

17. All private foundations must submit a copy of Form 990–PF to the

attorney general in each state in which it is registered or otherwise doing business. Care should be taken to be sure the foundation mails the form to the attorney general *before* filing Form 990–PF with the IRS.

18. There are certain advantages to being an "operating" foundation. See pages 407–408.

19. Questions 10 through 14 are designed to determine whether the foundation is engaged in any "prohibited" transactions. See pages 406–407 for a discussion of prohibited transactions, and the footnote on page 398 for a definition of disqualified persons.

20. In most instances the foundation will have paid compensation to the foundation manager and perhaps others who fit the definition of a "disqualified person." In that case, the answer to question 10(a) (4) will be "yes" but this transaction is not a prohibited transaction as long as the compensation paid is not unreasonable. A "yes" answer to question 10(b) confirms that this is the case.

21. A foundation is expected to follow a "prudent man" approach to investments. However, this does not preclude a foundation from making "program-related" investments. Typically these investments involve a high element of risk and probably would not meet the "prudent man" test. The distinguishing feature of a program-related investment is that it is made to accomplish the exempt function of the organization and not for the purpose of generating income. In reality, these investments are in the nature of a grant.

22. Effectively, question 14(a) (4) is asking whether the foundation has made a grant to an organization other than a publicly supported organization (see pages 397–400). Where grants are made to other than publicly supported organizations the foundation is required to exercise "expenditure control" to ensure that the grant is actually spent for the charitable purpose within the required time limit. Expert tax counsel should be obtained to ensure that the procedures followed by the foundation to exercise this "expenditure control" are adequate to meet the requirements.

23. See the footnote on page 398 for a definition of "substantial contributor." The only substantial contributors who need be listed in the schedule called for by question 15 are those who became substantial contributors in the current taxable year (1981 in this instance).

24. Capital gains or losses are now subject to an investment income excise tax. This section provides a place to record all sales during the period and to calculate taxable gains.

25. One of the major bookkeeping problems created by the Tax Reform Act of 1969 is that the foundation must determine the donor's basis on all gifts acquired after December 31, 1969, and all prior gifts where the fair market value at December 31, 1969, was less than the donor's tax basis. Gains from the sale of donated property

are based on the donor's original tax basis. As was illustrated in Chapter 25, if the donor's tax basis is very low, the foundation could have a substantial gain and this gain would be subject to the excise tax. The amount in Part VII, column h refers to donor's tax basis for donated securities.

26. The cost basis shown in column h is the cost at which the foundation is carrying this security for purchased securities.

27. The gain or loss in column i would normally be the "book" amount of the gain which the foundation calculates based on the amounts entered in its records. Where this is the case, the total of all the figures shown in this column will be the amount reported on line 7 (column A) on page 1. The major exception to this would be where the security sold had been donated to the foundation (in which case the donor's tax basis—which will be different from the foundation's cost basis—would be reflected in column h).

28. Private foundations are not subject to tax on the gain on securities held prior to December 31, 1969, which had accrued as of December 31, 1969. For computing gain on the sale of securities, the foundation uses the higher of its adjusted basis (column k) or the fair market value on December 31, 1969 (column j).

29. Adjusted basis at December 31, 1969, will probably be the same as cost (column h) in the case of securities and similar assets. However, in the case of depreciable assets the tax basis at that date will reflect depreciation and it is for this reason that this column is provided.

30. The net capital gain is taxable, but if, instead, there is a net loss, this net loss is not deductible from investment income to determine the amount which is taxable.

31. Part IX calculates the "distributable amount" and that calculation requires the minimum investment return calculation in Part VIII. See pages 404–405 for a definition of distributable amount. Note that the minimum investment return calculation is based upon fair market value and not on book value. Also observe that the calculation provides for a *monthly* average. Starting with taxable years beginning after December 31, 1981, the rule for computation of the distributable amount changes (as described on page 404) and lines 1 and 3 of Part IX will no longer be needed.

32. Part X is fairly straightforward. Line 1(b) refers to program-related investments, which are discussed in comment 21 above.

33. Very few foundations will qualify under the caption "Amounts set aside for specific projects which are for charitable, etc., purposes." Foundations wishing to do so should refer to tax counsel for assistance.

34. Part XI (Figure 26–14) is a complex schedule which requires patience on the part of the preparer. The purpose of this schedule is to determine whether the foundation has made the required dis-

tributions for each of the applicable years. Foundations which have distributed the required amounts will find that the amounts shown on lines 6(d), (e), and (f) will be zero.

35. The first step in filling out this Part is to record the distributable amount in line 1. Note that this amount comes directly from Part IX.

36. The next step is to record the excess or deficit distributions for the years 1976–1980 in lines 3(a) through 3(e). These amounts should be extracted from the 1980 return.

37. Of the $854,485 distributed during 1981 (line 4), $219,163 will be allocated on line 4(d) to meet the current year's distribution requirement. The excess distributions for 1981, or $635,322, are shown on line 4(e).

38. Line 6(a) is used to accumulate the excess distributions for 1981 and 1976–1980. Lines 8–10 are used to determine the excess distributions carryover to 1982. Since there is a five-year limitation on carryovers, the 1976 carryover of $109,357 is deducted on line 8, leaving $972,357 for carryover to 1982.

Most of page 7 is filled out only by private operating foundations. The Christiansen Foundation is not a private operating foundation so this page is not illustrated. Page 407–408 discuss the general requirements for being a private operating foundation and the advantages of that status.

39. The attached schedule would be similar to that illustrated in Figure 26–8.

40. Here the form requires an itemized list of "securities and all other assets" held at the close of the year. All assets must be listed, including cash, accounts receivable, securities, and real estate. Because this foundation keeps its investments at market there is no difference between "book" and "market."

41. The notice referred to here is the newspaper notice of availability of Form 990–PF for public inspection.

FORM 990–T—EXEMPT ORGANIZATION BUSINESS INCOME TAX RETURN

Form 990–T must be filled out if an exempt organization has unrelated business income and the gross (not net) income was $1,000 or more. What constitutes unrelated trade or business income was discussed in Chapter 25, pages 408–410, and it was noted that *all* exempt organizations are subject to this tax. Form 990–T is due 4½ months after the end of the fiscal year.

The complete Form 990–T is four pages long, and is complicated. Page 1 and two questions on page 2 must be completed by all filing organizations, but the remainder of page 2 and pages 3 and 4 must be

Form **990-T**	**Exempt Organization Business Income Tax Return** (Under Section 511 of the Internal Revenue Code)	OMB No. 1545-0047
Department of the Treasury Internal Revenue Service	For calendar year 1981 or fiscal year beginning................................, 19 1981, and ending................	**1981**

Name of organization The First Inter-Faith Church of Sprang Valley	**A** Employer identification number (employees' trust see instruction for Block A)
Address (number and street) 632 Main Street	13-1211947
City or town, State, and ZIP code Sprang Valley, New York 10799	**B** Enter unrelated business activity codes from page 11 of instructions 5600 | 5700 |

C Check box if address changed . . . . . . ▶ ☐   **D** Exempt under section . . . . . ▶ 501 (c)(3)

E Check applicable box . . . . ▶ ☒ Corporation   ☐ Trust   ☐ Section 401(a) trust

F Group exemption number (see instructions for Block F) ▶

If the unrelated trade or business gross income is $10,000 or less, complete only page 1, Part III on page 2, and sign the return.
Complete all applicable parts of the form (except lines 1 through 4) if unrelated trade or business gross income is over $10,000.

Taxable Income

1	Unrelated trade or business gross income. (State sources ▶ Thrift Shop (1)) .	1	9,670
2	Deductions (Complete Part II instead of line 2 if you have gross income over $10,000) (2) .	2	4,135
3	Unrelated business taxable income before specific deduction (Subtract line 2 from line 1.) (3)	3	5,535
4	Specific deduction (see instructions for line 4) .	4	1,000
5	Unrelated business taxable income (subtract line 4 from line 3 or enter amount from line 33, page 2) (4)	5	4,535

Organizations Taxable as Corporations (See Instructions for Tax Computation)

6 (a) Are you a member of a controlled group? . . . . ☐ Yes . . . . ☒ No

(b) If Yes, see instructions and enter your share of the $25,000 in each taxable income bracket:

(i) $..........   (ii) $..........   (iii) $..........   (iv) $..........

7 Income tax on amount on line 5, above. Check here ▶ ☐ if alternative tax from Schedule D (Form 1120) is used. (Fiscal year corporations should use the worksheet in the instructions) . . . . . (5) | 7 | 771

Trusts Taxable at Trust Rates (See Instructions for Tax Computation) (6)

8 Tax: Check applicable block and enter on line 8 whichever is less:

(a) ☐ Tax from tax rate schedule ▶................................

Multiply the tax by .9875 and enter the result on line 8, or

(b) ☐ Tax from attached Schedule D (Form 1041) . . . . | 8 |

Total Income Tax

9 (a)	Foreign tax credit (corporations attach Form 1118, trusts attach Form 1116)	9(a)	-0-	
(b)	Investment credit (attach Form 3468)	9(b)	-0-	
(c)	Work incentive (WIN) credit (attach Form 4874)	9(c)	-0-	
(d)	Other credits (see instructions)	9(d)	-0-	
10	Total (add lines 9(a) through (d))		10	-0-
11	Subtract line 10 from line 7 or line 8		11	771
12	Tax from recomputing prior year investment credit (attach Form 4255) . . .		12	-0-
13	Minimum tax on tax preference items (see instructions for line 13)		13	-0-
14	Alternative minimum tax (see instructions for line 14)		14	-0-
15	Total tax (add lines 11 through 14)		15	771
16	Credits and payments: (a) Tax deposited with Form 7004	16(a)	-0-	
(b)	Tax deposited with Form 7005 (attach copy)	16(b)	-0-	
(c)	Foreign organizations—Tax paid or withheld at the source (see instructions) .	16(c)	-0-	
(d)	Credit from regulated investment companies (attach Form 2439)	16(d)	-0-	
(e)	Federal tax on special fuels and oils (attach Form 4136 or 4136-T) . . .	16(e)	-0-	
(f)	Other credits and payments (see instructions)	16(f)	-0-	
(g)	Total credits and payments (add lines 16(a) through 16(f))		16(g)	-0-
17	**TAX DUE** (Subtract line 16(g) from line 15). See instructions for depositary method of payment ▶		17	771
18	**OVERPAYMENT** (subtract line 15 from line 16(g))		18	

Please Sign Here

Under penalties of perjury, I declare that I have examined this return, including accompanying schedules and statements, and to the best of my knowledge and belief, it is true, correct, and complete. Declaration of preparer (other than taxpayer) is based on all information of which preparer has any knowledge.

	5/12/82	▶ Treasurer
Signature of officer	Date	Title

Paid Preparer's Use Only

Preparer's signature ▶	Date	Check if self-employed ▶ ☐	Preparer's social security no.
Firm's name (or yours, if self-employed) ▶ and address		E.I. No. ▶	
		ZIP code ▶	

For Paperwork Reduction Act Notice, see page 1 of instructions.

Fig. 26-16.

completed only for those having unrelated gross income of more than $10,000. Only persons who are familiar with the form should attempt to complete pages 2, 3, and 4.

Page 1—Illustration and Comments

Because of the complicated nature of Form 990–T, the only part of the return which is discussed is the first page. Figure 26–16 shows a completed return for an organization having less than $10,000 of gross income and a very small tax. The circled numbers refer to the comments below.

1. Notice the nature of the unrelated income—the operation of a small thrift shop. While the net income from this activity will be used for exempt purposes, the activity of operating a thrift shop does not directly contribute toward the exempt purposes of the church.
2. In addition to the direct expenses, indirect expenses and overhead (such as heat, light, building costs) can also be deducted to determine taxable income.
3. There is a specific deduction of $1,000 for all exempt organizations.
4. An organization with gross income of $1,000 or more is still required to file Form 990–T even if taxable income after this deduction is zero.
5. The mechanics of computing the tax are complicated because there are five tax rates on ordinary income (15 per cent of the first $25,000, 18 per cent on the next $25,000, 30 per cent of the next $25,000, 40 per cent of the next $25,000, and 46 per cent on all income over $100,000),* as well as alternative taxes if there are capital gains. In addition there are certain other taxes or tax credits such as those relating to tax preferences and investment credits.
6. This section of the form is not applicable to exempt organizations of the type we have been discussing in this book. This is for trusts that are treated as though they were "individuals."

CONCLUSION

All exempt organizations must be aware of the requirements of federal tax laws. All exempt organizations except churches and organizations with gross receipts of $25,000 or less must file tax returns with the Internal Revenue Service, and even churches and very small organizations may have to file returns under certain circumstances. For many, this is

---

* 1983 rates. The amount shown on the illustrated form is calculated using 1981 rates.

a traumatic experience because the principal forms which are used—Form 990, Form 990–PF, and Form 990–T—are written in technical language which requires expert knowledge. With few exceptions, exempt organizations are well advised to obtain competent tax advice not only at the time these returns are prepared, but also throughout the year as potential tax problems arise.

27

State Compliance Requirements

In addition to federal filing requirements, most states also require nonprofit organizations to register with and submit financial reports to one or more agencies of the state government. These requirements usually fall into one or more of three areas:

1. Registration requirements for organizations soliciting funds within the state.
2. Registration of nonprofit organizations (including trusts) holding property in the state.
3. Registration of organizations "doing business" in the state.

These requirements are basically concerned with legal matters and may vary significantly from state to state. If an organization has operations in, or intends to "do business" in, a state, it should consult with its attorneys to get competent advice. The comments that follow in this chapter are intended only as an "overview" of the compliance-reporting requirements as related to the first two areas listed above. It is hoped that this overview will give the reader an indication of the financial reporting and, in some cases, the auditing requirements of various states. Since the laws governing nonprofit organizations' compliance requirements are complex and rapidly changing, the following comments should not in any sense be considered as a substitute for consultations with competent legal and accounting advisors.

REGISTRATION FOR ORGANIZATIONS SOLICITING FUNDS

A number of states have laws requiring nonprofit organizations to register with a regulatory agency (or obtain operating licenses or permits) prior to soliciting any funds within the state. Most states make no distinction between resident and nonresident organizations, and it would appear in most instances that an organization soliciting funds by mail or through advertisements would have to register, even though it has no office or employees in that state.

This registration often requires yearly renewals, as well as a requirement that an annual financial report be filed. Starting in 1982, most states will accept a copy of IRS Form 990 as the basic financial statement. The financial statements included in this report must sometimes include an opinion of an independent public accountant, and in some instances the state will even specify the accounting principles to be followed. Obviously, where an organization must provide this type of information, particularly where the organization is not a resident in that state, considerable planning is required. These annual reports are usually due between three and six months after the end of the organization's fiscal year.

Exemptions

Most states exempt certain classifications of nonprofit organizations from their registration and reporting requirements. These exemptions are usually limited to one or more of the following organizations:

Category 1. Religious organizations

Category 2. Educational institutions, meeting certain standards

Category 3. Nonprofit hospitals

Category 4. Organizations that solicit funds solely from within their existing membership

Category 5. Organizations that solicit funds for the relief of any individual specified by name at the time of solicitation, and all or substantially all of the contributions are turned over to the beneficiary for his or her use

Category 6. Organizations that do not actually raise or receive more than a specified amount, or do not receive contributions from more than a specified number of persons, and where no paid fund raisers are involved, and, in some states, where the organization has no paid staff

(These exemption categories are referred to by number in this chapter's section on individual state requirements.)

Organizations in categories 2 and 3 usually are required to file a copy of the fiscal report filed with other state agencies such as the department of education or health.

There are other types of exemptions as well, and their applicability depends upon a number of factors, including dollar limitations on contributions and/or total income, use of professional fund raisers, etc. For example, in New York nonprofit organizations receiving annual contributions of less than $10,000 are not required to register at all (providing no professional fund raisers are used), although an annual affidavit must be filed. When more than $10,000 in contributions has been received, but before total income exceeds $50,000, a simplified form of reporting is required. When more than $50,000 has been received, a much more detailed, audited report is necessary.

REGISTRATION FOR ORGANIZATIONS HAVING ASSETS WITHIN THE STATE

In addition to the registration of organizations soliciting funds, some states also have laws requiring all nonprofit organizations or charitable trusts to register with a state agency if they have assets or are residents within the state, even if they do not solicit funds. Usually this registration is with the state attorney general. Also, many states require nonprofit corporations to file periodic reports with the Secretary of State. While these requirements are less widespread than laws requiring registration for organizations soliciting funds, each organization must be careful to comply with these requirements. Sometimes a different agency of the state is involved, and the reporting requirements may be different from the requirements under the solicitation law.

As with the requirements for organizations soliciting funds, an organization may be required both to register initially and to file an annual report. The principal interest of the state is the proper administration and disposition of assets held by the organization.

Moreover, the Internal Revenue Code and regulations provide that every private foundation be required to submit a copy of its Form 990–PF to the attorney general of each state in which it conducts activities. The intent of this requirement is to encourage state officials to oversee the activities of at least this type of exempt organization.

INDIVIDUAL STATE REQUIREMENTS

Summarized below are some of the basic requirements of each state with respect to registration and report filing of charitable and nonprofit organizations and trusts. (Exemption reference numbers are keyed to the listing on page 452.) As was noted earlier in this chapter, this summary should not be considered all-inclusive or authoritative; its purpose is simply to provide a brief outline of requirements as of the date of publication. Even as this book was in progress, a number of states had statutes pending which, if adopted, will change existing laws.

Alabama

No known requirements. Legislation is planned for 1983.

Alaska

No known requirements. However, tax-exempt organizations must file a copy of Form 990 with the State Department of Revenue.

Arizona

No known requirements of the State, although the city of Phoenix has a statute regulating charitable solicitations. However, all tax-exempt organizations with gross income in excess of $25,000 must file a return with the Department of Revenue within four months and fifteen days of the end of the fiscal year.

Arkansas

All organizations are required to register with the Secretary of State prior to soliciting funds, except for the following:
1. Categories 1, 4.
2. Category 6, with limitation of $1,000.

An annual report must be filed within 90 days of the end of the fiscal year. Information may be obtained from the Secretary of State, Little Rock.

California

All organizations holding property or having operations in the State are required to register with the Attorney General, except for the following:
1. Categories 1, 2, and 3.
2. Category 6, with limitation of $25,000 gross revenue or total assets. (These organizations must register, but need file an annual report only once every 10 years, unless certain specified events occur.)

An annual report must be filed within four months and fifteen days after the end of the fiscal year. Information may be obtained from the Registry of Charitable Trusts, Sacramento.

In addition, all tax-exempt organizations must file a return with the Franchise Tax Board within four and a half months of the end of the fiscal year.

In addition, most cities or counties in California have statutes regulating charitable solicitations.

Colorado

No known requirements of the state, although the City of Denver as well as other cities have statutes regulating charitable solicitations.

Connecticut

All organizations are required to register annually with the Department of Consumer Protection prior to soliciting funds except for the following:
1. Categories 1, 2, 3, 5.
2. Category 4, with limitation that 80 per cent must come from membership in both number of contributions and dollar amount.

3. Category 6, with limitation of $5,000, and 10 contributors.

4. Various other specified types of entities.

An annual report must be filed within five months after the end of the fiscal year. It must be audited by an independent public accountant if public support is $100,000 or more or if a professional fundraiser is used. Information may be obtained from the Attorney General, Department of Consumer Protection, Hartford.

Delaware

No known requirements.

District of Columbia

All organizations receiving contributions are required to register annually with the Department of Economic Development, except for the following:

1. Categories 1, 2, 4.

2. Category 6, with limitation of $1,500.

3. American Red Cross.

An annual report must be filed at the time of registration and within 30 days after the end of each annual licensing period. Information may be obtained from Business License Branch, Department of Economic Development, Washington, D.C.

Florida

All organizations are required to register annually with the Department of State prior to soliciting funds, except for the following:

1. Category 1.

2. Category 6, with limitation of $4,000 or 10 contributors.

An annual report must be filed within six months of the end of the fiscal year, and it must be audited by an independent certified public accountant if contributions are in excess of $25,000. Information may be obtained from the Department of State, Division of Licensing, Tallahassee.

In addition, the city of St. Petersburg has a statute regulating charitable solicitations.

Georgia

All organizations are required to register with the Secretary of State prior to soliciting funds, except for the following:

1. Categories 1, 2, 4, 5.

2. Category 6, with limitation of $15,000.

3. Various other specified types of entities.

An annual report must be filed within 90 days after the end of the fiscal year, and it must be audited by an independent certified public accountant if contributions are in excess of $50,000. Information may be obtained from the Secretary of State, Atlanta.

In addition, a copy of IRS Form 990 must be filed with the Department of Revenue within four and one half months after the end of the fiscal year.

Hawaii

All organizations are required to register annually with the Director of the Department of Regulatory Agencies prior to soliciting funds, except for the following:

1. Categories 1, 2, 3, 4, 5.
2. Category 6, with limitation of $4,000 or 10 contributors.
3. Various other specified types of entities.

An annual report must be filed at the time of registration. Information may be obtained from the Deputy Attorney General, Honolulu.

Idaho

No known requirements, although the Attorney General is empowered to supervise and examine charitable organizations.

Illinois

All organizations are required to register with the Attorney General prior to soliciting funds, except for the following:

1. Categories 1, 2, 4, 5.
2. Category 6, with limitation of $4,000.
3. Various other specified types of entities.

An annual report must be filed within six months after the end of the fiscal year, and it must be audited by an independent certified public accountant if contributions are in excess of $25,000, or if paid fundraisers are used. Information may be obtained from the Office of the Attorney General, Charitable Trusts and Solicitations Division, Chicago.

In addition, organizations holding assets in excess of $4,000 may be subject to requirements of the Illinois Charitable Trust Act.

Indiana

No known charitable solicitation requirements; however, all tax-exempt organizations must file a return with the Department of Revenue by the fifteenth day of the fifth month following the end of the fiscal year, and not-for-profit corporations must file a report with the Secretary of State by February 28.

Iowa

All organizations are required to register annually with the Secretary of State prior to soliciting funds (except for those soliciting only within their counties of residence).

An annual report must be filed in December of each year. Information may be obtained from the Secretary of State, Des Moines.

Kansas

All organizations are required to register with the Secretary of State prior to soliciting funds, except for the following:

1. Categories 1, 2, 3, 4, 5.
2. Category 6, with limitation of $5,000.
3. Various other specified types of entities.

An annual report must be filed by organizations receiving contributions in excess of $10,000 or which use paid fundraisers, and the report must be audited by an independent certified public accountant if contributions exceed $75,000. Information may be obtained from the Attorney General, Topeka.

Kentucky

Organizations soliciting orders for publications or other printed matter must register annually with the court clerks of the counties in which such solicitations are to occur. Information may be obtained from the Office of the Attorney General, Consumer Protection Division, Frankfort.

Louisiana

All organizations are required to register with the Governor's Consumer Protection Division prior to soliciting funds, except for the following:

1. Categories 1, 2, 3.
2. Voluntary health organizations.

Information may be obtained from the Consumer Protection Division, Baton Rouge.

Maine

All organizations are required to register with the Secretary of State prior to soliciting funds, except for the following:

1. Categories 1, 2, 3, 4, 5.
2. Category 6, with limitation of $10,000 or 10 contributors.

An annual report must be filed within six months after the end of the fiscal year if gross contributions exceed $30,000, and it must be audited by an independent public accountant. Information may be obtained from the Attorney General's Department, Consumer and Antitrust Division, Augusta.

Maryland

All organizations are required to register annually with the Secretary of State prior to soliciting funds, except for the following:

1. Categories 1, 2, 3, 4, 5.
2. Category 6, with limitation of $5,000.
3. Various specified types of entities.

The above exemptions apply only to organizations which do not employ a professional fundraiser or do not mail more than 500,000 solicitations for contributions in a fiscal year. An annual report must be filed within 90 days after the end of the fiscal year, and it must be audited by an independent certified public accountant if gross income is $100,000 or more. Information may be obtained from the Secretary of State, Annapolis.

Massachusetts

All organizations are required to register annually with the Division of Public Charities prior to soliciting funds, except for the following:

1. Categories 1, 2, 3, 4, 5.
2. Category 6, with limitation of $5,000 or 10 contributors.
3. Various other specified types of entities.

An annual report must be filed (by all public charities except Category 1) by June 1 (or within 60 days after the end of fiscal years ending in April or May), and it must be audited if gross receipts are $100,000 or more. Information may be obtained from the Director of Public Charities, Department of the Attorney General, Boston.

Michigan

All organizations are required to register with the Attorney General prior to soliciting funds, except for the following:

1. Categories 1, 2, 3, 4, 5.

2. Category 6, with limitation of $8,000.

3. Various other specified types of entities.

An annual report must be filed each fiscal year, and it must be audited by an independent certified public accountant if contributions are in excess of $50,000. Information may be obtained from the Department of Attorney General, Lansing.

Minnesota

All organizations are required to register annually with the Securities Division, Department of Commerce except for the following:

1. Categories 1, 2, 5.

2. Category 4 (provided no professional fundraiser is engaged).

3. Category 6, with limitation of $10,000.

An annual report must be filed within six months after the end of the fiscal year, unless amounts received are less than $10,000 and no professional fundraiser is engaged. The financial statements included in the report must be audited by a certified public accountant if gross contributions exceed $50,000. Information may be obtained from the Office of the Attorney General, St. Paul.

In addition, a copy of IRS Form 990 must be filed with the Department of Revenue within 10 days after filing with IRS, and with the Department of Commerce within four and one half months of the end of the fiscal year.

Mississippi

No known requirements.

Missouri

All organizations must file an annual registration report by December 31 of the year following solicitation of funds with the Secretary of State, Jefferson City.

Montana

No known requirements.

Nebraska

All organizations are required to register annually with the Secretary of State prior to soliciting funds, except for those organizations soliciting solely within their home county or for "churches and like charitable organizations," in the immediately adjoining counties where part of their membership resides.

An annual financial report must be filed by all voluntary health and welfare organizations within six months after the end of the fiscal year. Information may be obtained from the Secretary of State, Corporation Division, Lincoln.

Nevada

All organizations must file an annual report by July 1 of each fiscal year with the Secretary of State, Carson City. In addition, larger cities and counties require registration prior to soliciting funds.

New Hampshire

All organizations are required to register with the Secretary of State (Division of Welfare) prior to soliciting funds. Certain cities also have statutes regulating charitable solicitations.

An annual report must be filed with the Director of Welfare within four months and fifteen days of the end of the fiscal year. Information may be obtained from the Office of the Attorney General, Consumer Protection Division, Concord.

New Jersey

All organizations are required to register annually with the Attorney General prior to soliciting funds, except for the following:

1. Categories 1, 2, 4, 5.
2. Category 6, with limitation of $10,000.
3. Various other specified types of entities.

An annual report must be filed within six months after the end of the fiscal year, and it must be audited by an independent public accountant if contributions are in excess of $50,000. Information may be obtained from the Office of the Attorney General, Division of Consumer Affairs, Newark.

New Mexico

No known requirements.

New York

All organizations holding property for charitable purposes must register with the Attorney General unless otherwise exempted. The registration form must be filed within six months after any property held or income therefrom is required to be applied to charitable purposes. Information may be obtained from the Office of the Attorney General, World Trade Center, New York City.

In addition, all organizations are required to register with the Department of State prior to soliciting funds, except for the following:

1. Categories 1, 2, 5.
2. Category 4, limited to certain enumerated types of organizations.
3. Category 6, with limitation of $10,000.
4. Various other specified types of entities.

An annual report must be filed within four months and fifteen days after the end of the fiscal year with the Department of State, with a copy to the Attorney General. If total income received is in excess of $50,000, or if paid fundraisers are used, a comprehensive report audited by an independent accountant must be filed. Information may be obtained from the Department of State, Office of Charities Registration, Albany.

North Carolina

All organizations are required to register annually with the Department of Human Resources prior to soliciting funds, except for the following:

1. Categories 1, 2, 3.
2. Category 6, with limitation of $10,000.
3. Public broadcasting stations.

An annual report must be filed with the initial registration and within 120 days after the end of the fiscal year, and it must be audited by an independent public accountant if total support and revenue exceed $250,000. Information may be obtained from the Department of Human Resources, Division of Facility Services, Raleigh.

In addition, all tax-exempt organizations must file a return with the Department of Revenue within four and one half months of the end of the fiscal year.

North Dakota

All organizations are required to register annually with the Secretary of State prior to soliciting funds, except for Categories 1 and 2.

An annual report must be filed within 60 days after the end of the fiscal year. Information may be obtained from the Secretary of State, Bismarck.

In addition, all tax-exempt organizations must file a return with the Tax Commissioner within four and one half months of the end of the fiscal year.

Ohio

All organizations are required to register with the Attorney General (or the county clerks of counties in which solicitations are made) prior to soliciting funds, except for the following:

1. Categories 1, 2, 4, 5.
2. Organizations with annual fundraising expenses of less than $500.

An annual report must be filed with the initial registration and within 90 days after the end of the fiscal year, and it must be audited by an independent public accountant, if gross receipts exceed $10,000. Information may be obtained from the Office of the Attorney General, Charitable Foundations Section, Columbus.

Oklahoma

All organizations are required to register annually with the State Auditor and Inspector prior to soliciting funds, except for Categories 1, 2, 4, and 5, and category 6 with limitation of $10,000.

An annual report must be filed within 90 days after the end of the fiscal year. Information may be obtained from the State Auditor and Inspector, Oklahoma City.

In addition, all tax-exempt organizations must file a return with the Tax Commission within four and one half months of the end of the fiscal year.

Oregon

All organizations are required to register with the Attorney General prior to soliciting funds, except for the following:

1. Categories 1, 2, 3, 4.
2. Various other specified types of entities.

An annual report must be filed within four months and fifteen days after the end of the fiscal year when contributions are in excess of $500. Information may be obtained from the Charitable Trust Section, Department of Justice, Portland.

Pennsylvania

All organizations are required to register annually with the Department of State prior to soliciting funds, except for the following:

1. Categories 1, 2, 3.
2. Various other specified types of entities.

An annual report must be filed with the initial registration and for each fiscal year thereafter, and if gross contributions are over $50,000 the financial statements must be audited by an independent public accountant. If contributions are between $15,000 and $50,000, the financial statements must be reviewed or audited. If contributions are under $15,000 or if the organization is in Categories 4, 5, and 6 (limit $15,000), a short-form registration may be used. Information may be obtained from the Department of State, Commission on Charitable Organizations, Harrisburg.

Rhode Island

All organizations are required to register annually with the Department of Business Regulation prior to soliciting funds, except for the following:

1. Categories 1, 2, 3, 4, 5.
2. Category 6, with limitation of $3,000 or 10 contributors.
3. Various other specified types of entities.

An annual report must be filed within 90 days after the end of the fiscal year, and it must be audited by an independent certified public accountant. Information may be obtained from the Department of Business Regulation, Providence.

South Carolina

All organizations are required to register annually with the Secretary of State prior to soliciting funds, except for the following:

1. Categories 1, 2, 3, 4, 5.
2. Category 6, with limitation of $2,000 or 10 contributors.

An annual report must be filed within six months after the end of the fiscal year. Information may be obtained from the Department of State, Division of Public Charities, Columbia.

South Dakota

All organizations are required to register annually with the Department of Commerce prior to soliciting funds, except for the following:

1. Categories 1, 2, 3, 4, 5.
2. Category 6, with limitation of $2,000 or solicitation of no more than 100 persons in the state.
3. Various other specified types of entities.

An annual report must be filed each fiscal year, and it must be audited by an independent public accountant if contributions exceed $10,000. Information may be obtained from the Division of Commercial Inspection and Regulation, Pierre.

Tennessee

All organizations are required to register annually with the Secretary of State prior to soliciting funds, except for the following:

1. Categories 1, 2.
2. Category 6, with limitation of $5,000.

An annual report must be filed within six months of the end of the fiscal year, and it must be audited by an independent public accountant if gross receipts are in excess of $10,000. Information may be obtained from the Secretary of State's Office, Division of Charitable Solicitation, Nashville.

Texas

There is no requirement that organizations register, but they must maintain detailed accounting records and prepare an annual report conforming to AICPA standards (to be made available for public inspection). Organizations exempted from the requirements of the statute include the following:

1. Categories 1, 2, 4.
2. Category 6, with limitation of $10,000.
3. Various other specified types of entities.

Utah

No known requirements; however, all tax-exempt organizations must file a return with the Tax Commission within three and one half months of the end of the fiscal year.

Vermont

No known requirements; however, a copy of IRS Form 990 must be filed with the Department of Taxation.

Virginia

All organizations are required to register annually with the Department of Agriculture and Consumer Services prior to soliciting funds, except for the following:

1. Categories 2, 3, 4, 5.
2. Category 6, with limitation of $5,000 or 10 contributors.
3. Various other specified types of entities.

An annual report must be filed with the initial registration and before the first day of the fourth month of each fiscal year thereafter. The report must be audited by an independent public accountant. Information may be obtained from the Office of Consumer Affairs, Richmond.

Washington

There are no advance registration requirements. There is a requirement to maintain financial records. The Attorney General or a county prosecutor may require the filing of financial information. Organizations exempted from the requirements are Categories 1, 3, 4, 5, and 6 with limitation of $10,000 or 10 contributors. Information may be obtained from the Division of Professional Licensing, Charities Section/Department of Licensing, Olympia.

West Virginia

All organizations are required to register annually with the Secretary of State prior to soliciting funds, except for the following:

1. Categories 1, 2, 3, 4, 5.
2. Category 6, with limitation of $7,500 or 10 contributors.
3. Various other specified types of entities.

An annual report must be filed each year, and it must be audited by an independent public accountant if contributions are in excess of $50,000. Information may be obtained from the Office of the Secretary of State, Charleston.

Wisconsin

All organizations are required to register with the Department of Regulation and Licensing prior to soliciting funds, except for the following:

1. Categories 1, 2, 3, 4, 5.
2. Category 6, with limitation of $500.
3. Various other specified types of entities.

An annual report must be filed within six months after the end of the fiscal year, and it must be audited by an independent certified public accountant if contributions are in excess of $50,000. Information may be obtained from the Department of the Attorney General, Madison.

Wyoming

No known requirements.

PART VI

SETTING UP AND
KEEPING THE BOOKS

28

Cash Basis Bookkeeping

Bookkeeping is the process of recording in a systematic manner transactions that have taken place. It is that simple. There is nothing mysterious or complicated about bookkeeping. It is simply maintaining records in a manner that will facilitate summarizing them at the end of a period in the form of financial statements. For small cash basis organizations there is little need to know a great deal about accounting theory. Common sense will dictate the records that must be kept. The purpose of this chapter is to discuss bookkeeping in its simplest form—where everything is recorded on a cash basis.°

THREE STEPS IN A BOOKKEEPING SYSTEM

There are basically only three steps involved in any bookkeeping system, whether a simple cash system or a more involved accrual basis system. These are:

1. Recording each transaction in a systematic manner when it occurs. In a simple cash basis system only cash transactions are recorded. This recording could be on the checkbook stub or, for organizations with many transactions, it might be an entry in either the "cash disbursement record" or the "cash receipts record." In accrual basis bookkeeping, transactions not involving cash are also recorded.
2. Summarizing transactions so that all "like" transactions are grouped together. This summarizing can be informally done on a simple columnar worksheet, or it can be more formally handled in a sys-

° Cash basis accounting and financial statements were discussed in Chapters 3 and 10.

tem in which transactions are posted to a formal book called the "general ledger." In either case, the objective is to bring "like" transactions together.

3. Preparing financial statements from the "summary" prepared in step 2. These financial statements can be a simple listing of all the major categories in the summary or they can involve some rearrangement of the figures into a more meaningful presentation. In either case, the financial statements are the end product of the bookkeeping system.

Illustrative Statements

Bookkeeping is truly a matter of common sense. If a little bit of thought is given, almost anyone can devise a simple bookkeeping system that will meet the needs of a small, cash basis organization. The best way to illustrate this is by showing how two organizations keep their records. The first is the Cromwell Hills Swim Club, and the second is All Saints Church. The financial statements of both organizations were illustrated in Chapter 10. The Cromwell Hills Swim Club uses the checkbook system of bookkeeping. All Saints Church uses a somewhat more formal system utilizing a cash receipts book, a cash disbursements book, and a general ledger.

CHECKBOOK SYSTEM

Most people are familiar with the first step in checkbook record keeping since almost everyone keeps a personal checkbook. The process of recording each check and each deposit on the checkbook stub is the first step in a checkbook system of bookkeeping—the step of initially recording the transaction. The checkbook becomes the "book of original entry." Obviously, it is important to write down enough description on the stub to properly identify what the receipt or disbursement was for. In the case of disbursements, there is usually reference to a vendor's invoice or some supporting documents. It is also important to keep track of receipts by noting whose checks are included in each deposit, perhaps using the back of the check stub if there isn't room on the front. Or, alternatively, this information can be put on the copy of the deposit slip which can then be kept with the bank statement or in a separate file.

Since the checkbook becomes the source of all bookkeeping entries, it is important that all receipts be deposited intact and all disburse-

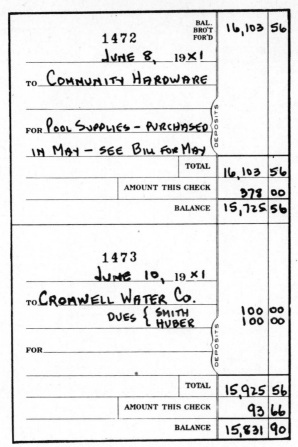

Fig. 28–1.　An example of a checkbook stub.

ments be made by check. This will ensure that a record is established of all transactions. Figure 28–1 shows an example of a checkbook stub.

Worksheet Summary

The second step of summarizing all the transactions for the period is almost as easy. Most organizations use a worksheet which has many columns, one for each major category of income or expense. Figure 28–2 shows a worksheet for the Cromwell Hills Swim Club.

It should be noted that on this worksheet each month's transactions have been summarized from the checkbook stubs and entered in total. Instead, each individual transaction could have been entered on this

Cromwell Swim Club
Worksheet Summarizing Checkbook Stubs By Month
For the Year Ended December 31, 19x1

Month	Deposits				Expenditures						
	Dues	Capital Contributions	Loan from Bank	Interest	Salaries	Payroll Taxes	Mortgage Interest	Mortgage Principal	Pool Supplies	Other Description	Amount
January											
February											
March	1000000	1000000									
April	1200000	4000000									
May	300000			7500						Land	2500000
June			4000000						200000	Pool Const.	3250000
July					542000		20000				3000000
August					158000	41000	20000			Misc.	30000
September					542000		20000			"	40000
October				5000	158000	41000	20000			"	380000
November							20000			"	20000
December							20000	380000		Lawn Furn.	80000
Total	2500000	5000000	4000000	12500	1400000	82000	120000	380000	200000		8968000

Total Deposits 11512500
Total Expenditures 11150000

Reconciliation of Cash

Balance at Beginning of Year	-0-
Total Deposits	11512500
Less: Expenditures	(11150000)
Balance at End of Year	362500

Fig. 28–2. Worksheet summarizing checkbook stubs by month.

worksheet. If this were done the worksheet could have been many pages long, depending on the number of transactions. However, if an organization has many similar transactions in a period, the bookkeeper can probably run an adding machine tape of all like items and enter only the total each month from the checkbook stubs, which would be faster than copying each transaction onto the worksheet. Either approach, or even a combination, is appropriate and is a matter of preference.

Notice the reconciliation of the cash account at the bottom of this worksheet. This is the bookkeeper's proof that a mistake hasn't been made in summarizing the transactions on this worksheet. While this is shown for the entire year, in practice the worksheet would be totaled either every month or every time financial statements were prepared. At that point, the bookkeeper would want to prove the cash position in this manner. This reconciliation should not be confused with the bank reconciliation which should be prepared monthly to prove out the checkbook balance.

Payroll Register

The payroll presents a problem because the club must also keep track of the payroll taxes it has to withhold, and it must pay these amounts plus the employer's share to the government, through the local bank. Figure 28–3 shows a typical payroll register. A payroll register in a form similar to this one can be obtained from many large stationery stores.

Since the club is following cash basis accounting, no attempt is made to record the liability for the unpaid payroll taxes between the date they were "withheld" and the date they were actually paid. In our example, employees are paid their summer wages in two equal installments on July 25 and September 5. Notice on the worksheet in Figure 28–2 that the net payroll of $5,420.00 is shown as the payroll expense in July. The payroll tax deductions of $1,580.00 are not shown since they weren't paid until August. In August when these withheld taxes are paid, the club will also have to pay employer FICA taxes of $410.00. This is also recorded when paid in August.

Unpaid Dues

The club will also need to keep track of which members have paid their dues. This can be handled by simply keeping a list of members and indicating the date "paid" after each member's name when pay-

Cromwell Hills Swim Club

PAYROLL MONTH ENDING JULY, 19X1

	WAGES			EMPLOYEE DEDUCTIONS				
NAME OF EMPLOYEE	REGULAR	OVER-TIME	TOTAL WAGES	F.I.C.A.	FED. WITH. TAX	OTHER WITH.	TOTAL DEDUCT.	NET AMOUNT PAYABLE
Jones, W. (Pool Mgr.)	1000.00	—	1000.00	58.00	170.00	—	228.00	772.00
Smith, J. (Lifeguard)	750.00	—	750.00	44.00	125.00	—	169.00	581.00
Brown, J. ,,	750.00	—	750.00	44.00	125.00	—	169.00	581.00
Samuels, A. ,,	750.00	—	750.00	44.00	125.00	—	169.00	581.00
McNair, S. ,,	750.00	—	750.00	44.00	125.00	—	169.00	581.00
Williams, A. ,,	750.00	—	750.00	44.00	125.00	—	169.00	581.00
Huber, W. ,,	750.00	—	750.00	44.00	125.00	—	169.00	581.00
Miller, C. ,,	750.00	—	750.00	44.00	125.00	—	169.00	581.00
McDonald, W. ,,	750.00	—	750.00	44.00	125.00	—	169.00	581.00
Total	7000.00	—	7000.00	410.00	1170.00	—	1580.00	5420.00

Fig. 28–3.   Payroll Register.

ment is received. This common sense approach should be used with any other type of information that the club must keep.

Financial Statements

The third step in the bookkeeping system is preparing financial statements. They can be prepared directly from the worksheet summary of the checkbook stubs (Figure 28-2). Look at the Statement of Cash Receipts, Disbursements, and Cash Balance . . . shown on page 130. It will be seen that this statement agrees with the totals on this worksheet. This worksheet becomes, in essence, the general ledger. This in conjunction with the checkbook and payroll register would become the "books" of the club.

Advantages and Disadvantages

The checkbook system of record keeping is very satisfactory for many organizations, but it has limitations on the number of transactions it can handle before it becomes more cumbersome than useful. This system has the disadvantage that it is not a recognized or formal system of bookkeeping and while it may work perfectly well for one treasurer, the next treasurer may find it awkward and too informal. Further, the use of worksheets to summarize the period's transactions has the disadvantage that they are just worksheets, and are likely to get lost or destroyed. So when an organization starts to have any volume of financial activity it should start to consider a more conventional and formal set of records.

CASH BASIS SYSTEM

The basic difference between the checkbook system and a more formal cash basis system is that in the latter transactions are recorded and summarized in a more formal manner. Otherwise the bookkeeping process is the same.

Basic Records

In the checkbook system we had only the checkbook stubs, worksheets summarizing transactions, and a payroll register. In a more formal cash basis system we would have the following records:

Cash Disbursement Book—in which each check disbursed is recorded in almost the same manner as on a checkbook stub.

Cash Receipts Book—in which each cash receipt is recorded in almost the same manner as on a checkbook stub.

General Journal—in which noncash transactions are recorded. The principal noncash entry is the entry to close the books at the end of the year.

General Ledger—in which all transactions are summarized.

Trial Balance—which lists all accounts in the general ledger and proves that the total of the "debits" and "credits" in the general ledger is equal.*

Each of these five records is discussed and illustrated below. Before doing so, however, it is necessary to discuss briefly the concept of a "double entry" bookkeeping system and to introduce the terms "debits" and "credits."

---

* Actually the trial balance is not part of the "set of books" as such. Rather it is something prepared from the books. However, since it is important that the trial balance be prepared, it is considered part of the books for this discussion.

Double Entry System

There are five major categories of accounts which a bookkeeping system keeps track of: expense accounts, income accounts, asset accounts, liability accounts, and the net worth or fund balance of the organization. For the moment only the first four will enter into our discussion. The principle of double entry bookkeeping is that every transaction affects two accounts and usually two of these four categories of accounts. For example:

An organization spends $100 to hire a secretary. The two categories affected are assets and expenses. The asset account is the cash balance (it is decreased) and the expense account is payroll expense (it is increased).

An organization receives a contribution of $50. The two accounts affected are contribution income (it is increased) and cash account (it is increased).

An organization spends $10 for stationery supplies. The two accounts affected are stationery supplies expense (it is increased) and cash (it is decreased).

An organization borrows $100 from the bank. The two accounts affected are cash (it is increased) and loans payable (it is increased).

An organization provides Jones with $100 of service which Jones agrees to pay for at the end of next month. The two accounts affected are the income account—sales of services—(it is increased) and accounts receivable from Jones, an asset account (it is increased).

Jones pays the organization the $100 owed. The two accounts affected are cash (it is increased) and accounts receivable (it is decreased).

Thus every transaction affects two accounts. This is why the words "double entry" bookkeeping are used. Each bookkeeping entry must affect two accounts.

Debits and Credits

The words "debit" and "credit" are bookkeeping terms which refer to the two sides of a transaction. Asset accounts and expense accounts normally have debit balances. Liability accounts and income accounts normally have credit balances. To increase an asset or expense account one would add a debit amount (i.e., the account would be "debited");

to increase an income or liability account one would add a credit amount (i.e., the account would be "credited"). Here is a summary which shows these debit and credit rules:

Category of account	To increase you would add a	To decrease you would add a	Balance is normally a
Assets (cash, accounts receivable, inventory, prepaid expenses, fixed assets)	debit	credit	debit
Liabilities (accounts payable, accrued liabilities, bank loans payable, long term debt) ...	credit	debit	credit
Income (contributions, sales, receipts)	credit	debit	credit
Expenses (salaries, supplies, cost of goods sold, taxes)	debit	credit	debit

All that needs to be remembered is that assets and expenses normally are debits and liabilities and income are credits, and that to decrease an account you would reverse the designation. It is also important to remember that there are both debits and credits to every transaction and that in total they must be equal in amount.

Many people are confused by the rule that an asset is a debit. After all, they point out, when you have a credit balance in your account with the local department store this is certainly an asset. How does this reconcile with the rule that an asset normally has a debit balance? The answer is the perspective from which one looks at a transaction. For every borrower there is a lender. On the borrower's books the amount borrowed shows up as a liability (credit balance). When a housewife returns some merchandise and gets credit she is getting credit on the department store's books—they owe her—a liability that is a credit on "their" books. If the housewife kept her own set of books they would show that the department store owed her and this is an asset to her, and would be a debit. So when someone talks about having a credit balance with someone what he is really saying is that on the other person's books he has a credit balance.

Debits on the Left

When there are two columns, the debits are always represented on the left side, and the credits on the right side. The general ledger pages illustrated here use a three-column format—a debit column, a credit column, and a "balance" column. Here is what it looks like:

SHEET NO.						ACCOUNT NO.			
TERMS		NAME	Cash Account						
RATING		ADDRESS							
CREDIT LIMIT									

Date 19 XI		ITEMS	FOL.	✓	DEBITS	CREDITS	BALANCE
Jan	1	Balance beginning of period			100 00		100 00
	31	Receipts for month			300 00		400 00
	31	Expenditures for month				200 00	200 00

This illustrates both the position of debits and credits, and also how, following the rules above, an asset account would be increased or decreased. Notice that since cash is an asset account it would normally have a "debit" balance. Notice that the beginning balance is a debit. The increase in cash from receipts is also a debit. The decrease in cash from expenditures is a reduction of a normally debit account and therefore must be a credit. The final column is merely a running balance to aid the bookkeeper.

Some general ledgers do not have this "balance" column and are set up on a somewhat different format. Here is this same general ledger account in this other form:

SHEET NO.							ACCOUNT NO.			
TERMS				NAME	Cash Account					
RATING				ADDRESS						
CREDIT LIMIT										

Date 19 XI		ITEMS	FOLIO	✓	DEBITS	Date 19 XI		ITEMS	FOLIO	✓	CREDITS
Jan	1	Bal. beginning			100 00	Jan	31	Expenditures			200 00
	31	Receipts			300 00		31	To balance			200 00
		total			400 00			total			400 00
	31	Balance			200 00						

This form of general ledger is a little more difficult for the inexperienced person to work with primarily because a running balance is more difficult to obtain. For this reason, it is not recommended. However, either form is equally acceptable.

That is all you must know about the theory of double entry bookkeeping. The rest follows from these relatively straightforward rules.

Don't try to figure out logically why assets and expenses are debits, or why liability and income accounts are credits. These are the rules by definition.

With the foregoing explanation about double entry bookkeeping, and debits and credits, let us now turn to the set of books that would be kept by an organization that keeps its records on a simple cash basis. The two principal books that will be substituted for the "checkbook stub" are the Cash Disbursements Book and the Cash Receipts Book. As the names indicate, one is for recording cash disbursements and one for recording cash receipts.

Cash Disbursements Book

The cash disbursements book is a book which provides a place to record all disbursements. Usually this is a wide book with ten to fifteen columns, each column of which represents one of the major categories of expense. As each check is written it is recorded in the cash disbursements book. The amount of the check is "posted" * in two places. The first is in the total column which at the end of the month will be "footed" † and then posted to the cash account in the general ledger to reduce the cash balance. The second posting will be in the column showing the category of expense which the disbursement represents. At the end of the month each of these expense category columns is footed to get the total disbursements for that particular category. These totals, in turn, are posted to the general ledger. Normally at the start of each month, a new cash disbursements page is started. Figure 28-4 shows an example of a cash disbursements book for All Saints Church.

Cash Receipts Book

The cash receipts book is very similar to the cash disbursements book and is used in the same manner. It also has a number of columns to provide for direct posting to the appropriate category of income. Figure 28-5 shows an example of a cash receipts book for All Saints Church.

* The word "post" means to record or to transfer an amount from one record to another. In this instance the check is "posted" or recorded initially in the cash disbursements book. At the end of the month the column totals are posted or "transferred" in total to the general ledger.

† Footed means added together. The Appendix discusses the rules for footing and ruling.

All Saints Church
Cash Disbursements Book
January 19x1

Page 1

Date	Payee	Check No.	Total Disbursements	Clergy	Music	Education	Church Office	Building Maint.	Miscellaneous Amount	Description
Jan. 3	Community Lumber	125	3851.6					3851.6		
5	Montana Telephone Co.	126	81.15				81.15			
6	S & S Stationary	127	115.83				115.83			
7	Mrs. Jones	128	100.00		100.00					
7	Ace Piano Repair Co.	129	85.85		85.85					
10	Parish House Publish. Co.	130	500.00		500.00					
11	Bismarck Water Co.	131	23.16						23.16	Water
13	Montana Oil Co.	132	216.15						216.15	Fuel
15	Rev. Williams	133	615.89	615.89						
15	Julian Dennison	134	318.50		318.50					
15	D. D. Bell	135	218.75					218.75		
15	A. J. James	136	419.36				419.36			
17	Miss Smith	137	387.45			387.45				
17	S & S Stationary Co.	138	74.43			74.43				
20	R & R Roofing	139	250.00					250.00		
20	U. S. Post Office	140	150.00				150.00			
20	Bismarck Nat'l Bank	141	235.05	84.11	31.50	37.55	50.64	31.25		
23	Community Leader	142	15.00					15.00		
23	Acme Plumbing Co.	143	39.45					39.45		
23	City Lighting		15.89					15.89		
24	S. S. Stat		12.45				12.45			
28	Ace Piano Repair Co.	173	13.45		13.45					
31	Thompson's Hardware	175	23.00					23.00		
31	Mutual Insurance Co.	176	36.25						36.25	Insurance
			4766.66	950.00	1131.63	518.07	841.83	908.32	41.681	

Fig. 28—4.   A simple cash disbursements book.

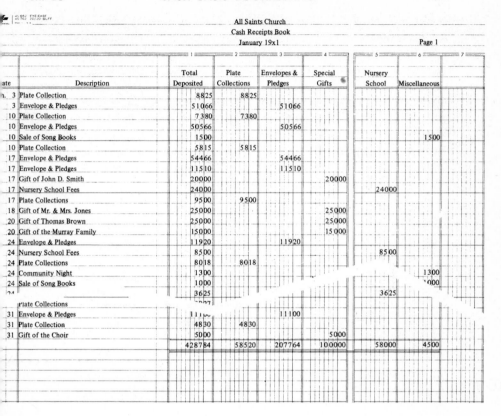

All Saints Church
Cash Receipts Book
January 19x1
Page 1

ate	Description	Total Deposited	Plate Collections	Envelopes & Pledges	Special Gifts	Nursery School	Miscellaneous
n. 3	Plate Collection	88 25	88 25				
3	Envelope & Pledges	510 66		510 66			
10	Plate Collection	73 80	73 80				
10	Envelope & Pledges	505 66		505 66			
10	Sale of Song Books	15 00					15 00
10	Plate Collection	58 15	58 15				
17	Envelope & Pledges	544 66		544 66			
17	Envelope & Pledges	115 10		115 10			
17	Gift of John D. Smith	200 00			200 00		
17	Nursery School Fees	240 00				240 00	
17	Plate Collections	95 00	95 00				
18	Gift of Mr. & Mrs. Jones	250 00			250 00		
20	Gift of Thomas Brown	250 00			250 00		
20	Gift of the Murray Family	150 00			150 00		
24	Envelope & Pledges	119 20		119 20			
24	Nursery School Fees	85 00				85 00	
24	Plate Collections	80 18	80 18				
24	Community Night	13 00					13 00
24	Sale of Song Books	10 00					10 00
24		36 25				36 25	
	Plate Collections						
31	Envelope & Pledges	111 00		111 00			
31	Plate Collection	48 30	48 30				
31	Gift of the Choir	50 00			50 00		
		4287 84	585 20	2077 64	1000 00	580 00	45 00

Fig. 28–5.   A simple cash receipts book.

Notice that there is a miscellaneous column for those items of receipts that do not fit into one of the income categories for which there are columns. At the end of the month the bookkeeper can either post all of these amounts in total to a miscellaneous category of income in the general ledger, or alternatively can analyze this column and then post to individual general ledger accounts based on this analysis. It should be observed that there is a similar column in the cash disbursements book for expenses that do not fall under one of the other categories.

General Journal

There are occasions where an entry must be made that does not involve cash. While this is not often necessary for cash basis organizations, there are times when adjustments must be made or when the books are "closed" at the end of the year. A general journal is merely a separate journal (or even a separate section of the cash receipts or cash disbursements book) in which all noncash entries are made. These entries are made in traditional bookkeeping fashion showing the name of the account being "debited" and the name of the account being "credited," the amounts involved and then some explanation of the purpose of the entry. The general ledger account involved is then posted directly from this general journal entry. Here is an example of a journal entry that is being made to correct a misposting in the previous month's cash disbursements register which had already been posted to the general ledger when the mistake was discovered:

February 28
Entry #1

Debit Education expense $500.00
    Credit Music expense $500.00

> To correct error made in posting to the cash disbursement register in January. Music books purchased for the nursery school were charged to music expense instead of education expense.

Journal entries follow a prescribed format:

1. They are dated and consecutively numbered for identification purposes.
2. The name of the account being debited is entered first and is shown at the left margin. The amount is entered in the left hand column of the two columns. If there is more than one account being debited, all debit entries would be entered before entering the credits. All debit amounts on the page should line up in the same column.
3. The name of the account being credited is indented to the right of the left margin to distinguish it from a debit. The amount is likewise entered in a column to the right of the debit column.
4. A brief narrative explanation is given describing the purpose or reason for the entry.

An example of a general journal entry to close the books at the end of the year is illustrated on page 485. This journal entry has a number of debit and credit amounts within the same entry.

General Ledger

The general ledger is a book or ledger in which all categories of transactions are summarized by specific account. The general ledger will contain a separate page for each of the various asset, liability, income, and expense accounts. Transactions are posted to the general ledger from the cash disbursements and cash receipts books and from the general journal entries at the end of each month. The format of the general ledger account was illustrated on page 478.

The general ledger will also have an account called "fund balance" or "net worth" which will represent the cumulative net worth of the organization. The income and the expense accounts are closed out at the end of each year into this "fund balance" account. This is discussed below. New ledger sheets are started at the beginning of each year.

Trial Balance

A "trial balance" should be taken from the general ledger each month after the cash disbursements book, the cash receipts book, and individual entries from the general journal have been posted to the general ledger. A trial balance is simply a listing of every account in the general ledger along with the balance in each account. The trial balance is shown with the debit balance amounts in one column and the credit balance amounts in the other. Again, the debit column is on the left side, and the credit is on the right side. Here is an example of a trial balance.

ALL SAINTS CHURCH
TRIAL BALANCE
January 31, 19X1

	Debits	Credits
Cash...................................	$3,859.18	
Fund balance (January 1)		$4,300.00
Plate collections		585.20
Nursery school fees		580.00
Envelopes and pledges....................		2,077.64
Special gifts		1,000.00
Other income............................		83.00
Clergy expense..........................	950.00	
Music expense	1,131.63	
Education expense.......................	518.07	
Church office expense	841.83	
Building maintenance	908.32	
Missions	—	
Other expenses	416.81	
Total	$8,625.84	$8,625.84

After the trial balance is prepared, the two columns should be footed. If everything has been posted correctly, the debit and credit columns should be equal. If they are not, it is because an entry has been mis-posted, or perhaps because there is an arithmetical error in arriving at the balance on an individual ledger account.

The trial balance is the bookkeeper's check to make sure that every-thing has been properly posted and summarized. Once it "balances"—that is, the debits and the credits in total are in agreement—the book-keeper can then prepare financial statements directly from the trial balance.

Closing the Books at the End of the Year

One of the bookkeeping chores that can cause a great deal of con-fusion is how to close the books at the end of the year. It is not difficult. Here is the December 31, 19X1, trial balance for All Saints Church before the books are closed.

ALL SAINTS CHURCH
PRECLOSING TRIAL BALANCE
December 31, 19X1

	Debits	Credits
Cash	$ 5,307.00	
Fund balance (January 1)		$ 4,300.00
Plate collections		4,851.00
Envelopes and pledges		30,516.00
Special gifts		5,038.00
Nursery school		5,800.00
Clergy expense	14,325.00	
Music expense	8,610.00	
Education expense	6,850.00	
Church office expense	5,890.00	
Building maintenance	4,205.00	
Missions	2,000.00	
Other expenses	3,318.00	
Total	$50,505.00	$50,505.00

The process of closing the books is simply the transferring of the bal-ances in each of the income and expense accounts to the "fund balance" account. The effect is to transfer the net income into the fund balance. To make the transfer, the debit balance expense accounts must be re-duced to zero by "crediting" them in the same amount. This is done for every expense account. The same process is followed with the income accounts, but since they have a credit balance in them, they are "debited." The difference between the aggregate debits and credits will be the amount of excess of income for the year and would be "credited" to the fund balance account.

While separate entries could be made to accomplish this transfer, usually a single journal entry is prepared. Using the trial balance above, the entry would look like this:

December 31, 19X1

Entry 1

Debit	Plate collections	$ 4,851.00	
"	Envelopes and pledges	30,516.00	
"	Special gifts	5,038.00	
"	Nursery school fees	5,800.00	
Credit	Clergy expense		$14,325.00
"	Music expense		8,610.00
"	Education expense		6,850.00
"	Church office expense		5,890.00
"	Building maintenance		4,205.00
"	Missions		2,000.00
"	Other expenses		3,318.00
"	Fund balance (excess of income over expenses for year)		1,007.00

To close the books for the year 19X1 by closing out all income and all expense accounts into the Fund Balance Account.

Each debit and credit above, once posted, would reduce the income and expense account to zero and the accounts would thus be "closed out." The fund balance account after posting the net income of $1,007.00 would then show a balance of $5,307.00, which is the net worth of the organization at December 31, 19X1, on a cash basis.

Other Records

As with the checkbook system discussed earlier, a payroll register must be kept in order to keep track of employees' gross salaries, deductions, and withholdings. The same type of payroll register used with a checkbook system of bookkeeping should also be used. In addition, there are forms on which to record such items as employees' salaries and deductions, needed to facilitate preparation of the quarterly payroll tax returns and the annual W-2 statement of wages given to each employee for tax purposes. These forms also can be obtained from stationery suppliers.

This chapter has not discussed some of the supporting information which the bookkeeper should maintain, giving details of disbursements and receipts. Some organizations follow the practice of making a "voucher" package for each disbursement and assigning it a consecutive number which is cross-referenced on the cash disbursement register. The voucher would contain the vendor's invoice, receiving reports, or other supporting information to show any interested person why the disbursement was made. Other organizations merely file the paid invoices by vendor name, or in check order sequence. A bank reconciliation must, of course, be prepared promptly upon receipt of the monthly bank statement. The internal controls surrounding bank reconciliations were discussed in Chapter 22.

CONCLUSION

Cash basis bookkeeping is basically a very simple way of keeping records since the only transactions entered into the records are those affecting cash. The principal records in such a system are the records of disbursements and receipts. These records can be informal as in the checkbook system or can be more formal as with the cash receipts and cash disbursements books. What is important is that systematic records be kept and that they be summarized into meaningful classifications. Both the checkbook system and the more formal set of cash basis records presented in this chapter meet these requirements.

29

Simplified Accrual Basis Bookkeeping

Many nonprofit organizations keep their records on a basically cash basis but record accrual entries at the end of each reporting period to convert these records to an accrual basis. These accrual entries are recorded by these organizations because they recognize that their financial statements would be distorted if unpaid bills or uncollected income at the end of the month weren't recorded. At the same time they want to keep their records as simple as possible. They do this by using what is referred to in this chapter as a simplified accrual basis system. It combines much of the simplicity of cash basis bookkeeping and the advantages of accrual basis reporting.

This chapter discusses such a simplified accrual basis system of bookkeeping. This approach will be appropriate for many small or medium-sized organizations that need accrual bookkeeping with a minimum of sophistication.

BOOKS AND RECORDS

The following records constitute a "set" of books under the simplified accrual basis system discussed in this chapter:

Cash Disbursements Book. The same basic format discussed in the previous chapter (Figure 28–4) is used. A separate payroll register is used to record payroll expenses and withholding amounts.

Cash Receipts Book. The format for this book is identical to the one illustrated in Chapter 28 (Fig. 28–5). The number of columns for the various categories of income can be expanded as appropriate.

General Journal. The same format illustrated in Chapter 28 is followed. In this accrual system, a number of general journal entries will be made at the end of each month.

General Ledger. The format illustrated in Chapter 28 is used. However, because of the greater number of general ledger accounts, the account structure is formalized through a "chart of accounts," discussed below.

Payroll Register. The format of this register differs from that illustrated in the previous chapter in that this register now records directly the cash disbursement of payroll tax and withholding obligations. This will be discussed and illustrated in this chapter.

Fixed Asset and Depreciation Ledger. This is a summary of all fixed assets and related depreciation. Fixed assets and depreciation cause some bookkeeping problems; these are also discussed below.

Investments Ledger. This is a summary of all investments.

Similarity to Cash Basis

As can be seen from this summary of the records kept, most were discussed in the previous chapter on cash basis accounting. The simplified accrual system is not much more difficult than the cash basis system. To a large extent the simplified accrual system is the worksheet adjustment approach discussed on pages 20–22. However, in the system discussed in this chapter the adjustments are formally entered in the records.

The handling of cash receipts and disbursements is not discussed in this chapter. The reader should refer to the previous chapter to see the general format of the cash receipts book and the cash disbursements book and the mechanics of their use. In this chapter only the records and procedures not discussed in the previous chapter will be covered.

CHART OF ACCOUNTS

A chart of accounts is a formal listing of all the different accounts being used by the organization. Usually the chart of accounts has numbers assigned to each account to facilitate account identification and to more readily locate the account in the general ledger. Every account in the general ledger is listed in the chart of accounts—all assets, liabilities, income, and expenses. The chart of accounts is an index to facilitate bookkeeping.

Illustrative Example

In Chapter 11 the financial statements of Camp Squa Pan were presented to illustrate simple accrual basis financial statements. The chart of accounts for Camp Squa Pan is shown in Figure 29–1. This is a simple and straightforward chart of accounts. It uses a two-digit number, and each type of account is grouped together. Thus, all assets are shown in numbers 1–30; liabilities in numbers 31–40, and so forth.

CAMP SQUA PAN, INC.
CHART OF ACCOUNTS

Assets (1-30)

1	Cash in bank
3	Petty cash
4	U.S. Treasury bills
5	Marketable securities
7	Accounts receivable from campers—19X3
8	Accounts receivable from campers—19X4
9	Employee accounts receivable
10	Other accounts receivable
11	Prepaid insurance
12	Other current assets
13	Food inventory
15	Land
16	Buildings
17	Furniture and fixtures
18	Automobiles
19	Canoes
20	Other camp equipment
21	Accumulated depreciation—building
22	Accumulated depreciation—furniture and fixtures
23	Accumulated depreciation—automobiles
24	Accumulated depreciation—canoes
25	Accumulated depreciation—other camp equipment

Liabilities (31-40)

31	Accounts payable
32	Accrued salaries payable
33	Withholding and employer taxes payable
34	Accrued expenses
36	Bank loans payable
38	Camp deposits
39	Deferred compensation payable

Fund balances (41-50)

41	Original contribution
42	Retained earnings

Income (51-60)

51	Camp fees
55	Interest income
56	Other income
57	Gain or loss on sale of assets

Expenses (61-99)

61	Salaries—counselors
62	Salaries—food
63	Salaries—camp director
64	Salaries—office
65	Salaries—other
69	Payroll taxes
70	Food
75	Repair and maintenance—buildings
76	Repair and maintenance—automobiles
77	Repair and maintenance—equipment
80	Horse care and feed
90	Insurance
91	Advertising and promotion
92	Depreciation
95	Miscellaneous expenses

Fig. 29–1.   A simple chart of accounts for an accrual basis organization.

Some numbers are skipped within each grouping; for example, account "1" is cash in bank, but there is no account "2." Instead it skips to account "3." The reason for this is to allow for future expansion of the chart of accounts as the organization expands. If Camp Squa Pan opens up a second bank account, account "1" might be for the original bank account and account "2" could then be used for the new bank account.

Notice that there are more accounts in the chart than there are accounts listed on the financial statement. This is so detail can be maintained for internal purposes. There is no reason to burden the reader of the financial statements with more details than are needed since they may detract from an overall understanding of the financial picture.

There is no "magic" way to develop a chart of accounts. The important thing is to sit down and think about the financial statement structure, the accounts which will be shown, and the detailed information that might be desired in the books. Then it is a simple matter to group like accounts together and assign numbers to them. The end product of an accounting system is the financial statements, and if the chart of accounts is properly put together it should be possible to prepare the statements directly from the general ledger without numerous reclassifications.

A chart of accounts can obviously be changed from time to time but it is difficult to make major changes in the middle of the year without creating chaos. New accounts can always be added by assigning the new account a number not previously assigned. Examples of more complex charts of accounts are shown in Chapters 30 and 31.

MONTHLY ACCRUAL ENTRIES

The basic approach to this simplified accrual basis system is to keep all records on the cash basis during the month in the manner discussed in the previous chapter but at the end of the month to make adjustments to record accrual items.* These adjustments are made through general journal entries following the format discussed in the previous chapter. For most small or medium-sized organizations, there will be six to fifteen recurring journal entries each month. The recurring journal entries most commonly recorded are:

1. An entry to record unpaid bills

---

* If financial statements are prepared less frequently than monthly, the accrual entries suggested here would be made only at the end of the period covered by the financial statements.

2. An entry to record unpaid salaries
3. An entry to record uncollected income from the sale of goods or services
4. An entry to record uncollected pledge income
5. An entry to record depreciation expense
6. An entry to record inventory and prepaid expenses

Each of these entries and the mechanics involved in determining the amount of the "accrual" are discussed below. For some organizations, only two or three of these entries will be appropriate. If the amounts involved are not material, no adjustment need be made.

Accrual for Unpaid Bills

An estimate must be made at the end of the month as to the amount of all unpaid bills. This is not difficult to do since most bills from vendors are received around the first of the month. Large expenditures of an unusual nature are usually known well in advance and bills for recurring services such as water, electricity, etc., can normally be estimated. The bookkeeper should gather all of this information together and summarize the total of these unpaid amounts, and the expense accounts to be charged.

The accrual entry itself is straightforward. The expense accounts for the estimated or actual bills should be debited ° and "accounts payable" should be credited for the total. Here is an example using the chart of accounts for Camp Squa Pan.

July 31
Entry No. 1 *

Debit No. 70	Food	$485.00
76	Repairs—automobile	116.89
80	Horse care and feed	259.00
95	Miscellaneous	184.62
17	Furniture and fixtures	250.00
19	Canoes	485.00
20	Other camp equipment	618.46
Credit No. 31	Accounts payable	$2,398.97

To record the liability for unpaid bills at the end of July and to charge the appropriate expense and asset accounts.

* Journal entries can be numbered consecutively from the beginning of the year, from the beginning of the month, or, as here, by individual date. In this instance, if there were six entries dated July 31, they would be numbered from 1 to 6.

° Debits and credits are discussed on pages 476–479.

The bookkeeper will post each of these amounts directly to the general ledger from this journal entry.

Reversal of Accrual. The related problem is how to handle the actual disbursement when the bills are paid. Since the expense account has already been "charged" as a result of this accrual entry, it cannot be charged a second time when the bill is actually paid. To avoid this double charging, the accrual entry is reversed at the beginning of the following month. In this way all bills can then be paid and recorded in the usual manner on the "cash" basis. The effect of these accrual entries and the reversal in the following month is to record the accrual only for financial statement purposes.

To reverse the accrual entry shown above, the entry's debits and credits are reversed. Here is how the reversal entry would look:

August 1
Entry No. 1

Debit No. 31 Accounts payable		$2,398.97
Credit No. 70 Food		$485.00
76 Repairs		116.89
80 Horse care and feed		259.00
95 Miscellaneous		184.62
17 Furniture and fixtures		250.00
19 Canoes		485.00
20 Other camp equipment		618.46

To reverse accrual entry No. 1 set up at July 31.

If at the end of August several of the bills from July are still unpaid, these bills should be added to the new unpaid bills and recorded as an August 31 accrual. During August when paying bills, no distinction is made between bills which were accrued at the end of July and bills which relate only to August.

Here is the general ledger page for account No. 70, Food Expense. It shows both the accrual at the end of each month and the reversal of the accrual at the beginning of the month. Note that actual expenditures for food are posted directly from the cash disbursements book.

In a full accrual system, the organization would use a somewhat different approach which would not require this type of reversal of the accrual entries each month. However, that type of system is more complex. The full accrual system is discussed in Chapter 30.

Accrual for Unpaid Salaries

The easiest way to avoid having to record accruals for unpaid salaries is to pay salaries on the last day of the month. To do this, all employees

Food Expense—Account No. 70

			(Debit)	(Credit)	(Balance)
June	30	Cash disbursements	$ 6,151.00		$ 6,151.00
	30	Accrual of unpaid bills	315.00		6,466.00
	30	To record inventory of food *		$4,000.00	2,466.00
July	1	Reversal of accrual		315.00	2,151.00
	1	Reversal of food inventory	4,000.00		6,151.00
	31	Cash disbursements for July	13,163.00		19,314.00
	31	Accrual of unpaid bills	485.00		19,799.00
	31	To record inventory of food		5,000.00	14,799.00
August	1	Reversal of accrual		485.00	14,314.00
	1	Reversal of food inventory	5,000.00		19,314.00
	31	Cash disbursements for August	10,161.00		29,475.00
	31	Accrual of unpaid bills	1,156.00		30,631.00
	31	To record food inventory		1,000.00	29,631.00

* The entries to record food inventory are discussed below.

would have to be paid on a monthly or semi-monthly payroll basis. This should be done, when practical, to avoid the bookkeeping problem of setting up an accrual. This is not always possible, and where it is not, an accrual entry should be set up at the end of the month for the unpaid portion of salaries.

There is usually no problem in determining the amount of the payroll accrual. By the time the bookkeeper is ready to make this accrual, the payroll covering the last week in the month will probably have been paid and the actual expense known. Unless there were unusual payroll expenses during that period, a simple proration based on the number of workdays is all that is needed. For example, Camp Squa Pan pays its employees every other Monday covering the two weeks ending on that date. The last pay date in July was on the 22nd and the first one in August was on the 5th; therefore 9 days of the 14 days paid on August 5th are applicable to July. If the August 5 payroll totaled $14,000, the 9/14, or $9,000, would be applicable to July and should be recorded in an accrual entry.

The accrual entry that would be made to record this payroll would be:

July 31

Entry No. 2

Debit No. 61 Salaries—counselors $6,000
          62 Salaries—food help 1,000
          63 Salaries—office 1,000
          64 Salaries—other 1,000
  Credit No. 32 Accrued salaries payable $9,000

To record accrued salaries payable at July 31, 9/14 of the August 5 payroll is applicable to July

As with the accrual entry for unpaid bills, this entry should be reversed in August. The August 5th payroll should be recorded in the same manner as any other payroll.

Withholding taxes and the employer's share of payroll taxes are special problems that can cause difficulty. They are discussed on pages 496 to 499.

Accrual for Uncollected Income

The accrual for uncollected income is made in the same manner as the accruals for unpaid bills and salaries. The bookkeeper must accumulate the appropriate information to determine the estimated amount of uncollected income. In the case of Camp Squa Pan, there are always a few campers who sign up for the first two weeks of the camp season but then stay on for additional weeks. The parents are billed for these additional amounts as soon as they decide to let their children stay for additional periods, but there is often a delay before payment is received. At the end of July, there was a total of fifteen campers who had been scheduled to leave on July 15 but had stayed through July 31, and whose fees were still unpaid. Camp fees are $100 a week, so each camper owes $228.57—and a total of $3,428.55 should be recorded as income:

July 31

Entry No. 3

Debit No. 8 Accounts receivable—campers $3,428.55
  Credit No. 51 Camp fees $3,428.55

To record unpaid camp fees at July 31 arising from extended camp periods

This accrual should also be reversed in August, and all receipts from these campers' parents should be handled in the same manner as all other receipts. A formal accounts receivable subsidiary ledger * is not suggested. Instead an informal system should be used keeping a copy of the unpaid bill sent to the parent in a folder until paid. Once paid, the bill should be filed with the paid copies of campers' bills.

Accrual for Pledges

As discussed in Chapter 9, accrual basis organizations should record all significant pledges. Pledges are not applicable to Camp Squa Pan, but if they were, the entry to record the pledge would be made in exactly the same manner as the other accruals discussed above. The accrual would likewise be reversed in the following month, and all payments received on the pledges would be treated as any other contribution.

Accrual To Record Depreciation

If depreciation is a significant expense for the organization, it should be recorded on a monthly basis. If it is not, depreciation can be recorded every six months, or even annually.

The easiest way to determine the amount of depreciation that should be recorded is to calculate the annual amount at the beginning of the year and then divide by twelve to get the amount to record each month.† This method ignores depreciation on fixed asset purchases during the year. Unless purchases or disposals are sizable, they can be ignored on a monthly basis; at the end of the year an adjustment should be made for such items. The calculation of depreciation itself is discussed on pages 499–502.

The accrual entry that should be made monthly would be as follows:

July 31
Entry No. 4

Debit No. 92 Depreciation	....	$6,600
Credit No. 21 Accumulated depreciation—building	....	$1,200
22 Accumulated depreciation—furniture and fixtures	.....	600
23 Accumulated depreciation—automobiles	....	3,000
24 Accumulated depreciation—canoes	....	1,200
25 Accumulated depreciation—other camp equipment	...	600

To record depreciation for the month of July

---

* An accounts receivable subsidiary ledger is discussed in Chapter 30.

† In the case of Camp Squa Pan, depreciation would be recorded over the camp season of two months rather than over twelve months.

This entry, unlike others discussed so far in this chapter, is not reversed in the following month. Instead, depreciation continues to accumulate until such time as it is equal to the cost of the fixed asset, or until the asset is sold. The entries to record the sale of depreciable assets are discussed later in this chapter.

Accrual for Inventory and Prepaid Expenses

Some organizations purchase inventory for resale, part of which may still be on hand at the end of the period. Other organizations prepay certain categories of expenses, such as insurance premiums. The disbursement for these items should be treated as any other category of expense in the cash disbursement book. This means that the full amount is "expensed" at the time it is paid for. At the end of each month, it is necessary to record the amount of any remaining inventory, and the unexpired portion of insurance or similar expense. The entry that should be made would be similar to this:

July 31
Entry No. 5

Debit No. 11 Prepaid insurance	$2,800	
13 Food inventory	5,000	
Credit No. 90 Insurance expense		$2,800
70 Food expense		5,000

To record as an asset prepaid insurance premiums and food inventory at July 31

This entry should be reversed in the following period in the same manner as the other accruals discussed above.

PAYROLL TAXES

Probably the most difficult "accrual" that has to be made for an organization trying to keep its books on a simple accrual basis is the entry to record payroll taxes. In the previous chapter it was recommended that payroll taxes be handled strictly on a cash basis. These taxes were recorded when they were paid and not before, and the amount recorded as salary expense on payday was the net amount of payroll after withholding deductions. At the later date when the withholding and payroll taxes were paid, this additional amount was recorded as salary expense.

This is awkward because most organizations split their payroll into two or more categories of salary expense. If payroll withholding taxes and the employer's share of taxes have to be allocated between salary categories it is easier to do this at the time the payroll is prepared than at the end of the month in an accrual entry, or in the following month when the taxes are actually paid. In the simplified accrual system recommended in this chapter, a separate payroll disbursement register is used which is designed to record this withholding at the time the payroll is paid.

Illustrative Treatment

Figure 29–2 shows an illustration of the payroll register for Camp Squa Pan.

Notice in Figure 29–2 that the amount shown in the salary expense columns for each employee is the full gross amount of salary. The net amount paid after deductions is shown in the net paid column. The withholding taxes are posted in total at the end of the month to the liability account in the general ledger. When such withheld taxes are paid, they are entered as a disbursement in the cash disbursements book with the offset to the withholding tax account. In the cash disbursements book in Chapter 28 (Figure 28–4), the offset (or debit) would be recorded in the miscellaneous column (account No. 33—withholding taxes payable). The total payment of withheld taxes for the month will be posted from the cash disbursement book to the general ledger as an offset to the liability account. At any month end the remaining amount in the liability account should represent the unpaid taxes.

Unlike the payroll register illustrated in Chapter 28 (Figure 28–3), the payroll register in Figure 29–2 is actually used to record the disbursement of the net pay to each employee. Notice that there is a space for the check number to be indicated. At the end of the month the total amount disbursed will be posted to the general ledger cash account.

Employer Taxes.   There is one final problem. In addition to withholding taxes, there are some taxes which are employer taxes. An example is the employer share of FICA taxes. These amounts will be paid at the same time as the withholding taxes are paid and probably as part of the same payment. These employer tax amounts should be recorded at the end of each month in an accrual entry similar to the entry recording unpaid bills. The debit, in this illustration, would be to payroll tax expense (account No. 69) and the credit account would be to taxes payable (account No. 33). This entry should *not* be reversed at the beginning of the following period since when payment is recorded in

Camp Squa Pan
Payroll Disbursement Register
19x4

Date	Payee	Check No. (1)	Net Pay (2)	Counselors (61) (3)	Kitchen (62) (4)	Camp Director (63) (5)	Office (64) (6)	Other (65) (7)	Income (8)	FICA (9)
July 8	John Harris	187	80.00	100.00					15.00	5.00
8	Tom Hannagan	188	80.00	100.00					15.00	5.00
8	Betty Thompson	189	80.00	100.00					15.00	5.00
8	Jim Heary	190	80.00	100.00					15.00	5.00
8	Ken Samuels	191	100.00					125.00	18.75	6.25
8	Tim Bradley	192	60.00		75.00				11.25	3.75
8	Steve McNair	193	240.00			300.00			45.00	15.00
8	Bill Huber	194	100.00				125.00		18.75	6.25
8	Brian Hogan	195	96.00				120.00		18.00	6.00
8	Karl Miller	196	160.00					200.00	30.00	10.00
8	Dave Johnson	197	80.00	100.00					15.00	5.00
8	Adam Smith	198	80.00	100.00					15.00	5.00
8	Elaine Michaels	199	80.00	100.00					15.00	5.00
8	Susan Bradley	200	60.00		75.00				11.25	3.75
8	Bob McDonald	201	96.00				120.00		18.00	6.00
8	Henry Faber	202	144.00	180.00					27.00	9.00
8	Ted Morris	203	100.00	100.00					15.00	5.00
8	Byron Sullivan	204	100.00				125.00		18.75	6.25
8	Brian Collins	205	68.00		85.00				12.75	4.25
8	Al Davidson	206	144.00	180.00					27.00	9.00
8	Steve Kline	207	80.00	100.00					15.00	5.00
8	..h Henderson		..00	100.00	80.00				12.00	4.00
			4116.88.59	37545.00	1480.00	600.00	3602.00	8234.00	77200.44	25711.97
22	Ken Samu..	270	100.00					125.00	18.75	6.25
22	Karl Miller	271	160.00					200.00	30.00	10.00
22	Jim Heary	272	80.00	100.00					15.00	5.00
22	Brian Hogan	273	96.00				120.00		18.00	6.00

Fig. 29–2. A payroll disbursement register.

the cash disbursements book, the "debit" entry will be directly to the taxes payable account as discussed above.

FIXED ASSET REGISTER AND DEPRECIATION SCHEDULE

Every organization, including those on a cash basis, should keep a ledger of fixed assets. As was discussed in Chapter 22, the board has a fiduciary responsibility to effectively control the organization's assets. The first step in controlling fixed assets is to know what assets the organization owns. A fixed asset ledger is merely a listing of these assets in a systematic manner. Figure 29–3 shows an example of the type of ledger that might be kept by a nonprofit organization. The first part records details on the asset itself; the second part records the calculation of depreciation.

A separate page of the fixed asset register is usually kept for each major category of asset. This categorization should follow the general ledger account description. For example, Camp Squa Pan has separate ledger accounts for buildings, furniture and fixtures, automobiles, canoes, and other camp equipment. Thus there would be a separate page for each of these categories.

Every time an asset is acquired it should be entered on this ledger. The total dollar amount shown in this ledger should agree with the general ledger account. Thus at December 31, 19X3, the total of the assets listed in the automobile account will equal $13,456, the amount shown on the Balance Sheet on page 137.

In order to do this, entries must be made in the fixed asset ledger to not only record additions but also to record when an asset is sold or junked. Two entries must be made. The first is to record the date of disposal on the line in this ledger on which the original entry was recorded at the time it was acquired. This will indicate that the asset has been disposed of. The second entry is recorded in the current period to remove the original cost of the asset. To do this, the original cost is shown in the amount column, in parentheses to indicate that it should be subtracted rather than added. In this way the amount column should agree with the general ledger. These two entries can be seen in Figure 29–3 where an automobile is sold.

At the time a fixed asset is acquired, the bookkeeping entry to set the asset up in the general ledger will be made automatically through the cash disbursements book. The account charged in the cash disbursements book will be the asset account, using the miscellaneous column.

The entries to record a sale of fixed assets are discussed below.

Camp Squa Pan

Fixed Asset Ledger—Automobiles

Date Acquired	Description	Tag Serial No.	Location	Cost	Depreciable Life	Date Disposed of
		1	2	3	4	5
(19x3)						
Jan. 1	Balance Forward			875600		
May 16	Ford Pick-up Truck	117611517		420000	5	
July 1	Plymouth Station Wagon	3165171—AE		350000	5	
July 1	Trade-in Ford Purchased in 19x0	G117661		(300000)		6/15/x4
Dec. 31	Balance			1345600		
(19x4)						
June 15	Ford Station Wagon	61875G1		421900	5	
	Trade-in Plymouth Purchased in 19x3	3165171—AE		(350000)		
Dec. 31	Balance			1417500		

Depreciation Schedule—Automobiles (5 Yrs):

Date Acquired	Description	Total Cost	Depreciation by Year						
			19x3	19x4	19x5	19x6	19x7	19x8	19x9
(19x3)									
Jan. 1	Balance Forward	875600	175100	175100	127700	60000	20000		
May 16	Pick-up Truck	420000	42000	84000	84000	84000	84000	42000	
July 1	Plymouth Station Wagon	350000	35000	70000	70000	70000	70000	35000	
July 1	Sale of 19x0 Ford	(300000)	(30000)	(60000)	(30000)	—			
Dec. 31	Balance	1345600	222100	269100	251700	214000	174000	77000	
(19x4)									
June 15	Ford Station Wagon	421900		42190	84380	84380	84380	84380	42190
	Sale of 19x5 Plymouth	(350000)		(70000)	(70000)	(70000)	(70000)	(35000)	
Dec. 31	Balance	1417500	222100	241290	260080	228380	188380	126380	42190

Fig. 29–3. A fixed assets ledger and depreciation schedule.

Depreciation Schedule

The second part of this fixed asset ledger shows depreciation and is used only for accrual basis organizations that capitalize and depreciate fixed assets.° This schedule is used to spread depreciation expense over the depreciable life of an asset using a columnar format. As with the fixed asset ledger, a separate page should be used for each general ledger category of assets, and often, as illustrated here, it is shown on the same page as the fixed asset register.

There are many equally correct methods for calculating depreciation in the year of acquisition. If an organization wants to be accurate to the last penny, depreciation should start in the month the asset is acquired. This degree of accuracy is usually not necessary. A more practical approach that many organizations follow is to assume that all assets are purchased half way through the year and therefore charge one half year's depreciation in the year the asset was acquired. Thus, for the automobile with a five-year life, the first year's depreciation in 19X3 would be $350 ($3,500 ÷ 5 years × $\frac{1}{2}$ year = $350). In 19X4 depreciation would be $700.

Depreciation Spread Year by Year

All acquisitions for the year for each category should be summarized and entered on this schedule at the end of the year.† All assets with the same depreciable life can be summarized and entered as one amount or each asset can be entered separately. The bookkeeper then calculates the amount of depreciation applicable to each future year and enters these amounts in the columns for that year. For example, if an automobile with a five-year life is acquired on July 1, 19X3, for $3,500, $350 depreciation would be shown in the column for 19X3, $700 in each of the columns for 19X4, 19X5, 19X6, and 19X7 and $350 in the column for 19X8. To determine the amount of total depreciation for each year the bookkeeper refers to the total depreciation in each column. In our illustration, depreciation is $2,221.00 for 19X3 and $2,412.90 for 19X4.

An adjustment must also be made to this schedule if the automobile is sold before it has been fully depreciated. Depreciation for future periods must be removed from the appropriate years' columns. This

---

° Depreciation is the subject of Chapter 7.

† If there have been major acquisitions during the year, such as a building, they can be entered during the year to enable the bookkeeper to start depreciating them, as part of the monthly depreciation entry. If no entry is made until the end of the year, the additional depreciation for the current year is recorded at that time.

future depreciation is removed by subtracting it from these columns. Figure 29–3 shows the removal of depreciation on an automobile sold in 19X3 and one sold in 19X4.

Depreciation on Acquisitions During the Year

At the end of the year, the depreciation column for the current year is totaled. As indicated earlier, the amount of depreciation recorded in the monthly accrual entries will normally not be adjusted throughout the year as assets are purchased or sold. Instead, for the sake of simplicity the same amount is used each month. This means that the amount of depreciation actually charged during the year should be compared to the current year's depreciation column in this schedule. An adjustment should be recorded for any difference.

This is less complicated than it seems. It does require that the bookkeeper systematically keep track of acquisitions and disposals. Since purchases of fixed assets are usually not voluminous this should not be too difficult.

Entries for Disposal of Assets

Many bookkeepers have difficulty in preparing the bookkeeping entry to record the sale or disposal of a fixed asset. This entry is not difficult if the objective of the entry is kept in mind: namely, to remove the cost of the fixed asset and to remove the accumulated depreciation. Let's take a typical example of an automobile acquired in 19X0 at a cost of $3,000 with a five-year life. It was sold in July 19X3 for $800.

The biggest problem is to calculate the amount of depreciation that has been taken. In 19X0, the year acquired, one-half year's depreciation was taken, a full year's depreciation in 19X1 and 19X2, and half a year's depreciation through June 30, 19X3 (the asset is sold in July so depreciation has been charged only through June). In total that is three years' depreciation or $1,800 ($3,000 ÷ 5 years = $600 per year × 3 years = $1,800). Here is the entry that records this sale:

July 31
Entry No. 8

Debit No. 10 Accounts receivable	$ 800	
23 Accumulated depreciation—automobile	1,800	
57 Loss on sale	400	
Credit No. 18 Automobiles		$3,000

To record the sale of an auto acquired in 19X0 for $3,000, sold in July for $800, and to remove the accumulated depreciation.

Notice that we have debited accounts receivable for $800, the sales price of the automobile. When the cash is received it will be entered in the cash receipts book and the credit will be to accounts receivable. In this way the cash receipt is recorded in the cash receipts book.

A typical variation on the above entry occurs if instead of receiving cash for the old car, this $800 is allowed as a trade-in value on a car costing $3,500. The organization pays $2,700 and its old car and receives a later model. Here is the journal entry that would be made to record this transaction:

July 31

Entry No. 9

Debit No. 18	Automobile	$ 500	
23	Accumulated depreciation—auto	1,800	
57	Loss on sale	400	
Credit No. 31	Accounts payable		$2,700

> To record purchase of an automobile costing $3,500 and trade-in of old automobile with original cost of $3,000.

Notice that the automobile asset account has been increased by $500, the difference in cost between the two automobiles. Instead the entry might have shown a debit of $3,500 to record the purchase, and a credit of $3,000 to remove the old car. Either would be acceptable since the end result is the same. When the organization makes out its check for $2,700 it will be entered in the cash disbursement book in the same manner as any other disbursement except that the account debited will be accounts payable. This will be shown in the miscellaneous column.

With respect to the old automobile, the bookkeeper must not forget to remove the depreciation for future periods from the depreciation schedule. Notice that depreciation of $300 in 19X3, $600 in 19X4, and $300 in 19X5 has been removed in Figure 29–3. If the auto had been sold three months later, in October instead of July, the amount removed from the 19X3 column would have been $150 instead of $300. This amount is calculated right up to the end of the month prior to sale since the monthly accrual entry has recorded depreciation to that time.

INVESTMENT LEDGER

All organizations must keep a record of the investments they own. Often this record is not formalized and when questions are raised later, the organization has difficulty in providing details. Figure 29–4 shows

The Johanna M. Stannick Foundation
Investment Ledger

Date	Investment Description	1 No. of Shares/Par Value	2 Cert. No.	3 Location of Cert.	4 Cost or FMV at Date Rec'd.	5 Date Sold	6 Sale Proceeds	7 Gain or (Loss)	8 How Acquired	9 Donor's Name & Address	11 FMV at 12/31/69*	12 Donor's Tax Basis
7-14-x3	IBM	100	11734	Daytona Bank	1870000				Gift	J.M. Stannick, Daytona, Fla		2500000
7-14-x3	Polaroid	300	34104	"	3300000	2-13-x4	45755900	1275900	Gift	J.M. Stannick, Daytona, Fla		15000000
7-14-x3	Hercules	1775	10025	"	6072500				Gift	J.M. Stannick, Daytona, Fla		16000000
7-14-x3	Intl. Nickle	2225	21573	"	8185300				Gift	J.M. Stannick, Daytona, Fla		19000000
Total Dec. 31, 19x3					19427800							
2-13-x4	Polaroid	300	34104	Daytona Bank	(3300000)							
2-23-x4	U.S. Steel	935	G8156	"	2524100				Purchase			
Total Dec. 31, 19x4					18651900							

*Required only for securities held on that date.

Fig. 29-4. An investment ledger.

an example of the type of investment ledger that should be kept. The information on this schedule is pretty straightforward, except for information on the tax basis of investments received as gifts. This information is required only with respect to "private foundations" and results from the special tax rules for calculating gains for these organizations.* Other organizations can eliminate these columns.

CONCLUSION

Many organizations will find that the simplified accrual basis system presented here is a practical way to have the advantage of cash basis accounting throughout the period while still recording the necessary adjustments at the end of the period to convert to an accrual basis at that date. The only difficulty with this system is determining the amount of each of these accruals at the end of the period. Nevertheless this is not hard to do if it is done systematically. Most non-bookkeepers can keep books in this fashion if they carefully study and follow the examples shown in this and the previous chapter. Where problems arise that are not discussed, a common sense approach should be used.

* See Chapter 25 for a discussion of these requirements.

30

Full Accrual Basis
Bookkeeping

The simplified accrual system discussed in the previous chapter will meet the needs of many smaller, and even some medium-sized organizations. However, there are many other organizations for which this system is too cumbersome because they have a large number of transactions. For these organizations a "full" accrual system is more appropriate. This chapter discusses such a system and illustrates the principal records that must be kept.

BOOKS AND RECORDS

The following records constitute a "set" of books for an organization using a full accrual basis bookkeeping system. Listed first are the new or revised books or records discussed in this chapter:

Sales Register—this records all sales of goods and services at the time they are made (Figure 30–3).

Accounts Payable Register—this book records all purchases and other obligations at the time the bill or invoice is received from the vendor, rather than at the time paid, as in previous systems (Figure 30–6).

Accounts Receivable Subsidiary Ledger—this book records the details of all amounts that others owe to the organization (Figure 30–4).

Cash Receipts Book—this book changes from that discussed in the previous chapter because much of the information previously recorded in this book is now recorded in the sales register (Figure 30–5).

Cash Disbursements Book—this book changes also from that discussed in previous chapters because much of the information previously recorded in this book is now recorded in the accounts payable register (Figure 30–7).

Chart of Accounts—this chart is more complex than previously illustrated (Figure 30–1).

Next are books or records that were discussed elsewhere:

General ledger (Ch. 28)
General Journal (Ch. 28)
Trial Balance (Ch. 28)
Payroll Register (Ch. 29)
Fixed Asset Register (Ch. 29)
Investment Ledger (Ch. 29)

From this list it can be seen that there are some new "books" not previously discussed. These relate principally to books in which two types of transactions are now recorded at the time they take place rather than at the time cash is involved—the sales register in which all sales are entered and the accounts payable register in which all bills are entered at the time they are received from the vendors. The basic distinction between a full accrual system and the simplified accrual system discussed in the previous chapter is that transactions are recorded at the time they occur rather than at the end of the month in accrual entries. In all other significant respects the two systems are similar.

The reader should refer to the previous two chapters for a description of records discussed earlier and for an explanation of how they tie into a total bookkeeping system. These chapters are cumulative and closely interrelated.

Background for Illustrative Example

The full accrual system can best be illustrated by using a typical organization as an example, and in this chapter we will study some of the procedures followed by The Valley Country Club. The procedures discussed here are applicable to many other types of nonprofit organizations and careful readers will be able to see how the books and procedures illustrated here can be adapted to their own organization.

The Valley Country Club's budgeting problems and financial statements were discussed in some detail on pages 321 to 330 and the reader may want to refer to the financial statements shown on those pages. This club is a typical small-to-medium size club. It has an 18-hole course and an olympic-size swimming pool. The only public building is the clubhouse in which there is a restaurant, a separate bar, and locker rooms. There are several small maintenance buildings.

Members may bring guests to the club but the member must pay a greens fee of $5 and a swimming fee of $2 for each guest. The members pay no fees as this is part of the annual dues. Guests are welcome in the restaurant and bar but they must be accompanied by a member and in all cases the member is billed for the fees and charges incurred by a guest. No cash is handled and the member signs a "charge slip" for each charge incurred. No tips are allowed, since 5 per cent tax and 15 per cent gratuity are added to all charges. The members are billed in the first week of the month for the previous month's charges.

CHART OF ACCOUNTS

Figure 30–1 shows a chart of accounts for The Valley Country Club. This chart of accounts is considerably more complex than the chart shown in Chapter 29. It is complex not only because of the greater number of accounts, but because expenses are kept by type of club activity.

Coding

Look first at the top group of accounts under the major caption, "Expenses." These are the major expense groupings. The subcodes which are immediately below this group are used with each of the major codes. For example, if salaries are to be charged to golf activities the code number would be "410." If salaries are to be charged to the bar then account "710" would be used, and so forth. This type of classification allows the bookkeeper to learn quickly almost all account numbers since only the major group codes and the major subcodes must be learned. There are also a number of specific accounts, mostly involving general and administrative expenses, and these are listed separately.

The income and expense accounts are three-digit codes; the asset and liability accounts are two-digit codes. In this accrual system the code numbers frequently will be used instead of account names. This is one

THE VALLEY COUNTRY CLUB
CHART OF ACCOUNTS

Assets

10 – Cash in bank—main
11 – Cash in bank—payroll
12 – Cash in bank—savings

20 – Members' accounts receivable
21 – Employees' accounts receivable
22 – Other accounts receivable
23 – Allowance for bad debts

32 – Inventories—greens and grounds
35 – Inventories—pool supplies
36 – Inventories—restaurant
37 – Inventories—bar

40 – Prepaid expenses—insurance
41 – Prepaid expenses—taxes
42 – Prepaid expenses—other

50 – Land (original cost)
52 – Greens and grounds improvements
53 – Clubhouse
54 – Golf carts
55 – Swimming pool
56 – Restaurant equipment
57 – Bar equipment
58 – Automotive equipment
59 – Club furniture and fixtures

63 – Accumulated depreciation—clubhouse
64 – Accumulated depreciation—golf carts
65 – Accumulated depreciation—swimming pool
66 – Accumulated depreciation—restaurant and dining room
67 – Accumulated depreciation—bar
68 – Accumulated depreciation—automotive equipment
69 – Accumulated depreciation—club furniture

Liabilities

70 – Accounts payable
73 – Short-term loans payable
74 – Accrued expenses
75 – FICA and withholding taxes payable
76 – Sales taxes
77 – Real estate taxes
78 – Other taxes
79 – Wages payable
80 – Employees' tip fund

85 – Mortgages—long-term
87 – Member bonds due 1990

90 – Contributed capital

95 – Surplus

Income

110 – Initiation fees
111 – Dues—full members
112 – Dues—social members
120 – Golf fees
130 – Locker room fees
140 – Golf cart rentals
150 – Swimming fees
160 – Sales—dining room
170 – Sales—bar
180 – Other
190 – Discounts earned
191 – Interest income
192 – Cash over/short

Expenses

200 – Greens and grounds
300 – Clubhouse
400 – Golf activities
500 – Swimming pool
600 – Restaurant
700 – Bar
900 – Administrative

Subcodes

10 – Salaries
20 – Supplies
30 – Repairs and minor maintenance
40 – Other costs
60 – Depreciation

Specific Accounts

610 – Dining room salaries
611 – Kitchen salaries
620 – Food
720 – Liquor and mixes

911 – Club manager's salary
912 – Secretarial and clerical
913 – Bookkeeping
914 – Janitorial
915 – Other
940 – Interest expense
941 – Auditing and legal
942 – Postage
943 – Telephone
944 – Insurance
945 – Real estate taxes
946 – Income taxes
947 – Pension expense
948 – Electricity
949 – Water
950 – Unemployment insurance
951 – Bad debts
952 – Employer payroll taxes

Fig. 30—1. A chart of accounts for a country club.

505

of the advantages of having a chart of accounts. It cuts down on both the amount of writing and the space involved.

SALES REGISTER

Figure 30–2 shows an example of the charge slip used by The Valley Country Club. Notice that it is prenumbered to ensure that accountability is maintained. Charge slips are prepared for every charge to members.

THE VALLEY COUNTRY CLUB

MEMBER CHARGE SLIP

DESCRIPTION OF CHARGE:

1 Club Sandwich	$ 2.50
1 Ham Sandwich	1.50
1 Steak Sandwich	3.20
3 Coffees	.75

Sub Total	7.95
5% Sales Tax	.40
15% Gratuity	1.19
TOTAL	$ 9.54

Number in Party

Members 1
Guests 2

No. 04002

JUL 1 19X4

Name John Brillon
Member No. 89

Fig. 30–2. An example of a "charge slip" used by a country club.

Comments and Procedure

At the end of each day all of the charge slips are forwarded to the bookkeeper in numerical sequence for each activity or location. The bookkeeper should check the sequence carefully. If some of the charge slips were lost before they were recorded, the club would lose income since there would be no way to know whom to charge, or the amount.

After accounting for the sequence of all charge slips, the bookkeeper enters each charge slip in the sales register. Figure 30–3 shows an example of a sales register. Each charge slip has been entered individually in the sales register in order to establish a permanent record of all charges.* The distribution of the charge, sales tax, and gratuity is shown in the appropriate column.† The account numbers shown at the top of the page are the general ledger account numbers.

At the end of the month all columns are totaled and the totals posted to the general ledger. The total sales column figure is posted to the accounts receivable control account in the general ledger. The other columns are posted to the general ledger account indicated at the top of the column. In order to be sure that all accounts are posted, the bookkeeper puts a check mark ($\checkmark$) beside each column total as it is posted.

ACCOUNTS RECEIVABLE SUBSIDIARY LEDGER

After being posted to the sales register all charge slips should be sorted down by member number and accumulated together during the month. Either at the end of the month, or throughout the month as the

---

* Some clubs do not enter these charge slips individually in the sales register. Instead the bookkeeper using an adding machine runs a recap of the charge slips for each day, by account classification. Then only the total of these charges is entered in the sales register. When this procedure is followed, the charge slips will probably be microfilmed before being sorted by member number. In this way a permanent record is created to support the summary entry in the sales register.

† While in this illustration the sales tax and gratuity amounts have been posted separately for each charge slip, some time could have been saved by entering only the total amount of the member's charge (including the sales tax and gratuity) and the income account distribution. Since both the sales tax and the gratuity amounts are a fixed percentage (5 per cent and 15 per cent) of charges, these amounts can be calculated at the end of the month by multiplying the total of all income accounts by these fixed percentages. In Figure 30–3 the aggregate of the income accounts (accounts 120–180, or $62,505.27) multiplied by these two percentages would give the amounts shown in the sales tax column ($3,125.26) and gratuity column ($9,375.80). These last two columns could then be eliminated.

The Valley Country Club

Sales Register

Date	Member	Member No.	Charge Slip No.	Total Sales	a/c 120	Distribution a/c 130	a/c 140	a/c 150	a/c 160	a/c 170	a/c 180	a/c 76	a/c 80
1981 July 1	Jones	369	108861	960	500	100						40	120
1	Smith	700	108862	960	500	100						40	120
1	McDonald	607	108863	240			200					10	30
1	Stannick	720	87115	240			200	200				10	30
1	Mc Nair	605	87116	240			200	200				10	30
1	Riley	687	87117	240				200				10	30
1	Falvery	340	44400	460								23	69
1	Miller	625	44401	2104					368	1753		88	263
1	Brillon	89	44402	954						795		40	119
1	Brillon	89	22815	4339								180	542
1	Jackson	372	22816	5178					3617	4315		216	647
1	Allen	15	22817	5615						2180		234	701
1	Thompson	760	22818	1152	1000		1500	200	260			48	144
1	Peterson	665	22819	1584	500				1320			66	198
1	Davidson	275	150001	720					600			30	90
1	Kinney	402	150002	3000	1000				1500				375
1	Melon	615	150003	480				200				125	75
1	Howard	360	150004	1200	1000							25	150
				910									
31	Jamison	390	51112			100				210		161	
31	Benjova	81	51113	1987						1655		05	249
31	Williams	905	51114	2280							1900	83	285
31	Shames	701	51115	600					500			95	75
31	Jones	385	51116	1020					850			25	125
31	Harris	353	51117	5580								45	
31	Johnson	390		697								232	697
				7500633	7501117	15,1310	174971	16000	3633901	1500127	24101	312526	937580

Fig. 30–3. A sales register.

508

bookkeeper has time, an accounts receivable ledger card for each member should be posted. Figure 30–4 shows an example of the type of accounts receivable ledger which should be maintained. This accounts receivable ledger should be in duplicate, with one copy sent to the member as a monthly bill. This ledger card can be hand posted, or if the volume is sufficient, a small bookkeeping machine or one-write system ° can be used to post the charge slip to both the sales register and the ledger card simultaneously.

Usually the charge slips are sent to the member with the bill. A few organizations, however, prefer to keep the charge slips as a part of the organization's permanent records and only send the member a copy of the ledger card. They will send a photo copy of the charge slip to the

	THE VALLEY COUNTRY CLUB	MEMBER NAME		
		BRILLON, JOHN		
		MEMBER ADDRESS		
	P.O. BOX 144	2641 ADAMS STREET		
	DAYTONA BEACH, FLORIDA 32017			
			DAYTONA BEACH, FLA.	
	STATEMENT OF MEMBER'S ACCOUNT	MEMBER NUMBER		
		89		

DATE	DESCRIPTION	DEBIT	CREDIT	BALANCE
JUNE 30	BALANCE			345.18
JULY 1	# 4002	9.54		
1	22815	43.39		
3	4079	14.53		
3	23019	24.56		
8	11345	14.00		
8	4107	45.44		
14	4314	33.16		
14	PAYMENT		345.18	
22	# 4516	13.15		
22	23990	43.67		
31	BALANCE			241.44

Fig. 30–4. An individual accounts receivable ledger card.

° A one-write system is a system where through specially designed forms and carbon paper more than one record is prepared simultaneously.

member if there is a question. Obviously there will be fewer questions raised if the charge slip is sent with the bill. Until the Tax Reform Act of 1969 this was largely a matter of preference. But as noted on page 414 the Club must now document certain information for tax purposes. The charge slip is the most logical place to do so, and accordingly, the Club may prefer to keep these slips permanently. One alternative is for the charge slips to be prepared in duplicate or to be microfilmed.

There will be, of course, receipts during the month from the member paying a bill from the previous month. As discussed below, all receipts are entered in the cash receipts book and then posted to the accounts receivable ledger cards.* The individual accounts to be credited can be either posted directly from the cash receipts book or from a "credit advice" slip prepared at the time the receipt is entered in the cash receipts book. If the credit advice slip approach is followed, the slips are sorted and posted in the same manner as the charge slips. Either approach can be used, but it is important to "control" carefully the postings to be sure they are posted to the right account.

Accounts Receivable "Control" Account

The general ledger accounts receivable account becomes the "control" account for all the individual members' accounts. In the sales register in Figure 30–3, the total amount of all charges to the members ($75,006.33) is posted in one amount to the general ledger accounts receivable control account. The same is true with the cash receipts book; $70,001.65 would be posted (Figure 30–5). If no mistakes have been made in posting, the aggregate of the individual ledger card balances should be the same as the balance in this control account after all postings since the sources of the postings are the same. Before mailing the members' monthly bills, all individual bills should be added together to be certain that the total of these bills does agree with this general ledger control account. If there is a large volume of activity, this "balancing," as it is called, can be a major job each month. But it must be done, and the individual accounts should not be sent out until they are in agreement in total.

---

* Some clubs will find it impractical to post receipts individually to the cash receipts book because of the large volume. One alternative is to prepare the deposit slip for the bank with the name of the member shown alongside each check listed. A duplicate copy of the deposit slip could be kept permanently, and only the total of the deposit slip entered in the cash receipts book. The copy of the deposit slip would be the posting source for the credits to each member's accounts.

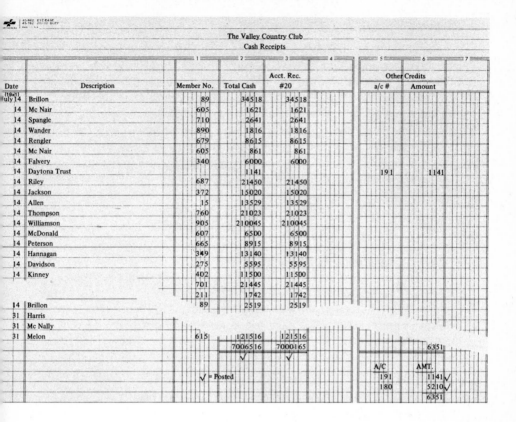

Fig. 30–5.   A Cash Receipts Book.

CASH RECEIPTS BOOK

As indicated above, the cash receipts book is the source of postings for the individual members' receivable accounts. This means that the form of cash receipts book discussed in the previous chapters must change in format. Figure 30–5 shows an example of the new format.

This is a very simple cash receipt register because The Valley Country Club makes sales only to its members, and only on a charge basis. Therefore there are seldom any receipts from sources other than the members. Since all receipts are posted to the members' accounts, the credit entry is usually to accounts receivable. There is an "other" column in this cash receipts book to provide for the occasional receipt from some other source.

Alternate Posting Procedures

As noted above, there are two ways to handle the posting to the members' accounts. The first is to post directly from the cash receipts book to an individual member's ledger card. This is probably the most common method where the volume is not too large. One alternative is to prepare an "advice slip" * at the time the cash receipts book entry is made and use this advice slip as a posting source.† Or, if a book-keeping machine or one-write system is used, the posting to the member's account can be made simultaneously at the time the posting to the cash receipts book is made.

ACCOUNTS PAYABLE REGISTER

An accounts payable register is a book in which all bills are formally recorded at the time they are received. In the process of recording these "payables" the expense classification to be charged is also entered, and this book becomes the primary source of charges to the various general ledger expense accounts. Figure 30–6 shows an example of the first page of an accounts payable register. The actual register could extend across a double page in order to provide enough columns for all major categories of expense. Using a double page would give about 20 columns.

Comments and Procedures

The date of actual payment is not of significance because the bill will show as an account payable until paid. The "date paid" and "check number" columns are provided in this register to show a record of which accounts have been paid, and which have not been paid. If there is no entry in these two spaces, the bill has not been paid and it is still an account payable. This is a control to keep track of the unpaid accounts payable. Each month after all general ledger postings have been made, an adding machine tape should be taken of these unpaid accounts and the total agreed with the amount in the general ledger. If the total does not agree, an error has been made and the bookkeeper

---

* An illustration of a credit advice slip is not shown. However, the format can be very simple. Some organizations even use the envelope in which payment was received as the advice slip, marking the amount of the payment on the envelope. The book-keeper can easily work out the preferred method.

† See the footnote on page 514 describing the use of a duplicate deposit slip as the posting source.

The Valley Country Club
Accounts Payable Register

Date 19x1	Payee	Check No. (1)	Date Paid (2)	Accounts Payable (70) (3)	—220— (4)	Distribution of Expense —320— (5)	—420— (6)	—520— (7)	—620— (8)	—720— (9)	Other Account (10)	Other Amount (11)	(12)
July 3	Allen's Lawn Needs	160	7/20	5 515 10	515 10								
3	All Pro's Invitational	162	7/21	184075			184075						
3	Aquarium Monthly	167	7/24	2500							# 340	2500	
3	Mc Given's Sporting Goods	169	7/26	245530		245530							
3	Best Food Inc.	170	7/26	112513					112513				
3	Jones Meat Market	173	7/26	201040					201040				
5	Ted's Frozen Foods	174	7/26	94630					94630				
5	Brown's Seed Supply	175	7/26	41200	41200								
5	Business Review	177	7/26	2000							# 340	2000	
5	A C Sporting Goods, Inc.	178	7/26	41200		41200							
5	Pickering Pool Supplies	179	7/26	35000				35000					
5	Morton Frozen Goods	181	7/27	85175					85175				
5	Bill's Produce Market	183	7/27	114190					114190				
6	Forrest Lawn Service	184	7/27	9510	9510								
6	Swimming Pool Goods	185	7/27	11575				11575					
6	Ludwig-Lawrence Agency	186	7/27	86150							# 944	86150	
6	A B C Stationery Store	187	7/27	511 74							# 920	511 74	
6	Donovin Bottled Liquors	201	7/27	201539						201539			
6	Cobb, Cole and Bond	226	7/31	100000							# 941	100000	
6	Martin & Ross Liquor Supplies		7/31	114050						114050			
6	The Lawn Goods Good		7/31	18590									
				4317956 ✓	175190 ✓	133236 ✓	559000 ✓	62030 ✓	2416144 ✓	618231 ✓		3544125 ✓	
6													
31	Apex Dry Goods			91 75					9 175				
31	Photo Copy Services			3445							# 915	3445	
31	Ted's Golf Goods			245510		245510							
31	Florida Golf Assoc.			100000			100000						
				4317956 ✓	175190 ✓	133236 ✓	559000 ✓	62030 ✓	2416144 ✓	618231 ✓		3544125 ✓	

Fig. 30—6. An Accounts Payable Register.

should go back and check to be sure that every cash disbursement involving accounts payable has been posted as being paid in the accounts payable register.

Although it is not necessary to do so, most organizations enter all bills in this register, even those they are going to pay the day they receive them. It is easier to record an expense in this register than in the cash disbursement book since the various expense classifications are in columnar form.

At the end of the month the accounts payable register is totaled by column. The total of the accounts payable column is posted to the accounts payable liability account. This liability account will be reduced as disbursements are made, through the cash disbursement book. The various expense account columns should also be posted, and if there are any amounts in the "other" column, they should be analyzed and posted individually.

CASH DISBURSEMENTS BOOK

With all bills being entered in the accounts payable register when received, there is no longer a need to have columns for the various expense categories in the cash disbursements register. In fact, the cash disbursements book becomes a much smaller book with only a few columns. Figure 30–7 shows an example of this book.

Comments and Procedures

Notice that there are two bank account columns. Many organizations have more than one active bank account and this is how the second bank account is handled. The amount of the check disbursed is entered in the appropriate column depending on the bank on which the check is drawn. The offsetting debit is normally accounts payable since all bills are entered in the accounts payable register. A column for this debit to accounts payable is provided. The total of the accounts payable column is posted to the general ledger at the end of the month which serves to reduce the accounts payable amount recorded as an obligation from the accounts payable register.

There is also a column for discounts earned. If payment is made within the time specified on the vendor's invoice for cash discounts, it should be taken. Thus the amount of the check will be less than the amount of the bill, and, therefore, less than the payable set up in the accounts payable register. The discounts earned column would be the

The Valley Country Club
Cash Disbursement Book

		1	2	3	4	5	6	7	8
			Disbursement		Accounts	Discount	Payroll	Other	
Date 19x1	Payee	Check No.	Daytona Bank	National Bank	Payable (Dr)	Earned (Cr)	Taxes (a/c 75)	Account	Amount
	Balance Forwarded from Previous Page		769502	1400375	1789492	4530	39875		3445040
July 26	McGiven's Sporting Goods	169	24530		24530				
26	Best Food Inc.	170		1112513	1112513				
26	Volusia Tax Board	171	348900						348900
26	Thompson's Hardware	172	8593		9045	452		#9045	
26	Jones Meat Market	173		201040	201040				
26	Ted's Frozen Foods	174		94630	94630				
26	Brown's Seed Supply	175	41200		41200				
26	Johnson's Lumber Co.	176	23750		25000	1250			
26	Business Review	177	2000		2000				
26	A C Sporting Goods, Inc.	178	41200		41200				
26	Pickering Pool Supplies	179	35000		35000				
27	Daytona Bank & Trust	180	489571				489571		
27	Morton Frozen Goods	181		85175	85175				
27	Williams Printers	182	7350		7500	150			
27	Bill's Produce Market	183		114190	114190				
27	Forrest Lawn Service	184	9510		9510				
27	Swimming Pool Goods	185	115575		115575				
27	Ludwig-Lawrence Agency	186	861150		861150				
27	A B C Stationery Repair Service	187	511174		511174				
31	Martin & Ross Liquor Supplies	225			...050	50			
31	Thomas Lawn Goods	226	18590		18590				
		227							
			21238849	24879940	3395598	7195	529446		6939440

Fig. 30–7. A Cash Disbursements Book.

place where this discount would be shown. In this way the amount entered in the accounts payable column will be the total amount owed. The "discounts earned" column is a credit or income item. For example, note that the July 26 payment to Thompson Hardware was less a 5 per cent discount of $4.52; but the credit to accounts payable was the total amount of the bill, $90.45.

A column has been provided to record the payment of FICA and withholding taxes. The obligation to pay these withholding taxes is recorded in the payroll register (Figure 29–2), and this column, when posted to the general ledger, serves to reduce the liability.

As with the other books, a column is provided to record transactions not reflected in one of the specific columns. There will be relatively few entries recorded in this column. In our illustration, payment of the sales tax collections in June has been recorded in this column. The actual liability entry setting up the obligation was recorded through the sales register (Figure 30–3).

MONTHLY ACCRUAL ENTRIES

Notwithstanding the use of the various journals and registers discussed above, several entries must still be made on a monthly basis in the general journal. These entries relate principally to adjustment of accounts not involving cash.

Employer Payroll Taxes

The payroll register provides a place to record the amount of withholding and FICA taxes withheld from employees' wages. It does not provide, however, for the recording of the employer's share of such taxes. An accrual entry must be made monthly to record such amounts. The amount of FICA taxes is usually exactly the same amount withheld from employees during the period. At the time the payroll register is totaled at the end of the month, the bookkeeper should note the amount of employee taxes and then make the following entry:

July 31
Entry No. 5

Debit No. 952 Payroll tax expense $2,117.89
    Credit No. 75 FICA and withholding taxes payable $2,117.89

      To record the employer's share of payroll taxes for the month of July.

In this illustration, all of this payroll tax expense was charged to a single account. Some organizations prefer to split this expense among all payroll expense accounts. If this is done, it can either be done monthly at the time the above entry is prepared, or it can be done at the end of the year by analyzing total payroll for the year and allocating the total employer taxes charged to account No. 952.

Depreciation

An entry must still be made monthly to record depreciation expense. The procedures outlined in Chapter 29 should be followed.

Inventories

Inventories can be handled in two ways. The first way, which is probably how it would be handled with The Valley Country Club, is to charge all inventory items to expense as the bills are received, and then to adjust, at the end of the month, for any inventory still on hand. This is the method used with the simplified accrual basis system discussed in Chapter 29. The other approach is to record all inventory purchases as assets (i.e., debit to the inventory asset account and credit to accounts payable) and then periodically to reduce the carrying value of this inventory as it is consumed. The entry for this adjustment would be a debit to expense and a credit to the inventory asset account.

Accrued Salary Payable

There is no automatic procedure to record accrued salary payable even with a full accrual system. Accordingly, an accrual entry must still be made for the portion unpaid at the end of the month. The procedures followed in this type of accrual are exactly as discussed in Chapter 29.

Prepaid Expenses

Insurance premiums, taxes, and similar items should be charged to the appropriate prepaid asset account at the time they are recorded in the accounts payable register. Then, at the end of the period, the portion of this prepaid expense which has expired by virtue of passage of time or usage should be written off to expense in a journal entry. The type of entry to be made would be:

July 31

Entry No. 6

Debit No. 944 Insurance expense $100.00

    Credit No. 40 Prepaid insurance $100.00

    To record as an expense that portion of the prepaid insurance applicable to July.

This type of entry might not be made on a monthly basis if the amounts involved were not large. Often quarterly or even semi-annual entries are all that are necessary.

Reserve for Bad Debts

From time to time a reserve for bad debts will be needed. This type of entry is also handled through the general journal. The entry in the case of The Valley Country Club would be:

July 31

Entry No. 7

Debit No. 951 Bad debts $200.00

    Credit No. 23   Allowance for bad debts $200.00

    To set up an allowance for bad debts for the portion of accounts receivable that are in dispute with estate of deceased member.

An alternative approach is to record the bad debt expense only at the time specific accounts receivable are written off. If this approach were followed, then the credit at the time of write-off would be to accounts receivable (account No. 20) rather than to the allowance account.

CONCLUSION

The two principal books that allow an organization to record certain transactions on an accrual basis are the sales register and the accounts payable register. Both have as their intent the recording of transactions as they occur rather than when cash is involved. As with the other records discussed in earlier chapters, they are basically common-sense types of records which are designed to record transactions in a systematic manner so as to allow like transactions to be grouped together.

31

Fund Accounting Bookkeeping

There is only one important difference between fund accounting and the other accounting methods used by nonprofit organizations. In fund accounting a number of separate accounting entities are maintained which are referred to as "funds." A fund accounting system presents no special difficulty, except for the problem of keeping the transactions of these funds separated while integrating all of the funds into a total bookkeeping system. An organization using fund accounting can be on the cash basis, a simplified accrual basis, or a full accrual basis. The same types of records discussed in the three previous chapters can be used in fund accounting. This chapter will discuss only the problems related to fund accounting.

For purposes of discussion an accrual basis research institute will be used as an illustration. The J. W. M. Diabetes Research Institute was discussed and financial statements were presented in Chapter 12 (Figures 12-6 to 12-11) and the reader may find it helpful to refer back to these statements. This organization uses fund accounting and has five fund "groupings" *—unrestricted general fund, unrestricted investment fund, fund for specified purposes, plant fund, and endowment fund. For purposes of reporting, the plant fund is combined with the unrestricted general fund.

---

* The reader should be careful to distinguish between a fund "grouping" and an individual fund. A fund "grouping" is all of the individual funds having similar characteristics, whereas a "fund" is an individual entity being accounted for as a separate unit. Another expression used in this chapter is "name" fund. A "name" fund is a fund that bears a name, usually of the principal donor. There may be other funds, with identical restrictions but the separate identification by "name" is maintained for any one of a number of reasons. These concepts were discussed in Chapter 4.

CHART OF ACCOUNTS

The key to a good bookkeeping system is a carefully thought out chart of accounts. This is especially true when fund accounting is used because there are a number of completely separate accounting entities each of which has its own accounts for assets, liabilities, income, expense, and fund balances. Yet these separate entities must be integrated carefully into an overall chart of accounts. Each fund grouping must have an account structure similar to the other groupings, both for ease in keeping the records and for ease in preparing financial statements.

Figure 31–1 shows the chart of accounts for The J. W. M. Diabetes Research Institute. This chart is basically a three-digit system with the first digit designating the fund grouping. These fund groupings are shown at the left-hand top column on the chart. All asset, liability, income, and expense codes are two-digit codes and are the second and third digits in the three-digit account code. These two-digit codes are used with the fund grouping code to designate the specific fund grouping they belong to. For example, code 107 is "unrestricted general fund marketable securities" while 507 is "endowment fund marketable securities."

Expense groupings are also used in a similar manner. There are four expense groups (instruction, research, administration, and maintenance). For each of these groups there are six single-digit expense codes and they are the third digit from the left. For example, "0" is salaries. Code 60 is "instruction salaries" while code 90 is "maintenance salaries." In addition to these codes there are a few other specific codes that are not applicable to these four major expense groups and they are listed separately.

One of the features of this chart of accounts is that it facilitates the preparation of financial statements in columnar format or, if desired, in a consolidated format. All similar items are coded with the same last two digits and this can be a time saver for the bookkeeper.

Interfund Accounts

In fund accounting, there are frequently interfund receivables and payables. In this chart of accounts all of these interfund balances are shown in five accounts for each fund grouping. The only distinction between a receivable or a payable with a particular fund is whether it is a debit (receivable) or a credit (payable). For example, if the unrestricted general fund owes the unrestricted investment fund $100, the unrestricted general fund would show a credit of $100 in account 142;

J. W. M. DIABETES RESEARCH INSTITUTE
CHART OF ACCOUNTS

Fund Grouping

100	Unrestricted general fund
200	Unrestricted investment fund
300	Fund for specified purposes
400	Plant fund
500	Endowment fund

Assets

01	Cash in bank
02	Cash in savings bank
03	Petty cash
05	U.S. treasury bills
06	Marketable bonds
07	Marketable securities
08	Investment real estate
09	Other investments
10	Contracts receivable—current year
11	Contracts receivable—prior year
12	Other receivables
13	Inventory—books
14	Inventory—supplies
15	Prepaid expenses
18	Land
19	Buildings
20	Accumulated depreciation—building
21	Equipment
22	Accumulated depreciation—equipment
23	Vehicles
24	Accumulated depreciation—vehicles

Liabilities

30	Accounts payable
31	Short-term loans
32	Payroll taxes
33	Salaries payable
34	Grants paid in advance
35	Other short-term liabilities
36	Long-term debts
38	Long-term pledges deferred

Interfund Receivables (Payables)

41	Unrestricted general fund
42	Unrestricted investment fund
43	Fund for specified purposes
44	Plant fund
45	Endowment fund

Fund Balances

46	Unrestricted
47	Unrestricted—allocated
48	Restricted

Income

50	Grant and contract income
51	Other fees
55	Contributions and gifts
57	Investment income
58	Interest income
59	Realized gains or losses

Expense Groups

6—	Instruction
7—	Research
8—	Administration
9—	Maintenance

Type Expense

—0	Salaries
—1	Retirement benefits
—2	Major medical
—3	Stationery and supplies
—4	Books
—5	Other

Specific Codes

86	Insurance
87	Bad debts
88	Depreciation
89	Legal and accounting and investment fees
97	Contracted services
98	Utilities and fuel

Fig. 31–1. A chart of accounts for a research institute that uses fund accounting.

the unrestricted investment fund would show a debit balance in account 241. Notice the account numbers "142" and "241." The first digit designates the fund in which the account belongs ("1" = unrestricted general fund, "2" = unrestricted investment fund), and the third digit designates the fund which either is owed, or owes, the $100. In the first instance, the "2" designates the unrestricted investment fund. In the other, the "1" designates the unrestricted general fund.

Likewise if the endowment fund owed $50 to the unrestricted general fund and $10 to the fund for specified purposes, the respective fund groupings would look like this in a columnar format:

Unrestricted General Fund		Fund for Specified Purpose		Endowment Fund		Total All Funds
145	$50			541	($50) credit	—
		345	$10	543	(10) credit	—

As can be seen, if all interfund receivables and payables are shown in columnar form in this fashion, the "total all funds" column will net out to zero.

"Name" Funds

No separate listing is shown for the various name funds within the fund for specified purposes or in the endowment fund. As can be seen from Figure 12–8, The J. W. M. Diabetes Research Institute has many such funds.

If there are only one or two name funds, probably no separate set of account numbers need be assigned. There are not usually many transactions in each such fund and it will be easier to analyze each name fund separately once or twice a year than to keep a separate set of accounts for each. But if there are many name funds, as is the case here, or if the bookkeeping is done on a bookkeeping machine where account numbers are really needed to facilitate posting, then a further account-number structure should be set up. The easiest way is to assign one more, or even two more, digits to the three-digit code to designate the specific fund involved. These would be the fourth or fifth digits reading from the left. Thus marketable securities in the Malmar endowment fund might be shown as code 507–1: the 507 being the code number for endowment fund marketable securities, and the "1" being the code number assigned to the Malmar Fund. There would be a complete balancing set of accounts maintained for this subcode "1." If more than ten such name funds were used then a second digit would be added (507–11).

The same procedure would be followed with the fund for specified purposes. In this way the organization can have any number of name funds all within the same chart of account structure.

BOOKS AND RECORDS

The books and records used by fund accounting organizations are basically the same records discussed in Chapters 28 to 30. A completely separate set of books is often maintained for each fund grouping rather than trying to integrate all of the fund groupings into a single set of books. With a separate set of books the unrestricted general fund would have its own cash receipts book, cash disbursement book, accounts payable register, general ledger, general journal, grant income ledger, etc. Each of the other fund groupings would also have its separate set of books, although not all of the books would be appropriate for each grouping. In the case of The J. W. M. Diabetes Research Institute, separate books are kept for each fund grouping, as shown below.

Even where a fund grouping requires one of these books, the actual format of the book may be much simpler than the format used by the unrestricted general fund. For example, the number of expense categories and volume of transactions applicable to the fund for specified purposes are relatively few, and the cash disbursement book may have only a debit and credit column with each expenditure being posted individually to the general ledger. In fact, if there are only a few cash transactions during the year, the cash receipts book and cash disbursements book may not be used at all. All entries, including cash entries, would then be entered in the general journal and posted directly and individually to the general ledger accounts.

Book	Unrestricted General Fund	Unrestricted Investment Fund	Fund for Specified Purposes	Plant Fund	Endowment Fund
General ledger ...	x	x	x	x	x
General journal ..	x	x	x	x	x
Cash disbursement.	x		x		
Cash receipts	x		x		
Accounts payable register	x				
Tuition income ledger	x				
Payroll register ...	x				
Investment ledger .	x	x			x
Fixed asset register	x			x	

The plant fund may or may not include assets other than plant or fixed assets. If the board places donor-restricted gifts for plant additions into the fund for specified purposes then only fixed assets would be shown in the plant fund. This type of decision, of course, affects the books that must be kept. In the case of our illustration, only fixed assets are shown in the plant fund.

Books of "Name" Funds

Each individual name fund within each fund grouping will also require separate records but these records will consist only of a set of general ledger pages for the accounts maintained for each name fund. For example, if the fund for specified purposes has two name funds, each with an opening fund balance represented by cash in a savings account and each having contributions and expenses during the year, then the general ledger accounts would be as follows:

	Name Fund No. 1	Name Fund No. 2
Savings cash	302—1	302—2
Fund balance	348—1	348—2
Contributions	355—1	355—2
Interest	358—1	358—2
Expenses	3---1	3---2

These general ledger accounts would be filed in account number order rather than being segregated by each of the name funds. When a trial balance of the general ledger of the entire fund grouping is needed, the bookkeeper will take a trial balance of the individual general ledger accounts for all of the name funds. For purposes of statement presentation these name accounts would be combined to get the figures for the fund grouping as a whole. Figure 31–2 shows an example of a combining worksheet for the endowment fund grouping. Notice how these figures tie into the financial statements in Chapter 12.

Single Set of Books

There is no reason why an organization cannot merge all of the fund groupings into one overall set of books in much the same manner discussed for the name funds above. The chart of accounts is arranged to permit this. If all accounts were combined, the general ledger would be fairly sizable but then it would only be necessary to keep one general journal, one cash disbursement book, one cash receipts book, etc.

J. W. M. DIABETES RESEARCH INSTITUTE

PRECLOSING WORKSHEET COMBINING NAME ENDOWMENT FUNDS
June 30, 19X1

Sub-Code		01/02	06/07	41/45	48	55	57/58	59	61/99
					Accounts				
-1	The Malmar Fund	$ 4,000	$ 108,655	($ 4,970)	($ 110,700)		($4,970)	$ 3,015	$ 4,970
-2	Clyde Henderson Fund		34,916		(25,601)		(1,150)	(8,165)	
-3	Evelyn I. Marnoch Fund		9,205		(10,871)		(490)	2,156	
-4	Roy B. Cowin Memorial Fund	4,496	1,850,173		(1,641,300)			(213,369)	
-5	Lillian V. Fromhagen Fund		60,076		(53,165)			(6,911)	
-6	Donna Comstock Fund		47,974		(28,160)	($ 16,153)		(3,661)	
-7	Josephine Zagajewski Fund		100,000			(100,000)			
-8	The Peter Baker Fund		20,081		(12,150)	(6,351)		(1,580)	
-9	The Alfred P. Koch Fund	7,119		(7,119)	(6,300)			(819)	7,119
	Total	$15,615	$2,231,080	($12,089)	($1,888,247)	($122,504)	($6,610)	($229,334)	$12,089

Net Assets $2,234,606

Fund balance after closing . . . . . ($2,234,606)

Fig. 31–2. An example of a preclosing worksheet in which individual "name" endowment funds are combined. For financial statement purposes, only the totals would be reported.

The principal advantage of a single set of books is that there is only one set of records, and this facilitates bookkeeping, particularly if the organization has enough volume to handle its bookkeeping on a book-keeping machine or some other form of mechanized system. With almost any type of mechanization, it is simpler to have one complex general ledger system than to have many separate general ledgers.

The principal disadvantage is that it is far easier to keep all transactions relating to one fund grouping together in a separate set of records. The bookkeeper is less likely to get confused and will be able to see what is happening more easily when separate books are used for each fund grouping. Accordingly, except when records are handled on some sort of mechanized system or where the organization has an especially competent bookkeeping staff, it is probably better to stick with a separate set of records for each fund grouping.

INTERFUND TRANSACTIONS

If all transactions involved a single fund, and there were no transactions between funds or fund groupings, the bookkeeping problems of fund accounting would be relatively easy. Unfortunately, these interfund transactions often cause more difficulty than they should partly because the bookkeeper is uncertain how to record such transactions. There are a number of fairly common interfund transactions, and each of these is discussed and illustrated in the following paragraphs.

Investment Income Transfer

The transfer of investment income from one fund to another is very common. Typically, investment income earned on an endowment fund is deposited by the custodian bank in an endowment fund income cash account. Then, from time to time the bookkeeper will transfer portions of this cash to the unrestricted general fund and if any of the income is restricted to a specified use, to the fund for specified purposes. Here are the journal entries that would be made if the endowment fund earned $250 of income, $200 of which is unrestricted and $50 is restricted for a specified purpose:

On endowment fund books:

Debit No. 501 (cash) $250
    Credit No. 557 (investment income) $250
      To record receipt of investment income.

Debit No. 557 (investment income) $250
　　Credit No. 541 (payable to unrestricted general fund) $200
　　Credit No. 543 (payable to fund for specified purposes) 50
　　　　To record transfer of investment income to unrestricted general fund
　　　　and fund for specified purposes.

On unrestricted general fund books:

Debit No. 145 (receivable from endowment fund) $200
　　Credit No. 157 (investment income) $200
　　　　To record transfer of investment income from endowment fund.

On fund for specified purposes books:

Debit No. 345 (receivable from endowment fund) .... $ 50
　　Credit No. 357 (investment income) .... $ 50
　　　　To record transfer of investment income from the endowment fund.

In due course when the cash is actually transferred from the endowment fund, the entry on the various books would be a debit or credit to cash and a corresponding debit or credit to the interfund payable or receivable account.

Interfund Borrowings

Another frequent interfund transaction is the temporary borrowing of cash by one fund from another fund. Here are the entries to record the unrestricted general fund's borrowing of $10,000 from the unrestricted investment fund.

On unrestricted general fund books:

Debit No. 101 (Cash) $10,000
　　Credit No. 142 (payable to unrestricted investment fund) $10,000
　　　　To record interfund loan from the unrestricted investment fund.

On unrestricted investment fund books:

Debit No. 241 (receivable from unrestricted general fund) $10,000
　　Credit No. 201 (cash) $10,000
　　　　To record interfund loan to the unrestricted general fund.

When this loan is paid off, the entries would be reversed.

Expenses Paid by One Fund for Another

The unrestricted general fund may pay expenses which are chargeable to another fund. A common example is payment of expenses out of the unrestricted general fund which are to be charged to the fund for specified purposes.

In the following example the unrestricted general fund paid $200 for library books, $75 of which can be charged to the fund for specified purposes. Here are the appropriate entries:

On unrestricted general fund books:

```
Debit No. 143 (receivable from fund for specified purposes) .......... $ 75
Debit No. 174 (library books) .................................   125
    Credit No. 130 (accounts payable) .................................   $200
        To record amount of library books purchased by unrestricted general
        fund, part of which is to be paid for by fund for specified purposes.
```

On fund for specified purposes books:

```
Debit No. 374 (library books) ................................... $ 75
    Credit No. 341 (payable to unrestricted general fund) ................. $ 75
        To record purchase of library books by the unrestricted general fund,
        out of the fund for specified purposes.
```

Contributions Transferred to Unrestricted Investment Fund

All contributions not restricted by donors must be shown in the unrestricted general fund. However, if the board wishes, it can always make transfers out of the unrestricted general fund into the unrestricted investment fund. The contribution must be reported first as income in the unrestricted general fund, so any transfer is effectively a transfer of a portion of the fund balance. Here are the entries that would be made to record a gift of $750 and the subsequent transfer to the unrestricted investment fund:

On unrestricted general fund books:

```
Debit No. 101 (cash) ......................................... $750
    Credit No. 155 (contributions) ...................................   $750
        To record receipt of an unrestricted contribution from Linda Jean Baker.
```

```
Debit No. 146 (unrestricted fund balance) ......................... $750
    Credit No. 142 (payable to unrestricted investment fund) ............... $750
        To record transfer to unrestricted investment fund of portion of unre-
        stricted general fund balance arising from gift of Linda Jean Baker
```

On unrestricted investment fund books:

Debit No. 241 (receivable from unrestricted general fund) $750
    Credit No. 246 (unrestricted fund balance) $750
        To record transfer from unrestricted general fund of portion of unre-
        stricted general fund balance arising from gift of Linda Jean Baker.

Several things should be noted about this entry. First, note that in the unrestricted general fund the transfer was out of the fund balance account and not out of the contributions received account. The gift of $750 must be reported as part of unrestricted general fund income, and accordingly the transfer cannot come from the contribution account. Second, note that in the unrestricted investment fund the $750 receipt was shown not as a contribution but, again, as a fund balance transfer. This is the important thing to remember about transfers. They don't create income; all they do is transfer portions of the fund balance or net worth from one fund to another. Transfers are discussed at length in Chapter 5.

Current Restricted Funds Expended Through the Unrestricted General Fund

A related type of transaction between funds takes place with those organizations following the accounting principle of placing all restricted contributions in a current restricted fund (the name often given to the fund for specified purposes) and then transferring to the unrestricted general fund such portion of these restricted contributions as is actually expended by the unrestricted general fund. This is the method recommended by a number of organizations for handling restricted contributions for current purposes.* Basically the entries to effect this transfer are quite straightforward. Assume $600 is received in the current year but only $500 is expended for the restricted purpose.

On fund for specified purposes books:

Debit No. 301 (cash) $600
    Credit No. 355 (contributions) $600
        To record receipt of $600 restricted contributions.

---

* See pages 100 to 107 for a complete discussion of alternative reporting practices for current restricted contributions. In addition, the application of this principle to hospitals is discussed at page 244.

Debit No. 355 (contributions) $500
    Credit No. 341 (interfund payable) $500
      To record transfer to the unrestricted general fund of a portion of restricted contributions for current operations that were expended during the year.

This entry appears more straightforward than it would actually be in practice because the mechanics of presentation recommended for handling current restricted contributions in this manner also provide that the initial receipt of the contribution ($600) be shown in a Statement of Fund Balances rather than in an Income Statement. Readers interested in more details on the presentation should refer to the pages indicated. In any event the entries above will accomplish the correct end objective of this transfer.

Allocation of Unrestricted Fund Balances

Allocations, or as they are often known, "appropriations," of part of the unrestricted general fund balance are occasionally made by the board. While the use of allocations is not recommended because they are seldom understood by the reader, some organizations still use this bookkeeping technique to segregate portions of the unrestricted general fund balance for future projects. This is an acceptable practice only if the rules outlined on pages 51 and 52 are followed. When the rules are followed, the entry that would be made to effect an allocation would be:

Debit No. 146 (unrestricted general fund balance) $1,000
    Credit No. 147 (unrestricted general fund balance—allocated $1,000
      To record an allocation of the unrestricted general fund balance for Project A.

Note that this entry merely transfers a portion of the unrestricted general fund balance to another unrestricted general fund balance. No income or expense is involved. At a future date when the expenditure is made for Project A, it will be charged to an expense account, and not to the allocated portion of the unrestricted general fund balance. At that time an entry will be made reversing the entry above.

TRIAL BALANCE

One final word of caution is in order. The usual way in which posting errors are caught is through the use of a trial balance. If the debits and the credits aren't equal, the bookkeeper is alerted to look for an error. The most likely posting error a bookkeeper will make, when fund accounting is involved, is to enter a transaction involving two funds in only one of the two funds. The use of a trial balance, however, will not catch this type of error since the debits and credits may be equal but a complete entry omitted (both debit and credit).

Balancing Interfund Transactions

It is easy to prevent this from going undetected. What is required is a balancing of the interfund receivables and payables. If they balance out to zero, then the bookkeeper knows that both sides of all interfund transactions have been recorded. This balancing is easy to do with the chart of accounts provided in Figure 31–1 because all of the interorganization accounts are classified in one series of account numbers. Usually all that is required is running an adding machine tape of the aggregate debit and credit balances of the interfund accounts to be sure they net out to zero; if they don't, then the bookkeeper can compare, account by account, the corresponding contra account in the other fund. Thus account 142 should be the same amount as 241 except one will be a debit and the other a credit. In this way it is easy to pinpoint differences.

CONCLUSION

Fund accounting is not difficult from a bookkeeping standpoint but it requires careful organization and a good chart of accounts. It also requires care to ensure that both sides of interfund transactions are recorded. Other than that, fund accounting follows the same principles used by nonfund accounting organizations.

Fund accounting can be applied to either cash or accrual basis organizations. The principal problem with fund accounting is not the bookkeeping, but the problem of presentation. This is where fund accounting frequently falls down. If the suggestions and recommendations that have been made throughout this book are heeded, the treasurer will be able to put together financial statements that are straightforward and clear to the unknowledgeable reader; in short, that will easily pass the "grandparent" test.

APPENDIX

Use of Rulings and Underscorings

One of the areas that causes confusion to the average reader of a financial statement is the number of rulings or underscores on a financial statement. What do they mean? When is something underscored? The rules are straightforward although somewhat complicated in application:

1. A figure is underscored when you want to indicate that you are adding all figures above the line to come to a total or subtotal which will be shown immediately below the line:

$$
\begin{array}{r}
1,139 \\
1,849 \\
590 \\
\hline
3,578
\end{array}
$$

The line here means that everything above the line adds down to the figure below the line (3,578).

2. A single row of figures is underscored where you want to indicate that this single row of figures is not going to be added into the figures immediately below the line. Notice that this occurs only when there is a single row of figures, and not several rows:

$$
\begin{array}{r}
1,139 \\
\hline
1,849 \\
590 \\
\hline
2,439
\end{array}
$$

The 1,139 is not added into the figures below because there is only the single row above the line.

3. A double underscore is used to indicate that absolutely nothing more is carried below this point in this column.

$$
\begin{array}{r}
1,849 \\
590 \\
\hline
2,439 \\
\hline\hline
\end{array}
$$

$$
\begin{array}{r}
23 \\
161 \\
\hline
184 \\
\end{array}
$$

4. If there are several sets of underscored figures which are sub-totals, and you want to add all these subtotals together, the figure directly above the final total will be underscored and the final total will be double underscored:

$$
\begin{array}{r}
1,139 \\
\hline
1,849 \\
590 \\
\hline
2,439 \\
\hline
3,578 \\
\hline\hline
\end{array}
$$

Here is a typical example showing all the possibilities:

Cash in bank	$ 1,000
Cash in petty cash	100
	1,100
Accounts receivable—trade	133,000
Accounts receivable—other	23,000
	156,000
Total current assets	157,100
Fixed assets:	
Land	25,000
Plant	116,000
Less reserve for depreciation	(65,000)
	76,000
Total assets	$233,100

The statements should be designed to avoid subtotals as much as possible to reduce possible reader confusion. If possible the use of two columns should be used to help avoid confusion. Here is the above statement in a two column approach:

Cash in bank	$ 1,000	
Cash in petty cash	100	$ 1,100
Accounts receivable:		
Trade	133,000	
Other	23,000	156,000
Total current assets		157,100
Fixed assets:		
Land	25,000	
Plant	116,000	
Less reserve for depreciation	(65,000)	76,000
Total assets		$233,100

As with most other reporting problems, care must be taken to minimize reader confusion. If the treasurer constantly keeps this in mind, the more complicated presentations can often be presented in a straightforward fashion that will increase reader comprehension without unduly cutting back on details.

Bibliography

Abingdon Clergy Income Tax Guide. Nashville: Abingdon Press, 1981 (updated annually), 80 p.

Accounting Advisory Committee Report to the Commission on Private Philanthropy and Public Needs. Washington, D.C.: Commission on Private Philanthropy and Public Needs, 1974, 36 p.

AMERICAN ACCOUNTING ASSOCIATION. Report of the Committee on Accounting Practices on Not-for-Profit Organizations, *The Accounting Review,* Supplement to Vol. XLVI, 1971, pp. 80–163.

AMERICAN CANCER SOCIETY. *Accounting Manual.* New York: Author, 1974, 70 p.

AMERICAN COUNCIL ON EDUCATION. *College and University Business Administration.* Rev. Ed. Washington, D.C.: Author, 1968, 311 p.

AMERICAN COUNCIL ON EDUCATION. *Planning for Effective Resource Allocation in Universities.* Prepared by Harry Williams of the Institute for Defense Analysis. Washington, D.C. 1966, 88 p.

AMERICAN HOSPITAL ASSOCIATION. *Budgeting Procedures for Hospitals.* Rev. ed. Chicago: Author, 1971, 68 p.

AMERICAN HOSPITAL ASSOCIATION. *Chart of Accounts for Hospitals.* Chicago: Author, 1976, 157 p.

AMERICAN HOSPITAL ASSOCIATION. *Cost Finding and Rate Setting for Hospitals.* Chicago: Author, 1968, 103 p.

AMERICAN HOSPITAL ASSOCIATION. *Internal Control and Internal Auditing and Operations Auditing for Hospitals.* Chicago: Author, 1979, 66 p.

AMERICAN HOSPITAL ASSOCIATION. *Uniform Hospital Definitions.* Chicago: Author, 1960, 50 p.

AMERICAN INSTITUTE OF CERTIFIED PUBLIC ACCOUNTANTS. *Audits of Certain Nonprofit Organizations.* New York: Author, 1981, 54 p.

AMERICAN INSTITUTE OF CERTIFIED PUBLIC ACCOUNTANTS. *Audits of Colleges and Universities, including Statement of Position issued by the Accounting Standards Division.* New York: Author, 1973, 1975, 137 p.

AMERICAN INSTITUTE OF CERTIFIED PUBLIC ACCOUNTANTS. *Audits of Voluntary Health and Welfare Organizations.* New York: Author, 1974, 51 p.

AMERICAN INSTITUTE OF CERTIFIED PUBLIC ACCOUNTANTS. *Hospital Audit Guide including Statements of Position issued by the Accounting and Auditing Standards Divisions.* New York: Author, 1973, 1978, 79 p.

AMERICAN INSTITUTE OF CERTIFIED PUBLIC ACCOUNTANTS. *Medicare Audit Guide.* New York: Author, 1969, 46 p.

AMERICAN INSTITUTE OF CERTIFIED PUBLIC ACCOUNTANTS. *Statement of Position No. 78–10: Accounting Principles and Reporting Practices For Certain Nonprofit Organizations*. New York: Author, 1978, 117 p.

AMERICAN NATIONAL RED CROSS. *Suggested Method for Keeping Chapter Financial Records*. Washington, D.C.: Author, March 1956, 27 p.

ANTHONY, R. N. *Financial Accounting in Nonbusiness Organizations, An Exploratory Study of Conceptual Issues*. Stamford: Financial Accounting Standards Board, 1978, 205 p.

ANTHONY, R. N. and HERZLINGER, R. E. *Management Control in Nonprofit Organizations*. Homewood, Ill.: Richard D. Irwin, 1975, 355 p.

ASPEN SYSTEMS CORPORATION. *Encyclopedia of Health Care Financial Management*. William O. Cleverly, editor. Rockville, Md. June 1982.

BARBOUR, H. O. *Private Club Administration*. Washington, D.C.: Club Managers Association, 1968, 630 p.

BASTABLE, C. W. "Evaluating Performance of Not-for-Profit Entities." *Journal of Accountancy*, Jan. 1973, p. 32.

BERMAN, H. J. and WEEKS, L. E. *The Financial Management of Hospitals*. 4th ed. Ann Arbor: Health Administration Press, 1979, 674 p.

BIERMAN, H., JR., and HOFSTEDT, T. R. *University Accounting: Alternative Measures of Ivy League Deficits*, n.p. April 1973, 20 p.

BORST, D. and MONTANA, P. J., Eds. *Managing Nonprofit Organizations*. New York: American Management Association, 1977, 328 p.

BRAMER, J. C., JR. *Efficient Church Business Management*. Philadelphia: Westminster Press, 1960, 150 p.

CANADIAN INSTITUTE OF CHARTERED ACCOUNTANTS. *Financial Reporting for Non-Profit Organizations, A Research Study*. Toronto: Author, 1980, 168 p.

CARY, W. L. and BRIGHT, C. B. "The Law and the Lore of Endowment Funds —Report to the Ford Foundation." New York: Ford Foundation, 1969, 82 p.

CARY, W. L. and BRIGHT, C. B. "The Developing Law of Endowment Funds: 'The Law and the Lore' Revisited." New York: Ford Foundation, 1974, 56 p.

CHAMBER OF COMMERCE OF THE UNITED STATES. *Financial Management Handbook for Associations*. Washington, D.C.: Author, 1973, 95 p.

CLUB MANAGERS ASSOCIATION OF AMERICA. *Expense and Payroll Dictionary for Clubs—For Use with the Second Revised Edition (1967) of the Uniform System of Accounts for Clubs*. Washington, D.C.: Author.

CLUB MANAGERS ASSOCIATION OF AMERICA. *Uniform System of Accounts for Clubs*. Rev. 2nd ed. Washington, D.C.: Author, 1967, 140 p.

COMMISSION ON PRIVATE PHILANTHROPY AND PUBLIC NEEDS. *Giving in America: Toward a Stronger Voluntary Sector*. Washington, D.C.: Author, 1975, 240 p.

CORPORATION FOR PUBLIC BROADCASTING. *Principles of Accounting and Financial Reporting for Public Telecommunications Entities*. Washington, D.C.: Author, 1980, 42 p.

CROWE, J. M. and MOORE, M. D. *Church Finance Record System Manual*. Nashville: Broadman Press, 1959, 48 p.

DAUGHTREY, W. H., JR. and GROSS, M. J., JR. *Museum Accounting Handbook*. Washington, D.C.: American Association of Museums, 1978, 158 p.

DEMAREST, ROSEMARY R. *Accounting: Information Sources*. Detroit: Gale Research Company, 1970, 420 p.

DERMER, JOSEPH. *How to Raise Funds from Foundations*. Public Service Materials Center, 104 East 40th St., New York, N. Y., 1971.

EVANGELICAL AND REFORMED CHURCH. *Handbook for the Finance Officers of a Local Church*. Philadelphia: Author, 1961, 28 p.

FAY, C. T., JR., RHOADS, R. C., and ROSENBLATT, R. L. *Managerial Accounting for the Hospitality Service Industries*. Dubuque, Iowa: 1971, 588 p.

FOUNDATION CENTER. *The Foundation Directory*. 8th ed. New York: Columbia University Press, 1981.

FOUST, O. Q. "Churches." In National Society of Public Accountants. *Portfolio of Accounting Systems for Small and Medium-Sized Business*. Vol. 1. Englewood Cliffs, N. J.: Prentice-Hall, 1968, pp. 297–322.

FREEMAN, D. F. *The Handbook of Private Foundations*. Washington, D.C.: Council on Foundations, 1981, 436 p.

GIBBS, G. *Manual for Parish Treasurers*. 3rd ed. Los Angeles: Protestant Episcopal Church in the Diocese of Los Angeles, 1971, 50 p.

GRAY, R. N. *Managing the Church*—Vol. 2, *Business Methods*. Enid, Okla.: Phillips University Press, 1970, 212 p.

GREEN, J. L., JR. and BARBER, A. W. *A System of Cost Accounting for Physical Plant Operations in Institutions of Higher Education*. Athens: University of Georgia Press, 1968, 103 p.

GRIFFITH, J. R., HANCOCK, W. M., and MUNSON, F. C. *Cost Control in Hospitals*. Ann Arbor: Health Administration Press, 1976, 447 p.

GROSS, M. J., JR. "An Accountant Looks at the 'Total Return' Approach for Endowment Funds." *CPA Journal*, Nov. 1973, pp. 977–84.

GROSS, M. J., JR. "Layman's Guide to Preparing Financial Statements for Churches." *Price Waterhouse Review*, Winter 1966, pp. 48–56. Also reprinted by the American Institute of CPA's.

GROSS, M. J., JR. and JABLONSKY, S. F. *Principles of Accounting and Financial Reporting for Nonprofit Organizations*. New York: Ronald Press, 1979, 415 p.

HARTOGS, N. and WEBER, J. *Boards of Directors; A Study of Current Practices in Board Management and Board Operations in Voluntary Hospitals, Health and Welfare Organizations*. Dobbs Ferry, N.Y.: Oceana Publications, 1974, 266 p.

HENKE, E. O. *Accounting for Non-Profit Organizations*. 2nd ed. Belmont, Calif.: Wadsworth Publishing Co., 1977, 211 p.

HENKE, E. O. "Evaluating Performance of Not-for-Profit Organizations." *Journal of Accountancy*, Jan. 1973, p. 34.

HENKE, E. O. *Introduction to Nonprofit Organization Accounting*. Boston: Kent Publishing Company, 1980, 500 p.

HENKE, E. O. "Nongovernmental Nonprofit Enterprises." In Warren, Gorham & Lamont, *Handbook of Accounting and Auditing*. New York: Warren, Gorham & Lamont, 1981, 49 p.

HENKE, E. O. "Performance Evaluation for Not-for-Profit Organizations." *Journal of Accountancy*, June 1972, pp. 51–55.

HOLCK, M., JR. *Accounting Methods for the Small Church*. Minneapolis: Augsburg Publishing House, 1961, 108 p.

HOLCK, M., JR. and HOLCK, M., SR. *Complete Handbook of Church Accounting*. Englewood Cliffs, N.J.: Prentice-Hall, 1978, 300 p.

HOLT, D. R., II. *Handbook of Church Finance*. New York: Macmillan, 1960, 201 p.

HOPKINS, B. R. *The Law of Tax-Exempt Organizations*. New York: Ronald Press, 1979, 653 p.

HUMMEL, J. *Starting and Running a Nonprofit Organization*. Minneapolis: University of Minnesota Press, 1980, 147 p.

LONGEST, B. B. *Principles of Hospital Business Office Management*. Chicago: Hospital Financial Management Association, 1975, 249 p.

LYNN, E. S. and FREEMAN, R. J. *Fund Accounting—Theory and Practice*. Englewood Cliffs, N.J.: Prentice-Hall, 1974, 1008 p.

MACLEOD, R. K. "Program Budgeting Works in Nonprofit Institutions." *Harvard Business Review*, Sept./Oct. 1971, pp. 46–56.

MARTIN, T. L. *Hospital Accounting Principles and Practice*. 3rd ed. Chicago: Physicians' Record Co., 1958, 296 p.

McCONKEY, D. D. *MBO for Nonprofit Organizations*. New York: Author, 1975, 223 p.

MEHTA, N. H. and MAHER, D. J. *Hospital Accounting Systems and Controls*. Englewood Cliffs, N.J.: Prentice-Hall, 1977, 265 p.

NATIONAL ASSOCIATION OF COLLEGE AND UNIVERSITY BUSINESS OFFICERS. *Annotated Tabulations of College and University Accounting Practices*. Washington, D.C.: Author, 1964, 55 p.

NATIONAL ASSOCIATION OF COLLEGE AND UNIVERSITY BUSINESS OFFICERS. *College and University Business Administration*. 4th ed. Washington, D.C.: Author, 1982, 527 p.

NATIONAL ASSOCIATION OF COLLEGE AND UNIVERSITY BUSINESS OFFICERS. *College and University Business Administration—Administrative Manual*. Washington, D.C.: Author, 1974. (Looseleaf.)

NATIONAL ASSOCIATION OF COLLEGE AND UNIVERSITY BUSINESS OFFICERS. *Planning, Budgeting and Accounting*. Prepared by Peat, Marwick, Mitchell & Co. Washington, D.C.: Author, 1970, 149 p.

NATIONAL ASSOCIATION OF INDEPENDENT SCHOOLS. *Accounting for Independent Schools*, 2nd ed. Boston: Author, 1977, 177 p.

NATIONAL BOARD OF YOUNG MEN'S CHRISTIAN ASSOCIATIONS. *Association Records—The Official Guide to YMCA Program Recording and Reporting*. New York: Association Press, 1964, 90 p.

NATIONAL CONFERENCE OF CATHOLIC BISHOPS. *Diocesan Accounting and Financial Reporting*. Washington, D.C.: Author, 1971, 142 p.

NATIONAL HEALTH COUNCIL, NATIONAL ASSEMBLY FOR SOCIAL POLICY AND DEVELOPMENT, INC. and UNITED WAY OF AMERICA. *Standards of Accounting and Financial Reporting for Voluntary Health and Welfare Organizations*. Rev. ed. New York: Authors, 1975, 135 p.

NATIONAL INSTITUTE OF MENTAL HEALTH. *Guidelines for a Minimum Statistical and Accounting System for Community Mental Health Centers*. Prepared by E. M. Cooper. Washington, D.C.: Government Printing Office, 1973, 133 p.

NELSON, C. A. and TURK, F. J. *Financial Management for the Arts: A Guidebook for Arts Organizations*. New York: Associated Councils of the Arts, 1975, 52 p.

NEW YORK (STATE) AUDIT AND CONTROL DEPARTMENT. *Uniform System of Accounts for Community Colleges*. Albany: Author, 1971, 31 p.

OLECK, H. L. *Non-Profit Corporations, Organizations, and Associations*. 3rd ed. Englewood Cliffs, N.J.: Prentice-Hall, 1974, 1000 p.

PEAT, MARWICK, MITCHELL & Co. *Planning, Budgeting and Accounting*. Washington, D.C.: National Association of College and University Business Officers, 1970, 149 p.

PELOUBET, MAURICE E. *The Financial Executive and The New Accounting*. New York: Ronald Press, 1967, 227 p.

PIERSALL, R. W. "Depreciation and the Nonprofit Organization." *New York Certified Public Accountant*, Jan. 1971, pp. 57–65.

PRICE WATERHOUSE. *The Audit Committee, the Board of Trustees of Nonprofit Organizations and the Independent Accountant.* New York: Author, 1980, 7 p.

PRICE WATERHOUSE. *Effective Internal Accounting Control for Nonprofit Organizations.* New York: Author, 1980, 26 p.

PRICE WATERHOUSE. *Position Paper on College and University Reporting.* New York: Author, 1975, 10 p.

PRICE WATERHOUSE. *A Survey of Financial Reporting and Accounting Developments in the Hospital Industry.* New York: Author, 1981, 33 p.

PRICE WATERHOUSE. *1982 Survey of Financial Reporting and Accounting Practices of Private Foundations,* New York: Author, 1982.

RYAN, L. V. *An Accounting Manual for Catholic Elementary and Secondary Schools.* Washington, D.C.: National Catholic Education Association, 1969.

SCHEPS, C. and DAVIDSON, E. E. *Accounting for Colleges and Universities.* Rev. ed. Baton Rouge: Louisiana State University Press, 1970.

SEAWELL, L. V. *Hospital Financial Accounting Theory and Practice.* Chicago: Hospital Financial Management Association, 1975, 569 p.

SEAWELL, L. V. *Introduction to Hospital Accounting.* Rev. ed. Chicago: Hospital Financial Management Association, 1977, 508 p.

SHARKEY, D. H. "Associations and Clubs." In National Society of Public Accountants. *Portfolio of Accounting Systems for Small and Medium-Sized Businesses.* Vol. 1. Englewood Cliffs, N.J.: Prentice-Hall, 1968, pp. 59–70.

SHERER, H. *Progress in Financial Reporting in Selected Universities Since 1930.* Urbana: University of Illinois, 1950, 120 p.

SILVERS, J. B. and PRAHALAD, C. K. *Financial Management of Health Institutions.* New York: Spectrum Publications, 1974, 339 p.

SIMMONS, H. *How to Run a Club.* New York: Harper Brothers, 1955, 380 p.

SKINNER, R. M. *Canadian University Accounting.* Toronto: The Canadian Institute of Chartered Accountants, 1969, 44 p.

SLADE, F. V. *Church Accounts.* 2nd ed. London: Gee and Co., 1974, 262 p.

SNYDER, P. C. and HOGAN, E. E. *Cost Accountability for School Administrators.* West Nyack, N.Y.: Parker Publishing Co., 1975, 222 p.

SWANSON, J. E., ARDEN, W., and STILL, H. E., JR. *Financial Analysis of Current Operations of Colleges and Universities.* Ann Arbor: Institute of Public Administration, University of Michigan, 1966, 443 p.

TAYLOR, P. J. and GRANVILLE, K. T. *Financial Management of Higher Education.* New York: Coopers & Lybrand, 1973, 122 p.

TOPPING, J. R. *Cost Analysis Manual.* Boulder, Colo.: National Center for Higher Education Management Systems at Western Interstate Commission for Higher Education, 1974, 325 p.

UNITED STATES DEPARTMENT OF EDUCATION. *The Blue Book. Accounting, Recordkeeping, and Reporting by Postsecondary Educational Institutions for Federally-Funded Student Financial Aid Programs.* Washington, D.C.: Author, 1981, 87 p.

UNITED WAY OF AMERICA. *Accounting & Financial Reporting; A Guide for United Ways and Not-for-Profit Human Service Organizations.* Alexandria, Va.: Author, 1974, 195 p.

UNITED WAY OF AMERICA. *Budgeting: A Guide for United Ways and Not-for-Profit Human Service Organizations.* Alexandria, Va.: Author, 1975, 55 p.

UNITED WAY OF AMERICA. *UWASIS—II—United Way of America Services Identification System.* Rev. ed. Alexandria, Va.: Author, 1976, 319 p.

VAN FENSTERMAKER, J. *Cash Management—Managing the Cash Flows, Bank Balances, and Short-Term Investments in Non-Profit Institutions.* Kent, Ohio: Kent State University Press, 1966, 59 p.

WALKER, A. L. *Church Accounting Methods.* Englewood Cliffs, N.J.: Prentice-Hall, 1964, 171 p.

WALZ, E. *Church Business Methods: A Handbook for Pastors and Leaders of the Congregation.* St. Louis: Concordia Publishing House, 1970.

WARSHAUER, W., JR., GROSS, M. J., JR., and MEYERSON, J. W. "Nonprofit Enterprises." In L. J. Seidler and D. R. Carmichael (Eds.), *Accountants' Handbook,* 6th ed., Vol. 2. New York: Ronald Press, 1981, 42 p.

WHEELEY, B. O. and CABLE, T. H. *Church Planning and Management: A Guide for Pastors and Laymen.* Philadelphia: Dorrance & Co., 1975, 218 p.

Index